MACMILLAN HISTORY O
General Editor : A. NORMAN JE

Macmillan History of Literature
General Editor: A. Norman Jeffares

Published

OLD ENGLISH LITERATURE
Michael Alexander

ENGLISH GOTHIC LITERATURE
Derek Brewer

SIXTEENTH-CENTURY ENGLISH LITERATURE
Murray Roston

SEVENTEENTH-CENTURY ENGLISH LITERATURE
Bruce King

EIGHTEENTH-CENTURY ENGLISH LITERATURE
Maximillian Novak

NINETEENTH-CENTURY ENGLISH LITERATURE
Margaret Stonyk

TWENTIETH-CENTURY ENGLISH LITERATURE
(Second Edition)
Harry Blamires

ANGLO-IRISH LITERATURE
A. Norman Jeffares

THE LITERATURE OF THE UNITED STATES
(Second Edition)
Marshall Walker

THE LITERATURE OF SCOTLAND
Roderick Watson

A HISTORY OF AUSTRALIAN LITERATURE
Ken Goodwin

A HISTORY OF CANADIAN LITERATURE
William H. New

Forthcoming

A HISTORY OF LITERATURE IN THE IRISH LANGUAGE
Declan Kiberd

A HISTORY OF LITERARY CRITICISM
A. H. Ashe

MACMILLAN HISTORY OF LITERATURE

THE LITERATURE OF THE UNITED STATES OF AMERICA

Marshall Walker

SECOND EDITION

MACMILLAN
EDUCATION

First published 1983
Second edition 1988

Published by
MACMILLAN EDUCATION LTD
Houndmills, Basingstoke, Hampshire RG21 2XS
and London
Companies and representatives
throughout the world

Printed in Hong Kong

ISBN 0–333–44326–8 (hc)
ISBN 0–333–44327–6 (pbk)

British Library Cataloguing in Publication Data
Walker, Marshall
    The literature of the United States.—
    2nd ed.—(Macmillan history of literature).
    1. American literature—History and
    criticism
    I. Title
    810.9   PS88
    ISBN 0–333–44326–8
    ISBN 0–333–44327–6 Pbk

Contents

TO NORA K. WALKER
AND IN MEMORY OF
HAROLD WALKER

This book is not written for the over-fed.
It is written for men who have not been able
to afford an university education or for young
men, whether or not threatened with universities,
who want to know more at the age of fifty than
I know today, and whom I might conceivably aid
to that object. I am fully aware of the dangers
inherent in attempting such utility to them.

Ezra Pound, *Guide to Kulchur*

Acknowledgements for the Second Edition

My chief obligation is to Stephanie Clark of the University of Waikato library. My thanks go also to her colleague, Geraldine Hay, for help with inter-library loans. Dr Lewis Fretz of the University of Waikato's Department of Politics has given invaluable advice on historical content. Alan J. Clark of Oxford has been generous in suggesting improvements to my account of the Nashville Fugitives. Once again I am especially indebted to Sonia Wells for her skill and endurance in preparing the new typescript, and grateful to Sue Cope for her scrupulous editing.

For encouragement, understanding and support over many years I thank Dr and Mrs J. R. F. Buchanan.

In revising this book for a second edition I have been guided by helpful criticism of the first edition. Some writers who fared poorly in the competition for space are now more amply represented. More coverage is given to drama and to science fiction. There are fuller discussions of work by Black and Jewish writers and of writing by women.

List of plates

Editor's Preface

THE study of literature requires knowledge of contexts as well as texts. What kind of person wrote the poem, the play, the novel, the essay? What forces acted upon them as they wrote? What was the historical, the political, the philosophical, the economic, the cultural background? Was the writer accepting or rejecting the literary conventions of the time, or developing them, or creating entirely new kinds of literary expression? Are there interactions between literature and the art, music or architecture of its period? Was the writer affected by contemporaries or isolated?

Such questions stress the need for students to go beyond the reading of set texts, to extend their knowledge by developing a sense of chronology, of action and reaction, and of the varying relationships between writers and society.

Histories of literature can encourage students to make comparisons, can aid in understanding the purposes of individual authors and in assessing the totality of their achievements. Their development can be better understood and appreciated with some knowledge of the background of their time. And histories of literature, apart from their valuable function as reference books, can demonstrate the great wealth of writing in English that is there to be enjoyed. They can guide the reader who wishes to explore it more fully and to gain in the process deeper insights into the rich diversity not only of literature but of human life itself.

A. NORMAN JEFFARES

The United States of America. Map © Macmillan Education.

90   70   60

C A N A D A

Quebec

Montreal   MAINE

Duluth   Augusta

ESOTA   MICHIGAN   L. Huron   Montpelier   Concord   Portland
nt Paul   WISCONSIN   L. Superior   Champlain   VERMONT   NEW   Boston
apolis   Milwaukee   Lansing   L. Ontario   Rochester   Mohawk   HAMPSHIRE   Providence
   Madison   Chicago   Detroit   Buffalo   Syracuse   Albany   MASS.   C. Cod
   IOWA   Mississippi   L. Erie   Hartford   CONN.   New York City
Des Moines   Gary   Toledo   Cleveland   PENNSYLVANIA   Jersey   Long Island
   ILLINOIS   INDIANA   OHIO   Pittsburgh   Harrisburg   NEW JERSEY   40
Springfield   Dayton   Columbus   Ohio   Washington   Baltimore   Philadelphia   DEL   Delaware Bay
Jefferson   Indianapolis   Cincinnati   WEST VIRGINIA   Annapolis   MARYLAND
City   Saint Louis   Evansville   Louisville   Charleston   Potomac   Richmond   Chesapeake Bay
MISSOURI   KENTUCKY   Frankfort   VIRGINIA   Norfolk
   Nashville   Roanoke   C. Hatteras
ARKANSAS   TENNESSEE   Raleigh
   Memphis   NORTH CAROLINA
Little Rock   Mississippi   Birmingham   Atlanta   SOUTH   Columbia
   MISSISSIPPI   ALABAMA   Chattahoochee   CAROLINA   C. Romain
LOUISIANA   Jackson   Montgomery   GEORGIA   Charleston
Baton   Alabama   Savannah   Savannah
Rouge   Mobile   Tallahassee   Jacksonville
alveston   New Orleans   C. San Blas   FLORIDA   C. Canaveral
   Gulf   of   Mexico   Tampa   COMM.
   Okeechobee   OF THE
   Miami   BAHAMAS
   Key West   Florida
   Keys

90   80

▬▬ International Boundaries	■ Capital City
─ ─ ─ State Boundaries	● State Capitals
‥‥‥ Major Roads	○ Other Important Towns

0   200   400 Kilometres
0   100   200 Miles

1

Terms of a Tradition

'THE land was ours before we were the land's', writes Robert Frost (1874–1963) in 'The Gift Outright' (1942). He is thinking about the effort early American settlers had to make to commit themselves to a vast new country 'vaguely realising westward'. The land itself could be appropriated by men and women of sufficient ingenuity, strength and determination. Transforming a frontier into 'home' took longer and required imagination. Every life lived in the new land brought home closer. Every artistic response to America acknowledged it as the artist's field of activity, his own place; and as artists of all kinds grew in number, the land increasingly possessed them.

The Pilgrims of the *Mayflower* who entered Cape Cod Harbor on 21 November 1620 and made a landing in snow at what is now Provincetown, Massachusetts, were still spiritually possessed by England. Separatists from the Church of England who sought to restore the church to its 'primitive order, liberty, and beauty', they were themselves shaped, even in their rebellion, by English life, language and ideas. Nothing in their past could have prepared them for the exotica of Indian culture, and nothing in England could have anticipated the sheer scale of the new country. They would become American only through generations of strenuous mental as well as physical adjustment and improvisation. The history of American literature is a sequence of spiritual appropriations of, and by, the land which the settlers and their descendants found and altered as it altered them.

The prime fact of America is its physical size, its huge distances. Gertrude Stein (1874–1946) says, 'In the United States there is more space where nobody is than where anybody is. That is what makes America what it is.' With an area of 3,615,122 square miles, America is slightly smaller than the People's Republic of China and less than half the size of the Soviet Union, but to settlers from Britain, Ireland and the populous countries of Europe it presented a varied, alien geography of awesome proportions and mysterious extent. The size of the country is the basis of its political organisation, a federal system of government in which the central authority of Washington is complemented by separate, largely autonomous administrations in each of the forty-eight contiguous states, in Alaska to the northern extreme of the continent, and Hawaii in the mid-Pacific.

A sense of space is fundamental to the work of writers as diverse as James Fenimore Cooper (1789–1851), Mark Twain (1835–1910), Willa Cather (1876–1947), Wallace Stevens (1879–1955), John Steinbeck (1902–68), William Carlos Williams (1883–1963) and Jack Kerouac (1922–69). It is there in the nineteenth-century panoramic landscape paintings of Thomas Cole, Albert Bierstadt and Frederick Erwin Church, as well as in the monumental effects of Thomas Hart Benton and Grant Wood. Size and distance are implicit in the grandiose polytonal music of Charles Ives and in the widely spaced chords and gapped arpeggio melodies of Aaron Copland. Towering images of space assert human ingenuity in city architecture from New York to Los Angeles. Perhaps the most spectacular response to the scale of American landscape was the attempt in 1971–2 by Christo, a Bulgarian-born artist, to construct his 'Valley Curtain' near Aspen, Colorado, a hawser slung between two mountains 1,250 feet apart and carrying an orange curtain weighing four tons.

There is still plenty of space 'where nobody is' in America. From some ten million people in 1820 the population has grown by more than twenty times, yet any substantial journey along the country's nearly four million miles of roads will bring the traveller – especially one accustomed to the congestions of Britain and Europe – a new sense of arrival and departure. Small towns and villages are definable incidents along the way; they do not just melt vaguely into each other. A small place makes its point, still, as a settlement in the great space of America. There is romance in this, and, outside the major cities, it fosters those local and regional characteristics which are, to a large extent, based on climate.

America's eastern seaboard runs from the northern climate of New England down to the semi-tropical states fringing the Gulf of Mexico. A journey down the centre of the country leads from the cutting winds of the Dakotas to the fetid airs of the Mississippi delta. Western climates range from the English affinities of Washington and Oregon to the hot, dry deserts of Arizona. There is a corresponding variety of flora and fauna, from timber-wolves to alligators and conifers to cactus. When to all this are added the diverse national origins of the thirty-five million people who emigrated to America between 1830 and 1914, the result is the supreme paradox of the post-Civil-War USA. It is both a single nation held together by a Federal government, transport lines, the English language, and coast-to-coast Coca-Cola, and many countries, none of which is uniquely indentifiable as the real America. Paul Simon's (b. 1941) wistful song 'America', popular in the late 1960s when to be young was to be nomadic, brings these elements together:

> 'Kathy', I said
> As we boarded a Greyhound in Pittsburgh,
> 'Michigan seems like a dream to me now
> It took me four days to hitch-hike from Saginaw.
> Ive come to look for America.'

Discovery and Settlement

Christopher Columbus was looking for the Indies, not for the America he is wrongly credited with discovering in 1492. Asiatics must have preceded him and possibly African and Egyptian voyagers. Norwegian archaeology has dated the foundations of seven buildings in the north end of Newfoundland at around the tenth century, and Scandinavian sagas of the eleventh and twelfth centuries refer to Norsemen who crossed the ocean. A world map drawn some fifty years before the voyage of Columbus, and now in Yale Unversity Library, shows a large island called Vinland, south-west of Greenland. A Latin inscription proclaims Leif Eriksson (son of Eric Rauthe, or Eric the Red) and his men as the discoverers of this island and says that Pope Paschall II sent Bishop Eric Gnupson to civilise it. Columbus himself got no further than an island in the Caribbean which he named 'San Salvador'. Believing he had attained his goal he called the natives 'Indians'.

The name 'America' derives from the Italian explorer Amerigo (or *Americus*) Vespucci who made four voyages to the New World. In 1502 Vespucci landed on the coast of Brazil, but in his report of a voyage of 1497 he mentions touching upon a coast 'which we thought to be that of a continent'. If he was right, the touch would give him precedence not only over Columbus in reaching the American mainland, but also over John Cabot whose voyage of 1497 under patent from Henry VII took him only to Cape Breton Island. It was in Cabot's second voyage the following year that he explored other parts of North America as a basis for England's claim to the continent.

The English were slow to begin their settlement of the New World. In 1583 Sir Humphrey Gilbert failed in an attempt to settle Newfoundland, and the 1585 expedition to what is now North Carolina, sponsored by Sir Walter Raleigh, survived only a year. Other attempts to settle 'Virginia', as the entire Atlantic seaboard of America was then called, also failed and it was not until 1607 that the first permanent colony was established by Captain John Smith at Jamestown. With this first successful settlement American literature properly begins and the first report is written of a 'fruitful and delightsome' virgin land of promise waiting for man to realise prelapsarian opportunities for ever lost to him in Europe.

A new Eden and the American Dream

The Irish philosopher, Bishop George Berkeley, expressed the yearning of fellow-intellectuals with his vision of a new world of 'innocence where nature guides and virtue rules'. Berkeley's plan for a Christian college for the natives in Bermuda failed, and, for the nine and a half million people who sailed the Atlantic in the first hundred years of America's history as a nation, reality was often a harsh climate, misfortune and enduring social inequality. The myths that kept them going and lured others form the basis of the American Dream. The New World would be an Arcadia, a new Eden, a Kingdom of Heaven on Earth where, uninhibited by the restraints of older societies, a man could practise his trade or his religion with freedom and control his political destiny – he could be Adam again.

John Smith's (1580–1631) *A Map of Virginia* (1612) says of Virginia that 'heaven and earth never agreed better to frame a place for man's habitation', and his *A Description of New England* (1616) develops the image of America as a Promised Land. Though under constant pressure from the many hardships of colonial life, the image is sustained with religious conviction by the Pilgrims of Plymouth, the first New England colony, and by the Puritans who founded the Massachusetts Bay Colony in 1629–30. More than half the Plymouth colonists died of disease, exposure or deprivation in the first American winter but, with help from the Indians, the year 1621 yielded a good harvest which prompted the first American Thanksgiving. William Bradford's (1590–1657) *History of Plymouth Plantation* (1620–50; pub. 1856) soberly narrates the hard facts of colonial survival, but is clearly the work of a man who deeply believes in the Christian destiny of the enterprise. Cotton Mather's (1663–1728) *Magnalia Christi Americana* ('The Great Deeds of Christ in America', 1702) confirms the New World as chosen by God for the purpose of rewarding faith with prosperity. When to this view was added the force of eighteenth-century confidence in the inevitability of man's intellectual and material progress, the Dream was firmly established as the foundation of American national consciousness, both religious and secular.

The possibilities seemed endless. In his first Inaugural Address on 4 March 1801 President Thomas Jefferson (1743–1826) spoke of the country's having 'room enough for our descendants to the 100th and 1000th generation'. The New World looked not to the past, where Europe lay mired in corruption, but to the present and the future. Corruption, of course, could seduce, as the characters of Henry James's (1843–1916) novels sometimes discover to their cost, though Europe invariably broadens their perceptions while it despoils them of their American innocence. Thomas Appleton (1812–84) is supposed to have made his most famous epigram from Europe's fatal attraction to lapsed Americans: 'Good Americans, when they die, go to Paris'. In 1825 Noah Webster (1758–1843), a descendant of William Bradford and originator of the famous 'Webster's Dictionary', announced that 'American glory begins at the dawn'. For the *Democratic Review* in 1839: 'Our national birth was the beginning of a new history . . . which separates us from the past and connects us with the future only'. Despite the internecine conflict of the Civil War, such apostolic confidence seemed validated by the rapid industrialisation of the nineteenth century and endorsed by the optimistic individualism of Ralph Waldo Emerson (1803–82), Henry David Thoreau (1817–62) and other 'Transcendentalist' writers. As society grew increasingly secular, material progress became at once the Dream's expression and proof. 'The business of America is business', Calvin Coolidge said in 1925. It was the most profitable business in history, and the American way of life became the envy of the world, a dream come true.

Even Emerson acknowledges that the world contains more than ideal states of being, but maintains his belief in the unity of things; 'All over the universe', he writes in his journal in 1842, 'there is just one thing, this old double'. There are aspects of the world which are ordinary or 'vulgar' and slavery was bad, but probably the only unalloyed evil Emerson could have recognised would have been that of seeing things differently from himself. The doubleness of things means simply higher and lower, not good and bad. A weed is a plant 'whose virtues have not yet been discovered'. Other worldlier men were less optimistic and the rhetoric of the Dream bred its own opposite. While Emerson cries, 'Here's for the plain old Adam, the simple genuine self against the whole world', Henry James senior (father of the novelist) inveighs against Emerson's 'unconsciousness of evil' and objects that 'nothing could be more remote . . . from distinctively *human* attributes . . . than this sleek and comely Adamic condition.' In *Moby-Dick* (1851) Melville (1819–91) makes his whale a symbol of Emerson's 'just one thing' but the thing includes evil at its most elemental. Realism was not the sole preserve of literary men. George Washington himself predicted that the thirteen states whose Declaration of Independence their Congress approved on 4 July 1776 would be rent by civil war. In 1803 Fisher Ames, a leading New England Federalist (that is, a supporter of strong central government even at the expense of the individual liberty so highly valued by Thomas Jefferson and his followers), rejected almost every aspect of the Dream: 'Our country is too big for union, too sordid for patriotism, too democratic for liberty.'

The last aphorism extracted from Pudd'nhead Wilson's Calendar in Twain's (1835–1910) *The Tragedy of Pudd'nhead Wilson* (1894) reads ambiguously:

> *October 12, the Discovery.* It was wonderful to find America, but it would have been more wonderful to miss it.

In *Democratic Vistas* (1871) even the profligately affirmative Walt Whitman (1819–92) admits that 'Society, in these States, is canker'd crude, superstitious, and rotten . . . . The problem of the future of America is in certain respects as dark as it is vast'. The vastness of things worries Saul Bellow's (*b.* 1915) hero in *Henderson the Rain King* (1959): 'America is so big, and every one is working, making, digging, bulldozing, trucking, loading, and so on, and I guess the sufferers suffer at the same rate.' A century after his country's birth, Henry Adams (1838–1918) is nostalgic for the splendid, clean potency of the American Adam: 'Stripped for the hardest work, every muscle firm and elastic, every ounce of brain ready for use and not a trace of superfluous flesh on his nervous and supple body, the American stood in the world a new order of man'. Early twentieth-century reality is the terrible energy represented by the Dynamo in Chapter XXV of *The Education of Henry Adams* (privately printed in 1907; published 1918), an immense mechanic power which brutally accelerates

America and the world towards disintegration. A soulless, mechanised America 'slides by on grease' in the giant, finned automobiles of Robert Lowell's (1917–77) poem 'For the Union Dead' (1965). William Burroughs (*b*. 1914), another enemy of technology, flatly denies the shibboleth of the American Dream in his novel *The Naked Lunch* (1959): 'America is not a young land: it is old and dirty and evil before the settlers, before the Indians. The evil is there waiting.'

Huckleberry Finn and his kind

Ernest Hemingway (1899–1961) says that 'all modern American literature comes from one book by Mark Twain called *Huckleberry Finn* (1884) . . . it's the best book we've had. All American writing comes from that.' In an introduction to an edition of the novel (1950), T. S. Eliot (1888–1965) calls Huck 'one of the permanent symbolic figures of fiction, not unworthy to take a place with Ulysses, Faust, Don Quixote, Don Juan, and other great discoveries that man has made about himself.' Huckleberry Finn's discovery is that American society has sunk from its original promise to the violence and hypocrisy that he meets along the banks of the Mississippi River; in making it he becomes, even more than Cooper's Natty Bumppo or Melville's Ishmael, the ancestor and model of many heroes of American fiction who, like him, refuse to be 'sivilized'.

Hemingway's heroes typically make what Nick Adams, the central figure in the best stories of *In Our Time* (1925), calls 'a separate peace' with society in order to realise themselves in their own ways. In J. D. Salinger's (*b*. 1919) *The Catcher in the Rye* (1951) Holden Caulfield, doggedly – and hilariously – honest adolescent loner in a deceitful society, ends his story in a sanatorium. J. P. Donleavy's (*b*. 1926) Sebastian Dangerfield, hero of *The Ginger Man* (1955) is almost as fleet of phrase as Twain's Huck. He lives by the darting lyrical language in which he expresses volleys of anxieties, quick angers, and sudden, bright perceptions. Alone in London, Sebastian wearies of his 'terrifying heart'. The last image in his mind is of horses 'running out to death'. On the last page of John Updike's (*b*. 1932) *Rabbit, Run* (1960) the hero runs from his shiftless wife and his uncomprehending pregnant mistress. Direction is unimportant, the flight is all: 'he runs. Ah: runs. Runs'. In *Rabbit is Rich* (1981) he is overweight, back with his wife, and sells Toyotas. Seen through the eyes of Michelangelo

Antonioni in the film *Zabriskie Point* (1969), social possibilities in modern America are reducible to two equally doomed options: conformity–even if to the protest movement in vogue–or flight. The eponymous hero of Saul Bellow's *Herzog* (1965) opts out of a society which, one of his friends observes, exacts heavy penalties for non-conformity: 'They'll put a meter on your nose and charge you for breathing. You'll be locked up back and front.' Joseph Heller's (*b.* 1923) best-selling *Catch-22* (1961) is ostensibly a Second World War novel about Captain John Yossarian and his ultimate refusal to fly any more bombing missions. Mike Nichols, who directed an excellent movie version of the book (1970), saw the subject differently: 'I don't think of this as a film about World War II. I think of it as a picture about dying and about when you get off and at what point you take control over your own life and say, "No. I won't. I decide. I draw the Line".' With self-control comes identity. The novelist Ralph Ellison (*b.* 1914) was once asked: 'Would you say that the search for identity is primarily an American theme?' He replied: 'It is *the* American theme.'

In each case the hero's rejection of dehumanising social institutions involves solitude. The Dostoevskian hero of Ralph Ellison's *Invisible Man* (1952) – still the best fable of the Black predicament since William Faulkner's (1897–1962) *Light in August* (1932) – is alienated by the refusal of American society to see an identifiable person inside a black skin. Heller's Yossarian takes control and asserts himself by escaping from the madness of war and making off, alone, for neutral Sweden, another Huck lighting out for 'the Territory' beyond the reach of a faulty society and its organisation men. Isolation is flaunted in the virtuoso ineptitudes of Woody Allen's movies. It is comically expressed in sexual terms by Philip Roth's (*b.* 1933) *Portnoy's Complaint* (1969), and in Erica Jong's (*b.* 1942) *Fear of Flying* (1973) the intrepid Isadora Wing takes raised female consciousness on a witty and audacious solo flight toward sexual satisfaction in a man's world. In *Falconer* (1977) John Cheever's (1912–82) college-professor hero is a drug addict and murderer. Behind the bars of Falconer prison he discovers both himself and the possibility of true human community. The hero of Walker Percy's (*b.* 1916) *Lancelot* (1977), confined to a cell in an asylum, rages not only at his wife's infidelity but also at the general 'whoredom' of modern America. Obsessed with the lack of 'proper geometry and theology' in the modern world, Ignatius J. Reilly, the gargantuan, eructating crusader of John Kennedy Toole's (1937–69) *A Confederacy of Dunces* (1980), wages lone war on the assorted excesses of the twentieth century. Yet 'we must have energy', says T. S. Garp in John Irving's (*b*. 1942) best-seller, *The World According to Garp* (1978). Paradoxically the best answer to the American novelist, preoccupied with the failings of his national culture, is the energy and accomplishment of his own work and that of his fellow artists.

The Dream and the past

The nostalgia of Henry Adams typifies much American literature. In an essay of 1879 on 'The Genius of Nathaniel Hawthorne' Anthony Trollope says:

> The creations of American literature generally are no doubt more given to the speculative, – less given to the realistic, – than are those of English Literature. On our side of the water we deal more with beef and ale, and less with dreams.

Notwithstanding such exponents of realism as William Dean Howells (1837–1920), Stephen Crane (1871–1900), Frank Norris (1870–1902), Theodore Dreiser (1871–1945), Sinclair Lewis (1885–1951) and John Dos Passos (1896–1970), American writers have always been more occupied with ideas and dreams than with manners or with the beef-and-ale surfaces of life. In *The Great American Novel* (1973) Philip Roth burlesques American myths, prejudices and history, particularly spoofing the portentousness with which American writers often invest their own culture. Roth's narrator, Word Smith, is a fractious old sporting columnist whose life has been devoted to the supremely American game of baseball. He now lives in an old folks' home called 'Valhalla', suffering from attacks of alliteration. From James Fenimore Cooper's 'Leather-Stocking' novels (1823–41) to Robert Coover's (*b*. 1932) *The Public Burning* (1977), which satirises the American myth in the bitter mood of the Watergate period, American literature repeatedly tries to define America.

Politicians, businessmen and technologists hail the present or the future, but ever since Washington Irving's (1783–1859) Rip Van Winkle awoke to discover that he had slept through his country's finest hour, the American Revolution, American writers have been concerned, often guiltily, with their own past and the need to acknowledge its failures. Holgrave, the man of today in Nathaniel Hawthorne's (1804–64) *The House of the Seven Gables* (1851), must accept that his blood is involved in that of his ancestors, the Maules: burning away the stains of the past would be to falsify the present and deny himself. William Faulkner's fictive Yoknapatawpha County, Mississippi, is obsessed with the guilt of slavery, the agonies of the Civil War, the ignominy of Reconstruction and the tawdriness of modernism. The most lyrical of all backward looks, perhaps the finest lament for lost opportunity in American literature, occurs in Nick Carraway's closing meditation at the end of Scott Fitzgerald's (1896–1940) *The Great Gatsby* (1925):

> . . . as the moon rose higher the inessential houses began to melt away until gradually I became aware of the old island here that flowered once for Dutch sailors' eyes – a fresh green breast of the new world. Its vanished trees, the trees that had made way for Gatsby's house, had once pandered in whispers to the last and greatest of all human dreams; for a transitory enchanted moment man must have held his breath in the presence of this continent, compelled into an aesthetic contemplation he neither understood nor desired, face to face for the last time in history with something commensurate to his capacity for wonder.

Whatever damage the Dream has sustained from Civil War and Civil Rights, Depression, Hiroshima, Korea, Vietnam, Watergate, the dwindling of the space programme and the decline of the cities, it persists in the imagination as a term central to the understanding of American culture. Nostalgia strengthens the documentary effects of Virgil Thomson's scores for *The Plow that Broke the Plains* (1936) and *The River* (1937). There is nostalgia as well as satire in Tom Wesselmann's plasticised nudes, and in Roy Lichtenstein's reminders of comic-book love and war. The pathos of British director John Schlesinger's culturally synoptic film *Midnight Cowboy* (1971) turns on American nostalgia for the raft of Huck and Jim and the anachronistic sanctity of the family. Nick Carraway's last words in *The Great Gatsby* sum up the condition of innumerable American artists: 'So we beat on, boats against the current, borne back ceaselessly into the past.'

The frontier

In July 1893 the Wisconsin historian Frederick Jackson Turner (1861–1932) presented a revolutionary paper to the American Historical Association on 'The Significance of the Frontier in American History'. Turner believed that the form and spirit of American democracy should be understood in terms of the frontier with its free lands and its stimulus to ingenuity and individualism. He stressed the usefulness of the continually advancing frontier as a 'safety valve'.

More recent historians and critics have sometimes disagreed with Turner. Henry Nash Smith (*b.* 1906) in *Virgin Land, the American West as Symbol and Myth* (1950) suggests that Turner was biased by his own captivity to a romantic, agrarian myth. Smith sees the degeneration of the Western novel in the twentieth century as evidence that the national imagination is characterised by new, industrial ideals. The resilience of the frontier as a metaphor eludes Smith; so does the popularity of Western movies, the global success of the television series based on Owen Wister's (1860–1938) novel *The Virginian* (1902), and the record-breaking paperback sales of pulp Western novels by Louis L'Amour. Even if Louis B. Wright's *Culture on the Moving Frontier* (1955) is right in its contention that frontier society followed Anglo-Saxon models, Turner's evaluation of the frontier as a key term in American culture remains sound. More useful responses to the Turner thesis expand it to a theory which finds Americans ready to move not only westward but also in all directions.

According to Frederic L. Paxson in his *History of the American Frontier* (1924) the frontier 'was a line, a region or a process'. There were four principal regions. The first frontier was the Atlantic seaboard where John Smith's Jamestown, Virginia and the Pilgrims' Plymouth, Massachusetts were succeeded in 1623 by the settlement of Manhattan Island. The second frontier was defined by the Appalachian Mountains, a broad ridge curving down from the St Lawrence almost to the Gulf of Mexico. Here pioneers of the eighteenth century had to modify their European ways and come to terms with bear, coyote and Indian. The majority of nineteenth-century immigrants headed beyond the mountainous territory of the Appalachians to the third or fourth region. The third was the vast interior plain of the Middle West which became the agricultural and industrial heartland of America with Chicago, as apostrophised by Carl Sandburg (1878–1967), its lustiest powerhouse:

> Hog Butcher for the World,
> Tool Maker, Stacker of Wheat,
> Player with Railroads and the Nation's Freight Handler;
> Stormy, husky, brawling,
> City of the Big Shoulders.

The fourth region is divisible into three parts, each one arguably a frontier in its own right: the high plains of the old cattle ranchers' wild west, the Rocky Mountains inhabited by fur traders and gold miners, and the lush coast of California. Each frontier prompted innovation and demanded adaptability. As R. A. Billington and J. B. Hedges show in their *Westward Expansion: A History of the American Frontier* (1949), the process that each involved was a 'rebirth of civilisation'.

Mark Twain's miscellany of desperadoes, vigilantes, pet tarantulas, drunks and newspapermen makes *Roughing It* (1872) the surrealistic classic of personal experience on the frontier. Francis Bret Harte (1836–1902) sentimentalises the same frontier in his short stories. The first substantial frontier fiction is the 'Leather-Stocking' sequence of novels by James Fenimore Cooper whose own youth was spent on the disappearing frontier of central New York State. Among other works that deal with frontier life are novels by Willa Cather – most notably *O Pioneers* (1913) and *My Antonia* (1918) – Edna Ferber's (1887–1968) *Cimarron* (1930), H. L. Davis's (1896–1960) *Honey in the Horn* (1935) and E. L. Doctorow's (*b.* 1931) *Welcome to Hard Times* (1960). The best-known poetry of the pioneer and the frontier is Walt Whitman's, particularly 'Song of the Broad-Axe' (1856) which celebrates 'The beauty of independence, departure, actions that rely on themselves,/The American contempt for statutes and ceremonies, the boundless impatience of restraint', and 'Pioneers! O Pioneers!' (1865):

> All the past we leave behind,
> We debouch upon a newer mightier world, varied world,
> Fresh and strong the world we seize, world of labour and the march
> Pioneers! O pioneers!

Much revealing verse about pioneering days is anonymous. The frontier songs not only reflect the dream of freedom and equality, but also tell of women robbed of youth and beauty, men lured to physical or moral destruction, and death at the hands of the Indians. 'Sioux Indians' tells of the frontier ordeal endured by followers of the Oregon Trail whose hazards included 'Sioux Indians all out on the plain,/A-killing poor drivers and burning their train,/A-killing poor drivers with arrow and bow,/When captured by Indians no mercy they'd show'. A variation on the Irish 'Bonny Boy' called 'The Jam on Gerry's Rock' became one of the most widely sung native American ballads. It tells the story of an accident that occurs at an unknown time and place when a band of loggers, professional timber-men, try to loosen a river log-jam:

They had not rolled off many logs, when the foreman
        he did say,
'I'll have you boys be on your guard, for the jam will
        soon give way'.
These words were scarcely spoken, when the jam did break
        and go
And with it went those six brave youths with their
        foreman, young Monroe.

The body of young Monroe is found crushed and bleeding. His girl laments – 'a maid from Saginaw town' – the boss pays Monroe's wages to her and her widowed mother, and the bold 'shanty-boys' are exhorted to pray for their dead comrades in a spirit of Christian fraternity.

The drowned logger is a hero, but the reckless men of the Californian Gold Rush are judged 'The Fools of Forty-Nine' in the ballad of that name and misguided losers in the revivalist verses of 'The Dying Californian'. The temptations and qualms of the pioneering era are illustrated with exceptional clarity by 'The Wisconsin Emigrant'. A New England husband addresses his wife:

'Since times are so hard, I've thought, my true heart,
Of leaving my oxen, my plough, and my cart,
And away to Wisconsin, a journey we'd go
To double our fortune as other folks do.
While here I must labour each day in the field,
And the winter consumes all the summer doth yield.'

For the ordinary man and his family life in nineteenth-century New England meant poor soil and hard work. The west could make a man rich, but, as the wife knows, it meant risks:

'Oh husband, remember, that land of delight
Is surrounded by Indians who murder by night.
Your house they will plunder and burn to the ground,
While your wife and your children lie murdered around.
Oh, stay on the farm, and you'll suffer no loss,
For the stone that keeps rolling will gather no moss.'

Wisely, perhaps, the husband capitulates, and in doing so neatly converts his preference for security into domestic romance:

'I never had thought of your dying before,
I love my dear children although they are small, –
But you, my dear wife, are more precious than all'.

A mural by Emmanuel Leutze entitled 'Westward the Course of Empire Takes Its Way' is a reproach to such timidity. It depicts American pioneers at their moment of triumph, looking down into the fertile valley that typifies the great nineteenth-century dream of the frontier. The details of the painting include struggling draught animals and bleached bones, but these emphasise the auroral message of a new life ahead. The earliest successes in American painting are either responses to the new landscapes which the pioneers were opening up, such as Inness's 'The Delaware Valley' and Bierstadt's 'Thunderstorm with Rocky Mountains', or memorials to the romantic aspects of frontier life, such as 'Advice on the Prairie' by William Ranney, 'Gold Rush Camp' by Erneste Narjot or 'American Frontier Life' by Arthur Tait. As a potent and enduring symbol the frontier has continued to shape American attitudes long after the age of the mining camp and the 'prairie schooner'. Behind the heroics and camaraderie portrayed by the artists lay a reality of commonplace misfortunes – crop failure, bankruptcy, health unequal to climate. On the first page of *Main Street* (1920) Sinclair Lewis says, 'The days of pioneering, of lassies in sunbonnets, and bears killed with axes in piney clearings, are deader now than Camelot'; but the myth of those days has survived as a condition of the American imagination. 'The shattering of the myth by economic distress', says Henry Nash Smith, 'marked the real end of the frontier period'; but it did not mark the end of the frontier mentality.

Before taking office in January 1961 President John F. Kennedy described his programme as 'The New Frontier', the intellectual, physical and moral challenge in contemporary American life that had replaced the old geographic frontiers. When Captain Kirk of the Star-ship 'Enterprise' invokes space as 'the final frontier' and reminds viewers of the television series 'Star Trek' that his mission is 'to go where no man has gone before' he speaks to a stock American sympathy – and one near enough the surface of popular consciousness to warrant repeating the appeal in every episode. In 1979 Tom Wolfe (*b*. 1931), America's quizzical analyst of cultural trends since the mid-1960s, published *The Right Stuff*, his history of the space programme. Wolfe finds that the material of which astronauts are made is a combination of stamina, guts, fast synapses and old-fashioned hell-raising. The men of the new frontier, where Russian Sputniks take the place of Indians, are cast in the mould of the pioneers.

2

The colonies

EARLY colonists had little time for art. Their first concern was survival, their second construction. Making a new life in Virginia or New England, even with God's help, required energy, resourcefulness, stamina, and fostered utilitarian forms of expression in the prose of reports, histories, sermons and diaries. Verse, with a few notable exceptions, was occasional, and without merit.

When Sir Humphrey Gilbert, on his final voyage in 1583, disappeared with 5 ships and 260 men in the North Atlantic, Sir Walter Raleigh tried to establish a colony on Roanoke Island off the coast of North Carolina. By 1590 the settlers had mysteriously vanished and since 1937 their story has been told in annual performances of *The Lost Colony*, a pageant drama by the folklorist playwright Paul Green (*b*. 1894). A member of Raleigh's first expedition was Thomas Harriot (*c*. 1560–1621), a young Oxford graduate who returned to England before the settlement was destroyed. His *Brief and True Report of the New-Found Land of Virginia* (1588) describes the New World to potential colonists at home. It is especially remarkable for its objective account of early encounters with the Indians, 'a people clothed with loose mantles made of deer skins', armed with 'bows made of witch-hazel and arrows of reeds', living in 'houses made of small poles made fast at the top in round form after the manner as is used in many arbours in our gardens of England'. The alleged intimacy of Captain John Smith's contact with the Indians has brought some notoriety to his *Generall History of Virginia, New England, and the Summer Isles* (1624), which tells how the clubs of King Powhatan's courtiers were prevented from beating out Smith's brains when the king's daughter, Pocahontas, 'got his head in her arms and laid her own upon his to save him from death'. The Indian king was astonished into granting Smith a reprieve. There is more to Smith than this uncorroborated romantic episode. His earlier report of Jamestown experiences in *A True Relation* (1608) is scrupulously factual and *A Description of New*

England (1616) encourages new settlers by its persuasive depiction of America as a land of opportunity.

Pilgrims and Puritans

In 1609 a group of English nonconformists migrated to Holland in search of religious freedom. When the young William Bradford joined them he was dissatisfied with the lack of economic opportunity and organised an expedition to the New World. Under Bradford's leadership about a hundred 'pilgrims' left Plymouth, England on the *Mayflower* 'to plant the First Colony in the Northern Parts of Virginia'. *The Mayflower Compact*, signed during the voyage, is the first notable document of American political history. It established the Plymouth colony in New England as 'a Civil Body Politic', an independent republic, until 1691 when it merged with the Massachusetts Bay Colony. Bradford became the second and most famous of the Plymouth colony's elected governors. His *History of Plymouth Plantation* (1856), written between 1620 and 1650, is among the most amiable of early American narrations, although Bradford's Puritan orthodoxy is less likely to appeal to twentieth-century readers than the wit of Thomas Morton's (*c*. 1575–*c*. 1647) *New English Canaan* (1637). Morton lampoons both Bradford and John Winthrop (1588–1640), first Governor of the Massachusetts Bay Colony, as dour representatives of a way of life inferior to that of the Indians to whom he sold liquor and guns. His settlement at Merry Mount (Quincy, Mass.) is the setting of Hawthorne's story, 'The May-pole of Merry-Mount', in which Morton's merrymaking is seen as the anarchic spirit of paganism inevitably opposing the restrictive simplifications of Puritanism.

The Massachusetts Bay Colony began in 1630 with a group of about a thousand Puritan refugees from England under Governor John Winthrop. Before the outbreak in 1642 of civil war in England, Charles I's repressive High Church measures motivated many thousands of Puritans to join the theocratic colony and spread its population across the landscape of New England. The dullness of the good Winthrop's conscientious *History of New England* (1790; 1826) is partly relieved by its accounts of Roger Williams (1603–83) and Anne Hutchinson (1591–1643), two of the period's most vigorous proponents of individuality within the Puritan system. Both Williams and Hutchinson were rebels against the exclusive, authoritarian Puritan rule as laid down by John Cotton (1584–1652) in *The Way of Life*

(1641). The most prolific writer of sermons in the early settlement, Cotton migrated to Massachusetts in 1633 from Cambridge where he had been Dean of Emmanuel College. He was soon an acknowledged patriarch of the colony, became pastor of the First Church in Boston, and enjoined strict adherence to Puritanism as defined by the Five Points of John Calvin: [1] Total Depravity as a consequence of the fallen Adam's original sin which stains all mankind; [2] Predestined Election whereby God chooses the 'elect' for salvation irrespective of faith or works; [3] Limited Atonement according to the belief that Christ's death redeems only the 'elect'; [4] the Irresistible Grace of God which can be neither rejected nor earned; [5] the Perseverance of the Saints on the assumption that, while no one can know how he fits into God's plan, the Puritan 'Saints' might expect to be among the saved. The prime Puritan virtues were industry and acceptance of God's law revealed in the Scriptures by the interpretation of the colony's church ministers.

Cotton's inflexibly Calvinist theology was institutionalised by a narrowly prescriptive formula for church government. In *The Keyes of the Kingdom of Heaven* (1644), an apparently liberal compromise between the independence of the Plymouth separatists and conformity to the Church of England (as practised in Virginia), masks a rigidity calculated to deprive the individual of freedoms available both to the Pilgrims and to communicants of the established Church. Cotton's statement of congregational principles develops the argument of Richard Mather's (1596–1616) *Church Government and Church Covenant Discussed* (1643) by freeing church congregations from all outside control. Each congregation was empowered to call and ordain its clergy and to admit, judge or excommunicate its members.

Voices of dissent

The congregational principle of freedom from external state or ecclesiastical control meant in practice that members of a church were thrall to their clergy. State authority had been replaced by theocratic fascism. A minister's unchallengeable command of Scripture made him the prime influence on the lives of his congregation. Eden on the east coast of America grew austere as hopes of rediscovered innocence yielded to an obsession with sin. Naturally there was reaction against a regimen so grimly authoritarian and so claustrophobic.

Exiled from England for his nonconformity, Thomas Hooker (1586–1647) went to Massachusetts from Delft in Holland where he had ministered to an English church. After three years at Newtown (Cambridge, Mass.) he and his congregation withdrew from the power of the New England theocracy to Hartford, Connecticut. Hooker's sermon on 'A True Sight of Sin' (1659) exemplifies a decorative and psychologically skilful preaching style; it also shows an awareness of the limitations of language:

> We must see it [sin] clearly in its own nature, its native colour and proper hue. It's not every slight conceit, not every general and cursory, confused thought or careless consideration that will serve the turn or do the work here. We are all sinners: it is my infirmity, I cannot help it; my weakness, I cannot be rid of it. No man lives without faults and follies, the best have their failings, 'In many things we offend all'. But alas! all this wind shakes no corn, it costs more to see sin aright than a few words of course. It's one thing to say sin is thus and thus, another thing to see it to be such . . . .

Hooker's theology is orthodox Puritan – 'A True Sight of Sin' ends with images of the 'fury of an offended God', 'the Devil's roaring', and 'flames of everlasting burning' – but his opposition to the union of church and state, or to churches that behaved like miniature states, and to the rise of property and religious tests for the franchise, make him a genuine democrat in recognisably modern terms. 'The foundation of authority', he says, 'is laid, firstly, in the free consent of the people', and he would not comply with the practice by which the people were tacitly assumed to have abrogated their rights in favour of the clergy's superior wisdom.

One of the most attractive seventeenth-century colonists was the high-spirited Roger Williams who arrived from England in 1631. While pastor at Salem he angered the Puritan establishment by urging greater separatism from the Church of England and also by proclaiming the English King a 'public liar' for illegally bestowing on the early settlers land that rightfully belonged to the Indians. He maintained that God was averse to all organised forms of church and that the conscience of the individual was pre-eminent over all civil and ecclesiastical institutions. The General Court of Massachusetts banished Williams in 1635. He founded a settlement at Providence, Rhode Island, which became famous for religious toleration and gave refuge to Anne Hutchinson when John Cotton discredited her for antinomianism. Despite its clumsy style, Williams's pamphlet *The Bloudy Tenent of Persecution, for Cause of Conscience* (1644) effectively challenged John Cotton's right to deny anyone's liberty of conscience. A wan reply from Cotton was answered by Williams's impassioned *The Bloudy Tenent Yet More Bloudy* (1652):

> I must profess, while heaven and earth lasts, that no one tenent . . . is so heretical, blasphemous, seditious, and dangerous, to the corporeal, to the spiritual, to the present, to the eternal good of man, as the bloudy tenent (however washed and whited) . . . of persecution for cause of conscience.

By the middle of the seventeenth century the American dialectic was being shaped in New England by new men from the Old World. There was a strong Puritan establishment with Boston increasingly its cultural centre. Attempts to impose conformity met with resistance albeit within the Puritan system. From the defections of those who broke from the rigid Puritanism represented by John Cotton sightings may be taken of the many different fundamentalist churches that were to spring up throughout America, today the most vigorously sectarian of all Christian countries. Roger Williams's community of religious toleration anticipates more secular Utopian experiments such as George Ripley's Brook Farm Institute (1841–6) at West Roxbury – the basis of Hawthorne's novel *The Blithedale Romance* (1852) – and the Helicon Home Hall colony (1906–7) which Upton Sinclair (1878–1968) founded in New Jersey on the proceeds of *The Jungle* (1906), his influential novel of protest about the Chicago stockyards. Thomas Hooker and Roger Williams are the moral and political ancestors of Thoreau's 'Civil Disobedience' (1849) first an article in a journal, of the resistance to Senator Joseph McCarthy's rabid anti-Communist witch-hunt in the early 1950s, and of the Civil Rights movement in the 1960s and 1970s.

The Mather dynasty

The Mathers are the first outstandingly accomplished American family, like the Jameses, the Adamses, the Roosevelts, the Kennedys. Reference to one member of such a family inevitably evokes a dynasty, a span of cultural history. The most substantial body of colonial writing is by the Mathers and it made a prodigious contribution to Puritan culture. Richard Mather (1596–1669) helped to prepare *The Bay Psalm Book* (1640), a revision of the Book of Psalms from the

Hebrew. It became popular both in New England and in Britain, despite much graceless versification:

> The Lord to me a shepherd is,
>   want therefore shall not I.
> He in the folds of tender grass,
>   doth cause me down to lie:
> To waters calm me gently leads
>   Restore my soul doth He:
> He doth in paths of righteousness:
>   for his name's sake lead me.

Richard Mather's *A Platform of Church Discipline* (1649) strongly influenced the formulation of church rules and policy.

The youngest and most distinguished of Richard's six sons, Increase Mather (1639–1723), became Pastor of North Church in Boston, secured a charter from William III which gave Massachusetts a greater degree of self-government than any other colony of the British Crown in America, and was President of Harvard College from 1685 until 1701. His *Cases of Conscience Concerning Evil Spirits Personating Men* (1693) seeks to vindicate the Mathers' part in the Salem witchcraft trials of 1692 whose social and psychological complexities Arthur Miller's (*b*. 1915) play *The Crucible* (1953) explores for modern audiences in its treatment of the theme of freedom of conscience. Although Increase Mather believed in the reality of witchcraft and the need to punish witches, he opposed 'spectre evidence' according to which Satan could assume the likeness of an innocent person.

Increase's versatile and dynamic eldest son, Cotton Mather (1663–1728), inveighed fervently against heretics but joined his father in criticising the Salem judges' use of 'spectre evidence'. Probably the most learned American of his time, his scientific interests won him election to the Royal Society of London in 1713. He incurred popular disapproval of his courageous advocacy of smallpox innoculation: when he innoculated his own son, who nearly died as a result, a bomb was thrown through his bedroom window. Cotton Mather regarded himself as a pillar of the Puritan theocracy and the most obvious feature of his masterpiece *Magnalia Christi Americana* (1702) is the epic grandeur with which it invests the first person singular. Here is Cotton Mather, the author as hero, Miltonically recounting the manifestation of God's plan in New England:

I write the wonders of the Christian religion, flying from the depravations of

Europe to the American strand; and, assisted by the holy author of that religion, I do, with all conscience of truth, required therein by Him who is the truth itself, report the wonderful display of His infinite power, wisdom, goodness and faithfulness, wherewith His divine providence hath irradiated an Indian wilderness.

Uncompromisingly Calvinist, the Mathers were believers rather than bigots, their prominence in seventeenth-century New England is largely owing to their being so energetically not only of their time, but also ahead of it politically, scientifically and morally.

Personal narratives

Many Puritans wrote diaries or 'personal narratives' which recorded everyday events, kept account of God's dealings and monitored the state of the writers' souls. The *Personal Narrative* (1740) of Jonathan Edwards (1703–58) describes the author's spiritual growth towards a direct apprehension of God and the New Jersey Quaker John Woolman's (1720–72) *Journal* (1774) attests both his personal sense of God and the peaceful altruism of his sect. Woolman's reactions to unacceptable laws and social practices – passive resistance and economic boycott – anticipate the kinds of 'Civil Disobedience' recommended by Thoreau in the middle of the nineteenth century. John Winthrop's *History of New England* (1790; 1826) fastidiously chronicles settler life from the sailing of the *Arbella* from Southampton in 1630 until his death in 1649. A more spectacular journal by far is Mary Rowlandson's (c. 1635–78) *The Soveraignty and Goodness of God*, customarily known by its subtitle, *A Narrative of the Captivity and Restauration of Mrs Mary Rowlandson* (1682). The wife of the Congregational minister in Lancaster, Massachusetts, Mary Rowlandson was wounded and captured with her daughter by the Narragansett Indians on 10 February 1675. A fall from horseback and exposure to the February snows led to the daughter's death ten days later. During an ordeal that lasted for eleven weeks and five days, when she was ransomed by money raised by the ladies of Boston, Mrs Rowlandson was transported to twenty different camps according to the Indians' 'usual manner to remove, when they had done any mischief, lest they should be found out'. The record of her experiences is the first Indian captivity narrative and, with some thirty reprints after its posthumous publication in 1682, the first American best-seller by a woman. Captivity narratives soon became a definite literary genre and appeared until the late nineteenth century. Some were consciously 'literary', like Samuel Bownas's version (1760) of Elizabeth Hanson's *God's Mercy Surmounting Man's Cruelty* (1728), some sensational as in the gory details of *French and Indian Cruelty Exemplified in the Life and Various Vicissitudes of Peter Williamson* (1757). Mary Rowlandson's unliterary style is spare but graphic:

> No sooner were we out of the House, but my Brother-in-Law (being before wounded, in defending the house, in or near the throat) fell down dead, whereat the Indians scornfully shouted, and hallowed, and were presently upon him, stripping off his clothes, the bullets flying thick, one went through my side, and the same (as would seem) through the bowels and hand of my dear Child in my arms. One of my elder sister's Children, named William, had then his Leg broken, which the Indians perceiving, they knockt him on head. Thus were we butchered by those merciless Heathen, standing amazed, with the blood running down to our heels. My eldest Sister being yet in the House, and seeing those woeful sights, the Infidels hauling Mothers one way, and Children another, and some wallowing in their own blood: and her elder Son telling her that her Son William was dead, and myself was wounded, she said, And Lord, let me die with them; which was no sooner said, but she was struck with a Bullet, and fell down dead over the threshold.

Puritan habits of mind readily associated Indians with the Devil in the eternal conflict between Heaven and Hell. Mrs Rowlandson's natives, like those of Cotton Mather's Indian massacres in the *Magnalia Christi Americana* are pagan 'Wolves' descended upon Christian 'Sheep', 'Infidels', 'Barbarous Creatures'. Puritan resolution implausibly celebrates the mercy of God despite extreme adversity – 'Oh, I may see the wonderful power of God, that my Spirit did not utterly sink under my affliction' – but neither Mrs Rowlandson nor her contemporaries make any substantial effort to understand the culture of the Indians or their perception of whites as aliens. The Indian was being allocated his role in American mythology, a typecasting from which the popular imagination has scarcely allowed him to recover, even if Mrs Rowlandson does concede of her abductors that 'not one of them ever offered me the least abuse of unchastity to me, in word or action'.

The lively *Diary* of Samuel Sewall (1652–1730) is a detailed record of life in New England from 1674 to 1729 (with a break from 1677–85). After graduating from Harvard, Sewall rose to the position of chief justice of the superior court of judicature and although he helped to condemn to death some nineteen supposed witches at the Salem trials, he subsequently made a public confession of 'blame and shame' in the persecution. The *Diary* exhibits a man for whom Puritanism was not merely a set of rigid, unexaminable tenets, but an apparatus with which a Christian might try to live humanely and transact his business with fairness and efficiency. The homelier entries in the *Diary* show how simple things naturally prompted this honest, sensitive man to proportionate religious thought without supplanting domestic reality by Puritan theology or catapulting him into Bible-thumping rhetoric:

> Jan. 13, 1677. Giving my chickens meat, it came to my mind that I gave them nothing save Indian corn and water, and yet they eat it and thrived very well, and that that food was necessary for them, how mean soever, which much affected me and convinced what need I stood in of spiritual food, and that I should not nauseat daily duties of Prayer, & c.

> Oct. 19, 1717. . . . About a quarter of an hour past four, my dear Wife expired in the Afternoon, whereby the Chamber was fill'd with a Flood of Tears. God is teaching me a new Lesson; to live a Widower's Life. Lord help me to Learn; and be a Sun and Shield, to me, now so much of my Comfort and Defense are taken away.

Although orthodoxly Calvinist in his religion, Sewall was a compassionate man who believed that slaves and Indians should be kindly treated. His *The Selling of Joseph* (1700) is the first anti-slavery tract to be published in America. Shaped by the seventeenth century, his reasonableness and humanity took him beyond its limitations to anticipate the enlightenment of the succeeding age.

Bradstreet, Wigglesworth and Taylor

Most colonial poetry is bad. English models – often inferior ones – were ineptly copied and wit was scarce among the early settlers even when they had the leisure to cultivate it. America's first poet of intermittent talent, Anne Bradstreet (*c.* 1612–72), arrived with her husband at Massachusetts on the *Arbella* in 1630. Her poems, the first volume of collected verse by an American poet, were published in London in 1650 as *The Tenth Muse Lately Sprung up in America*, a title chosen without her knowledge by her brother-in-law. Most of the poems are long, and display at best a modest competence in emulating minor English writers. Her reputation today is founded on a few shorter pieces included in the posthumous collection, *Several Poems* (1678) and in J. H. Ellis's edition of *The Works of Anne Bradstreet in Prose and Verse* (1867). 'Verses upon the Burning of Our House' combines simple narrative efficiency with the religious conviction that her true home 'stands permanent' in heaven; but the poem's most touching feature is the inventory her 'sorrowing eyes' make of cherished furnishings and domestic pleasures gone for ever:

> Here stood that Trunk, and there that chest;
> There lay that store I counted best:
> My pleasant things in ashes lye,
> And them behold no more shall I.
> Under thy roof no guest shall sitt,
> Nor at thy Table eat a bitt.

'The Flesh and the Spirit' is a dialogue between two sisters, in which crisp octosyllabic couplets strengthen the spirit's assertion of the superior felicities of heaven. It is Mrs Bradstreet's more openly human poems, however, especially the tender love poems to her husband, that speak most affectingly to the modern reader and distinguish her from the repressions of her background. The heroine of John Berryman's (1914–72) *Homage to Mistress Bradstreet* ((1956) is the authoress of 'To My Dear and Loving Husband':

> If ever two were one, then surely we.
> If ever man were lov'd by wife, then thee;
> If ever wife was happy in a man,
> Compare with me ye women if you can.
> I prize thy love more than whole Mines of gold,
> Or all the riches that the East doth hold.
> My love is such that Rivers cannot quench,
> Nor ought but love from thee, give recompense.
> Thy love is such I can no way repay,
> The heavens reward thee manifold, I pray.
> Then while we live, in love lets so persever,
> That when we live no more, we may live ever.

The most popular poem by a colonist was Michael Wigglesworth's (1631–1705) Calvinist apocalypse, *The Day of Doom, or a Poetical Description of the Great and Last Judgement* (1662). James Russell Lowell (1819–91) ironically supposes that this bizarre and pretentious poem was 'the solace of every fire-side, the flicker of the pine knots by which it was conned perhaps adding a livelier relish to its premonitions of eternal combustion'. Published in the same year as the restoration of the repugnant Stuart dynasty, the 1,800-line poem brought a timely reminder of Puritan principles, drew attention away from the momentary triumph of the unrighteous and catered to the sado-masochistic elements of Puritan psychology. 'Carnal reason' would be confounded by the exaltation of the saints on Judgement Day when the ungodly, who 'put away the evil day and drowned their care and fears', would be 'swept away by vengeance unawares'. Today the poem reads like self-parody, nowhere more so than in the passage where Christ the Judge kindly awards unbaptised babies the 'easiest room in Hell'.

The highly wrought poetry of Edward Taylor (*c.* 1642–1729) was not published during his life. Fortunately his heirs did not obey his instruction to destroy his 400-page manuscript, and a grandson presented it to Yale University Library. In 1937 the manuscript was critically 'discovered' and editions of the poems followed – selected in 1937 and complete in 1960. A Congregationalist schoolteacher, Taylor was a refugee from the restored authority of the Church of England. He arrived in Boston in 1668, graduated from Harvard College, where he became a lifelong friend of Samuel Sewall, and for fifty-eight years served as both pastor and physician in the village of Westfield, Massachusetts. His poetry, similar to that of seventeenth-century metaphysical poets such as Donne, Herbert and Crashaw, is distinctly superior to any produced by his colonial contemporaries.

Taylor's works consist of a small number of miscellaneous poems and two main groups entitled 'God's Determinations Touching His Elect' and 'Preparatory Meditations'. The first group is a verse sequence which glorifies in dialogue form the 'Might Almighty' of God as a drama of sin and redemption. It sets out to justify the Puritan doctrine of God's covenant of Grace, by which all people may hope for salvation if they believe in Christ, whose spirit, predictably, renders impotent the 'Dreadfull Enemy', his 'Cur', Satan. If the sequence of varied stanzas and verse forms is uneven in quality, it achieves a strong cumulative effect because Taylor's metaphorical audacity commends itself as arising not from mere calculation but from genuine religious ardour.

The greater part of Taylor's manuscript comprises two series of poems, 217 in all, each of which is preceded by a Scriptural text. Taylor's habit was to compose a 'Meditation' as a way of compacting the argument of the Communion Sunday Sermon he was about to preach. Like George Herbert he appreciated the rhetorical value of analogies taken from everyday life, and like Donne he is adept at bringing heterogeneous elements into surprising coherence. If he is less intellectually distinguished than Donne, he is also less violent: the process of association is more fluent, the rhythm of thought gentler. In the well-known eighth 'Meditation' of the First Series, based on *John* 6: 51, 'I am the living bread', incongruous images blend, imparting quasi-allegorical meaning to each other, as the poet works his way from a sense of deprivation towards peace of mind. The soul, a 'Bird of Paradise', has been put in a 'Wicker Cage', the body, 'to tweedle praise' to God. Pecking the forbidden fruit, the Bird has fallen into 'Celestiall Famine sore':

> Alas! alas! Poore Bird, what wilt thou doe?
> The Creatures field no food for Souls e're gave:
> And if thou knock at Angells dores, they show
> An Empty Barrell: they no soul bread have.
> Alas! Poore Bird, the Worlds White Loafe is done,
> And cannot yield thee here the smallest Crumb.

God comes to the rescue by grinding the 'Bread of Life', his Son, and serving it as 'Heaven's Sugar Cake', a 'Food too fine for Angells'.

In his most anthologised poem, 'Huswifery', Taylor succeeds in employing the technique of the conceit only to transcend his own device at the climax of the poem. He begins by asking to be God's spinning wheel. His affections will be the flyers, his soul the spool, his conversation the reel. Metaphors of spinning are developed until the poet imagines himself no longer the machine for spinning but the completed garment, woven by God:

> Then mine apparell shall display before yee
> That I am cloathed in Holy robes for glory.

The Enlightenment and the Great Awakening

If the manuscript sermons of Edward Taylor reveal a fervently orthodox Puritan theologian, the poetry displays two symptoms of the eighteenth rather than the seventeenth century. One is the human emphasis, Taylor's particular joy in the fusion of human and divine natures in Christ, the other is the mixture – and range – of reason and emotion in the poetry's treatment of religious experience. There is a new openness here which looks to the future. The mental and emotional effort involved in each act of Communion preaching – biblical text, sermon, 'Preparatory Meditation' – presents a man for whom the theological dogmatism of the seventeenth century was not enough. There is as much personal as there is biblical exegesis in Taylor's verse. The preacher–poet who so often turned to 'The Song of Solomon' for his inspiration had to work with all his faculties to establish a secure, fully satisfying theological position from which to direct the Communion of his congregation. Taylor therefore illustrates the great shift of focus from the mind of God to the mind of man that is the essential feature of the Enlightenment. The passion and intensity of his writing also pre-figure the religious emotionalism of the Great Awakening stimulated in America by the teachings of the Methodists imported to the colonies in the late 1730s and 1740s by John and Charles Wesley and the spellbinding George Whitefield. In the secular aftermath of Descartes, Newton and Locke new status was accorded individual reason, and in the revivalism of the Great Awakening, the individual was exhorted to search his own heart. By either emphasis, individualism was on the march. Nowhere did it travel further or more rapidly than in America and nowhere has it taken more flamboyant forms.

Jonathan Edwards and other individualists

The most complex transitional figure of his time was Jonathan Edwards. In the latter part of the seventeenth century the Puritan church had admitted all its members to Communion in the belief that it might bring grace to the unregenerate. Edwards believed that only those who had experienced conversion were entitled to Communion. The astonishingly skilful rhetoric of the sermons he preached at Northampton, Massachusetts, often induced a state of frenzied ecstasy in his listeners. Edwards made hundreds of converts in four or five months in 1734–5, and was only temporarily discomfited by the shocked reaction to the suicide of Joseph Hawley, his uncle-by-marriage. For Edwards the death of his uncle was clearly the work of Satan, a sign that 'the spirit of God was gradually withdrawing from us', and that his people stood in urgent need of reclamation. In July 1741 he delivered his most famous sermon, 'Sinners in the Hands of an Angry God', to a congregation in Enfield, Massachusetts. The method of the style is an onslaught of closely packed, highly affective images, varied rhythms and changing tempi. With a shrewd sense of audience psychology, Edwards insinuates a parallel between the wrath of God and the familiar fear of Indian attack:

> The bow of God's wrath is bent, and the arrow made ready on the string, and justice bends the arrow at your heart, and strains the bow, and it is nothing but the mere pleasure of God, without any promise or obligation at all, that keeps the arrow one moment from being made drunk with your blood.

Having softened up his listeners by portraying their vulnerability in recognisable terms, Edwards then plays on their capacity for self-contempt and presses his rhetorical advantage to pure nightmare:

> The God that holds you over the pit of hell, much as one holds a spider, or some loathsome insect over the first, abhors you, and is dreadfully provoked: his wrath towards you burns like fire; he looks upon you as worthy of nothing else, but to be cast into the fire; he is of purer eyes than to bear to have you in his sight; you are ten thousand times more abominable in his eyes, than the most hateful venomous serpent is in ours.

The people of Enfield moaned and screamed; two hundred years later the force of Edwards's language and imagery moved Robert Lowell to write his poem 'Mr Edwards and the Spider'.

There is, however, more to Edwards than hell-fire. In 1751 the Northampton congregation voted him out of his pastorate. He went to the remote parish of Stockbridge, did missionary work among the Housatonic Indians, and wrote the great theological studies which established his scholarly reputation. These studies place Edwards intellectually on the isthmus of a middle state between the beliefs and mentalities of two eras. It is conventional Puritan dogma to assert, as Edwards does in 'The Nature of True Virtue', that true virtue (as distinct from 'secondary virtue') is a mysterious gift of God; but it is an eighteenth-century mentality which seeks to prove this by un-remittingly logical procedures. A concern to systematise Puritan theology leads Edwards to develop his allegorical theory of types (objects of nature) and anti-types (divine things); but it is a more individual and modern imagination which sees visible and mundane 'types' as lively images of the spiritual 'anti-types' and which, therefore, respects the senses as crucial faculties of apprehension.

Something of Edwards' ability to combine faith and reason in reverence for both God and the natural world is found again in the Quaker explorer William Bartram (1739–1823), son of the first American botanist. Bartram became known in America and Europe by his *Travels through North and South Carolina, Georgia, East and West Florida* (1791) and despite his florid style was apparently read with pleasure by Coleridge, Wordsworth and Chateaubriand. Wide savannahs, mighty forests, unscaled mountains and even traces of nobility among Indians are all signs of a beneficent God, but they are also accurately observed by a scientific eye. A traveller more thoroughly of the Enlightenment was the enterprising Mrs Sarah Kemble Knight (1666–1727), a Boston schoolteacher who journeyed alone on horseback from Boston to New York and back in 1704–5. Her *Journal* (1825) notices bad roads, gimcrack bridges, hard beds in sleazy inns, and delineates a rich gallery of character types: the city slicker, the debauched Indian, the slatternly inn hostess, the gawky

Connecticut Yankee, and the rustic 'Bumpkin Simpers' who 'spit a Large deal of aromatic tincture'. Despite danger, discomfort and indigestible food, Madam Knight is irrepressible: she even has a method for silencing a tavern brawl that threatens to keep her from sleeping:

> I could get no sleep, because of the Clamor of some of the Town topers in next Room, who were entered into a strong debate concerning the Signification of the name of their Country, (viz.) *Narraganset*. One said it was named so by the Indians, because there grew a Brier there, of a prodigious Height and bigness, . . . His Antagonist Replied no – It was from a Spring it had its name . . . He utter'd with such a Roaring voice and Thundering blows with the fist of wickedness on the Table, that it pierced my very head . . . I set my Candle on a Chest by the bedside, and setting up, fell to my old way of composing my Resentments, in the following manner:
>
> > I ask thy Aid, O Potent Rum!
> > To charm these wrangling Topers Dumb.
> > Thou hast their Giddy Brains possesst –
> > The man confounded with the Beast –
> > And I, poor I, can get no rest.
> > Intoxicate them with thy fumes:
> > O still their Tongues till morning comes!

And I know not but my wishes took effect, for the dispute soon ended with t'other Dram; and so Good Night!

The South

Early Southern colonists were English, French and Spanish settlers with more worldly attitudes and ambitions than those of the English, Dutch and German immigrants who established themselves in the North. The plantation system, the traumas of Civil War and Reconstruction, and the rise and fall of the cotton economy combined to make the South become the most unified and self-conscious region of the United States. Conventionally eleven states are included in the South – Virginia, North and South Carolina, Georgia, Florida, Alabama, Mississippi, Louisiana, Kentucky, Tennessee and Arkansas – and sometimes Maryland, Missouri and Delaware.

It was not until the twentieth century that the South's preoccupation with itself yielded a substantial body of imaginative writing of rare variety and accomplishment. If more fiction was read in the colonial South than in the Puritanical North, few novels were written and poetry of aesthetic worth was virtually non-existent. Like the North the region produced sermons and historical records. The Wesleys and

George Whitefield were active in Georgia and Virginia, the new spirit of Methodism promoting 'Trances, Visions, and Revelations, both among Blacks and Whites, in abundance'. Nathaniel Bacon's (1647–76) rebellion against Sir William Berkeley, Governor of Virginia, is documented in the so-called 'Burwell Manuscript'. It led to the destruction of Jamestown by Bacon and his followers in 1676, and exposed seventeenth-century colonial life as far from paradisal. Bacon was incensed by social conditions in the colony: 'The poverty of the country is such that all the power and sway is got into the hands of the rich, who by extortious advantages, having the common people in their debt, have always curbed and oppressed them in all manner of ways'. A more literary malcontent was the shadowy Ebenezer Cook (c. 1672–1732), probably an Englishman, whose breezy satirical poem, *The Sot-Weed Factor; or, A Voyage to Maryland* (1708) may have helped him to earn the title of 'Laureate' from Lord Baltimore and records his failure to succeed as a tobacco merchant because of the fraudulent practices of mendacious colonists. The verse is modelled on Samuel Butler's *Hudibras*, and the poem ends with a curse:

> May Cannibals transported o'er the Sea
> Prey on these Slaves, as they have done on me;
> May never Merchant's trading Sails explore
> This Cruel, this Inhospitable Shore;
> But left abandon'd by the World to starve,
> May they sustain the Fate they well deserve:
> May they turn Savage, or as Indians Wild,
> From Trade, Converse, and Happiness exil'd;
> Recreant to Heaven, may they adore the Sun,
> And into Pagan Superstitions run
> For Vengeance ripe –
> May Wrath Divine then lay those Regions waste
> When no Man's Faithful, nor a Woman Chaste.

John Barth (b. 1930) brilliantly reanimates Cook as the angular, mercurial hero of his satirical novel *The Sot-Weed Factor* (1960).

Enterprising sons of middle-class tradesmen and younger sons of English gentry created the economic basis of the South's early development. They grew their tobacco, rice and indigo on fifty-acre farms until the slave-trade boom in the eighteenth century enabled a single man to supervise the cultivation of large areas of land. William Byrd (1674–1744) was the son of an unusually astute Virginia planter and local politician who, by the time of his death in 1704, had increased his estate to over 26,000 acres. Byrd spent much of his life in

England, where he studied law at London's Middle Temple and served as an agent of the colony. Although he incurred heavy debts in building his Georgian mansion at Westover and further extending his lands, he was the leading public figure of his time in the colony and epitomised the Virginia aristocrat. He died in possession of nearly 180,000 acres, a library of over 3,600 volumes, and a private diary in shorthand, recently decoded, whose entries for the years 1717–21 distinguish the leisure pursuits of the Southern grandee from those of his Puritan contemporaries:

> 29 May, 1719, London . . . After dinner we played at faro and I won forty shillings. About 6 o'clock I went to Will's Coffeehouse, and from there to Lady Guise's and then returned to Will's where Margaret G–t–n called on me and I went with her to the bagnio where I rogered her three times with vigour, twice at night and once in the morning. I neglected my prayers.

A royal commission to survey the boundary between Virginia and North Carolina issued in a *History of the Dividing Line* (1728) in which Byrd writes with the man of wit's concision about the unashamedly casual living he found on the small-holdings of North Carolina farmers and backwoodsmen. The title of his less tolerant *A Journey to the Land of Eden* (1733) is ironic. Now the independence of the feckless North Carolina settlers strikes him as wasteful and dangerous. This is not Eden, but an uncivilised, boorish 'Lubberland'.

If the South was slow to produce poetry or fiction of quality, men from Virginia led America in the literature of politics. Edmund Randolph's 'Virginia Plan' to centralise government and include a triumvirate of executives from three regions contributed to the Constitutions' eventual compromise between centralisation and local autonomy. James Madison's (1751–1836) writings in *The Federalist* helped win support for the Constitution in the separate states. Above all, Thomas Jefferson's knowledge of the philosophy of Locke together with his forceful, sophisticated prose helped to make the Declaration of Independence the foremost literary work of the American Revolution.

3

The revolution

AMERICA was propelled into the first phase of defined nationhood by the greed of the government in London and Britain's propensity for underestimating her colonists. The second phase was initiated by the Civil War which, European influences notwithstanding, was an American production. Eighteenth-century imperial arrogance blinded a series of George III's ministries to the economic and political maturing of the American colonies. Though accustomed to contributing to the wealth of the mother country, the colonists increasingly objected to remote control of their lives by taxes and regulations imposed by a government three thousand miles away. Particularly repressive and humiliating were the taxes levied by the Sugar Act (1764), the Stamp Act (1765) and the Townshend Acts (1767), which charged duties on imported glass, lead, paint, paper and tea. Resistance led to the Boston massacre in 1770, a skirmish between British troops and a crowd in Boston in which five protesters, including Crispus Attucks, a Black sailor and former slave, were shot and killed by harassed British troops. Although most of the Townshend Acts were repealed, the tax on tea remained to provoke the defiance of the Boston Tea Party in 1773.

There were public rallies, press agitation and economic boycotts. In 1772 Samuel Adams (1722–1803) organised the first Committee of Correspondence at Boston, and within a few months some eighty such groups had been formed throughout Massachusetts. Their original function was to correspond with colonial agents in Britain, but they rapidly became more useful as agencies of co-operation between the thirteen colonial legislatures. These committees, together with Virginia's legislative standing committees, promoted unity among the colonies and were largely responsible for organising the First Continental Congress, which was the earliest formal expression of unified resistance to British authority. With Boston under British military jurisdiction, the Congress met in Philadelphia on 5 September

1774, rejected a plan for reconciling colonial freedom with British rule and drew up a declaration of rights and grievances. Parliamentary regulation of American commerce was accepted, but taxation without representation was denounced as was the British military presence. Boycott of British goods was called for, and a second Congress scheduled for the following year.

New members of the Second Continental Congress included Benjamin Franklin (1706–90) and Thomas Jefferson but before it met, the War for Independence had begun at Lexington and Concord when British troops engaged in gunfire with 'embattled farmers'. Congress appointed George Washington commander-in-chief of the Continental Army. His determination was largely responsible for keeping the war going despite a succession of military failures and the difficulty of recruiting enough soldiers among colonists who were traditionally opposed to regular armies, and farmers whose first allegiance was to their fields. The conflict was initially a civil war within the empire, but as colonial resentment was fed by British contempt, and by the Crown's use of some 30,000 mercenaries bought from German princes, the popular demand grew for independence.

On 2 July 1776 Congress declared that 'these United Colonies are, and of right, ought to be, free and independent states'. The Declaration of Independence was approved two days later. General Burgoyne's surrender at Saratoga in 1777 emboldened the French to increase their support of the colonists from secret financial and material aid to formal alliance in 1778. Lord Cornwallis's defeat at Yorktown in 1781 effectively ended the war on land, and by the Treaty of Paris on 3 September 1783 Great Britain recognised the independence of the United States. Immediately after Washington's early defeat at the Battle of Long Island in August 1776, the first pamphlet of Thomas Paine's (1737–1809) *The American Crisis* series began with the words, 'These are the times that try men's souls'. In the thirteenth pamphlet Paine recalled his own words, triumphantly inaugurating the new era: '"The times that tried men's souls" are over – and the greatest and completest revolution the world ever knew, gloriously and happily accomplished.' The ground was ready for the Frenchman, Hector St John de Crèvecoeur's (1735–1813) influential romantic myth of the American character in *Letters from an American Farmer* (1782). Identifying with the revolutionary American's idea of himself, de Crèvecoeur writes: 'We have no princes for whom we toil, starve and bleed: we are the most perfect society now existing in the world. Here man is free as he ought to be.'

The affinity of aesthetic to religious sensibility meant that artistic imagination was subdued in a period when religion was suspect. Ethics prevailed over theology, although the men of the Enlightenment were not, as a rule, atheists. They tended, like John Adams (1735–1826) and Benjamin Franklin, to call themselves deists. In a letter written in his last year to the President of Yale, Franklin defines the benevolent deism by which he sought to live:

> I believe in one God, Creator of the Universe. That he governs it by his Providence. That he ought to be worshipped. That the most acceptable service we render to him is doing good to his other children. That the soul of Man is immortal, and will be treated with Justice in another life respecting its conduct in this. These I take to be the fundamental Principles of all sound Religion, and I regard them as you do in whatever Sect I meet with them.

In relation to seventeenth-century Puritanism, this resembles 'the Religion of Sentiment and Reason' professed by a man like Robert Burns in opposition to the strict Calvinism of his upbringing. The bias of the new age was secular, its preoccupation not with the nature and authority of God, but with the power of human reason, the natural rights of man and the forms of society which would best express and guarantee them. Especially in America it was a time not for art but for politics. Thomas Jefferson held the novel a 'great obstacle' to education and James Madison thought that 'poetry, wit, and criticism, romances, plays, etc., deserve but a small portion of a man's time'.

The ablest minds of the Revolutionary years concentrated on making a nation. In addition to the Declaration of Independence, the great texts of the time are speeches, political essays and pamphlets such as *Common Sense* (1776), Thomas Paine's eloquent, inflammatory manifesto excoriating monarchy and clamouring for 'the rights of mankind and of the free and independent states of America'. There is more specific and intricate political philosophy in the papers of *The Federalist* (1787–8) by Alexander Hamilton (1757–1804), John Jay (1745–1829), and James Madison. Hamilton wrote some two-thirds of the eighty-five papers, arguing for the superiority of the 1787 Constitution over the Articles of Confederation which Congress had adopted in 1781, and which provided only a feeble and ineffective central government. Madison too urged adoption of the Constitution which he had been largely responsible for framing.

Much distinction is to be found in public and private letters from John Dickinson's (1732–1808) denunciation of colonial taxes in *Letters from a Farmer in Pennsylvania to the Inhabitants of the British Colonies* (1767–8; 1773), printed in Pennsylvania newspapers, to the rich correspondence between the conservative John Adams and the liberal Thomas Jefferson. It is above all the name of Jefferson which, with that of Benjamin Franklin, stands out during this volatile period of American cultural history.

Benjamin Franklin

Printer and publisher, author, scientist, inventor and diplomat, Benjamin Franklin (1706–90) became a symbol of the Enlightenment in America and one of the most famous and respected men in the world. From 1757 until 1785 he lived mostly in England or in France, keenly and effectively promoting American interests. As Philadelphia's delegate to the Second Continental Congress he helped to draft the Declaration of Independence and in 1776 elicited French aid for the colonists. At the end of the war he was chosen as one of the diplomats responsible for negotiating terms of peace with Great Britain. Best known in America during his lifetime for his publication of *Poor Richard's Almanack* (1732–57), he also invented the Franklin stove, the lightning rod, the smokeless chimney and bifocal spectacles. As successful in business as in the scientific experiments which made him a world authority on electricity – 'the new Prometheus' as Emmanuel Kant called him – his exemplary civic energies brought Philadelphia a fire department, street lighting and a sewage system, a lending library and a college that became the University of Pennsylvania. To writings on religious, philosophical, political and economic matters, he added the whimsy of his *Bagatelles* (1776–85) and gradually, from 1771 until shortly before his death, the memoirs that became known as *The Autobiography of Benjamin Franklin* (1791; 1868).

Born in Boston, tenth son of an English tallow chandler and soap-maker, Franklin was apprenticed at twelve to his half-brother James, a printer, after one year of formal schooling. His literary debut was as 'Silence Dogood' whose sniping comments on local affairs Franklin slipped under James's office door for publication in the *New England Courant*. After a quarrel with his brother he broke his indentures and left for Philadelphia where he gained employment in the print shop of Samuel Keimer. Encouraged by Governor Keith of Pennsylvania he went to England to obtain his own printing equipment. While abroad he wrote the narrowly rationalistic *Dissertation on*

Liberty and Necessity, Pleasure and Pain (1725), disallowing the distinction between good and evil and denying the moral responsibility of the individual on the ground that all things are predetermined. Thus delivered at nineteen of this chill adolescent intellectuality, he went on full-bloodedly to oppose in everything he did and wrote all forms of deterministic philosophy.

Back in Philadelphia, Franklin set up his printery, manipulated Keimer into selling him *The Pennsylvania Gazette*, and in 1732 published the first issue of the phenomenally successful *Poor Richard's Almanack*, compiled under the *nom de plume* of Richard Saunders. In annual sales of some ten thousand copies *Poor Richard* conveyed throughout the colonies a uniquely influential mixture of information, practical advice and geniality to people who read little else but the Bible. In three editions, each with specifically local data for New England, the middle colonies and the South, the *Almanack* brought its readers facts about weather and astronomy, simple accounts of eighteenth-century science and philosophy, and maxims for living which Franklin often took from other writers but altered to make them crisper. Thus 'A Man in Passion rides a horse that runs away with him' becomes 'A Man in Passion rides a mad Horse'; 'Fresh fish and new come guests, smell by they are three days old' is sharpened to 'Fish and visitors stink in three days'. All this, and a serial too, for Dick Saunders, living in the country with his wife Bridget, provided pre-comic-strip continuity from year to year. *The Way to Wealth*, originally in the form of a letter to the *Almanack* for 1758, proved one of Franklin's most popular writings. In it Richard describes a public auction where he heard an old man, Father Abraham, recommending financial caution with the support of quotations from *Poor Richard's Almanack*: 'Nothing gives an author so great Pleasure, as to find his Works respectfully quoted by other learned Authors'.

If *Poor Richard* illustrates a pragmatic flair for harmonising commercial talent with missionary purpose, Franklin's literary sophistication is evident in two short pieces in the manner of Swift. 'An Edict by the King of Prussia' and 'Rules by which a Great Empire may be reduced to a Small One', both published in 1773, satirise British exploitation of the colonists. Franklin's 'Rules' include the taxes and restrictions currently imposed by the government in London. In the 'Edict' the Prussian monarch decrees that fifth-century German emigration, which gave Britain its Anglo-Saxon stock, entitles eighteenth-century Prussia to tax the English. The final insult of the mock analogy is aimed at Britain's use of the colonies as a dumping ground for criminals:

And lastly, being willing farther to favour our said colonies in Britain, we do hereby also ordain and command, that all the thieves, highway and street robbers, house-breakers, forgerers, murderers, s–t–tes [i.e. sodomites], and villains of every denomination, who have forfeited their lives to the law in Prussia; but whom we, in our great clemency, do not think fit here to hang, shall be emptied out of our goals into the said island of Great Britain, for the better peopling of that country.

The candid self-portrait of the *Autobiography*, intended for his son William, was begun when Franklin was sixty-five. Additions were made in 1783–4 and 1788 which more than doubled the size of the manuscript but brought the story of Franklin's life only to the years 1757–9, when his international career was just beginning. The record of his years as a statesman is known from his large correspondence and from other private and public papers. The *Autobiography* provides useful information about Franklin's earlier years and reflects the tastes, morality and psychology of the period; but the book's chief attraction is the balanced humanity that underlies everything he says and the civilised tones of his comfortable voice as he recalls matters of fact and offers opinions. Mild but never bland, the book is frank, and unfailingly well-mannered without being precious. From his acquisition of a 'good and faithful helpmate' in Deborah Read – preferable to 'intrigues with low women that fell in my way' – the narrative flows on to his proposal for a subscription library, recollection of meetings with kings, reflections on his Presbyterian upbringing, and his 'bold and arduous project of arriving at moral perfection'. Franklin drew up a list of thirteen virtues and 'annexed to each a short precept which fully expressed the extent I gave to its meaning'. Thus Temperance is glossed: 'Eat not to dullness. Drink not to elevation'; Frugality: 'Make no expense but to do good to others or yourself, i.e., waste nothing'; Moderation: 'Avoid extremes. Forbear resenting injuries so much as you think they deserve'. If this borders on archness, Humility, the thirteenth virtue, prompts a disarmingly wry comment:

My list of virtues contained at first but twelve. But a Quaker friend having kindly informed me that I was generally thought proud; that my pride showed itself frequently in conversation; that I was not content with being in the right when discussing any point but was overbearing and rather insolent, of which he convinced me by mentioning several instances; I determined endeavouring to cure myself, if I could, of this vice or folly among the rest, and I added humility to my list . . . I cannot boast of much success in acquiring the *reality* of this virtue, but I had a good deal with regard to the *appearance* of it.

Thomas Jefferson

Almost as versatile as Franklin, and equally devoted to the American cause, Thomas Jefferson (1743–1826) differed from his older compatriot in background, temperament and philosophy. The self-educated Franklin's origins were humble, his character gregarious and his view of life pragmatic. Jefferson came from a well-to-do Virginia family, graduated from the College of William and Mary, was of retiring disposition, and an idealist. His belief that man was by nature 'endowed with a sense of right and wrong' gave American democracy its basic premise as his rhetoric gave it voice.

Although Jefferson's wide-ranging interests in science, history, education, architecture and language are recorded in a voluminous collection of letters and papers, he was not a literary man in the sense that Franklin was. Yet the Declaration of Independence, supreme text of the period, remains substantially his, despite revisions by the committee appointed to draft it and further emendations by Congress. However questionable philosophically, Jefferson's central assertion is the idea of America which expresses the colonists' impetus towards nationality and states the principles to which American politics must always refer:

> We hold these truths to be self-evident: that all men are created equal; that they are endowed by their Creator with certain inalienable rights; that among these are life, liberty, and the pursuit of happiness.

Jefferson's only book is *Notes on the State of Virginia* (1784–5), an answer to questions from the secretary of the French legation at Philadelphia about the character of the American people and their land. The idealised picture Jefferson gives in *Notes* of the small farmer reflects the convictions about rustic virtue and urban depravity expressed in a famous letter of 1757 to James Madison:

> This reliance [i.e. on the will of the majority of the people] cannot deceive us as long as we remain virtuous; and I think we shall be so, as long as agriculture is our principal object, which will be the case, while there remains vacant lands in any part of America. When we get piled upon one another in large cities, as in Europe, we shall become corrupt as in Europe, and go to eating one another as they do there.

By an almost Wordsworthian equation of agrarianism and the life of simple virtue Jefferson believed that agriculture would shield Americans from the complex fate of Europe. A benign nature would be the nourishing context for a republic of yeoman farmers. The impact on the American imagination of Jefferson's authoritative views of man and nature can hardly be over-estimated. His belief in nature's fundamental goodness and the natural integrity of the individual set precedents for the philosophy of Emerson – and other Transcendentalists of the nineteenth century – which moved Hawthorne and Melville to fruitful contradiction and instated moral ambiguity as a recurrent theme in American literature.

Poetry

It took the War of 1812 to elicit 'The Star-Spangled Banner' from Francis Scott Key (1779–1843), but the passionately anti-Federalist Philip Freneau (1752–1832) was dubbed 'The Poet of the American Revolution' for his patriotic verses and satires against the British like 'George the Third's Soliloquy' in which the harassed King wonders what action is left to him now that France has allied herself with the colonists and the tide of the war has turned against him:

> France aids them now, a desperate game I play,
> And hostile Spain will do the same, they say;
> My armies vanquished, and my heroes fled,
> My people murmuring, and my commerce dead,
> My shattered navy pelted, bruised, and clubbed,
> By Dutchmen bullied, and by Frenchmen drubbed,
> My name abhorred, my nation in disgrace,
> How should I act in such a mournful case!
> My hopes and joys are vanished with my coin,
> My ruined army, and my lost Burgoyne!

In the end the King realises that defeat in the war is not the worst that could happen:

> I must submit, and that with bloody nose,
> Or, like our James, fly basely from the State,
> Or share, what still is worse – old *Charles's* fate.

Here Freneau echoes Patrick Henry's famous speech of 1765 to the Virginia House of Burgesses: 'Caesar had his Brutus, Charles the First his Cromwell and George the Third may profit by their example.' Imprisoned twice by the British for revolutionary activities, Freneau denounced his captors in the three cantos of 'The British Prison Ship' (1780) and he so vigorously opposed the Federalist politics of Alexander Hamilton and John Adams that Washington

claimed he had saved the American Constitution 'when it was galloping fast into monarchy'. Hating the English, Freneau became
obsessively nationalistic and in later life refused to wear clothing or
eat food not of native American origin.

There are auguries of romanticism not only in Freneau's life but
also in poems like the early 'The Beauties of Santa Cruz', 'The Wild
Honey Suckle' and in 'On a Honey-Bee'. His most effective later
poem is 'The Indian Burying Ground'. The poet contemplates the
sitting position in which Indians bury their dead:

> His imaged birds, and painted bowl,
> And venison, for a journey dressed,
> Bespeak the nature of the soul,
> ACTIVITY, that knows no rest.

Indian 'Shadows and delusions' triumph over 'Reason's self' and
scepticism wilts before so strong an intimation of the afterlife:

> By midnight moons, o'er moistening dews,
> In habit for the chase arrayed,
> The hunter still the deer pursues,
> The hunter and the deer, a shade!

By comparison with the mature Freneau's passionate intensities,
John Trumbull's (1750–1831) *McFingal: A Modern Epic Poem* (1776) is
crude burlesque, although the tarring and feathering of its caricatured
Tory hero was effective propaganda and made the poem popular.
Timothy Dwight's (1752–1817) ill-advised epic in eleven books *The
Conquest of Canaan* (1785), offered as 'the first epic poem to have
appeared in America', clumsily allegorises Washington's victory as
Joshua's conquest of the Promised Land. The strained artificialities of
the poem are at odds with the reputation Dwight shared with others of
the so-called Hartford, or Connecticut Wits, staunch Federalists who
produced a creditable body of acrimony towards all aspects of
Jeffersonian republicanism. Heavily influenced by Samuel Butler and
Alexander Pope, *The Anarchiad: A Poem on the Restoration of Chaos and
Substantial Night* (1786–7), is not great satire, but it is at least enterprising, barbed and aware of its own literary form. One of its co-
authors was probably Joel Barlow (1754–1812), whose often deft
mock-heroic 'The Hasty Pudding' (1793), written in France, indulges
the poet's nostalgia in exile by celebrating the essentially Connecticut
experience of a dish of Indian corn-meal mush. Other American
dishes please well enough, but none can compare:

Some talk of Hoe-cake, fair Virginia's pride,
Rich Johnny-cake this mouth has often tri'd;
Both please me well, their virtues much the same;
Alike their fabric, as allied their fame,
Except in dear New-England, where the last
Receives a dash of pumpkin in the paste,
To give it sweetness and improve the taste.
But place them all before me, smoaking hot,
The big round dumplin rolling from the pot;
The pudding of the bag, whose quivering breast,
With suet lin'd leads on the Yankey feast;
The Charlotte brown, within whose crusty sides
A belly soft the pulpy apple hides;
The yellow bread, whose face like amber glows,
And all of Indian that the bake-pan knows –
You tempt me not – my fav'rite greets my eyes,
To that lov'd bowl my spoon by instinct flies.

The novel

By 1820 America had produced nearly a hundred novels. Most of
them were sentimentally moralistic, Gothic or purportedly historical
tales, and nearly all were derivative. This is hardly surprising if by
'novel' is meant prose fiction of extended length, and if a prerequisite
for the form is an established society in which the narrative may be
set. The novel in English took its great leap forward only when the
eighteenth century was well begun. Defoe's *Robinson Crusoe* came
early, in 1719, but Richardson's *Pamela* did not follow until 1740, and
Fielding's picaresque masterpiece *Tom Jones* in 1749.

The influence of Richardson's epistolary form gives *The Power of
Sympathy* (1789) a place in the genealogy of American fiction. Published
anonymously and probably by William Hill Brown (1765–93) this
dull, sensational novel was long attributed to Sarah Wentworth
Morton (1759–1846), 'the American Sappho', because its mixture of
seduction, near incest and suicide corresponded to scandalous events
in the Morton family. The ingredients of the plot reflect the taste
which made a best-seller of Susanna Rowson's (1762–1824) *Charlotte
Temple* (1791), the Richardsonian story of an English girl's seduction
by a British officer whom she follows to New York. Richardson is
again the exemplar for *The Coquette* (1797) a popular epistolary novel
of seduction and sentimentality by Hannah Webster Foster
(1759–1840). A more substantial effort than any of these is *Modern*

Chivalry; or The Adventures of Captain Farrago and Teague O'Reagan by the Scottish-born Federalist Hugh Henry Brackenridge (1748–1816). Modelled on *Don Quixote* and published in instalments from 1792 to 1815, the book offers a commentary on American politics by a man who believed in democracy but deplored the degeneration of liberty into license.

The post-Revolutionary topicality of *Modern Chivalry* accounts for Henry Adams's calling it 'a more thoroughly American book than any written before 1833', but Brackenridge's over-long and loosely structured satire is much less of a novel than any of the four books which Charles Brockden Brown (1771–1810) produced between 1798 and 1800. Brown was much more of a pioneer than is often realised. His rejection in the preface to *Edgar Huntly* (1799) of the 'superstitions and exploded manners, Gothic castles and chimeras' in favour of 'incidents of Indian hostility and perils of the Western Wilderness' prepared the way for James Fenimore Cooper; his use of symbols anticipates the work of Hawthorne and Melville; his fascination with individual and aberrant psychology in *Wieland* (1798) and *Edgar Huntly* foreshadows Edgar Allan Poe (1809–49) and brings realistic subtleties not found in English Gothic writers such as Horace Walpole, 'Monk' Lewis and Mrs Radcliffe. The almost Dickensian story of initiation in *Arthur Mervyn* (1799–1800) precedes numerous elaborations of the theme throughout the American novel's history, from Cooper and Melville, via Hemingway and Robert Penn Warren (*b.* 1905) to John Irving. Under the influence of Voltaire, Rousseau and William Godwin, Brown was a rationalist, but his preoccupation is with mystery and the critique of rationalism implied by the power of Carwin in *Wieland*, and by the career of Constantia Dudley in *Ormond*, makes him less an eighteenth-century writer than a forerunner of the great American imaginations of the romantic age.

4

The waiting poem

THE Revolutionary War left America a confederation of independent states. Adoption of the Constitution in 1789 defined the political nature of the new government and affirmed a determination to overcome state differences for the sake of the advantages that union alone could bring. The purchase of the Louisiana territory from France in 1803, the War of 1812 and the Monroe Doctrine of 1823 promulgated the image of America as expansionist within its own continent and detached from the internal affairs of Europe.

Slavery was established as a way of life in the South, but in 1831 Nat Turner, a thirty-year-old slave who believed he was a Black Messiah, led a revolt in Virginia, killing ten men, fourteen women and thirty-five children. What became known as the Southampton County Insurrection was the most violent slave rebellion in American history. It provided William Styron (*b.* 1925) with the basis for his novel *The Confessions of Nat Turner* (1967). As a direct result of the episode, an anti-slavery lobby urged the Virginia legislature to support a programme of emancipation; but a boom in prices of tobacco, cotton and slaves led to a conservative reaction which outvoted the motion.

The rapid westward movement of population led in 1828 to the Presidential election of Andrew Jackson, hero of the 1812 War, a citizen of Nashville, Tennessee and the first President from a region west of the Appalachians. The Jackson years favoured the common man, and the national preoccupation was now with economics instead of religion, living rather than fighting. Hard-working farmers were eager to exploit technological innovations such as the mechanical reaper invented by McCormick in 1834, and the railroad which enabled them to reach wider markets and enjoy a steadily rising standard of living.

Literature lagged behind. Newspapers proliferated – some twelve hundred were being published by 1830 – as did magazines; their columns exhorted writers to celebrate the developing national character in a truly native literature. The English preacher, Sydney Smith, scored a palpable hit in 1820 with his question in *The Edinburgh Review*:

> In the four quarters of the globe, who reads an American book? or goes to an American play? or looks at an American picture or statue?

As late as 1842, in his essay on 'The Poet', Emerson called for a poet discerning and confident enough to make art out of the real America:

> We have yet had no genius in America, with tyrannous eye, which knew the value of our incomparable materials, and saw, in the barbarism and materialism of the times, another carnival of the same gods whose picture he admires so much in Homer; then in the Middle Age; then in Calvinism. Banks and tariffs, the newspaper and caucus, Methodism and Unitarianism, are flat and dull to dull people, but rest on the same foundations of wonder as the town of Troy and the temple of Delphi, and are as swiftly passing away. Our log-rolling, our stumps and their politics, our fisheries, our Negroes and Indians, our boats and our repudiations, the wrath of rogues and the pusillanimity of honest men, the northern trade, the southern planting, the western clearing, Oregon and Texas, are yet unsung. Yet America is a poem in our eyes; its ample geography dazzles the imagination, and it will not wait long for metres.

Despite the native ingredients and romantic features of William Cullen Bryant (1794–1878), the music of Poe (1809–49) and the scope of Cooper, America had to wait for metres until Longfellow's (1807–82) mid-century verses about Hiawatha and Miles Standish. It had to wait until Whitman for a truly 'metre-making argument' commensurate with Emerson's panorama of 'incomparable materials'. Sydney Smith, however, was answered by four writers in the first half of the nineteenth century: Washington Irving, Bryant, Cooper and Poe were read both at home and overseas.

Irving, Bryant and Cooper

Washington Irving (1783–1859) was born into a prosperous merchant family in New York City. He read law and passed the bar examination, but practised the profession only desultorily. Literary interests supervened, and the attractions of Europe lured him to periods of residence in England, where he was a great social success, travel in Germany and France and spells of government service in Spain. In 1807–8, with his brother William and the lively James Kirke Paulding

(1778–1860), he issued the periodical *Salmagundi; or, The Whim-Whams and Opinions of Launcelot Langstaff & Others* which happily proved less pretentious than its intention to 'instruct the young, reform the old, correct the town, and castigate the age'. Irving's piece, 'Of the Chronicles of the Renowned and Antient City of Gotham' accorded New York City the enduring nickname of Gotham by which a reputation for foolish behaviour was transferred from the original Gotham village in Nottinghamshire, England. The light satire of the *Salmagundi* papers is directed at pedantic scholarship and the Dutch settlers of New Amsterdam in *A History of New York from the Beginning of the World to the End of the Dutch Dynasty* (1809), which Irving offered to the public under the name of Diedrich Knickerbocker, thereby initiating the term 'Knickerbocker School' for authors like himself, Paulding, Fitz-Greene Halleck (1790–1867) and Joseph Rodman Drake (1795–1820), who wrote about 'little old New York' in the years before the Civil War. The *History* caricatures Jefferson as Governor Kieft under whom greedy Yankees attempt 'to get possession of the city of Manhattoes', and there is an ironic apologia for the unyielding Peter Stuyvesant, cast here as Peter the Headstrong:

> a ruler who follows his own will pleases himself; while he who seeks to satisfy the wishes and whims of others runs great risk of pleasing nobody. There is nothing too like putting down one's foot resolutely, when in doubt, and letting things take their course. The clock that stands still points right twice in the four-and-twenty hours: while others may keep going continually and be continually going wrong.

Irving's early manner and style are derived from the eighteenth-century fluencies of Addison and Goldsmith. Later works show a more romantic strain. *Bracebridge Hall, or, The Humorists* (1822) is a sentimental evocation of the England of landed gentry; only the story of 'The Stout Gentleman', a romance of the English stagecoach, is worthy of Irving at his best. Self-conscious attempts at the imaginative short story in *Tales of a Traveller* (1824) yield only one memorable tale, 'The Devil and Tom Walker', which deploys the Faust theme in a contest between the devil and a Yankee not quite wily enough to get out of an awkward bargain. More pleasure is to be had from the sketches and stories of *The Legends of the Alhambra* (1832), based on Irving's 1829 residence in the thirteenth-century Moorish palace and full of genuine feeling for the romance of an alien and exotic past. The romance of the frontier, but none of its rigours, is stressed in both *A Tour of the Prairies* (1835) and *Astoria* (1836). The latter also idealises the business tycoon, John Jacob Astor, who commissioned Irving to memorialise the founding of Astoria, Oregon.

While he lived Irving was the pre-eminent man of American letters; today he would interest only the cultural historian but for *The Sketch Book of Geoffrey Crayon, Gent.* (1819–20), an immediately popular collection of essays and stories, including two small masterpieces, 'Rip Van Winkle' and 'The Legend of Sleepy Hollow'. Both stories illustrate Irving's skill as a genial miniaturist with a gift for satire tempered with whimsy. Neither the influence of Sir Walter Scott nor probable sources in German folklore can detract from Irving's success in turning the lazy, hen-pecked Rip's discovery of little men in Dutch costume, bowling at ninepins in the Catskill Mountains of New York State, into a myth of America before and after the Revolution. In 'The Legend of Sleepy Hollow', the story of the superstitious Yankee Ichabod Crane's besting by the headless horseman of Brom Bones the extrovert Dutchman, sets American types in the context of a perfect expression of the endangered pastoral ideal:

> . . . it is in such little retired Dutch valleys, found here and there in the great State of New York, that population, manners, and customs remain fixed, while the great torrent of migration and improvement, which is making such incessant changes in other parts of this restless country, sweep by them unobserved. They are like those little nooks of still water which border a rapid stream; where we may see the straw and bubble riding quietly at anchor, or slowly revolving in their mimic harbor, undisturbed by the rush of the passing current.

The first American to achieve an international reputation as a poet was the New Englander, William Cullen Bryant (1794–1878). Transitional English writers such as Gray, Young, Cowper and Thomson lie behind the diction and feeling of the much-anthologised 'Thanatopsis' (view of death), but the absence of God and the injunction to live by the dictates of nature indicate a more than incipient romanticism. The concluding image of reabsorption into nature is Wordsworthian in idea if not in language or intensity:

> So live, that when thy summons comes to join
> The innumerable caravan, which moves
> To that mysterious realm, where each shall take
> His chamber in the silent halls of death,
> Thou go not like the quarry-slave at night,
> Scourged to his dungeon, but sustained and soothed
> By an unfaltering trust, approach thy grave
> Like one who wraps the drapery of his couch
> About him, and lies down to pleasant dreams.

American rather than English materials are used to lyrical effect in 'The Yellow Violet', 'A Winter Piece' and 'The Prairies'. If sentimentality spoils 'The Indian Girl's Lament', at least the poet sees instructive value and dignity in attitudes hitherto all too often dismissed as heathen. Bryant's fervent patriotism is stirringly revealed in 'Song of Marion's Men' (General Francis Marion, known as the 'Swamp Fox', fought a guerrilla campaign against the British), 'The Battle-field' and 'Abraham Lincoln', a commemorative public tribute to the assassinated President as liberator and martyr.

Lectures on poetry and innumerable reviews established Bryant as a considerable literary critic. His preference of feeling and imagination to imitation and metaphysics aligns him with English and European romanticism rather than eighteenth-century neo-classicism, despite a pragmatic insistence on the moral role of literature. 'To a Waterfowl', often considered his finest poem, shows him practising what he preached. Bryant remains an observer – he lacks Keats's empathic ability to enter into the life of another creature – but sympathy is strong as he imagines the bird flying beyond the range of 'the fowler's eye', searching for its summer home:

> All day thy wings have fanned,
> At that far height, the cold, thin atmosphere,
> Yet stoop not, weary, to the welcome land,
> Though the dark night is near.

The 'Power' that shows the bird where to go is no God of Puritan imagining, even if the third person is used to compact the message of the last stanza:

> He who, from zone to zone,
> Guides through the boundless sky thy certain flight,
> In the long way that I must tread alone,
> Will lead my steps aright.

The five 'Leather-Stocking' novels which won James Fenimore Cooper wider international fame than Irving or Bryant, and praise from Goethe, Scott, Thackeray and Balzac, amount to less than a third of his output as a novelist. After *Precaution* (1820), a clumsy imitation of Jane Austen, written in answer to a challenge from his wife, Cooper scored a popular success with *The Spy: A Tale of the Neutral Ground* (1821) in which adventure and romance are combined after the manner of Sir Walter Scott. A melodramatic story of the

Revolution insists on the permanence of moral values in a changing world. *The Spy* brought Cooper praise from the *North American Review* as 'the first who has deserved the appellation of a distinguished American novel writer'. Yet Cooper's distinction is not in his writing, which is often laborious, pompous and turgid, but rather in his choice of subjects and his industry in proffering them to a public avid for a literary heritage. A sailor and naval officer from 1806 until his marriage five years later, Cooper was dissatisfied with Sir Walter Scott's *The Pirate* (1822). *The Pilot* (1823) is the first of a series of sea stories intended to appeal in terms of their nautical authenticity. The plot of *The Pilot* is ungainly, the writing stilted, and the characterisation thin; even the admired Long Tom Coffin, a sea-going Leather-Stocking, is an improbable caricature. The book was successful in its day because it brought the sea into American literature and contrasted Tory ineffectuality with the Pilot's practical competence. Better still, the mysterious Pilot, 'a Quixote in the behalf of liberal principles', could voice the ideal, American democratic boast: 'I was born without the nobility of twenty generations to corrupt and deaden my soul.'

Cooper not only wanted to out-do Scott, but also intended his novels to be read as social criticism in parallel with *Notions of the Americans* (1828) and *The American Democrat* (1838) which, as H. L. Mencken (1880–1956) says, 'went into the defects and dangers of democracy with acrid realism'. The American public did not want Cooper's admirably independent if tactless diatribes against almost every aspect of Jacksonian society and vilified him as a 'spotted caitiff' and 'leprous wretch'; but they welcomed his frontiersman, his Indians, his wilderness, his prairie, and despite Mark Twain's derisory remarks about the fakery of 'Cooper Indians', have stuck to them.

The publication chronology of the Leather-Stocking series does not follow its narrative chronology which begins with the early eighteenth-century youth of Natty Bumppo and ends with his death on the prairies in 1806. In *The Deerslayer* (1841) – last written, but first in narrative sequence – Natty's blood brotherhood with the Indian chief Chingachgook confirms his natural affinity with the Edenesque forest where innocence is threatened by the white man's reduction of Indians to the bounties their scalps will bring. By comparison Natty is made ill when forced to kill his first Indian. *The Last of the Mohicans* (1826) further celebrates the grandeur of the forest, the equation of natural integrity and woodland expertise in Natty – now in his thirties, known as Hawkeye – and, in contrast to the barbarous Iroquois, the nobility of Chingachgook and his son Uncas whose death gives the book its title. In *The Pathfinder* (1840) Natty protects the unlikely Mabel Dunham from assorted perils, but relinquishes her hand in marriage to remain true to his wild element. The laws and customs of so-called civilisation erode the primeval innocence of the wilderness in *The Pioneers* (1823) and the ageing Leather-Stocking sets off to be a trapper on the western prairies.

At times vague, often prolix, there is an amplitude in Cooper's work that makes it a genuine if flawed response to Emerson's 'poem' of America. The whole is larger than the sum of its ineptitudes. In its minting of American archetypes, the cumulative power of the Leather-Stocking saga makes narrow-eyed criticism look mean. Who wants to topple Wordsworth from his Snowdon because of the prosaic glosses with which he intersperses his 'spots of time' in *The Prelude*; and who seriously denies Spenser's achievement because of what C. S. Lewis calls the 'flat passages' in *The Faerie Queene*? Mark Twain loathed Natty Bumppo for talking 'like an illustrated, gilt-edged, tree-calf, hand-tooled, seven-dollar *Friendship's Offering*, in the beginning of a paragraph, and like a Negro minstrel at the end of it'. This is clever talk, but beside the point. Natty is a great fictional character, like Melville's Ishmael, Twain's Huck, Dreiser's Carrie, Faulkner's Sutpen and Warren's Willie Stark, because he takes hold of the imagination and will not let go. With Chingachgook he is first in a line of comrade heroes that includes Melville's Ishmael and Queequeg, Twain's Huck and Jim, Kerouac's Sal Paradise and Dean Moriarty, and Wyatt and Billy of the nostalgic film *Easy Rider* (1969). The creaking plot and crude dialogue of *The Prairie* (1827) are irrelevant to a reader who has approached the novel through the building chronology of Natty Bumppo's life. What matters are the relationship between Natty and the good Pawnees, their victory over the wicked Ishmael Bush and his Sioux allies, and Cooper's evocation of the vast prairie itself as a backdrop for his solitary, self-possessed natural democrat. Natty's death, a last, grand entry into nature, dramatises the 'unfaltering trust' of Bryant's 'Thanatopsis':

> The trapper had remained nearly motionless for an hour. His eyes alone had occasionally opened and shut. When opened, his gaze seemed fastened on the clouds which hung around the western horizon, reflecting the bright colours and giving form and loveliness to the glorious tints of an American sunset. The hour, the calm beauty of the season, the occasion – all conspired to fill the spectators with solemn awe. Suddenly . . . the old man, supported

on either side by his friends, rose upright to his feet. For a moment he looked about him as if to invite all in presence to listen (the lingering remnant of human frailty), and then, with a fine military elevation of the head and with a voice that might be heard in every part of that numerous assembly, he pronounced the word 'Here!'

Poe

The South is lucky to have had Edgar Allan Poe (1809–49). He deflects attention from the paucity of good southern writing before the twentieth century. John Pendleton Kennedy's (1795–1870) light-weight *Swallow Barn* (1832) earned praise from V. L. Parrington (1871–1929) for its portrayal of plantation life. The prolific William Gilmore Simms (1806–70) did obeisance to Scott with a seven-volume epic of the Revolution, and achieved popularity with *The Yemassee* (1835), a romantic tale of conflict between colonists and Indians. Both Kennedy and Simms were deeply committed to the South, although Kennedy opposed secession while Simms passionately defended it. Poe was never so involved. He thought of himself as a Virginian, worked for the raising of Southern literary standards and held abolitionist Boston in contempt; but his mind was its own place.

As the narrator in 'The Fall of the House of Usher' enters the gloomy mansion he observes that 'the carvings of the ceilings, the sombre tapestries of the walls, the ebon blackness of the floors, and the phantasmagoric armorial trophies which rattled as I strode, were but matters to which, or to such as which, I had been accustomed from my infancy'. The narrator, of course, is a device: such things were not 'ordinary images' in the home of John Allan, the Richmond merchant who became the orphaned Poe's legal guardian (without formally adopting him) and gave him his middle name. Such furnishings come from Poe's true region, the lurid, synthetic, Gothic Europe of his imagination.

Between the ages of six and eleven Poe lived in England, where his foster father had business. At eighteen he entered the University of Virginia, learned to gamble and left after a year, believing himself denied sufficient funds by Allan. He returned to Boston, the town of his birth, issued his first volume *Tamerlane and Other Poems* (1827), and joined the army, rising to the rank of sergeant-major. A short spell at West Point and further estrangement from Allan completed the inauspicious prologue to a meteoric literary career in the brief course of which he made the tale of terror his own special preserve, invented the modern detective story, was the first outstanding American literary theorist and became, in the words of W. B. Yeats, 'always and for all lands a great lyric poet'. After his death he was disparaged by those whom he had offended by his critical candour. His originality could hardly be denied, even posthumously, but it was easy to denigrate the personality of one so morbidly inclined, so opinionated and apparently so frequently the worse for drink or drugs. Recent scholarship has rehabilitated Poe. There is evidence to suggest that he was diabetic and that his drug-taking amounted to no more than the use of laudanum to alleviate pain or grief. Under the pressure of modern biography the fell Poe yields to the Freudian Poe; but, whatever may be done with the life, the works remain unimpeachable evidence of four obsessions: woman, guilt, death and art.

A journey to the moon makes *The Unparalleled Adventures of One Hans Pfaal* (1835) an early example of science fiction, but the best of Poe's imaginary voyages is *The Narrative of Arthur Gordon Pym of Nantucket* (1838). The explorer J. N. Reynolds was a vociferous champion of J. C. Symmes's theory that the earth was hollow with a habitable centre, and open at the Poles. Inspired by information supplied by Reynolds, Poe devised a tale of initiation in the form of a symbolic sea story which takes its protagonist from innocence, through the chaos of mutiny and the shock of aboriginal savagery, to the Antarctic, the world's remaining *terra incognita*. As a chasm opens ahead of Pym and his companion, a huge snow-white figure rises up in their pathway. The narrative ends teasingly, with destruction and revelation both impending. Although he attempted one other extended fiction, *The Journal of Julius Rodman* (1840), Poe came to believe that a piece of literature should be consumed at a sitting; poems should be of moderate length and stories short. He gives his own game away in a review of Hawthorne's *Twice-Told Tales*. The literary artist aims, first, for effect and, second, for unity:

> Having conceived, with deliberate care, a certain unique or single *effect* to be wrought out, he then invents such incidents – he then combines such events as may best aid him in establishing this preconceived effect . . . In the whole composition there should be no word written, of which the tendency, direct or indirect, is not to the one pre-established design.

If this looks like objective theorising, it is also workshop criticism, a rationale of the method by which Poe's stories excel in achieving their characteristic effect of making the flesh creep. The method works because it serves a higher power, Poe's ability to disintegrate the rational world into the obscene delights of dread and guilt. D. H.

Lawrence, himself a connoisseur of 'the disintegrative vibration', understood the rigours and the value of such power:

> Doomed to seethe down his soul in a great continuous convulsion of disintegration, and doomed to register the process. And then doomed to be abused for it, when he had performed some of the bitterest tasks of human experience, that can be asked of a man. Necessary tasks, too. For the human soul must suffer its own disintegration *consciously* if it is ever to survive.

'The Cask of Amontillado' is a model of catharsis. Poe's perfectly calculated understatement brings an aesthetic pleasure which is absorbed in the emotional pleasure of participating simultaneously in Montresor's evil triumph and in the terror of Fortunato as he is walled into the vault that will be his tomb. At the end of 'The Pit and the Pendulum' the prisoner, a victim of the Inquisition, is about to fall into the pit. When he is rescued by the French General Lasalle the relief is as anti-climactic as order restored at the end of a Shakespearean tragedy. It is the hissing blade of the pendulum, the moving red walls, the rats and the black pit that stay deliciously in the mind to prolong the terror of struggling along with the prisoner and the guilt of enjoying his agony. 'The Tell-Tale Heart' and 'The Black Cat' are only superficially moral tales. Alarmed conscience terrifies both murderers into the panic of confession; but the fascination of each story is its display of hatred, destruction and self-destruction by men whose abnormal states of mind express common feelings normally repressed. Both stories exemplify the truth of Oscar Wilde's observation that 'each man kills the thing he loves'. The narrator of 'The Tell-Tale Heart' begins by admitting that there was neither 'object' nor 'passion' in his murder of the old man:

> I loved the old man. He had never wronged me. He had never given me insult. For his gold I had no desire. I think it was his eye! yes, it was this! He had the eye of a vulture – a pale blue eye with a film over it. Whenever it fell upon me, my blood ran cold; and so by degrees – very gradually – I made up my mind to take the life of the old man, and thus rid myself of the eye forever.

Is this credible? How could he love the old man, yet plan to kill him? Perhaps the narrator is motivated by physical revulsion from the eye 'all a dull blue, with a hideous veil over it' that chills the marrow of his bones on the night of the murder. Many find physical distortion hard to accept and might even murder to destroy it, as in some primitive societies, but for the restraints of conventional morality and the check of law. Poe's effect depends partly on such guilty recognition, but the word 'vulture' and the imagined heartbeat of the dead man suggest the horror of a paranoia so overmastering that it remains mysterious even when it has been named. Mystery ousts morality: the killer's being brought to book is of little interest, but his frantic efforts to cover the noise of the beating heart are as thrilling as the prisoner's terror in 'The Pit and the Pendulum'. Explanation is equally otiose in 'The Black Cat'. 'The instrumentality of the Fiend Intemperance' cannot explain why a man cuts out the eye of a favourite cat and kills both the cat and his wife. The narrator realises this himself and gives as good an account as any of Poe's recurrent theme:

> ... then came, as if to my final and irrevocable overthrow, the spirit of PERVERSENESS. Of this spirit philosophy takes no account. Yet I am not more sure that my soul lives, than I am that perverseness is one of the primitive impulses of the human heart – one of the indivisible primary faculties, or sentiments, which give direction to the character of Man ... It was this unfathomable longing of the soul *to vex itself* – to offer violence to its own nature – to do wrong for the wrong's sake only – that urged me to continue.

In 'Ligeia' and 'The Fall of the House of Usher' Poe's vexed souls are caught in a nightmare web of sex and death. The third stanza of Ligeia's poem 'The Conqueror Worm', offers a serviceable epigraph for both stories: 'much of Madness and more of Sin/And Horror the soul of the plot.' As a monument to Poe's dictum in his essay on 'The Philosophy of Composition' (1846) that 'the death of a beautiful woman is, unquestionably, the most poetical topic in the world', Ligeia is much more impressive than lost Leonore of 'The Raven', whom Poe had in mind when he wrote his essay. The poem made Poe famous, largely because of its structure, metre and refrain as well as its ebony bird and tolling melancholy; but the merely 'rare and radiant' Leonore is no match for Ligeia's passionate eyes and 'more than womanly abandonment'. Hallucination or not, the return of Ligeia after death to inhabit the body of Rowena reproaches the narrator for the sexual dishonesty of his second marriage, vindicates his passion for the superior woman and punishes the Lady Rowena for her failure to love. If there are intimations of necrophilia here, 'The Fall of the House of Usher' provides an incestuous *Liebestod* as Roderick and Madeline die in each other's arms while the decayed mansion sinks into the black waters of the tarn.

Generations of imitators have obscured the originality of Poe's detective stories. His unflappably analytical detective, Monsieur Dupin, and the narrator's role, as a comparatively slow-witted intermediary between detective and reader, give the formula used by Sir Arthur Conan Doyle in the Sherlock Holmes stories. Poe prided himself on the 'ratiocination' of 'The Murders in the Rue Morgue' (1841), 'The Mystery of Marie Rogêt' (1842–3) and 'The Purloined Letter' (1845). As the genre he invented has developed, its potential for character and atmosphere has been more fully realised in the 'hard-boiled' mysteries of Dashiell Hammett (1894–1961) and the incomparable romantic thrillers of Raymond Chandler (1888–1959). The prolific Erle Stanley Gardner's (1889–1970) Perry Mason stories extend the sheer logic of Poe's Dupin to legal expertise and courtroom strategy.

Poe's reputation as a poet has suffered both from his cool, theoretical approach to composition and from his unashamedly romantic dedication to verbal music and ideal beauty. 'The Bells' is a uniquely successful *tour de force*, but sense is too often disrupted by rhythm, as in 'The Raven', or displaced by sound as in Mallarmé's favourite 'Ulalume':

> The skies they were ashen and sober;
> The leaves they were crisped and sere –
> The leaves they were withering and sere;
> It was night in the lonesome October
> Of my most immemorial year

Yet, detached from its dullingly hypnotic context, this 'lonesome October' lives, as do many of Poe's lines: 'the glory that was Greece,/ And the grandeur that was Rome' ('To Helen'); 'The viol, the violet, and the vine' ('The City in the Sea'); 'But we loved with a love that was more than love – / I and my Annabel Lee' ('Annabel Lee'). It hardly matters that the poetic superiority of Poe's stories to his verse puts him out of step with his own literary theory. His critical writing injected Coleridgean principles into the American cultural bloodstream, anticipated the twentieth century's emphasis on textual analysis and challenged moralistic assumptions about the function of literature by proposing new aesthetic standards. He was at his most American as a literary crusader, notably in his editorial work for Richmond's *Southern Literary Messenger*. He was the first great professional American man of letters. His constant subject was his own vexed soul, a thing without nationality. Emerson's poem of America was still waiting; but Poe helped to create the conditions in which others might rise to its measure.

5

Renaissance

THE Jackson era's promotion of the common man gave democracy a momentum that kept going throughout the nineteenth century, but not without doubts and defections. In *Democracy in America* (1835–40) the Frenchman Alexis de Tocqueville (1805–59) wondered if the will of the majority could function as efficiently as the influence of the old privileged classes in preventing the possible abuse of power by centralised government. Men might become equal, but it remained to be seen whether the principle of equality would lead them 'to servitude or freedom, to knowledge or barbarism, to prosperity or wretchedness'. The pragmatic Orestes Brownson (1803–76) began as a Socialist, lost his faith in the common people and argued for a ruling élite. Emerson's essay 'Politics' warned that the ideal social system had not yet been realised – the aim of democracy was not the perfect state but the fulfilled individual: 'We think our civilisation near its meridian, but we are yet only at the cock-crowing and the morning star!' A few years later Melville's Ishmael was ecstatic about the God-given condition of equality, visible everywhere:

> Thou shalt see it shining in the arm that wields a pick or drives a spike; that democratic dignity which, on all hands, radiates without end from God; Himself! The great God absolute! The centre and circumference of all democracy! His omnipresence, our divine equality!

Walt Whitman heard the voices of Americans, 'Each singing what belongs to him or her and to none else'; but his own songs in *Leaves of Grass* (1855) were for all with whom he shared a common humanity: 'Thou throbbest with life and pride and love the same as I/ Therefore for thee the following chants'.

Humourists and Brahmins

Delight in the eccentricities of ordinary life is the common factor among the humourists of New England and the south-west. Their writings often throb with greater vitality than the more long-bearded productions of the genteel tradition developing in the east. Pious literary history must acknowledge the good intentions of the Brahmins, as they came to be called after Oliver Wendell Holmes (1809–94) had referred to the cultural aristocracy of New England as 'The Brahmin Caste' in his novel *Elsie Venner* (1861). They promoted literary consciousness, but their works have not worn well. Henry Wadsworth Longfellow (1807–82), the most popular American poet of his time, was a learned man and a gifted versifier who brought distinctive metres to the poem of America in the hexameters of *Evangeline* (1847) and *The Courtship of Miles Standish* (1858), as well as in the incantatory rhythm of *The Song of Hiawatha* (1855). His 'spreading chestnut tree' and 'village smithy' ('The Village Blacksmith') will, no doubt, stand as monuments to an honest man of letters, but for the most part Longfellow is fluent and forgettable. Dr Oliver Wendell Holmes should be remembered more for his paper on *The Contagiousness of Puerperal Fever* (1843), which saved lives, than for the overrated urbanity of *The Autocrat of the Breakfast-Table* (1858). John Greenleaf Whittier (1807–92) achieved more as a committed abolitionist than as a poet, although 'Skipper Ireson's Ride' (1828) is a crisp ballad with effective dialect touches and the nostalgic 'Snow-Bound: A Winter Idyll' (1866) is often compared to Robert Burns's 'The Cotter's Saturday Night'.

James Russell Lowell (1819–91), first editor of the influential *Atlantic Monthly*, tried to be profound but succeeded in a lighter vein with the two series of *The Biglow Papers* (1848; 1865) which advanced new claims for the use of American dialect and used it to satirise politicians, slavery and the war with Mexico. Even Lowell's clever way with worthy purposes looks pale, however, by comparison with the tall tales of Tennessee's legendary Davy Crockett (1786–1836), 'the coonskin Congressman' and killer of 'b'ars', who could 'hold a buffalo out to drink, and put a rifle-ball through the moon'; or with Augustus Baldwin Longstreet's (1790–1870) *Georgia Scenes* (1835) viewed through the eyes of his egregious Ransy Sniffle. Seba Smith's (1792–1868) satirical 'Jack Downing' letters were enjoyed by a huge public including President Jackson, and, under the pen name of Artemus Ward, Charles Farrar Browne (1834–67) boosted Yankee dialect to noble heights of absurdity: 'I girdid up my Lions & fled the Seen'; 'Did you ever have the measels, and if so how many?'; 'The female woman is one of the greatest institooshuns of which this land can boste'. His epigrams are deathless: 'The Mormon's religion is singular, and his wives are plural'; 'I prefer temperance hotels – although they sell worse liquor than any other kind of hotels.'

The Transcendentalists

Such as it was, the romanticism of the Brahmins was superficial. Sentimental responses to nature and revulsion from the blatant degradations of slavery were aspects of a broad humanitarianism which owed little to the new definitions of life and art current in Europe. The romanticism of the New England Transcendentalists was radical. It was indebted to the Unitarian movement in the church which had developed out of eighteenth-century deism, and dissolved the Puritan concept of the Trinity. Unitarianism reached its fullest expression in the work of William Ellery Channing (1780–1842) who made God and the human mind daringly similar: 'God is another name for human intelligence raised above all error and imperfection, and extended to all possible truth . . . We see God around us, because he dwells within us' ('Likeness to God', 1828). Transcendentalism stressed the individualism implicit in Unitarian thinking. Under the influence of idealist German philosophers like Kant, Hegel and Schelling, it preferred intuition to reason, and freedom to institution. The transcendentalist position developed by Emerson, Thoreau and others was judged heretical by staunch Unitarians. It is to the credit of Theodore Parker (1810–60), Unitarian minister of West Roxbury, that he retained a loyal congregation while active in the Transcendental Club, whose leading members included Emerson, Thoreau, Bronson Alcott (1799–1888) and Margaret Fuller (1810–50).

German ideas about the status of intuited truth often reached the Transcendentalists indirectly, through Coleridge's *Biographia Literaria* (1817), where 'the primary imagination' supersedes reason as 'the living power and prime agent of all human perception'. Coleridge's belief in the faculty of imagination as 'a repetition in the finite mind of the eternal act of Creation in the infinite I AM' endowed individual human perception with God-like authority. With the addition of what Coleridge calls 'the One Life within us and abroad', Emerson had the precedents he needed for his 'infinitude of the private man' and the 'Over-soul' defined in *Nature* as an all-pervading spiritual essence. For Emerson and Thoreau as for William Blake in *America, a Prophecy* (1793), 'every thing that lives is holy, life delights in life'. Margaret Fuller, Emerson's co-editor on the Transcendentalist journal *The Dial*, enjoyed a leaner version of the faith, to judge by her cryptic announcement, 'I accept the universe'. (Thomas Carlyle is alleged to have commented, 'By God! She'd better!') Bronson Alcott was regarded by his contemporaries as leader of the movement, although today he is chiefly remembered for fathering Louisa M. Alcott (1832–88), author of *Little Women* (1868–9) and other best-selling juvenile fictions. Alcott was only moderately successful in disseminating Transcendentalist principles in New England schools. 'Fruitlands', his vegetarian farm co-operative at Harvard, failed within a year.

In *American Renaissance* (1941) F. O. Matthiessen (1902–50) examines the 'extraordinarily concentrated moment of expression' that occurred in the middle of the nineteenth century:

> The half-decade of 1850–55 saw the appearance of *Representative Men* (1850), *The Scarlet Letter* (1850), *The House of the Seven Gables* (1851), *Moby-Dick* (1851), *Pierre* (1852), *Walden* (1854), and *Leaves of Grass* (1855). You might search all the rest of American literature without being able to collect a group of books equal to these in imaginative vitality.

The American renaissance was not a re-birth of something that had existed before. With hindsight it is easy to see it as a product of cultural tendencies in evolution through religious and political debate, as well as historical circumstance, since colonial times. In the freer, more confident ethos of the romantic era a new maturity was possible. In the works of Emerson, Thoreau, Hawthorne, Melville and Whitman, American literature gained an argument, a historical centre and a new beginning.

Emerson and Thoreau

Both Ralph Waldo Emerson (1803–82) and his friend Henry David Thoreau (1817–62) were Harvard graduates, lifelong students of consciousness in what Emerson called 'the age of the first person singular', and solitaries. Thoreau was born in the Massachusetts town of Concord. Emerson lived there most of his life, becoming its 'Sage', enjoying his garden, his orchard and possession of the woods in which Thoreau built his cabin at Walden Pond. Both men held to Emerson's idea that 'every real man must be a nonconformist'. In 1832 Emerson resigned his pastorate of Boston's Old Second Church. He could no longer conscientiously administer the Sacrament because he did not believe Christ had intended it to be a regular observance. 'It is my desire, in the office of a Christian minister', he told his congregation, 'to do nothing which I cannot do with my whole heart'. Thoreau's 'Civil Disobedience' is based on a similar view of personal integrity: 'The only obligation which I have a right to assume is to do any time what I think right'. Nature as apprehended by Emerson seemed to guarantee protection from the grosser varieties of egotism:

> Standing on the bare ground – my head bathed by the blithe air and uplifted into infinite space – all mean egotism vanishes. I become a transparent eyeball; I am nothing; I see it all; the currents of the Universal Being circulate through me; I am part or parcel of God.

'The American Scholar', Emerson's 1837 Phi Beta Kappa address at Harvard, was hailed by Oliver Wendell Holmes as 'Our intellectual Declaration of Independence'. 'We have listened too long to the courtly muses of Europe', Emerson insists, exhorting his listeners to turn from imitation to confident originality. The active process of becoming connects the self to a continuing present. Religion, as specified in the Harvard 'Divinity School Address' (1838), must stress the contemporary union of God, humanity and nature: 'It is the office of a true teacher to show us that God is, not was'. In 'The Problem', a poem published in the first issue of *The Dial* (1840), Emerson acknowledges that the traditional adjuncts of religion appeal to him:

> I like a church; I like a cowl;
> I love a prophet of the soul;
> And on my heart monastic aisles
> Fall like sweet strains, or pensive smiles;
> Yet not for all his faith can see
> Would I that cowlèd churchman be.

The past has charm, but the poet opts for the present in which the word of old 'Still floats upon the morning wind,/Still whispers to the willing mind'. The scholar must be 'Man Thinking' in the present, pushing beyond convention and institution to learn directly from life:

> Life is our dictionary. Years are well spent in country labours; in town; in the insight into trades and manufactures; in frank intercourse with many men and women; in science; in art; to the one end of mastering in all their facts a language by which to illustrate and embody our perception.

The key to Emerson's manifesto in 'The American Scholar' is self-respect. Books are good when they inspire, bad when they threaten to warp the individual out of his own orbit, making him 'a satellite instead of a system'. 'Imitation is suicide', in the essay, 'Self-Reliance', which examines the proposition that 'No law can be sacred to me but my own nature'; after all, an institution is only 'the lengthened shadow of one man'. Fidelity to oneself precludes submission to precedent or custom, even to a previously held position of one's own: 'A foolish consistency is the hobgoblin of little minds'.

With no visible logic – for he was a writer of *pensées*, not an arguer – but with taking audacity touched by oriental mysticism, Emerson swoops from the self to God. Since 'self-existence is the attribute of the Supreme Cause', self-fulfilment is enjoined by 'the ever-blessed ONE' in which all things are resolved. Emerson's divinity is strongly reminiscent of the 'motion' and 'spirit' that 'impels' and 'rolls through all things' in Wordsworth's 'Tintern Abbey' (1798). The orthodox Christian God is replaced in 'The Over-Soul' by the Platonic concept of an all-including primal spirit which both contains man and is to be found within him: this is 'the soul of the whole; the wise silence; the universal beauty, to which every part and particle is equally related; the eternal ONE'. To wisdom and beauty is added love which 'works at the centre' in 'The Sphinx', and in 'Art' the Over-Soul inspires the artist to attest its presence. 'Brahma' (Divine Reality) echoes the idea of a supreme immanence given in the Hindu *Bhagavadgita*:

> Far or forgot to me is near;
>   Shadow and sunlight are the same;
> The vanished gods to me appear;
>   And one to me are shame and fame.

Denial of petty human distinctions by a transcendent immanence is all very well, but Emerson's blurring of good and bad into personal preference is philosophically disconcerting and morally dangerous: 'Good and bad', he says in 'Self-Reliance', are 'but names very readily transferable to that or this; the only right is what is after my constitution; the only wrong what is against it'. The thrusting, staccato rhetoric of the essays and the startlingly fresh imagery compacted into the poems brought American literature a fresh voice as well as a new harmony of nature, God and humanity. Emerson's insistence on self-determination made him an oracle in an age of expansion, and

Representative Men (1850) gratifyingly implied that the qualities of great men like Plato and Napoleon were potentially present in all Americans. Hitching their wagons to a star or exulting in snow puddles at twilight doubtless helped the literati of New England to expand their consciousness, but held less utility for the suppressed Indian, the battered Mexican or the enslaved Negro. Emerson was not a practical man, despite his membership of the Concord Fire Association and eventual involvement in the abolitionist cause. Henry Adams remarks in his *Education*: 'Unless education marches on both feet – theory and practice – it risks going astray'. Emerson was a theorist; as a practitioner Thoreau was more impressive.

Emerson encouraged Thoreau to keep the journal from which his books were made. The first book was *A Week on the Concord and Merrimack Rivers* (1849) which records the boating and hiking holiday Thoreau took with his brother John in the late summer of 1839. Thoreau's quest for understanding is remembered in a simple flow of description and digression. He is 'Man Thinking', on the move. The unexpected sound of a drum beating on the bank of the Merrimack prompts an extended reflection on the links between man and the universe, the nature of music – 'thought coloured and curved, fluent and flexible' – and the ironic discrepancy between the morning wind's music in the telegraph wires and the news of cotton and flour prices which the wires are made to carry. Thoreau was aware that this is 'extravagance', but it has helped him to grow a little too. Freely associating with frogs, sharing his mountain observatory with mice – 'They nibbled what was for them; I nibbled what was for me' – he earns his Transcendentalism by contacting the eternal in the particular. The essay on friendship in the 'Wednesday' chapter and the relaxed, rhapsodic lyricism sustained throughout the miscellany of fact, poetry and philosophy, make the book a worthy predecessor to *Walden* (1854).

In relation to society Thoreau's life followed a rhythm of alternating entry and withdrawal. The school he ran with his brother was forced to close in 1841 because of John's poor health. Both brothers loved and lost Ellen Sewall, but remained each other's best friend, and John's death at twenty-seven was a deep bereavement for Thoreau. He lived with Emerson, did some tutoring, contributed a useful graphite process to his father's pencil business and developed skills as a surveyor and botanist. After his period of retreat at Walden Pond, from 1845–7, he became 'a sojourner in civilised life again' but in 1853 went north to sample the woods of Maine. The social conscience evident in 'Civil Disobedience' led him to assist fugitive slaves and to speak publicly in defence of John Brown. In an essay written in his senior year at Harvard he had written, 'Our Indian is more of a man than the inhabitant of a city. He lives as a man, he thinks as a man, he dies as a man'. The year before tuberculosis killed him, Thoreau visited Minnesota in search of better health and to consider the Indians. At his death the words 'Moose' and 'Indian' were among his last.

In July 1846 Thoreau spent a 'novel and interesting' night in gaol for refusing to pay his poll tax. He was resisting the constitutional principle by which Massachusetts gave Congressional support to Southern leadership in the imperialistic Mexican War that followed the annexation of Texas to the United States in 1845. According to Bronson Alcott, Emerson thought Thoreau's going to gaol 'mean and skulking, and in bad taste', but 'Civil Disobedience' (first published in the short-lived Transcendental journal *Aesthetic Papers*, 1849) expounds the doctrine of passive resistance which found favour with Mahatma Gandhi, Martin Luther King and countless protesters for a better society in the 1960s and early 1970s. Reminiscent of William Godwin's *Political Justice* (1793), the essay is applied Transcendentalism. It sharpens Emerson's heady individualism to a specific social point according to the formula given in Theodore Parker's 'Transcendentalism': 'The conscience of each man is to him the moral standard'. Contemptuous of a government which has 'never of itself furthered any enterprise', Thoreau's refrain is the need for a thinking minority and the seminal role of individual conscience. If government is for and by the people, 'must the citizen ever for a moment, or in the least degree, resign his conscience to the legislator?' The best government is the least government, and 'Under a government which imprisons any unjustly, the true place for a just man is also prison'. Having practised what he preached, Thoreau paid his tax. His essay is a persuasive argument for the status of individual conscience and defines an instrument of resistance for minority opinion. It does not adequately consider the social and political consequences of its own proposals, but brilliantly clarifies the fallacies of American democracy for 'statesmen and legislators', who, 'standing so completely within the institution, never distinctly and nakedly behold it'.

Thoreau went to Walden convinced that 'the mass of men lead lives of quiet desperation' and determined to find out what might be 'necessary of life'. Emerson had said 'Things are in the saddle,/ And ride mankind'; Thoreau would not be ridden by materialism. Keen observation of nature enables him to portray the beetle-like absurdity of man struggling with the burden of his possessions:

> How many a poor immortal soul have I met well nigh crushed and smother-ed under its load, creeping down the road of life, pushing before it a barn seventy-five feet by forty, its Augean Stables never cleansed, and one hundred acres of land, tillage, mowing, pasture, and wood-lot!

The strength of *Walden* is its style and the descriptive detail from which Thoreau makes his analogies. The parallel between the seasons and the cycle of human life holds no surprises, and the pond predict-ably reflects states of mind. Work on the bean field provides a ready lesson on self-discipline, ice a symbol of purity; but there is nothing routine about the writing itself, genial yet provocative, poetry without metre:

> Time is but the stream I go a-fishing in. I drink at it; but while I drink I see the sandy bottom and detect how shallow it is. Its thin current slides away, but eternity remains. I would drink deeper; fish in the sky, whose bottom is pebbly with stars.

Animals and birds illuminate eternal verities of human behaviour, from foxes that look like 'rudimental burrowing men' to the woodchopper, a bonhomous, tender-hearted creature, if light in intellect, possessed of a 'mirth without alloy', and 'so genuine and unsophisticated, that no introduction would serve to introduce him, more than if you introduced a woodchuck to your neighbour'. The red squirrel is an inveterate performer whose motions, 'even in the most solitary recesses of the forest, imply spectators as much as those of the dancing girl'. The type of all battles is fought between red and black ants. 'I have no doubt', Thoreau sardonically opines, 'that it was a principle they fought for, as much as our ancestors, and not to avoid a threepenny tax on their tea.' The analogies work in both directions: if Thoreau saw people in animals, *Walden* makes it impossible to avoid seeing animals in people. Walt Disney must have read Thoreau.

The aphorisms are well known: 'As if you could kill time without injuring eternity'; 'Beware of all enterprises that require new clothes'. Such pith gains from context. A paragraph towards the end of the 'Solitude' chapter begins with a paradox: 'I have a great deal of company in my house; especially in the morning, when nobody calls.' The imagery in which Thoreau refutes all thought of loneliness takes his tone from wisecrack to paean, and justifies the paradox by con-necting man to nature's detail and its elements:

> I am no more lonely than a single mullein or dandelion in a pasture, or a bean leaf, or sorrel, or a horse-fly, or a humble-bee. I am no more lonely than the Mill Brook, or a weather-cock, or the north star, or the south wind, or an April shower, or a January thaw, or the first spider in a new house.

After the god-like solitudes of the north star and the south wind, how lightly that well-judged spider sets the thought down in the modesty of a house, albeit a new one. No wonder Robert Frost said *Walden* was his 'favourite poem'. Thoreau's blend of transcendence and particularity makes him a forebear of contemporary poets as different as Gary Snyder (*b*. 1930), Robert Bly (*b*. 1926), A. R. Ammons (*b*. 1926) and Philip Booth (*b*. 1925).

The vision of Emerson and Thoreau gained nature a new dimension as the repository of moral laws to be grasped intuitively, but also diminished it from the authoritative art of God to an operation of the human mind. An early entry in Emerson's journal says, 'Make your own Bible', and James Russell Lowell observed that the Sage of Concord was a man 'In whose mind all creation is duly respected/As parts of himself – just a little projected'. Nature eventually lost its own objective existence and became a human projection, in precocious anticipation of the appropriations of modern science. It followed, in the inevitable progress of American romanticism, that increasing autonomy and power were attributed to the individual mind. With increasing numbers pushing west, a spirit of independence was in the air at all levels of American life. The way was open for the solipsism of Melville's Captain Ahab, or the homicidal fanaticism of John Brown, who went marching on until his attack on the Federal armoury at Harper's Ferry in West Virginia in 1859 brought him martyrdom, Negroes some hope as well as much vexation, and Civil War nearer. Both Hawthorne and Melville criticised Transcendentalism in their fiction. Whitman swallowed it whole and made it into a national poem.

Hawthorne

Like the Puritans before them, the Unitarians and Transcendentalists dealt in certainties. The Puritans knew that God was in his heaven, though they might not be elected to join him; the Transcendentalists knew that the world was charged with the grandeur of an Over-Soul of which they were parts. Nathaniel Hawthorne (1804–64) was repelled by the moral naïvety of the Transcendentalists and appalled by the psychological and social effects of Puritan obsession with sin. Melville wrote admiringly of him that he could 'say no in thunder', and that it was the 'blackness' of his work that fixed and fascinated him. Hawthorne said himself that *The Scarlet Letter* (1850) 'was positively a hell-fired story, into which it is almost impossible to throw any light'; Henry James found it 'densely dark with a single spot of vivid colour'. There is no disputing Hawthorne's darkness. It is there to say no to Transcendental ebullience and to express the dark sides of Puritanism.

Despite a decaying maritime trade and somnolent colleagues, Hawthorne's position as Surveyor of the Salem Customs House from 1845 to 1849 was a more agreeable way of providing for his family than the communal life of George Ripley's Brook Farm whose defects are examined in *The Blithedale Romance* (1852). Salem was his birthplace, and original American home of the Hathornes (the 'w' was added to the name by the author). 'The Custom House' chapter introductory to *The Scarlet Letter* refers to 'the persecuting spirit' of William Hathorne, who emigrated from England in 1630, and of his son John. Hawthorne means it when he says that he takes their shame upon himself. Edgar Allan Poe imaginatively revelled in guilt, but Hawthorne experienced it with abomination. His art is an attempt to remove the curse brought down on the family by John Hathorne's participation in the Salem witchcraft trials of 1692.

Under misleadingly demure titles – *Twice-Told Tales* (1837) and *Mosses from an Old Manse* (1846) – Hawthorne's short stories expose the corrupting powers of guilt and pride. In 'The Minister's Black Veil' Parson Hooper's obsession with guilt severs him from the human community: viewing the world through the veil of his own guilt, he thinks he sees a black veil on every face around him. A satanic figure leads the credulous 'Young Goodman Brown' to consort with witches among whom he recognises pillars of Salem's Puritan society as well as his wife, Faith. '"Welcome, my children", said the dark figure, "to the communion of your race. You have found thus your nature and your destiny. By the sympathy of your human hearts for sin ye shall scent out all the places . . . . Evil is the nature of mankind. Evil must be your only happiness".' Henceforth Brown can trust neither himself nor anyone else. Hester Prynne's scarlet 'A' stands not only for 'Adultress', but also for 'A' in the seventeenth-century school primer: 'In Adam's fall/We sinned all'. Sin is everywhere in *The Scarlet Letter*, as tangibly present as the prison, the church and the graveyard, each of which stands as a symbol of the others. The church preaches sin and guilt, the prison and the scaffold punish them and the graveyard opens a gateway to everlasting damnation for victims of the group conscience.

At the age of seven Hawthorne injured his foot during a ball game. Several years of lameness disposed him to habits of reading and meditation, and sensitised him to the hazards of solitude as well as its pleasures. The gap between Miles Coverdale and the action of *The Blithedale Romance* accords with his narrative role as spectator; it is also symptomatic of a life impoverished by timidity. Coverdale loves Priscilla but is not man enough to break into the circle of involvement:

> It was both sad and dangerous, I whispered to myself, to be in too close affinity with the passions, the errors and the misfortunes of individuals who stood within a circle of their own, into which, if I stept at all, it must be as an intruder, and at a peril that I could not estimate.

More usually Hawthorne associates isolation with victims – Hester Prynne, Clifford Pyncheon in *The House of the Seven Gables* (1851), Donatello in *The Marble Faun* (1860) – or sinners. Miles Coverdale flinches from involvement; 'Ethan Brand' is about a man who repudiates it. The 'Unpardonable Sin' Brand seeks is the one he commits in separating intellect from feeling as a 'cold observer, looking on mankind as the subject of his experiment, and, at length converting man and woman to be his puppets, and pulling the wires that moved them to such degrees of crime as were demanded for his study'. Although Roger Chillingworth is motivated by revenge, he too commits the Unpardonable Sin in manipulating Hester, Pearl and Dimmesdale in his attempt to dominate the minister's soul. The hypnotic Westervelt commits similar violations in *The Blithedale Romance*. The sin of intellectual pride is exemplified by the monomaniacal botanist of 'Rapaccini's Daughter', who breeds a garden of beautiful but poisonous flowers which so thoroughly infect his daughter that she dies when given an antidote to the poison. The death of Georgiana in 'The Birthmark', when Aylmer tries to remove her only blemish, is a symbolic judgement of the pride implicit in both Puritan intolerance and Transcendental presumption.

Puritans considered their lives allegorical reflections of the mighty conflict between God and Satan. Hawthorne apologised for his own 'inveterate habit of allegory', and in *Moby-Dick* Melville calls allegory 'hideous and intolerable'. Both writers rejected Puritan modes of perception, and both avoid the typically allegorical one-for-one correspondence of object for abstract idea. Melville's whale is at once the most solid of physical things and the most reverberant symbol in American literature. (In *Herman Melville* [1950] Newton Arvin suggests that if the word 'symbolism' in its literary bearing had been fashionable when Melville was writing he would have used it in his own thinking about his books.) Hawthorne's use of allegory in 'The Celestial Railroad' and 'Dr Heidegger's Experiment' is exceptional; his method, like Melville's, is typically symbolic. Rappacini's garden of flowers, Hester Prynne's blazing 'A' and the character of Miriam in *The Marble Faun* (1860) are too ambiguous for reduction to the simple equations of the Puritan mind. Hawthorne chooses the latitude of the Romance not merely because he wishes to exploit what T. S. Eliot calls his 'ghost sense' of the supernatural, or manage atmosphere freely, but because the technique of the form enables him to show an ambivalent world in which Puritan and Transcendentalist certainties are replaced by a symbiosis of good and evil.

In 'Lady Eleanore's Mantle' a splendid garment carries smallpox germs. The beautiful Georgiana's single flaw in 'The Birthmark' represents imperfection that must be accepted. Rappacini's garden of poison becomes the only element in which the innocent Beatrice can live; she is a passive victim both of her father's perverse experiment and of Giovanni's wholesale rejection of a world in which good and evil are so intermingled. The figure who meets Goodman Brown in the forest bears 'a considerable resemblance to him', and the story develops the hint of an evil *alter ego* which only faith can control in any man of mixed proclivities. The complexity of human passions undermines the Utopian ideal of the Blithedale community: Hollingsworth is isolated by his obsession with criminal reform, but he wins the fair Priscilla. Hester Prynne is at once sinner and noble heroine. Pearl, her daughter by Dimmesdale, is a 'demon offspring', 'an elfin creature' and the 'one pearl of great price' of Matthew's Gospel. Bending over the dying Dimmesdale, Roger Chillingworth is a shrivelled devil, thwarted in his bid to possess a soul, yet he bequeaths a substantial legacy to Pearl. 'It is a curious subject of observation and inquiry', Hawthorne comments, 'whether hatred and love be not the same thing at bottom.' Uncertainty about the cause and alleged appearance of the scarlet letter on Dimmesdale's chest refers the theme of ambiguity to the problem of perception. Thus, in his masterpiece, Hawthorne confronts the enigma that fixed and fascinated his great contemporary, Herman Melville.

Melville

In 1876 Melville (1819–91) published *Clarel*, a long philosophical narrative poem about the future of Western civilisation. It was, he said, 'eminently adapted for unpopularity'. He had become accustomed to hostility and neglect. Even *Moby-Dick* (November 1851), or *The Whale* (October 1851) in its first English edition, failed to win him general recognition as a writer of the first rank despite favourable reviews on both sides of the Atlantic. The influential New York critic and editor Evert A. Duykinck (1816–78) had difficulty in classifying the mixture of fact, fiction and philosophy; the book was 'a remarkable sea-dish – an intellectual chowder'. Duykinck thought Ishmael inconsistent and Ahab 'too long drawn-out' but praised Melville's 'acuteness of observation', 'freshness of perception' and 'salient imagination'. Noticing distinctively American excellencies in the book as in the works of Poe, Emerson and Hawthorne, the London *Leader* asked, 'Who knows the horrors of the seas like HERMAN MELVILLE?' The American *Southern Quarterly Review* admired 'much vigorous description', but ridiculed the pseudo-Shakespearean extremes of Melville's rhapsodic prose: 'The style is maniacal – mad as a March hare – mowing, gibbering, screaming, like an incurable Bedlamite, reckless of keeper or strait-waistcoat'. *Moby-Dick* is incomparably superior to Melville's other books, yet at the time of his death it was almost forgotten. His achievement is largely a twentieth-century discovery.

After less than four years of formal schooling, Melville tried clerking and elementary-school teaching before shipping in 1839 aboard the packet boat *St Lawrence*. The voyage to Liverpool provided the story of initiation in *Redburn: His First Voyage* (1849), a calculated pot-boiler which glances at the discrepancy between appearance and reality. In January 1841 Melville embarked on the most formative experience of his life by signing his name on the register of the *Acushnet*, a three-masted whaler bound for the South Seas. Ishmael speaks for Melville himself in *Moby-Dick* when he says at the end of Chapter 24, 'a whale-ship was my Yale College and my Harvard'. A year and a half later he jumped ship in the Marquesas with a fellow sailor and lived for about four weeks among the reputedly cannibal natives. A fiction-alised version of this experience, *Typee: A Peep at Polynesian Life* (1846), was received as a tale of adventure among exotic primitives; but it shows signs of Melville's characteristic interest in contraries. There is kindness as well as cannibalism among the Typees and an innocence which accentuates the brutality of life on the whaler deserted by Tom and his friend and calls civilised morality in question. *Omoo: A Narrative of Adventures in the South Seas* (1847), a sequel to *Typee*, goes to Tahiti to make a point of the corrupting effect of white missionaries on the Polynesian islanders. The success of these first two books brought Melville a respite from material anxiety, but *Mardi: and a Voyage Thither* (1849) was a financial disaster.

It is immediately obvious that *Mardi* is to be a different kind of book:

> We are off! The courses and topsails are set; the coral-hung anchor swings from the bow; and together the three royals are given to the breeze that follows us out to sea like the baying of a hound. Out spreads the canvas – alow, aloft – boom-stretched on both sides with many a stun' sail, till like a hawk, with pinions poised, we shadow the sea with our sails and reelingly cleave the brine.

This is prose with a mission. Fact subserves imagery, sonority and rhythm in a bombardment of feeling. From the abrupt, implicating 'We are off!' – similar in effect to the buttonholing of *Moby-Dick*'s opening 'Call me Ishmael' – to the image of the hawk, Melville keys his language to the theme of quest. The hero Taji searches unendingly for Yillah, an incarnation of truth and love, through a foam of allegory, symbolism and Melville's most muddled plot. Disjointed and too long, the book was nevertheless an experiment which developed the muscles Melville would need for managing the mad captain and his whale. With the evil-eyed Jackson of *Redburn*, a man of 'even more woe than wickedness', he had the prototype for both Ahab and the satanic Claggart, of *Billy Budd, Sailor* (1924). *White-Jacket; or The World in a Man-of-War* (1850) provided the ambiguous white jacket emblematic of egoism, isolation, hatred and innocence, as a symbolic model for the white whale. Although *Redburn* was an immediate success and *White-Jacket* commanded favourable terms from his publishers, Melville still needed money. *Moby-Dick* began as a story of whaling intended to appeal to a paying public. With Ishmael's profusion of 'hints touching the plain facts' it sometimes resembles a handbook of whaling, but the intended tale of adventure turned into a gigantic prose-poem, an epic of the sea, a tragedy of the mind. When Ishmael presents his 'systematised exhibition of the whale' in Chapter 32 he essays nothing less than 'the classification of the constituents of a chaos'. The chaos, of course, is life. Melville is giving substance to his metaphor; a myth is in the making.

On its most obvious level Ahab's sin is his sacrifice of other men for the sake of vengeance on the whale that has 'dismasted' him:

> 'Vengeance on a dumb brute!' cried Starbuck, 'that simply smote thee from blindest instinct! Madness! To be enraged with a dumb thing Captain Ahab, seems blasphemous!'

Greater than the blasphemy of revenge is that of interpreting creation exclusively in terms of personal experience: Melville's notion of beatitude is remote from that of Emerson's 'Self-Reliance'. Ahab creates the image he defies. Believing that his injury represents the meaning of life, he sees demonism as an expression of universal nature. Thus, on his own terms, he wages war on the limitations of the human condition. This is the upper level of his sin, his *hubris*:

> What I've dared, I've willed; and what I've willed I'll do! They think me mad – Starbuck does; but I'm demoniac, I am madness maddened! That wild madness that's only calm to comprehend itself! The prophecy was that I should be dismembered; and – Aye! I lost this leg. I now prophesy that I will dismember my dismemberer. Now, then, be the prophet and the fulfiller one. That's more than ye, ye great gods, ever were.

The dualism Ishmael discovers in 'The Whiteness of the Whale' contradicts the sedative morality of the Transcendentalists; but there is more to the whale than malice. In the appalling purity of Moby-Dick's whiteness lies absolute terror, yet the colour is emblematic of 'the innocence of brides, the benignity of age'. While it has been made the symbol of 'divine spotlessness and power', it also 'strikes more of panic to the soul than that redness which affrights in blood'. In his momentous whiteness, Moby-Dick represents the ultimate ambiguity. Coloured with the traditional hue of sanctity, 'the very veil of the Christian's Deity', and at the same time with 'a colourless all-colour of atheism', he embodies 'the great principle of light', which 'forever remains white or colourless in itself'. Thus, at the core of his metaphor, Melville places a symbol of the fusion of opposites. With the blessing and curse of his whiteness Moby-Dick is an amalgam of the heavenly and the infernal, the 'one portentous something' at the heart of the world and the book.

In Chapter 11 Ishmael enjoys the warmth of bed in contrast to the chill outside, 'for there is no quality in this world that is not what it is merely by contrast. Nothing exists in itself'. Contrast makes things easy: it does not take Stubb long to spade out the fragrant ambergris from the *Rose-Bud*'s foul-smelling, blasted whale, and there is no problem of recognition. The central point of *Moby-Dick* is that definition is normally more difficult, because the line of demarcation between opposites is harder, if not impossible, to see. The ambiguity of experience in 'Benito Cereno', one of Melville's best *Piazza Tales* (1856), may be broken down into Old World corruption and New World innocence. In his poem 'The Maldive Shark' doubleness is the straightforward paradox whereby the serrated teeth of the shark afford a haven for its pilot-fish. Neither *Pierre, or the Ambiguities* (1852) nor *The Confidence-Man: His Masquerade* (1857) can be so easily glossed. In the midst of the Jacobean intensities of *Pierre*, a warning is issued not to over-simplify. Pierre Glendinning has read many novels, but rejects 'their false, inverted attempts at systematising eternally unsystematisable elements; their audacious, intermeddling impotency, in trying to unravel, and spread out, and classify, the more than thin gossamer threads which make up the complex web of life'. At the end of his story it is still impossible to judge Pierre. Symbolically mothered into death by the vial of poison hidden in his saintly or fiendish wife–sister's bosom, the meaning of his life remains, in his own phrase, 'ambiguous still'. *The Confidence-Man* may be read as a recommendation of universal distrust, or as a lesson in the supreme virtue of charity.

Unfinished when Melville died, *Billy Budd, Sailor* appears to polarise absolute good in Billy against absolute evil in Claggart. Such a reading is supported by much of the imagery, by Captain Vere's verdict that Claggart has been 'Struck dead by an angel of God! Yet the angel must hang!' and by the doggerel ballad 'Billy in the Darbies'. Yet the point of the story is that this simple polarity is too neat, an illusory refuge from more complex and disturbing doubleness. The depraved Claggart sometimes looks 'like the man of sorrows'; Billy may be an angel but he is clearly 'not yet quite a dove', and his stammer, on Melville's own terms, is a mark of the arch interferer who is always 'sure to slip in his little card'. Chapter 29, describing Billy's trial and conviction, begins with speculation about Captain Vere's sanity. It can be difficult to tell where sanity becomes its opposite; after all, 'Who in the rainbow can draw the line where the violet tint ends and the orange tint begins?' Violet has already been given as the colour of Claggart's eyes in his climactic moment of evildoing, and Billy's indurated hand has been described as 'orange-tawny'. Good and evil oppose each other in the Adamic sailor and the depraved master-at-arms, but they mysteriously blend into each other too. This is the essential enigma of Melville's vision, an insoluble riddle as tantalising as the tattooed mysteries on Queequeg's pagan skin. Like Taji and Ishmael, man is driven to seek a truth he can never fully apprehend. At the end of Melville's poem 'The Lake', the spirit enjoins acquiescence, 'Since light and shade are equal set/And all revolves'. The phantom is grand but hooded. Unable, in Simone Weil's phrase, to 'wait for God', Ahab is like the nihilist Verhovensky in Dostoevsky's *The Possessed* who, 'when he was excited, preferred to risk anything rather than remain in uncertainty'. 'Ungraspableness' is anathema to Ahab: with Manichaean ferocity he arrests the flow of ambiguity, splits the moral atom, and blows up the microcosmic *Pequod* and himself.

The angelic prophecy to Hagar in *Genesis* 16: 11–12 leads us to expect a character called Ishmael to be 'a wild man' and an outcast. Melville's Ishmael progresses from the anti-social behaviour of his moody isolation to a sense of community. The men of the *Pequod* achieve a perverse community through their common submission to a monomaniac, 'federated along one keel' in the vortex of Ahab's Promethean aggression. Early in the book Ishmael admits that the magnetism of Ahab's personality had attracted him: 'Ahab's quenchless feud seemed mine'. In his 'Squeeze of the Hand' he discovers fellowship with other men, and, afloat at the end on Queequeg's coffin, is symbolically preserved by his capacity for love. Through his participation in the metaphor of the novel, Ishmael achieves the balanced vision signified by the 'equatorial' doubloon Ahab nails to the *Pequod*'s mast. Few works of fiction equal Melville's nineteenth-century fable in expressing essential features of the post-romantic agony. In the hyper-romantic terms of Jean-Paul Sartre's existentialism in *Being and Nothingness* (1943), Ahab magnificently acts out the terrifying project of human reality: 'To be man means to reach toward being God', Sartre writes, 'or, if you prefer, man fundament-ally is the desire to be God'. Both Ahab and Ishmael know that a man is locked into his own subjectivity, but while Ahab tries to hoist his into godhead, Ishmael sees that human reality includes the claims of 'the other' and requires relationship. Ahab's 'desire to be God' must be modified through 'the very milk and sperm of kindness'. We must live according to the 'elongated Siamese ligature' by which we are joined to our fellow-beings, as in 'The Monkey-rope', Ishmael is joined to Queequeg. 'Every mortal man that breathes . . . has this Siamese connection with a plurality of other mortals'.

Walt Whitman and the Civil War

Moby-Dick is a critique of the romantic emphasis on the assertion of self as the basis of authentic human experience. Release into brother-hood means escape from the centripetal egoism most obviously exemplified by Captain Ahab, but present too in Starbuck and Stubb. The achievement of Melville's contemporary, Walt Whitman (1819–92), is to be at once nonchalantly individualistic and insatiably fraternal. With unprecedented gusto he bestows dignity on the commonplace. Containing 'multitudes', his classless soul is nothing if not expansive, for the extreme Emersonian stance of his poetry is that man is God. In a different temperament consistent adherence to such a belief might appear either simple-minded or dauntingly rigorous; in the case of Whitman it is a process of joy, love, nationalism and egoism of disarming candour. He is the bard of democracy.

Whitman was born in rural Long Island, grew to manhood in Brooklyn, and through his early years worked as a printer, journalist, teacher and building contractor. By the 1840s he was editing news-papers, notably the Democratic Brooklyn *Daily Eagle*. He supported United States expansion into South America, opposed slavery and advocated immigration and free trade. In 1848, while working on the New Orleans *Crescent*, he published 'The Mississippi at Midnight'. Portentous imagery and atmosphere press hard against constrictingly neat rhymes:

> Now drawn nigh the edge of the river,
>   Weird-like creatures suddenly rise;
> Shapes that fade, dissolving outlines
>   Baffle the gazer's staring eyes.

Two years later 'Blood-Money' appeared in the New York *Tribune Supplement*. The line is now the unit of construction, and rhythm is freely determined by rhetorical purpose:

> Of olden time, when it came to pass
> That the beautiful God, Jesus, should finish his work on earth,
> Then went Judas, and sold the divine youth,
> And took pay for his body.

With the addition of frequent parallelism and the use of sonority to give the verse momentum, this is the tumescent, quasi-Biblical style of Whitman's *Leaves of Grass*, first published anonymously in 1855.

Until the so-called 'Death-bed' edition of 1892 (the text referred to here) Whitman revised and enlarged the book. New poems published separately, for example, the volume entitled *Drum-Taps* (1865), served to nourish the larger work. The Preface to the 1855 edition offers the work as a poetic incarnation of Whitman's spiritual response to the meaning, geography and natural life of his country. Here, at last, was something commensurate with Emerson's poem of America. Accordingly the Sage of Concord acknowledged his complimentary copy of *Leaves of Grass* by calling it 'the most extraordinary piece of wit and wisdom that America has yet contributed', and hailing Whitman 'at the beginning of a great career'.

The longest poem in *Leaves of Grass* is the seminal 'Song of Myself'. The poem's opening lines boom out the premise of Whitman's life and work:

> I celebrate myself, and sing myself,
> And what I assume you shall assume,
> For every atom belonging to me as good belongs to you.

The 'I' is the healthy, mercurial, thirty-seven year-old poet who unabashedly delights in the smoke of his own breath, the 'no sweeter fat than sticks to his own bones', his kisses, comradeship and the 'play of light and shade' as he finds it throughout creation. 'Read these leaves', the 1855 Preface urges, 'in the open air every season of every year of your life, re-examine all you have been told at school or church or in any book, dismiss whatever insults your own soul.' In its first version the poem was untitled and unsectioned, but Whitman later divided it into fifty-two parts as if to provide a weekly portion for the recommended annual year-long reading. His purpose is to 'reckon' the earth and renew contact with nature's 'original Energy'. The second part of the poem develops the injunction of the Preface:

> You shall not look through my eyes either,
>   nor take things from me,
> You shall listen to all sides and filter them
>   from yourself.

Whitman is not disingenuous when he says this, or insists, against the evidence, that he is 'not stuck up'. His tone is undeviatingly assertive, but his target is the reader's faculty of cognitive feeling, not his reason. His song enjoins shared exaltation in the common atoms, not agreement with definitions or discriminatory moral positions. There are certainly irritants to be tholed: 'Trippers and askers' ply him with pettily untranscendent questions about his life and opinions. There are suicides, runaway slaves sweating with fear and fatigue, traitors, murder, war. So be it: 'All truths wait in all things'. The poet becomes 'Walt Whitman, a Kosmos', by assimilating everything, good and bad, like Emerson's Brahma incarnate, into himself and his amazing hymn:

> I am the poet of the Body and I am the poet
> of the Soul,
> The pleasures of heaven are with me and the
> pains of hell are with me,
> The first I graft and increase upon myself,
> the latter I translate into a new tongue.

Lacking 'mockings or arguments' Whitman is the most permissive of Messiahs, celebrating the grass both as the hopeful 'flag of my disposition' and as 'a uniform hieroglyphic' that symbolises immortality and universality: 'The smallest sprout shows there is really no death'. After his ecstatic participation in the teeming life around him, 'of every hue and caste . . . of every rank and religion', he bequeaths himself to be recycled in the perpetual process of nature:

> I bequeath myself to the dirt that grows
> from the grass I love,
> If you want me again look for me under your boot-soles.

The optimism of 'Song of Myself' is sustained in the additions Whitman made to *Leaves of Grass* in its third edition (1860). 'Chants Democratic', which included 'By Blue Ontario's Shore', 'Song of the Broad-Axe' and 'I hear America Singing', celebrates the nationalistic spirit advocated in the Preface of 1855. 'Enfans d'Adam' (later entitled 'Children of Adam') rejects the traditional Christian view of the Fall of Man, glories in the innocence of Adam and Eve, sings the 'Body Electric', and graphically praises physical love. The main theme of 'Calamus' is 'the manly love of comrades', which prompted the banning of *Leaves of Grass* in Boston as well as much irrelevant comment on Whitman's capacity for homosexual love. The idea of universal camaraderie is developed to especially telling effect in the urgent forward movement of 'Song of the Open Road' – 'Allons! whoever you are come travel with me! . . . Allons! the road is before us!' In 'Crossing Brooklyn Ferry' Whitman asserts consanguinity with the future by prefacing 'I too' to aspects of his background and character. All who cross the ferry or walk the earth derive from one 'eternal float of solution'. Such all-encompassing optimism was soon put to the test. At 4.30 a.m. on 12 April 1861 a ten-inch mortar shell burst inside the red-brick building of Fort Sumter, South Carolina, calling in question not merely Walt Whitman's transcendent belief in kinship, but the very Union itself. The South's eleven Confederate States of America, under the presidency of Jefferson Davis, were at war with the twenty-three states of the North, under Abraham Lincoln.

At the beginning of hostilities each side expected the engagement to be short and decisive. The North had the advantages of numbers, a comparatively stable economy and a navy. The Confederacy had self-righteousness and a cause. By the concept of 'States rights' the United States was a confederation of states any of which was free to secede if it objected to Federal interference. The slave-holding states' insistence on their rights was chiefly motivated by economics. Without slave labour Southern economy would collapse. John Brown's raid on Harper's Ferry in 1859 gave the anti-slavery movement a martyr and the South all the evidence it needed to prove that Northern abolitionists would stop at nothing. Some 1,200,000 copies of Harriet Beecher Stowe's (1811–96) *Uncle Tom's Cabin* (1852) had convinced the North of the iniquity of slavery, although the novel is fairer to the South than is often realised, and Mrs Stowe's villainous overseer, Simon Legree, is a Yankee from Vermont. On 6 November 1860 Lincoln was elected President on a Republican platform which condemned the African slave trade and denied the legal status of slavery in the territories. In December South Carolina started the landslide of state secessions.

Lincoln's objective was to preserve the Union, but the Confederacy gained the upper hand in the early stages of the war. The rupture of American unity was not to be healed save by a long and agonising struggle. After the Union defeat at the Second Battle of Bull Run (called Second Manassas by the South) in the summer of 1862 General Robert E. Lee advanced into Maryland with designs on the Federal Capitol in Washington. Halted at Antietam on 17 September 1862 in the bloodiest battle of the war, Lee was forced to retreat to Virginia and Lincoln issued a preliminary Emancipation Proclamation: slaves would be freed if the South did not surrender before 1 January 1863, the date on which the final Proclamation was made. Within a few days the world knew that slavery in America was doomed and the war became a paradigmatic struggle for human freedom. Union victories at Gettysburg and Vicksburg on 3 and 4 July 1863 left the Confederacy trapped by the Union armies to the west and north and by the Union navy to the east and south. Ulysses S. Grant, the Union hero of Vicksburg, mounted an assault on Richmond, while William T. Sherman marched through Georgia and Philip Sheridan suppressed resistance in the Shenandoah Valley. On 9 April 1865, after a brave defence of Richmond, Robert E. Lee surrendered to Grant at the Court House in Appomattox, Virginia.

The North had its rallying song in Julia Ward Howe's (1819–1910) 'Battle Hymn of the Republic' (1862), and the South had Dan Emmett's (1815–1904) 'Dixie'. By the time of Margaret Mitchell's (1900–49) death some eight million copies of *Gone With the Wind* (1936) and its movie adaptation (1939) had mythologised the war for audiences world-wide and immortalised Scarlett O'Hara as the embodiment of a fleshly South's indomitable spirit. The realism of John W. De Forest's (1826–1906) *Miss Ravenel's Conversion from Secession to Loyalty* (1867) anticipates the more graphic evocations and psychological precision of Stephen Crane's *The Red Badge of Courage* (1895). Supreme battlefield realism was achieved, and photographic history made, by the pictures of Mathew Brady and his assistants who covered the entire war using outsize and unwieldy plates that had to be rushed immediately after exposure to the wagon dark-room for development. Melville's *Battle-Pieces and Aspects of the War* (1866) laments the national tragedy and the ironies of a war in which Federal soldiers watching the enemy through a telescope see 'a baseball bounding sent' and wish they could join the game ('The Armies of the Wilderness'). The young men of both armies are 'swept by the winds of their place and time' ('On the Slain Collegians'), which render ethical distinctions meaningless:

> Warred one for Right, and one for Wrong?
> So be it; but they both were young –
> Each grape to his cluster clung,
> All their elegies are sung.

'Real, terrible, beautiful days!', Whitman exclaimed towards the end of his life, recalling the war. Sympathy for the South, advocacy of free soil and a deep-seated passivism did not prevent him from writing the recruiting poem 'Beat! Beat! Drums!' on the outbreak of hostilities. Contact with the sick and wounded changed his tune, as he admits in 'The Wound-Dresser':

> Arous'd and angry, I'd thought to beat the
> alarum, and urge relentless war,
> But soon my fingers fail'd me, my face droop'd
> and I resign'd myself,
> To sit by the wounded and soothe them, or
> silently watch the dead.

Rushing down to Virginia in 1862 to nurse his wounded brother George, Whitman was so moved by the sight of the injured that he stayed on in Washington as a hospital volunteer. The collection of poems published as *Drum-Taps* is the record of his wartime moods and impressions. The sequence moves from the depiction of soldiers in battle formation ('Cavalry Crossing a Ford'), the scattering of camp-fires ('Bivouac on a Mountain Side'), and the personal pain of war in the effect of a soldier's death on comrades and relatives ('Come up from the Fields, Father' and 'Vigil Strange I Kept on the Field One Night') to the vision of a reunified America ('To the Leaven'd Soil They Trod').

Washington itself swarmed with politicians, 'well-drest, rotten, meagre, nimble and impotent, full of gab, full always of their thrice-accursed *party*'; but, Whitman noted in a letter, the war the politicians had contrived also brought:

> this other other freight of helpless worn and wounded youth, genuine of the soil, of darlings and true heirs to me the first unquestioned and convincing western crop, prophetic of the future, proofs undeniable to all men's ken of perfect beauty, tenderness and pluck that never race yet rivalled.

In 'Song of Myself' Whitman had seen himself as 'the mashed fireman with breast-bone broken'; now optimism grew again from his identification with the young warriors in their pain:

> Many a soldier's loving arms about this neck
> have cross'd and rested,
> Many a soldier's kiss dwells on these bearded lips.

The bravery, grace and responsiveness of the young war-wounded comprise a greater and more enduring truth than the temporary cause of their suffering. 'When Lilacs Last in the Dooryard Bloom'd', an elegy on the death of Lincoln, published in *Sequel to Drum-Taps* (1865), expresses the recovered optimism in Whitman's finest symbolism. By working through his own grief for Lincoln, the 'great star', and covering the fallen leader's coffin with lilacs as emblems of eternal spring, the poet – symbolised by the hermit thrush – reconciles the tension between life and death in the chant of his own representative soul. The suffering is over, the land still beautiful and the eternal cycle of life continues in terms of the three symbols of the star, the lilac and the bird. The world is, in the words of 'Passage to India' (1871), a 'vast Rondure, swimming in space,/Cover'd all over with visible power and beauty'.

Any view of the mid-nineteenth century as a time of American renaissance must include the Civil War as part of the process. At enormous cost of life and resource the war gave America a history it could call intrinsically and exclusively its own. After the war unionism was no longer either an ideal or a fragile realisation of one; it was ready to quicken into the incontrovertible fact described by Robert Penn Warren in *The Legacy of the Civil War* (1961):

> a fact so technologically, economically, and politically validated that we usually forget to ask how fully this fact represents a true community, the spiritually significant communion which the old romantic unionism had envisaged.

In 'Long, too Long America' Whitman unjustly accuses his country of learning 'from joys and prosperity only'. He is prescience itself when he sees the Civil War as an opportunity to learn 'from crises' and 'to conceive and show to the world' what its 'children en-masse really are'. The process of education, of course, continues. A hundred years after the Emancipation Proclamation, most Americans were acutely aware of how much was still to be done to achieve equality for all citizens regardless of colour. Even Lincoln's interest in the welfare of the Negro was subsidiary to his concern for the threatened ideals of democratic federalism. The unfulfilled promises of the Proclamation were in President Kennedy's mind in 1963 when he asked Congress to enact a new Civil Rights bill: 'Surely in 1963, one hundred years after emancipation, it should not be necessary for any American to demonstrate in the streets for opportunity to stop at a hotel, or to eat at a lunch counter'. It should not have been necessary, but it was. Yet without the war and the Emancipation Proclamation, the language of Kennedy's appeal would have been impossible. The Civil War and the works of Emerson, Thoreau, Hawthorne, Melville and Whitman gave the people of the United States new terms of reference in which to develop their conception of themselves.

6
Realisms

AFTER Lincoln's momentous Proclamation of New Year's Day, 1863, emancipation celebrations were shared by Negroes and whites from Boston to San Francisco. Humane values had triumphed, and European support of the South dwindled rapidly. Union victory in the Civil War gave the abolitionists their moral apotheosis, but created massive new problems in the South. The plantation system was destroyed, Simon Legree an impossible anachronism, but the Southern states now became a vast stagnant region where impoverished whites and destitute Blacks lived in debt and ill-health as oppressed sharecroppers. An intricate socio-economic system had been dismantled at a stroke, and there was nothing to replace it. Alternative employment for casualties of disabled agrarianism was not available in southern towns and cities as it was to some extent in New England. The South exacerbated its poverty and compounded its guilt by persecuting its Blacks and bearing the heavy costs of segregation. The official dissolution of the Ku Klux Klan in 1871 was, as the world knows, not effective.

The frontier moved westward and, towards the end of the nineteenth century, was transubstantiated from reality into metaphor. Huddled in reservations, defeated Indians starved and grew desperate. 'They made us many promises,' said Sioux Chief Red Cloud of the white man's negotiators, 'more than I can remember, but they never kept but one; they promised to take our land, and they took it.' In south-western Dakota the Teton Sioux Indians performed the Ghost Dance of Wovoka, a Paiute prophet, to propitiate the removal of the white people and the return of native lands replete with buffalo. Federal intervention led to the death of Chief Sitting Bull, the humiliation of Chief Big Foot, and on 29 December 1890 the massacre of over 200 Sioux men, women and children at the 'Battle' of Wounded Knee. In *Bury My Heart At Wounded Knee* (1970), Dee Brown (*b.* 1908) observes that the Indians knew 'that life was equated with the earth and its resources, that America was a paradise, and they could not comprehend why the intruders from the East were determined to destroy all that was Indian as well as America itself'.

Farmers throughout the country were burdened by loans to buy the machinery without which they could not compete. They knew that the earth and its resources had been pawned to capital. They knew the lure of the Montgomery Ward and Sears Roebuck mail-order catalogues, cornucopious displays of tempting products. It was an era of the city of breathtaking industrial expansion, of science and finance. These were the post-Civil-War gods Americans chose to guide them into a paradisal twentieth century. Andrew Carnegie built his empire of steel; Cornelius Vanderbilt made over a hundred million dollars from railroads and shipping; J. Pierpont Morgan created a similar fortune in banking; John D. Rockefeller formed the Standard Oil Company and became 'the richest man in the world'. In 1879 James Ritty invented the cash register.

The money market crashed in 1873 and 1893; thousands of new immigrants lived in slum conditions in New York, Boston, Philadelphia and Chicago. Corrupt politicians and robber barons gave capitalism a bad name; but America achieved prodigious feats of progress between the end of the Civil War and entry into the First World War in 1917. Chicago received the Tacoma Building, America's first skyscraper in 1889, and New York the 792-foot Woolworth Building in 1913. America's first transcontinental railway, the Union Pacific, was completed in 1869. E. Remington and Sons were manufacturing and selling the first commercially successful typewriters, designed by Sholes and Glidden. Alexander Graham Bell invented his telephone, Thomas Edison the phonograph, William Stanley the transformer, George Eastman the roll-film, William Burroughs the adding machine, W. L. Judson the zip fastener, King C. Gillette the safety razor. The Massachusetts Institute of Technology was founded in 1865 and the following year Mary Baker Eddy propounded the concept of Christian Science. New York City's Brooklyn Bridge was opened in 1883; Orville and Wilbur Wright made the first flight in a heavier-than-air machine in 1903, the year in which Henry Ford founded his motor company. (In *The Magnificent Ambersons* (1918) the popular novelist, Booth Tarkington (1869–1946) describes the victory of the automobile industry over real estate as a source of wealth in America). The first real cinema opened at Pittsburgh in 1905. H. L. Higginson founded the Boston Symphony Orchestra in 1881; Edward Macdowell composed his

Indian Suite in 1896; W. C. Handy's 'Memphis Blues' (1911) and 'St Louis Blues' (1914) affected the prevalent ragtime with nostalgia peculiar to the music of Southern Blacks. In 1911 Irving Berlin set America and the world dancing to 'Alexander's Rag-time Band'.

Regionalists

Regional consciousness is a marked feature of much of the writing done during this explosive period of change. As the old America faded into history, sectional pride fostered literature which mixed committed realism with sentiment and nostalgia. New England's Sarah Orne Jewett (1849–1909) and Mary Wilkins Freeman (1852–1930) both write about the decay of their region. Sarah Orne Jewett's work laments the passing of rural New England and of the era of family ties responsible and tolerant enough to ensure the continuity of a place in terms of its succeeding generations. The city is her villain. In the title story of *A White Heron and Other Stories* (1886) a town-bred girl, now living in the country, chooses not to show the nest of the white heron to a beguiling young sportsman who has offered her ten dollars for the information. Sight of the bird makes Sylvia realise her own affinity with nature in contrast to the urban value system represented by the young man's bribe. A sequence of loosely connected tales *The Country of the Pointed Firs* (1896) memorialises Jewett's fictional town of Dunnet Landing, once a port, now a forgotten backwater. In a style of muted realism, she allows land and sea to bestow a timeless dignity and grace on the lives of her unexceptional townspeople. Mary Wilkins Freeman's psychological insight and realistic landscapes compensate for her narrower range. The stories collected in *A Humble Romance* (1887) and *A New England Nun* (1891) specialise in spinsters. The call of the west – or of Australia in 'A New England Nun' – has drained away the vigorous young men of the east.

New York's Harold Frederic (1856–98) attempts a more ambitious realism in several novels which anticipate the work of Stephen Crane, Frank Norris and Theodore Dreiser. In the best of them, *The Damnation of Theron Ware* (1896), Frederic uses an intricate plot to reveal the disintegration of Protestant orthodoxy and the inadequacy of religious fashions from the arid Methodism of Theron Ware's own congregation to Ledsmar's sceptical Darwinism, and the volatile Celia's late nineteenth-century aestheticism. Pennsylvania's Margaret Deland (1857–1945) was best known for her anti-Calvinist novel *John Ward, Preacher* (1888), but achieves more in *The Awakening of Helena Richie* (1906), a novel about a woman's growth towards independence in the context of the repressive morality of 'Old Chester', a fictional town near Pittsburgh.

Not surprisingly the post-Civil-War South produced a large crop of regionally conscious writers in whom realism is more or less modified by the romantic, backward look. In *The Grandissimes* (1880) and *Madame Delphine* (1881) Louisiana's George Washington Cable (1844–1925) foreshadows William Faulkner's treatment of race relations in a decadent, often violent society. Cable's first and most enduring literary success was *Old Creole Days* (1879), seven stories, previously published in *Scribner's Monthly*, about miscegenation, smuggling, courageous or coquettish women, and proud or cunning men of the old Spanish–French Creole society of New Orleans. Plotting is thin, but Cable brings his characters to brilliant life by his expert use of Creole dialect. In 'Jean-Ah Poquelin' a proud French Creole smuggler and slave-trader turns recluse and protests against the building of a new road through his fetid marshland. A natural aristocrat, he takes his complaint to the top and visits the Governor:

> I come to you. You is *le Gouverneur*. I know not the new laws. I ham a Fr-r-rench-a-man! Fr-rench-a-man have something *aller au contraire* – he comes at his *Gouverneur*. I come at you. If me not had been bought from me King like *bassals* [vassals] in the hold time, ze King gof-France would-a-show *Monsieur le Gouverneur* to take care his men to make strit in right places. *Mais*, I know; we billong to *Monsieur le Président*.

The Governor relegates the problem to the appropriate municipal official who finds Mr Poquelin's 'impudence refreshing' and remarks that the new street will increase the value of his property 'ten dollars to one'. The building of the street leads to Poquelin's death and the exposure of his secret reason for attempting to keep progress at bay. The ghost supposedly haunting his ramshackle property is his younger brother, whitened by leprosy. 'Belles Demoiselles Plantation' centres on Colonel De Charleau's efforts to provide for his daughters by trading his beloved but heavily mortgaged property on an eroding bank of the Mississippi. The bank finally caves in and the splendid house sinks into the river like Poe's House of Usher, symbolising the demise of Creole aristocracy in Louisiana:

> Belles Demoiselles, the realm of maiden beauty, the home of merriment, the house of dancing, all in the tremor and glow of pleasure, suddenly sank, with one short, wild wail of terror – sank, sank, down, down, down, into the merciless, unfathomable flood of the Mississippi.

Under the name of Charles Egbert Craddock, Mary Noailles Murfree (1850–1922) commemorates the traditional austerities of her home state's mountain folk in *In the Tennessee Mountains* (1884) and *The Prophet of the Great Smoky Mountains* (1885). Two generations later, Mildred Haun (1911–66) captures the Southern oral tradition's distinctive tones, rhythms and natural flair for simple figurative speech. Set in the Smoky Mountains of East Tennessee, her stories, collected by Herschel Gower in *The Hawk's Done Gone, and Other Stories* (1968), convey Southern Appalachian passion, fatalism and superstition with exemplary directness and economy, art concealing art to create a regional balladry in prose. A mountain midwife narrates the family chronicle of the title story:

> I've been Granny-woman to every youngon born in this district for nigh sixty years now. I've tied the navel cords of all the saints and sinners that have seen their first daylight in Hoot Owl District. They all have bellies about alike. There's not much difference.

She can't climb the hills that fence her in as she used to, but still readily evokes them:

> Letitia Edes Mountain climbs up over there in the west, and Reds Run Mountain is in front of the house, jig-jagging up to the top like a stair-step, covered with spruce pine that stay green all winter long. And on the east side of the house there's that little old haystacky-looking hill Ma always calls Sals King Mountain. I have a time hunting heart leaves and ginseng on it. It goes straight up into a point and is harder to climb than a greased pole.

James Lane Allen (1849–1925) did not publish his best-known novel *A Kentucky Cardinal* (1894) until ten years' residence in New York had disposed him to a more lyrical than realistic depiction of the blue-grass region. John Esten Cooke (1830–86) produced some thirty volumes of fiction, biography and history. *The Heir of Gaymount* (1870), which treats the South's changing environment, is a useful complement to the work of his fellow Virginian Thomas Nelson Page (1853–1922), a vociferous spokesman for the prewar era. 'That the social life of the Old South had its faults I am far from denying,' Page said, 'but its virtues far outweighed them; its graces were never equalled . . . It was, I believe, the purest, sweetest life ever lived.' If the stories of *In Ole Virginia* (1887) depict plantation life as an implausibly Utopian system of benevolent masters and cheerfully loyal slaves, Page's work is distinguished by authentic Negro speech, and remains an illuminating if partisan account of humane elements which the Civil War all too often rendered obsolete. Page was not a bigot: the Northerners are people of honour in his novel *Red Rock* (1898); the villain is bureaucracy.

When Georgia's Joel Chandler Harris (1848–1908) was thirteen he went to work as a printer's devil on *The Countryman*, a weekly newspaper issued from the plantation, 'Turnwold', where he became familiar with Negro lore and dialect. A series of newspaper jobs culminated in a twenty-four-year-long position with the Atlanta *Constitution* which printed the first 'Uncle Remus' stories based on Harris's memories of 'Turnwold' and the work of William Owens on Negro folklore. Implicit in the framework of the stories – the sagacious Negro filling his pipe, threading a needle or peeling a yam while he delivers his homiletic legends to 'Miss Sally's' seven-year-old boy – is a salute to the equilibrium of the Old South. Harris makes the point in his introduction to the first collection of his stories:

> I trust I have been successful in presenting what must be, at least to a large portion of American readers, a new and by no means unattractive phase of negro character – a phase which may be considered a curiously sympathetic supplement to Mrs. Stowe's wonderful defence of slavery as it existed in the South.

If Harris gives the South its Aesop, the strength and appeal of *Uncle Remus, His Songs and His Sayings* (1880) and *Nights with Uncle Remus* (1883), which introduces the less successful Coast Negro, Daddy Jack, are not in their didacticism. Lighter moralities are not to be found, but it is Uncle Remus's genial wisdom and the colloquial freshness of his condensed, homespun poetic speech that continue to draw generations of readers to the escapades of Brer Rabbit, Brer Fox, Brer Wolf and Brer Terrapin. With his hands, feet and head stuck in the wonderful Tar-Baby, and Brer Fox, 'lookin' des ez innercent ez one er yo' mammy's mockin' birds', Brer Rabbit exemplifies the hazards of pride. The language of his conversation with the Tar-Baby runs from jaunty courtesy to incongruous anger, taking the sketch beyond any simple moral, as Harris builds up his comic nemesis to the refrain of Brer Fox keeping his cool:

> 'Mawnin!' sez Brer Rabbit, sezee – 'nice wedder dis mawnin'', sezee.
> Tar-Baby stay still, en Brer Fox, he lay low.
> 'How duz yo' sym'tums seem ter segashuate?' sez Brer Rabbit, sezee.
> Brer Fox, he wink his eye slow, en lay low, en de Tar-Baby, she ain't sayin' nuthin'.
> 'How you come on, den? Is you deaf?' sez Brer Rabbit, sezee, 'Kaze if you is I kin holler louder', sezee.

Tar-Baby stay still, en Brer Fox, he lay low.
'Youer stuck up, dat's w'at you is', sez Brer Rabbit sezee, 'en I'm gwineter
kyore you, da't w'at I'm a gwineter do', sezee.
Brer Fox, he sorter chuckle in his stummuck, he did, but Tar-Baby ain't
sayin' nuthin'.
'I'm gwineter larn you howter talk ter 'specttuble fokes ef hit's de las' ack',
sez Brer Rabbit, sezee. 'Ef you don't take off dat hat en tell me howdy, I'm
gwineter bus' you wide open', sezee.
Tar-Baby stay still, en Brer Fox, he lay low.

Francis Bret Harte (1836–1902) was born in Albany, New York,
but went to California at eighteen. By thirty he was nationally known
for his work on western newspapers and in 1870 accepted an unprecedented offer of ten thousand dollars a year from *The Atlantic
Monthly*. In a brisk, elegant style Harte mythologises the romantic
California of the 1850s, where innocence flames in the inhospitable
circumstances of frontier experience. Gamblers, whores and
blaspheming miners evince hearts of gold in *The Luck of Roaring Camp
and Other Stories* (1870) which brought world fame to Harte's blend of
wit and sentiment. Taking his cue from the French critic Hippolyte
Taine that 'the artist of originality will work courageously with the
materials he finds in his own environment', Indiana's Edward
Eggleston (1837–1902) based his novel *The Hoosier Schoolmaster* (1871)
on his brother George's experience of a one-man school. The realistic
portrayal of a coarse and bigoted society of Indiana farmers is
alleviated by an improbably ideal hero and impeccable heroine. The
adversities of life in the Midwest receive more realistic treatment in
the work of Hamlin Garland (1860–1940). *Main-Travelled Roads*
(1891) and *Prairie Folks* (1893) focus on the hardships endured by
farmers in Iowa and the Dakotas. Frank Norris (1870–1902) of
Chicago explores the Californian wheat industry in *The Octopus* (1901)
and the struggle for power between the ranchers and the railroad, the
'octopus' whose tentacles surround and strangle them. A sequel, *The
Pit* (1903), about speculation on the Chicago wheat exchange, was the
second volume of an intended trilogy which Norris did not live to
complete.

Imaginary worlds and wishful thinking

Although realism soon became the dominant mode in American
writing after the Civil War, there were romantics and escape artists
too in the closing decades of the nineteenth century. Lew Wallace's

(1827–1905) biblical romance, *Ben Hur, a Tale of Christ* (1880) sold over three million copies and provided Hollywood with material for two epics in 1926 and 1959, both of which did justice to 'the most terrific chariot race in the world'. Frank R. Stockton (1834–1902) specialised in whimsical stories for children, but achieved international fame with a short story called 'The Lady or the Tiger', which evinces a psychological penetration worthy of Poe or Henry James. Horatio Alger's (1834–99) *Ragged Dick* (1867), *Luck and Pluck* (1869) and *Tattered Tom* (1871) books for boys perpetuated the great American myth that industry, frugality and clean living will bring wealth and honour. Edward Bellamy (1850–98) imagines a Utopian future in *Looking Backward: 2000–1887* (1888) and *Equality* (1897). Bellamy's fantasies incorporate serious social comment and a programme for reform, but Francis Marion Crawford (1854–1909) declared the novel a 'pocket-stage' for entertainment, and used non-American settings for the majority of his forty-five romantic novels. The historical novels of Winston Churchill (1871–1947) enjoyed a wide readership around the turn of the century, but few American writers have entertained as successfully as 'O. Henry', the *nom de plume* of William Sydney Porter (1862–1910). His romanticism is especially committed to New York City – 'Baghdad-on-the-Subway' – as he makes clear in the introduction to *The Four Million* (1906). A master of the form of the short story, O. Henry's sentimentality is almost invariably absorbed into the effectiveness of his surprise endings. The tales gathered in *The Collected Works of O. Henry* (1953) amply realise his intention to refute the allegation that only four hundred people in New York were worth knowing.

Owen Wister (1860–1938) went to Wyoming for the sake of his health and re-invented the west in *The Virginian* (1902), one of the steadiest best-sellers in America's literary history. Wister created a new image. A crack shot, cool gambler and knight to the rescue of Molly Wood, the New England schoolmistress, from her marooned stagecoach, the Virginian became the prototype of all cowboy heroes, authority perfectly compressed into his immortal retort to the irredeemable villain, Trampas: 'When you call me that, smile.' Zane Grey (1875–1939) gave up dentistry for the western and developed the Wister formula in a large output of novels, including *Last of the Plainsmen* (1908) and *Riders of the Purple Sage* (1912). The hero of Jack Schaefer's popular *Shane* (1949) is especially reminiscent of the Virginian, and won existentialist praise from Jean-Paul Sartre's journal, *Les Temps Modernes* as 'that nostalgic outlaw of a Racine-like modesty'. While fictional cowboys multiplied, Edgar Rice Burroughs (1875–1950) turned from stories about life on Mars to transpose the ethos of the west into the African jungle with *Tarzan of the Apes* (1914) and its numerous sequels, thereby creating the most popular folk hero of the early twentieth century, until Tarzan's supremacy was challenged by Superman, Batman and other blue-haired, caped crusaders of the comic-book.

Twain

Samuel Langhorne Clemens (1835–1910) took the *nom de plume* of 'Mark Twain' from the river-boat leadsman's sounding call for two fathoms' depth of navigable water. Chapter 7 of *Life on the Mississippi* (1883) gives the call its context when Horace Bixby, the veteran pilot to whom Twain apprenticed himself, negotiates a hazardous crossing in the dark:

> Mr. Bixby pulled the cord, and two deep mellow notes from the big bell floated off on the night. Then a pause, and one more note was struck. The watchman's voice followed, from the hurricane deck:
> 'Labboard lead, there! Stabboard lead!'
> The cries of the leadsmen began to rise out of the distance, and were gruffly repeated by the word-passers on the hurricane deck.
> 'M-a-r-k three! .... M-a-r-k three! .... Quarter-less-three! .... Half twain! .... Quarter twain! .... M-a-r-k twain! .... Quarter-less –!
> Mr. Bixby pulled two bell ropes, and was answered by faint jinglings far below in the engine room, and our speed slackened. The steam began to whistle through the gauge cocks. The cries of the leadsmen went on – and it is a weird sound, always, in the night. Every pilot in the lot was watching now, with fixed eyes, and talking under his breath. Nobody was calm and easy but Mr. Bixby.

Maestro of the international lecture circuit, Twain was so conscious of being typed by his contemporaries as a literary comedian that he published the now-forgotten *Personal Recollections of Joan of Arc* (1896) as by 'The Sieur Louis de Conte', to ensure that it would be taken seriously. For the devotee of romance he offers a hyperbolic west in *Roughing It* (1872), boyish idealism and melodrama in *The Adventures of Tom Sawyer* (1876), sixteenth-century England in *The Prince and the Pauper* (1882), the river-boat pilot as hero in *Life on the Mississippi*, Huck and Jim 'free and easy and comfortable' on their raft in *The Adventures of Huckleberry Finn* (1884), and Camelot with Hank Morgan, American virtuoso as 'Boss' in *A Connecticut Yankee in King Arthur's Court* (1889).

His best invention, however, is the flexible authentically vernacular voice of Huckleberry Finn, which particularly warrants William Dean Howells' comment on the fluidity of his style: 'So far as I know, Mr Clemens is the first writer to use in extended writing the fashion we all use in thinking, and to set down the thing that comes into his mind without fear or favour of the thing that went before or the thing that may be about to follow.' His chief vein is satire; it runs through his work from his adaptation of a popular oral tale of the gambler outwitted in 'Jim Smiley and His Jumping Frog' (1865) to the misanthropy of 'The Man That Corrupted Hadleyburg' (1900) and the acrid pessimism of *The Mysterious Stranger* (1916). The means may be caricature, symbol, pseudo-history or fantasy, but the end is always an expression of his vision of the reality of American society and the nature of man.

After brief formal schooling and apprenticeship to a printer, Twain became at eighteen an itinerant journeyman printer, learning the manners and methods of popular journalism in St Louis, New York, Philadelphia, Keokuk (in Iowa) and Cincinnati. In 1847 he met Horace Bixby under whose tutelage he learned the river and gained his own pilot's licence. When the Civil War put a stop to Mississippi river-boat traffic and his own career as a pilot, he served with a vaguely defined Confederate company of Missouri irregulars, and left for Nevada for a brief spell as secretary to his brother Orion, and an unsuccessful career as a prospector, thereby acquiring the raw material for *Roughing It*. Failing to achieve instant wealth by a goldstrike, he became a professional journalist, first with the Virginia City *Territorial Enterprise*, then with San Francisco papers and magazines. His talent for mixing fact and anecdote emerged in travel sketches of Hawaii for the Sacramento *Union* (1866) and earned him engagements as a lecturer. With a story-telling technique partly derived from George Washington Harris's (1814–69) 'Sut Lovingood' yarns and T. B. Thorpe's (1815–78) vigorous tall tale of 'The Big Bear of Arkansas', Twain was equipped for his own developing life as a writer.

The Celebrated Jumping Frog of Calaveras County, and Other Sketches (1867) was his first book, but it was *The Innocents Abroad* (1869) that established him before an appreciative national public in the persona of an American traveller self-confident enough to pass judgement on overrated and outmoded aspects of the Old World, even if, at times, a little too brashly materialistic to appreciate the merits of tradition. Twain's trip aboard the *Quaker City* not only produced material for his book. A fellow passenger, Charles Langdon, showed him a miniature of his sister, Olivia. Twain married her in 1870 and she dubbed him 'Youth'. The nickname held throughout their marriage, but Twain's youthful vision of life was growing darker. His first novel *The Gilded Age: A Tale of Today* (1873), written in collaboration with the popular writer Charles Dudley Warner (1829–1900), blatantly denounces post-Civil War materialism and political corruption, although Twain clearly enjoys the scheming, irrepressibly optimistic, Micawber-like character of Colonel Beriah Sellers. He was something of a Sellers himself, but his optimism was less robust.

Like Benjamin Franklin, though less productively, Twain was fascinated by technology. He speculated on a chalk-engraving process called Kaolatype and on various gadgets from grape scissors to steam pulleys and bed clamps. In 1885 his Charles L. Webster publishing company brought out the *Memoirs* of Ulysses S. Grant and the first American edition of *The Adventures of Huckleberry Finn*. Neither book was as successful as Twain had hoped, although the first royalty cheque for $200,000 paid to Grant's widow was the highest single payment to date in the history of publishing. Webster company profits were swallowed up by other publishing projects and by Twain's investment in the expensive and impractical Paige Type-setting Machine. *The Gilded Age* coined the definitive title for Twain's own times, and he despised the 'money-lust' which seemed to him to have undermined America, yet he longed for wealth and was rescued from complete financial disaster by Henry H. Rogers of the Standard Oil Company. Unable to manage money, he was expert in making it at his own game. The proceeds of a world lecture tour and profits from *Following the Equator* (1897) enabled him to repay his creditors in full, but this triumph over adversity did not keep him from depression. Intellectually and emotionally he evaded responsibility for his business failures by taking refuge in a determinism which mixed Darwinism with the guilt of his Calvinist background, and exhorted his readers to cynicism.

Before writing *The Prince and the Pauper* (1882), Twain summarised the idea in his notebook: 'Edward VI and a little pauper exchange places by accident a day or so before Henry VIII's death. The Prince wanders in rags and hardships and the pauper suffers the [to him] horrible miseries of princedom, up to the moment of crowning in Westminster Abbey, when proof is brought and the mistake rectified.' The book emerged as a story for children, but it reveals Twain's interest in heredity, accidental social differences and the influence of environment. These are the themes of *The Tragedy of Pudd'nhead Wilson*

(1894), a more complex case of switched identities, which questions the dichotomies of human nature in terms of race as well as social circumstances. The plot's most obvious irony is that the Negro slave, Roxy's switching of the two infants – one white, one her own – initiates a sequence of events which leads to her son's selling her 'down the river' at her own instigation, to pay off his gambling debts. In Chapter 10, shortly after his mother's revelation that he is a Negro, Tom has a bitter seizure of self-awareness:

> 'Why were niggers *and* whites made? What crime did the uncreated first nigger commit that the curse of birth was decreed for him? And why is this awful difference made between white and black? . . . How hard the nigger's fate seems, this morning! – yet until last night such a thought never entered my head.'

Tom's capacity for moral outrage is no match for his conditioning as a privileged white man; his mother's endearments are horrible to him, but he offers little resistance to her appalling offer to be sold for six hundred dollars. The scene in Chapter 16 in which the sacrifice is conceived, accepted and made compresses a devastating critique of slavery into the brief interchanges between mother and son. The majestic Roxy's maternal selflessness is her triumph; Tom's opportunism, like that of the townsfolk of Hadleyburg, is his, and mankind's doom:

> Tom was dazed. He was not sure he had heard aright. He was dumb for a moment; then he said:
> 'Do you mean that you would be sold into slavery to save me?'
> 'Ain't you my chile? En does you know anything dat a mother won't do for her chile? Dey ain't nothin' a white mother won't do for her chile. Who made 'em so? De Lord done it. En who made de niggers? De Lord made 'em. In de inside, mothers is all de same. De good Lord he made 'em so. I's gwine to be sole into slavery, en in a year you's gwine to buy yo' old mammy free ag'in. I'll show you how. Dat's de plan.'
> Tom's hopes began to rise, and his spirits along with them. He said:
> 'It's lovely of you Mammy – it's just –'
> 'Say it ag'in! En keep on sayin' it! It's all de pay a body kin want in dis worl', en it's mo'den enough. Laws bless you, honey, when I's slavin' aroun', en dey 'buses me, if I knows you's a-sayin' dat, 'way off yonder somers, it'll heal up all de sore places, en I kin stan' 'em.'

There is poetic justice in Tom's murder of Judge Driscoll, his supposed father, as a symbolic act of vengeance for Southern white aristocracy's abuse of slave women. There is a note of hope in David 'Pudd'nhead' Wilson's disproving the town's false estimation of him by using fingerprints to establish Luigi Capello's innocence; but justice makes Roxy a murderer's mother and ruins Chambers, Driscoll's real heir. Raised as a slave, he is merely deprived of the only environment in which he can function. Elevated, he is lost. Twain's concluding account of him is the image that seals the novel into its own cynicism towards the power of circumstance and the malignancy of truth:

> His gait, his attitudes, his gestures, his bearing, his laugh – all were vulgar and uncouth; his manners were but the manners of a slave. Money and fine clothes could not mend these defects or cover them up; they only made them the more glaring and the more pathetic. The poor fellow could not endure the terrors of the white man's parlor, and felt at home and at peace nowhere but in the kitchen. The family pew was a misery to him, yet he could nevermore enter into the solacing refuge of the 'nigger gallery' – that was closed to him for good and all.

When he was fifty-five Twain wrote to an unknown correspondent: 'I can't go away from the boyhood period & write novels because *capital* [i.e. personal experience] is not sufficient by itself & I lack the other essential: interest in handling the men & experiences of later times'. Born in Florida, Missouri, Twain was four when his family moved to nearby Hannibal. The world of the small river-town populated his boyhood and youth with colourful characters and lively frontier incident. With the five-hundred-acre farm of his uncle John A. Quarles – 'a heavenly place for a boy', as he calls it in his *Autobiography* (1924) – Hannibal became his imaginative centre. It is the St Petersburg of *Tom Sawyer* and *Huckleberry Finn*, Dawson's Landing in *Pudd'nhead Wilson*, Eseldorf in *The Mysterious Stranger*. The Hannibal years and his intimacy with the Mississippi River as boy and pilot were the 'capital' on which he drew for *The Adventures of Huckleberry Finn*. Twain's masterpiece, the book is episodic in the picaresque manner; but its parts cohere to depict the complexities of American life in terms of the rival appeals of realism and romantic illusion.

If the book's first attraction is Huck himself, the second is the image of his long, comradely journey down the Mississippi with Jim, through a sequence of towns and villages, colourful encounters, narrow escapes and starspeckled night skies. 'It's lovely to live on a raft', says Huck, and each contact with the depravities of life ashore makes it lovelier. Along the river banks the American dream has declined to the perverted moral and legal values of slavery, religious 'soul butter and hogwash', cowardly ambushes and murders. The arts are represented by the Grangerford parlour's squeaking ornaments, crockery fruit and sentimental pictures, and by Emmeline Grangerford's doggerel verse, a parody of the banalities Twain despised in the writing of Julia A. Moore (1847–1920), popularly known as 'The Sweet Singer of Michigan'. The idyll of the raft survives fog, separations, misunderstandings and sinking, but it is not equal to the king's greed, which returns Huck and Jim to dry land and replaces the illusion of freedom with the charade of Tom Sawyer's plot to 'free' Jim. From the first chapter the novel is packed with warnings about romantic expectations: the much-debated ending may disappoint, but it should not come as a surprise.

The story begins with Widow Douglas and Miss Watson labouring under the illusion that Huck can be 'sivilized' with new clothes, a ban on smoking, the story of 'Moses and the Bulrushers', spelling and a fundamentalist heaven and hell. The reality of Huck's discomfiture is too strong for all this: 'I felt so lonesome I most wished I was dead', he says, almost meaning it, but doing the best he can to ward off the ill-luck of the dead spider accidentally incinerated in his candle-flame. Eager for companionship, he subscribes briefly to the romance of Tom Sawyer's robber band and is 'most ready to cry' because he has no family to be killed if he should divulge its secrets, but resigns for lack of action. Tom's make-believe contains as much reality as prayers bring fish-hooks. 'It had', he concludes, 'all the marks of a Sunday-school.' The idealistic new judge and his wife are brought down from their elation at Pap's tearful promises of reform, to the realistic conclusion that 'a body could reform the old man with a shotgun, maybe'. Chapter 12 begins with the lyricism of Huck and Jim drifting down the river at night, and ends with their eaves-dropping on an impending murder. The Grangerford–Shepherdson feud recalls Shakespeare's Montagues and Capulets to make the point that mindless bloodthirstiness, not a capacity for tragic grandeur, lies behind the postures of Southern aristocracy. Sympathy for the drunken, foul-mouthed Boggs, shot dead by Colonel Sherburn, is soon allayed by the realisation that the death of Boggs and the proposed lynching of Sherburn are no more than entertainments to the idle citizens of a feckless, one-horse town.

In his relationship with Jim, Huck learns that his intuition is superior to the deformed conscience inculcated by a slave-holding value system. Twain's satire of Southern attitudes is at its sharpest in the Swiftian inversions of Chapters 16 and 31. In Chapter 16 Huck paddles for shore 'all in a sweat' to tell on Jim, when he meets two men in a skiff searching for five escaped Negroes. They ask Huck the colour of the man he has left on his raft, and plunge the boy's heart into conflict with his conscience:

> I didn't answer up prompt. I tried to, but the words wouldn't come. I tried, for a second or two, to brace up and out with it, but I warn't man enough – hadn't the spunk of a rabbit. I see I was weakening; so I just give up trying, and up and says –
> 'He's white.'

This scene anticipates the climactic choice of human feeling over conscience in Chapter 31. Thinking of Jim's kindness, affection and gratitude, Huck finds himself in 'a close place' morally, but tears up his note to Miss Watson, opts for loyalty and friendship across the colour line, and pronounces judgement on himself from the point of view of his culture: 'All right, then, I'll *go* to hell.' Achieving such moral eminence, why does he collaborate with Tom Sawyer in the heartless make-believe of the Phelps farm episode?

In the last fifth of the book, Huck's behaviour is defensible on grounds of form, consistency and realism. T. S. Eliot finds the formal justification enough: 'it is right that the mood of the end of the book should bring us back to the beginning'. This is valid comment, not because there is special virtue in a circular form, but because Twain's ending finishes the story in a 'mood' of provocative realism towards which it has tended from the first chapter. Huck's participation in Jim's 'evasion' is consistent with his admiration for Tom Sawyer. Although he is disenchanted with the robber band, he still defers to Tom's flair for illusion. In Chapter 7 he does a thoroughly efficient job of scene-setting for his 'murder', reporting it in matter-of-fact detail that augurs the style of Hemingway; but he regrets that Tom Sawyer is not there to 'throw in the fancy touches'. In Chapter 28 he reflects that Tom 'would a throwed more style' into his plot to help the Wilks girls. It is hardly surprising that Tom's cadenza of 'fancy touches' overcomes Huck's scepticism in the final episode.

Huck lies whenever he has to and condones the king's exploitation of the revival meeting in Chapter 20 and the deception of 'The King's Cameleopard' in Chapter 23; but he plays his last mean trick on Jim as early as Chapter 15 when he tries to fool him into thinking their separation in the fog was only a dream. Jim's reproof teaches him not to behave like 'trash'. He accepts the duke's excessively histrionic transformation of Jim into a 'Sick Arab – but harmless when out of his head' in Chapter 24, because the spectacle of a blue-faced King Lear will deter unwelcome visitors and keep Jim safe. The trick demeans Jim, but has a worthy purpose. Similarly his acceptance of Tom

Sawyer's elaborations is a compromise between regard for his white friend and affection for his Black one. The outrageous plotting is a trick too painful to be in Jim's best interest but satisfies Tom, and will eventually bring Jim freedom. Huck will embrace perdition for the sake of one Negro, but he is still a product of the Mississippi Valley, no abolitionist. To have liberated him more than this from the thinking of his region would have been sentimentality, a 'fancy touch' worthy of Tom Sawyer himself. The compromise is Twain's final stroke of realism in expressing the ambiguities of Huck's situation. Disappointment with the ending of the book is justifiable only on aesthetic grounds: the Phelps episode is funny and painful, as it is meant to be; it is simply too long.

'Real Life'

Robert Louis Stevenson quite properly thought William Dean Howells a 'zealot' for dreaming 'of an advance in art like what there is in science'. In thirty-five novels that issued regularly from his fertile mind Howells sought to refine the 'scientific decorum' he advocated first in the editorial columns of *The Atlantic Monthly* and then of *Harper's Magazine*. He early declared his unblinkered allegiance to realism in his first novel *Their Wedding Journey* (1872): 'Ah, poor Real Life, which I love, can I make others share the delight I find in thy foolish and insipid face?' Dismissing the 'false theory and manners' of the British novelists who had so long dominated American writers, he commended the superior truth to life of Turgenev, Ibsen, Hardy, Zola and Tolstoy, and drew attention to the virtues of Norris, Crane and Garland, as well as those of his friends, Mark Twain and Henry James.

Howells's development of a realism of the commonplace within the tradition of the novel of manners yielded a first outstanding success in *A Modern Instance* (1882). The novel's original title was *The New Medea* because of the resemblance between the passionate Marcia Gaylord's love for Bartley Hubbard and Medea's for the self-centred Jason. One of the earliest American novels of social realism, it is a perceptive study of marital love souring into divorce. Except for the aesthetic pleasure of accuracy, no palliative is offered for the waste of Marcia's life as she stiffens into loneliness. Bartley Hubbard's decline from ambitious young editor to pariah, to tawdry death in a western feud foreshadows the moral decay of Theodore Dreiser's Hurstwood in

Sister Carrie (1900) and Scott Fitzgerald's Dick Driver in *Tender is the Night* (1934). *A Modern Instance* is not as lively a work as Howells's best-known novel *The Rise of Silas Lapham* (1885), but it does achieve a higher degree of essential realism. The 'fidelity to experience and probability of motive' that Howells proposes as 'essential conditions of a great imaginative literature, are present in the self-made Silas's business dealings and in his efforts to ingratiate himself and his daughters into the Brahmin society of Boston. American literature affords no clearer picture of the *parvenu's* shaky social position than the Corey's dinner party in Chapter 14 at which Silas gets drunk and makes a fool of himself. In the following morning's scene between Silas and Tom Corey, Howells skilfully combines the business man's remorse with his characteristic brusquerie, in contrast to the humane young Brahmin's moral elegance:

> 'I was the only one that wasn't a gentleman there!' lamented Lapham. 'I disgraced you! I disgraced my family! I mortified your father before his friends!' His head dropped. 'I showed that I wasn't fit to go with you. I'm not fit for any decent place. What did I say? What did I do?' he asked, suddenly lifting his head and confronting Corey. 'Out with it! If you could bear to see it and hear it, I had ought to bear to know it!'
> 'There was nothing – really nothing,' said Corey. 'Beyond the fact that you were not quite yourself, there was nothing whatever. My father *did* speak of it to me,' he confessed, 'when we were alone. He said that he was afraid we had not been thoughtful of you, if you were in the habit of taking only water; I told him I had not seen wine at your table. The others said nothing about you.'

Silas's further rise from tycoon ruthlessness to a recognition of good manners and moral standards and Penelope Lapham's eventual marriage to Tom Corey soften the book by transposing it from the plane of realism to that of moral fable.

From 1886 to 1892 Howells's regular *Harper's Magazine* feature 'The Editor's Study' gave him a platform for 'thundering at the gates of Fiction in Error' with particular reference to 'the welter of over-whelming romance' from Sir Walter Scott to Lew Wallace. A selection of his essays for *Harper's* provided the text of *Criticism and Fiction* (1891), and during this period he wrote *A Hazard of New Fortunes* (1889), which he thought 'the most vital of my fictions'. He was right. Broadest in scope of all his works the book portrays the world of big-city journalism and dramatises the conflict between Dryfoos's late-nineteenth-century capitalism and Lindau's socialism in memorably particularised characters and vivid scenes like the ideological jousting between Dryfoos and Lindau in Part Four,

Chapter 6, and Conrad's death in the street-car strike in Part Five, Chapter 5. Its thematic concern with social inequalities and its truth of detail and circumstance make *A Hazard of New Fortunes* Howells's most complete expression of the realism he calls 'democracy in literature':

> It wishes to know and to tell the truth, confident that consolation and delight are there; it does not care to paint the marvellous and impossible for the vulgar many, or to sentimentalize and falsify the actual for the vulgar few. Men are more like than unlike one another: let us make them know one another better, that they may all be humbled and strengthened with a sense of their fraternity.

Henry James

Superficially there are few similarities between William Dean Howells and Henry James (1843–1916). Both were thorough professionals for whom writing was a vocation of the highest seriousness. Both exerted powerful influence through critical writing as well as by example, Howells during his own life, James more particularly in the twentieth century. The differences between them are more obvious. Howells avows a belief in human likeness, and considers the individual in a carefully realised social context. James's passion is 'the special case' in the context of increasingly involved moral situations which usually seem detached from the everyday world of getting and spending. Howells is direct, where James is oblique. Uninterested in social justice, though attentive to the ethical effects of class, James is fascinated by 'marvellous' contortions of human psychology, and this imparts a secular mysticism to his work. He evokes a vaguely obscene 'gross blackness' underneath the surfaces of behaviour that demands to be called 'evil' even when it emanates from individual consciousness as in the *alter ego* phenomenon of 'The Jolly Corner' (1908), the egoism of Gilbert Osmond in *The Portrait of a Lady* (1881) or, almost indecipherably, in the vampire-like machinations of Grace Brissenden in *The Sacred Fount* (1901). Yet, as editor and critic, Howells may be said to have discovered James's genius, and James generously acknowledged his indebtedness in a letter of 19 February 1912:

> You showed me the way and opened me the door; you wrote to me, and confessed yourself struck with me – I have never forgotten the beautiful thrill of that. You published me at once – and paid me, above all, with a dazzling promptitude; magnificently, I felt, and so that nothing since has ever quite come up to it.

It is to Howells' great credit that he saw lifelike ambiguity in art so different from his own, and a sufficient 'air of reality' to sustain the psychological realism by which Henry James took the craft of fiction into new reaches of sophistication.

Through a period of extended European travel, the elder Henry James provided his children with an unusually cosmopolitan education and stimulated them to be, above all, aware of people, places, art and ideas. Both William James and Henry, his junior by a year, became students of awareness. Encouraged to value their own perceptions of the world, they both spent their lives considering the ways in which people see and react. William began his Harvard career as a physiologist, but by 1880 had turned philosopher and was pioneering the new science of psychology towards *The Principles of Psychology* (1890) and the evolution of the inclusive concepts defined in *Pragmatism* (1907). Henry, meanwhile, was 'drinking the tone of things' and turning psychology into art.

Like William, Henry studied painting briefly. He entered the Law School at Harvard but began to write reviews and short stories and left the university without taking a degree. In 1875 contact in Paris with Turgenev and the prominent French writers of the time – Flaubert, Maupassant, Zola and Daudet – induced 'weariness with the French mind'. He rejected Zola's brand of naturalism as *'merde au naturel* – simply hideous', but the French commitment of literary art to the reflection of life endorsed the seriousness of his own vocation. His devoted approach to the art of fiction is evident not only in his novels and stories, but also in the many essays he wrote about other writers and about the principles of 'The House of Fiction' whose innumerable windows – sometimes mere makeshift holes – overlook the human scene. Each aperture in the front of the 'House' is a literary form through which an individual artistic consciousness appraises what it can see of life. Settling in London in 1876, James looked out on America and Europe, and in bringing them into moral confrontation, devised his 'international theme'. This became his most famous subject, and occupied him almost exclusively during the first period of his work, from about 1870 to 1883.

Compared to Europe, America was still a new, innocent country, notwithstanding the shrewd Dr Sloper of James's *Washington Square* (1881). European subtleties of manners and morality, evolved over many centuries, baffled the visiting American, who was accustomed to more direct behaviour and clearer demarcations of right and wrong. The talented young sculptor discovered by Rowland Mallet in

Roderick Hudson (1876) is destroyed by Europe, where the expatriate American Christina Light is merely absorbed by it. In Italy Roderick neglects his talent, falls into dissipation and pursues Christina to the Swiss Alps even after her marriage to an Italian prince. He dies in an accidental or suicidal fall from a mountain; Christina lives on to mesmerise and undo Hyacinth Robinson in *The Princess Casamassima* (1886). Another innocent, Christopher Newman, hero of *The American* (1877) thinks that money can buy happiness in Europe as it does in America. Compared to the bickering poker-playing Tom Tristram and the puritanical Benjamin Babcock, the self-reliant Newman is at least capable of growth. Burning Mrs Bread's evidence of Madame and Urbain de Bellegarde's part in the death of Claire's father lifts him above the cheap satisfaction of revenge. He loses the girl but does attain a moral eminence, quite an achievement for an innocent abroad. The heroine of *Daisy Miller* (1878) does not understand that she cannot behave in Europe as she does in her home town of Schenectady, New York, and pays for her mistake with her life. The American girl in *The Portrait of a Lady* (1881) comes to wish for death as an escape from her mistake. Isabel Archer is determined to be free; she fails because her American background has not prepared her for the sophisticated evil that traps her in Europe.

In an essay on the life of George Eliot, James defines 'the basis of the story-teller's art' as 'the passion for the special case'. In *The Portrait of a Lady*, the crowning effort of his early period, his purpose is to reveal the special case of Isabel Archer by placing 'the centre of the subject in the young woman's consciousness'. The 'subject' of the novel is Isabel's progress from innocence to experience as she tries to live freely, fails, and achieves a deeper understanding of the meaning of freedom. The method is similar to that employed in painting the portrait of Christopher Newman. In the preface to *The American* which he wrote for the 'New York' edition of his novels and stories (1907–9) James describes his method of telling Newman's story:

> He was to be the lighted figure, the others . . . were to be the obscured; by which I should largely get the effect most to be invoked, that of a generous nature engaged with forces, with difficulties and dangers, that it but half understands.

In *The Portrait of a Lady* Isabel Archer is the 'lighted figure' whose character is revealed in detail from the beginning. All the other characters are kept more or less 'obscured', until the concluding chapters bring a rush of clarifications. James does interpolate authorial comment on Isabel's thoughts and feelings and, while retaining the mystery of other characters, gives the reader information about them that Isabel does not possess. This delicate balancing of awareness maintains the sense of Isabel's innocence, preserves the reader's sympathy for her as the victim of a conspiracy and keeps up the suspense.

Caspar Goodwood, the square-jawed Bostonian factory manager, cannot fulfil the requirements of an imagination like Isabel Archer's. Marriage to someone with such 'intense identity' and so dependably provincial would mean surrendering her power to choose her own fate before she has had an opportunity to discover other possibilities. As Lady Warburton Isabel would be obliged to end her free exploration of life and behave as an English aristocrat. The appeal of Gilbert Osmond is that he seems to live freely, according to his own exacting standards, detached from all worldly considerations and even from the artistic objects with which he has furnished his house near Florence. He seems 'a specimen apart', an original. Osmond is, of course, nothing of the kind. In 'the rich perfection' of Gardencourt Isabel is an American Eve before the Fall. The incarnation of evil in Osmond is made clear by the image that comes into Isabel's mind in Chapter 42: 'his egotism lay hidden like a serpent in a bank of flowers'. Caspar Goodwood echoes the satanic image of the serpent in the last chapter when he refers to Osmond as 'the deadliest of fiends.'

James's achievement in the last part of *The Portrait of a Lady* is to convert Isabel's defeat into victory. In Chapter 51, during the argument about her going to see her dying cousin Ralph Touchett, Osmond says: 'I think we should accept the consequences of our actions, and what I value most in life is the honour of a thing!' Isabel is mature enough to accept the truth of this, even though it is said by the diabolically false Osmond. The consequence of her promise to Osmond's daughter, Pansy, in Chapter 52 is an obligation to return to Rome. She could leave Osmond and break her promise to Pansy; instead she chooses the way of 'honour' and duty. James brings Warburton and Goodwood back into her life in order to make it clear that assistance and means of escape are available. Recoiling from the revelatory 'white lightning' of Goodwood's kiss, Isabel chooses honour; she does not have it thrust upon her.

In Chapter 19 Isabel disagrees with Madame Merle's opinion that everyone is made up of an 'envelope of circumstances . . . some cluster of appurtenances', because this would mean that no one is really free and Isabel is intent on believing in her own self-determination. To go away with Goodwood would imply that Madame Merle had been right after all, an admission by Isabel that the 'envelope' of her unhappy circumstances was powerful enough to make her run away from the consequences of her own actions with a man she has never loved. The decision to return to Rome must, therefore, be seen as a further refutation of Madame Merle's view. It is not quite the 'wind in her sails' Ralph Touchett had hoped to achieve by his father's bequest, but it is the greatest expression of Isabel's freedom. It marks her triumph over circumstances and over the immature ideal of freedom she had brought with her from America. That ideal had equated freedom with liberty of appreciation and self-fulfilment, yet it led her into marrying a man who seeks to extinguish her. It is not enough 'to be free to follow out a good feeling'. Freedom now means being perceptive enough to choose the right action with reference to all responsibilities, and in full awareness of probable consequences. In choosing to go back, Isabel transcends her circumstances, keeps her promises, and freely accepts responsibility for her own past and her own bleak future. The moral and aesthetic shapeliness of James's resolution is equalled only by the ending of *The Wings of the Dove* (1902), and helps to make *The Portrait of a Lady*, for many readers, the most completely satisfying of James's novels.

James returned to America for a visit shortly before his mother's unexpected death in 1882. By the end of the year his father died too, and in 1883 he lost his younger brother, Wilky. 'Sorrow comes in great waves,' he wrote in a letter of 1883, 'but it rolls over us, and though it may almost smother us it leaves us on the spot and we know that if it is strong, we are stronger, inasmuch as it passes and we remain.' James remained, but not in America. His sense of belonging to the United States was reduced to all but vanishing point by his parents' death. In the second period of his writing, from the mid-1880s to about 1900, he created mainly English settings and characters. *The Bostonians* (1886) is set entirely in America, but its purpose is satirical. Like *The Princess Casamassima*, published in the same year, the novel deals with the tension between private sensibility and political belief. The aggressive and self-deluding Olive Chancellor thinks she finds a kindred feminist in the beautiful Verena Tarrant. Impressionable and compliant at first, Verena succumbs to the superior attractions of Olive's emphatically masculine Mississippi cousin, Basil Ransom. *The Princess Casamassima* embodies the conflict between socialism and society in the character of Hyacinth Robinson. Illegitimate son of an English nobleman and a French prostitute,

Robinson's 'slashing about in the bewilderment' of his attraction to Christina Light, once-beloved of Roderick Hudson, and his belief in revolution, ends in his suicide. Although James says that the idea for the novel 'sprang up for me out of the London pavement', his focus is not radicalism itself but the motives of those who use it as a vehicle of self-expression. London poverty is a diversion for Christina Light, now separated from her husband and in need of occupation. Paul Muniment exploits Robinson, and displaces him with the Princess. Betrayed by his friends, Robinson is destroyed by the dilemma implicit in the mixed aristocratic and republican proclivities of his own blood.

A woman is again the pivotal character in *The Tragic Muse* (1890), in which the world of affairs clashes with the world of art. The clash splits the energies of Peter Sherringham, making him foil to the actress Miriam Rooth who embodies the fusion of these worlds, although her ideal blending of artistic and personal genius is somewhat diminished by excessive self-esteem and the devotion of her infatuated mother. Predictably James is on the side of art, but he is too much of a realist not to show its associations with inadequacy and humbug. The disproportion between Nick Dormer's sacrifice of a great fortune, a distinguished career and a good woman and his modest competence as a portrait-painter is underscored by the sympathy James creates for Julia Dallow and Lady Agnes. As a symbol of aestheticism, Gabriel Nash is Oscar Wilde at his fluffiest: 'merely to be is such a *métier*; to live is such an art; to feel is such a career!'

Rebecca West has suggested that the sense of something amiss in the world of James's fiction – as in that of his friend, Edith Wharton – arises from its proposition that 'the prime cause of sin is lack of taste, and that men and women of refined and educated perceptions can avoid the moral tarnish that dims coarser characters'. In *The Ambassadors* (1903) Lambert Strether's moral growth is defined in terms of his refinement away from the narrow attitudes of Woollett, Massachusetts into a less secure but more bountiful European morality. The education of Merton Densher in *The Wings of the Dove* makes him not only more 'refined and educated' but better. Clearly James values artistic sensibility and delights in the aesthetics of moral patterns; but none of his characters is more tarnished than the fastidious Gilbert Osmond, more intrinsically peripheral than Gabriel Nash, or less maternal than Nanda Brookenham's mother in *The Awkward Age* (1899). It is the fools who are tasteless, like the aimless Mr and Mrs Luce of *The Portrait of a Lady* or the Pococks of *The Ambassadors*. The arrogant ineffectuality of taste for its own sake is James's subject in *The Spoils of Poynton* (1897). Only Mrs Gereth and her young friend, Fleda Vetch, have the refinement and discrimination to see Poynton and its collection as the perfect expression of taste:

> While outside on the low terraces, she contradicted gardeners and refined on nature, Mrs Gereth left her guest to finger fondly the brasses, that Louis Quinze might have thumbed, to sit with Venetian velvets, just held in a loving palm, to hang over cases of enamels and pass and repass before cabinets. There were not many pictures and panels and the stuffs were themselves the picture; and in all the great wainscotted house there was not one inch of pasted paper. What struck Fleda most in it was the high pride of her friend's taste, a fine arrogance, a sense of style which, however amused and amusing, never compromised nor stooped.

But taste, by itself, is not formidable enough. Mona Brigstock may lack soul, but she is tough enough to win Mrs Gereth's malleable son, Owen, from the scrupulous Fleda who, after fire has destroyed the spoils, is left with a sixpenny pin-cushion. 'The free spirit,' James says in his 'New York' edition preface to *The Spoils of Poynton*, 'always much tormented, and by no means always triumphant, is heroic, ironic, pathetic or whatever, and, as exemplified in the record of Fleda Vetch, for instance, "successful", only through having remained free.'

Towards the end of his second period James secured his reputation as a short-story writer with 'The Aspern Papers' (1888), 'The Altar of the Dead' (1895) and 'The Great Good Place' (1900). Several of his stories are about writers and writing, such as 'The Lesson of the Master' (1888), 'The Middle Years' (1893), 'The Death of the Lion' (1894) and 'The Figure in the Carpet' (1896). His short-lived career as a playwright came humiliatingly to an end with *Guy Domville* at the St James's Theatre. The play never recovered from its riotous first night on 5 January 1895 when George Alexander, playing Guy Domville said 'I'm the last, my Lord, of the Domvilles', and a voice from the gallery replied, 'It's a bloody good thing y'are.' James's experiments with the theatre did help him to develop a dramatic technique for fiction. His mastery of scene and the manipulation of point of view to achieve maximum intensity are his chief exemplary contributions to literature.

Daisy Miller's tragedy of indiscretion is intensified and enlarged by its unfolding from the point of view of Frederick Winterbourne. The use of a child's consciousness in *What Maisie Knew* (1897) accentuates the horror of adult depravity which in turn infects the young heroine with a perverse sophistication. *The Turn of the Screw* (1898) depends for its intensity of terror on the fact that everything occurs in the mind of the governess who desperately needs corroboration in order to know that she is not mad in attributing corruption to the children, Miles and Flora. She is understandably jubilant when Miss Jessel's second appearance by the lake in Chapter 20 seems to be witnessed by Mrs Grose the housekeeper, and acknowledged by Flora. James's prose precisely catches the governess's rhythm of feeling: first the sudden presence of the apparition, then her joy in being proved right, and finally the suggestion of a bizarre emotional rapport with the evil ghost of her predecessor:

> Miss Jessel stood before us on the opposite bank exactly as she had stood the other time, and I remember, strangely, as the first feeling now produced in me, my thrill of joy at having brought on a proof. She was there, and I was justified; she was there, and I was neither cruel nor mad. She was there for poor scared Mrs Grose, but she was there most for Flora; and no moment of my monstrous time was perhaps so extraordinary as that in which I consciously threw out to her – with the sense that, pale and ravenous demon as she was, she would catch and understand it – an inarticulate message of gratitude.

The so-called 'Freudian' interpretation of *The Turn of the Screw*, most notably propounded by Edmund Wilson (1895–1972) in his essay 'The Ambiguity of Henry James' (1934), sees the ghosts as the hallucinations of a sexually repressed hysteric. James certainly intended to leave his *'amusette'* open to different readings. 'My values are positively all blanks', he says in the 'New York' edition preface. Post-Freudian readers for whom evil has been rendered obsolete will fill the blanks in their own way. In doing so they brush aside the fact that there is no satisfactory explanation for Mrs Grose's recognising Peter Quint in the governess's detailed description of the man she sees on the tower in Chapter 3 and through the dinning-room window in Chapter 4. They also ignore James's stated repudiation of the 'psychical' fashion in fiction, and his preference for 'the dear old sacred terror'.

At Lamb House, Rye, in Sussex, James embarked on the third period of his writing, reasserting the 'international theme' in the three complex novels of his 'major phase'. *The Ambassadors* (1903) was written in 1901, before *The Wings of the Dove* (1902) and *The Golden Bowl* (1904). In the opening paragraph of *The Ambassadors*, Lambert

Strether, the novel's hero, feels the first tremor of disaffection from the narrowly circumspect world of Woollett when he arrives at Liverpool and learns with pleasure that his stolid American friend Waymarsh has been delayed. An unaccustomed sense of personal freedom makes him receptive to the charms of England and France. Abandoning his mission – and with it his prospect of advantageous marriage to Mrs Newsome – he encourages Chad's liaison with Mme de Vionnet even to the point of instructing the young man that it would be 'the last infamy' if he ever forsook her. 'Live all you can', Strether says in Book 5, Chapter 2, provoked by Little Bilham to a sense of his own tentative life, 'it's a mistake not to. It doesn't so much matter what you do in particular, so long as you have your life. If you haven't had that what *have* you had?'

Milly Theale, the ailing young heiress of *The Wings of the Dove*, is motivated by her love for Kate Croy's secret fiancé, Merton Densher, to live more than seems possible. James gives his novel two opposing centres. Kate and Milly are superficially in harmony, but profoundly antithetical in character and purpose. This broadens the psychological stage, but prevents the novel from achieving the focal intensity of *The Portrait of a Lady* or *The Ambassadors*. The moral strenuousness of the interactions nearly makes up the deficit. The same cannot be said of *The Golden Bowl*, in which James's grace notes pre-empt his themes, although there is a certain eerie pleasure to be had from its mistily convolving intimacies. Action in *The Wings of the Dove* is still recognisable and resonant. Lord Mark's thwarting of Kate Croy's scheme to obtain Milly's money is one of many hints of a variation on Wagner's *Tristan und Isolde*. Milly's death soon after the revelation is followed by Merton Densher's receipt of a legacy large enough to make him at last an acceptable husband for Kate. But the 'wings' of Milly the 'dove' cover the guilty pair, protecting them from the union that would make them irredeemable. Densher cannot tell Kate that he is not in love with Milly's memory: *Liebestod* saves him from a sin of hideous venality.

Henry James died British. He was angry with America for hesitating to come to Britain's aid during the First World War, and wished to declare his allegiance to the country he had adopted. Naturalised in 1915, he was awarded the British Order of Merit shortly before his death on 28 February 1916. He left unfinished *The Ivory Tower* (1917), *The Sense of the Past* (1917), and the art of the novel more conscious of itself than it had ever been.

Women, war and money

In her own time Edith Wharton (1862–1937) was accused of imitating Henry James; but the reviewer who called her a 'masculine James' was outdone in irony by her admission that she could not read the Master's novels. 'It's a relief to know you can't read H. J.,' she wrote to their publisher in 1904. 'The efforts I made to read *The Ambassadors*! I broke one tooth after another on it.' James, in turn, called her 'The Angel of Devastation', referring not to her writing but to the 'rich, rushing, ravening' life she led on both sides of the Atlantic with her unsatisfactory husband and noisy automobile. Her writing is most Jamesian in its emphasis on character and its treatment of moral dilemmas; less so in its style, which is leaner and more direct. The brief *Ethan Frome* (1911) is the most famous of her novels, a grimly realistic fable of the ruinous power of New England duty. In *The House of Mirth* (1905) the mercenary values of New York high society cause the downfall of Lily Bart, a well-connected but impecunious aspirant to a wealthy husband. The specifically male shortcomings of America's aristocracy of wealth are satirised in *The Custom of the Country* (1913), Edith Wharton's subtlest and most provocative novel. Vulgar and insensitive, Undine Spragg prostitutes her beauty for money and position through a series of marriages and divorces. She mirrors the society whose customs have produced her by valuing women as merchandise.

Disgust with Midwestern vulgarity and the *nouveau riche* diffuses the focus of *The Custom of the Country* away from the novel's central feminist issue. There is nothing in Kate Chopin's (1851–1904) more naturalistic novel *The Awakening* (1899), to deflect attention from Edna Pontellier's awareness of a sexual capacity for 'the taste of life's delirium' at odds with the roles traditionally allocated to women. The exultantly sensuous moment in Chapter 10 when Edna discovers she can swim is followed in the next chapter by a new assertion of herself. Reclining in her hammock, she savours her newly acquired power to control 'the working of her body and her soul', and disobeys her uncomprehendingly querulous husband's instruction to come in from the night air:

> With a writhing motion she settled herself more securely in the hammock. She perceived that her will had blazed up, stubborn and resistant. She could not at that moment have done other than denied and resisted. She wondered if her husband had ever spoken to her like that before, and if she had submitted to his command. Of course she had; she remembered that she had. But she could not realise why or how she should have yielded, feeling as she then did.

The language may be unexceptional, but the pacing and exactness of observation in this sequence are worthy of D. H. Lawrence. The publication of Louisiana sketches and tales in *Bayou Folk* (1894) brought Kate Chopin popularity as a local colourist in the traditional sense. Several of the stories in her second collection *A Night in Acadie* (1897) – 'Athenaïse', 'A Respectable Woman', 'Regret' – together with *The Awakening* established female sensibility as her true locale, alienated her admirers and were almost forgotten until twentieth-century readers rediscovered her quality as well as her courage.

'Too much detail', said Willa Cather (1873–1947), 'is apt, like any form of extravagance, to become slightly vulgar.' It was her own judgement of her third book *The Song of the Lark* (1915) in which the main obstacle to Thea Kronborg's effort to become an opera singer appears to be the excessive detail in which her story is told. After *Alexander's Bridge* (1911), a stiff exercise in the genteel tradition, Cather had chosen a subject closer to her own experience for *O Pioneers!* (1913) in which she gave the Nebraska of her upbringing its literary *début* and embodied the spirit of the great plains in the monolithic figure of the Swedish girl, Alexandra Bergson. The inter-action between old world and new dramatised here by the immigrants' response to the challenge of a hard new country, receives further treatment in *One of Ours* (1922) and *The Professor's House* (1925). *Death Comes for the Archbishop* (1927) makes an inspiring Catholic legend from documentary accounts of the founding of the Santa Fé cathedral in New Mexico, a huge empty land of 'blazing sand, adobe town, red mountains, Indian ceremonials, hieratic mystery, violent colours, fire and ice'. Seventeenth-century Quebec is credibly evoked in *Shadows on the Rock* (1931), but it is in *My Antonia* (1918) that Willa Cather most successfully combines her themes in the fluently reminiscent narrative of Jim Burden.

The youthful innocence Jim shares with Antonia Shimerda is invaded by 'the ancient, eldest Evil' in the outsize rattlesnake he kills in Book 1, Chapter 7. Eden is replaced by a world in which their different struggles for survival take Jim from Lincoln to Harvard and a successful career in law, Antonia to men's work on the Shimerda farm, betrayal by Larry Donovan and ultimate contentment as wife of a fellow-immigrant. Antonia's natural dignity is expressed through-out the novel by her association with the majestic qualities of the prairies in descriptive passages which simultaneously paint the great spaces of the Midwest in realistic detail and work to unmistakable symbolic effect. All the 'hired girls' – Tiny Soderball, Lena Lingard, Anna Hansen, Antonia – and Jim himself are ennobled in their individual efforts by the spectacular image in Book 2, Chapter 14 of the single plough silhouetted against the setting sun:

> There were no clouds, the sun was going down in a limpid, gold-washed sky. Just as the lower edge of the red disk rested on the high fields against the horizon, a great black figure suddenly appeared on the face of the sun. We sprang to our feet, straining our eyes toward it. In a moment we realised what it was. On some upland farm, a plough had been left standing in the field. The sun was sinking just behind it. Magnified across the distance by the horizontal light, it stood out against the sun, was exactly contained within the circle of the disk; the handles, the tongue, the share – black against the molten red. There it was, heroic in size, a picture writing on the sun.

The naturalistic impressionism of Stephen Crane's (1871–1900) *Maggie: A Girl of the Streets* (1893) issues in a monotonously staccato prose of statement. Crane's admirably precise display of the realities of New York slum life testifies to his sympathy for the working class, its women in particular, as represented by the environmentally fore-doomed Maggie, hopelessly striving in sweat shop, in love and on the street. The nineteen scenes of the book follow each other like frozen movie frames, a jerky sequence of still lifes. Crane's concision works to better effect in *The Red Badge of Courage: An Episode of the American Civil War* (1895). Henry Fleming's point of view gives the narrative con-tinuity. Fuller and more flowing, the prose's tendency to freeze into moments of impressionistic arrest is balanced by the deadly move-ments of the fighting. If Crane is indebted to John William De Forest's emphasis on the vicious confusion of war in *Miss Ravenel's Conversion from Secession to Loyalty* (1867) and to the dry prose and suggestive realism of Ambrose Bierce's (1842–1914) *Tales of Soldiers and Civilians* (1891) – better known by its 1898 title *In the Midst of Life* – he surpasses both in economy and intensity. Like the sea in *Moby-Dick*, the river in *Huckleberry Finn* and the prairie in *My Antonia*, Crane's Civil War battlefield becomes a metaphor for the world into which the individual must be initiated. As 'a part of a vast blue demonstration', the Union infantryman Henry Fleming believes himself a realist in his approach to war:

> Greek-like struggles would be no more. Men were better, or more timid. Secular and religious education had effaced the throat-grappling instinct, or else firm finance held in check the passions.

After he has bolted from the unexpected reality of persistent, random savagery, Henry's moral regeneration comes through the 'solemn ceremony' of Jim Conklin's death in Chapter 9. Without breaking the realistic surface of his writing, Crane insinuates the association of Conklin with Christ by the wound in his side and the initials of his name. There is 'a resemblance in him to a devotee of a mad religion' and the first word uttered after he falls to the ground is 'God!' The sun bleeds with 'the passion of his wounds', fixing his anguished followers in a communion of pain: 'The red sun was pasted in the sky like a wafer'. No novel in English evokes war more lucidly, or more powerfully sanctifies the repudiation of its horrors.

War of a different kind is Frank Norris's subject in *The Octopus* (1901) and *The Pit* (1903), the two completed volumes of his projected 'Epic of Wheat' trilogy. There is dirty fighting by both the ranchers and the railroad entrepreneurs in *The Octopus*, and the ambitious Curtis Jadwin is a casualty of commercial war in *The Pit*. The imperishables in Norris's world are the vast, indifferent fields of wheat and the power of money, beside which men are but 'motes in the sunshine'. The prolific Jack London's (1876–1916) Nietzschean view of man is less persuasive. His gifts as a story-teller yielded some fifty books including a classic of animal literature in *The Call of the Wild* (1903), set in the Klondike of London's own experience, and a powerful melodrama in *The Sea Wolf* (1904). In *Martin Eden* (1909) the hero's Nietzschean aspirations give way to a view of materialism more in accord with Frank Norris's in *McTeague* (1899). Norris studied the Harvard Library's copy of *A Textbook of Operative Dentistry* so that he could substantiate his story with accurate dental minutiae. Heredity and environment play the role of fate. There is nothing vicious about McTeague, the gigantic dentist from the Big Dipper Mine: 'Altogether he suggested the draft horse immensely strong, docile, obedient.' Despite the huge gilded tooth hung outside his office as the sign of his profession and success, he is the only principal character in the novel who is not ruled by material greed. Gold is a mania for those who surround him, including his wife, Trina, whom he kills not for avarice but for revenge. It is the rapacity of others that brings out the latent viciousness McTeague has inherited from his father. When he escapes from the city back to the Big Dipper Mine, he regains the contentment of his boyhood, but ironically gold is waiting in the mountains to destroy him. Like London's autobiographical *Martin Eden*, Norris's Zola-esque moral experiment ends as a cautionary fable.

In January 1900 the publishing firm of Doubleday, Page & Company hired Frank Norris as a special manuscript reader. That summer Theodore Dreiser (1871–1945) submitted the manuscript of *Sister Carrie* (1900), his first novel. After Norris's enthusiastic recommendation had secured its acceptance, the publishers tried to persuade Dreiser to withdraw it, and when he refused, fulfilled their contract by issuing the novel without making any effort to sell it. The trouble with the book was its breach of popular literary decorum in echoing Horatio Alger's 'Luck and Pluck' formula only to ridicule it by omitting the crucial ingredient of virtue.

In writing *Sister Carrie* Dreiser assimilated influences as diverse as the prose impressionism of Crane, the realistic newspaper journalism of the 1890s, 'the exploration of the familiar' in the documentary photography of Alfred Stieglitz (1864–1946) who stalked the streets of New York with a hand-held 'detective' camera, and the image of affluence in the style and night-club fame of his eldest brother, Paul 'Dresser'. Arriving in the booming, brutal Chicago of the 1890s, Dreiser fell in love with the city, became a reporter and discovered its corruption. In *Sister Carrie* he records his impressions of cities that glitter, beckon and arbitrarily destroy without reference to moral deserts. It was not George Hurstwood's fall that made Doubleday, Page want to drop the book; a weak man, a thief and adulterer unable to adapt himself to the environment of New York, he deserved all he got. The offence was Carrie. When her 'average little conscience' questions her in Chapter 10, the reply is simple: 'The voice of want made answer for her'. Drouet's mistress before becoming Hurstwood's, she is not made to suffer, like Edith Wharton's Lily Bart in *The House of Mirth*, for violating social norms. At the end of the novel she is at the peak of her career in a world akin to that of Dreiser's flashy, envied brother, and she is not contrite. 'Not evil', Dreiser suggests, compounding the moral felony of his work, 'but longing for that which is better, more often directs the steps of the erring.'

Everything Dreiser wrote is a form of self-projection. Hurstwood is what he might become himself. Carrie, rocking as she dreams of happiness, but fated to know 'neither surfeit nor content', expresses his fear that both might elude him in a deterministic world where man pathologically wavers between beastliness and humanity, instinct and will:

> He is even as a wisp in the wind, moved by every breath of passion, acting now by his will and now by his instincts, erring with one, only to retrieve by the other, falling by one, only to rise by the other – a creature of incalculable variability.

With hindsight Dreiser's own variability is calculable as an inexhaustible capacity to absorb and identify with opposites. In terms of this his fiction after *Sister Carrie* is less remarkable as a series of individual books than as parts of a phenomenon that is symptomatic of the transitional age in which he lived. The Frank Cowperwood trilogy – *The Financier* (1912), *The Titan* (1914) and *The Stoic* (1947) – enabled him to identify with a Nietzschean superman of business (based on the character of the magnate Charles T. Yerkes), whose view of life is contained in his motto, 'I satisfy myself'. The 'survival of the fittest' ideas of Social Darwinism gathered from Spencer, Huxley and Loeb also led him to identify with the weak and victimised in *Jennie Gerhardt* (1911) and *An American Tragedy* (1925), which Dreiser based on the murder of Grace Brown by her lover, Chester Gillette, at Moose Lake, upper New York State in 1906. The long section of *An American Tragedy* devoted to Clyde Griffith's imprisonment and brief emergence as a hero of newspaper publicity implies a heavy emotional investment by Dreiser in ideas of redemption, self-knowledge and social reform, that pull against the pure determinism with which he is often credited.

In the autobiographical *Dawn* (1931) Dreiser looks back on the excitement of early days in Chicago:

> Hail Chicago! First of the daughters of the new world! Strange illusion of hope and happiness that resounded as a paean by your lake of blue! . . . Of what dreams and songs were your walls and ways compounded!

Romantic illusion indeed, according to the young Frank Cowperwood in *The Financier*, observing a tank in which a lobster and a squid are exhibited, until the lobster eats the squid. The moral seems clear:

> Things lived by each other – that was it. Lobsters lived on squid and other things. What lived on lobsters? Men, of course! Sure, that was it! And what lived on men?

Frank bases his life on the answer, 'Sure, men lived on men', but Dreiser was never so simply assured. His glorification of material success carries far more conviction than the disintegration of Cowperwood's grandeur in *The Stoic*; yet he was invited as a distinguished visitor to Soviet Russia in 1927, became an active leftist on his return to America, and expressed his faith in socialism in *Dreiser Looks at Russia* (1928) and *Tragic America* (1931). At the end of his life he was a Communist, yet he took communion on Good Friday, 1945. The 'wisp-in-the-wind' passage in *Sister Carrie* was a premonitory confession, for Dreiser wavered all his life. Running scared, he backed both sides of the day's great questions; but in his running he documented urban America in more realistic detail than any of his literary predecessors.

Gopher Prairie and West Egg

Both Sinclair Lewis (1885–1951) and F. Scott Fitzgerald (1896–1940) were students of contemporary manners. They had little else in common except birth in Minnesota and a capacity for personal disintegration. Lewis gave the outside world and his own countrymen a comprehensible picture of the uncharted new world of the middle-brow, middle-class Middle West. His prose can be swift and incisive when anatomising the small-town smugness of *Main Street*, the entrapment of *Babbitt* (1922) or the hypocritical evangelism of *Elmer Gantry* (1927). It is often dull and slapdash as in the over-plotted *Arrowsmith* (1925), *Ann Vickers* (1933) and *Cass Timberlane* (1945). Fitzgerald diagnosed and succumbed to the era he called the 'Jazz Age', either analysing the wealthy and neurotic lives of the 1920s in a cultured prose of inimitable grace and precision or calculatedly, and very professionally, diluting his talent to produce facile stories for sale to magazines. Of all his stories only 'The Diamond as Big as the Ritz' displays his imaginative power at full throttle. Patchily in *The Beautiful and the Damned* (1922), *Tender is the Night* (1934) and *The Last Tycoon* (1941), and consistently in *The Great Gatsby*, Fitzgerald is a writer's writer. Lewis, like James Fenimore Cooper or Theodore Dreiser, is a piece of America. His characters, seldom observed in depth, remain two-dimensional figures moving against a back-cloth painted by a clever journalist who could not make up his mind about the connection between sentiment and satire. He is, in the words of his biographer Mark Schorer, 'one of the worst writers in modern American literature', yet without his books 'one cannot imagine modern American literature'.

There is more subtlety in Sherwood Anderson's (1876–1941) sympathetic miniatures of small-town people in *Winesburg, Ohio* (1919) and more naturalistic satire in the free verses of Edgar Lee Masters' (1869–1950) *Spoon River Anthology* (1915) than in *Main Street*. Lewis's story of Carol Kennicott, young wife of the town doctor, her unsuccessful efforts to raise the cultural level of the community, her flight to Washington and her return, barely escapes banality but it is sufficient to convey the lawyer, Guy Pollock's illustration of 'The Village Virus':

The Village Virus is the germ which – it's extraordinarily like the hook-worm – infects ambitious people who stay too long in the provinces. You'll find it epidemic among lawyers and doctors and ministers and college-bred merchants – all these people who have had a glimpse of the world that thinks and laughs, but have returned to their swamp.

Towards the end of the novel Carol's 'active hatred' of Gopher Prairie has run out. Suddenly eager to return, she sees it afresh as 'a toiling new settlement'. This reassuringly sentimental vision cannot last. 'I've been making the town a myth', she realises; frontier vitality has degenerated to complacent insularity:

'This is how people keep up the tradition of the perfect home-town, the happy boyhood, the brilliant college friends. We forget so. I've been for-getting that Main Street doesn't think it's in the least lonely and pitiful. It thinks it's God's Own Country. It isn't waiting for me. It doesn't care.'

Luckily for Carol the romantic image of Gopher Prairie, waiting for her in the sunset, reasserts itself and she returns stocked with city sounds and colours to sustain her through 'the long still days' that lie ahead.

Gopher Prairie is more than a case of the provincial Village Virus; it represents the national disease of a country bent on mediocrity, 'taking pains to become altogether standardised and pure'. George F. Babbitt's Zenith City boasts some three or four hundred thousand inhabitants. As the hero gradually awakens at his 'Floral Heights' home, the towers of the city,

aspired above the morning mist; austere towers of steel and cement and limestone, sturdy as cliffs and delicate as silver rods. They were neither citadels nor churches, but frankly and beautifully office-buildings.

This, it seems, must be taken straight to justify Babbitt's loving 'his city with passionate wonder', but the promise of the early morning vision soon fades into the trivia of soggy towels in the bathroom, smelly toothpaste, unpressed trousers, and the homogenised Mrs Babbitt's genteel preference for 'dinner-jacket' to 'Tux'. The people of Zenith City are frustrated or content in relation to their achieve-ment of the standardised symbols of material or social success. Complacent acceptance of the symbols themselves is common to all. Zenith City is just Gopher Prairie with skyscrapers. As Dr Martin Arrowsmith discovers, the smug resistance to progress of a small Midwestern town is essentially the same dessication of spirit as he finds in the rigidly mercenary attitudes of Chicago's medical world. It takes a visit to Europe to persuade the eponymous hero of *Dodsworth* (1929) that there is real hope for cultural growth in America.

Sinclair Lewis went from Sauk Center via Oberlin College to an AB at Yale. Scott Fitzgerald was born at St Paul's, Minnesota, and proceeded from private schools to Princeton which he left with 'the sense of all the gorgeous youth that has rioted through here in 200 years', but without a degree. In 1920 after the publication of his first novel *This Side of Paradise*, which he described as 'a somewhat edited history of me and my imagination' – referring to its sequence of Princeton, war service, and involvement with a headstrong Southern girl – he married Zelda Sayer, belle of Montgomery, Alabama, and took up extravagant living. *The Beautiful and the Damned* followed in 1922, partly based on his tempestuous marriage, and in 1925 *The Great Gatsby*. He further examined the theme of disillusionment in the story of Dick Driver, the self-destructive psychologist of *Tender is the Night* (1934), and the status of the American dream in the unfinished manuscript of *The Last Tycoon* (1941). In Fitzgerald's own lifetime *The Great Gatsby* reached a far smaller audience than his *Saturday Evening Post* stories, and its sales were well below those of his first novel. Today it is not only acknowledged as his masterpiece, but also as a work fit to be mentioned with other great fables of American literature, by Hawthorne, Melville, Twain and Henry James.

Gatsby is an idealist who is compelled to a meretricious way of life in order to realise his dream in a society obsessed with money. 'The truth', Nick Carraway realises, 'was that Jay Gatsby of West Egg, Long Island, sprang from his Platonic conception of himself.' Gatsby does not only create himself; it is the force of his passion for Daisy Buchanan, his 'grace', that briefly recreates her. It brings her out of the bored conspiracy of sophistication she shares with her husband into the reality of her own tears at the gauche exhibitionist appeal of Gatsby's display of shirts and it presses her languor too hard in the confrontation at the Plaza Hotel. Lost, but never surrendered, Daisy as the ideal woman has committed Gatsby to making money and an absurd but valiant image. His solipsism is as complete as Ahab's and infinitely more pathetic. With a voice already 'full of money' Daisy can hardly be bought. Gatsby may 'look so cool' compared to the momentarily nonplussed Tom, but Tom has class, rights of possession and the arrogance of natural wealth.

After Chapter 7 the end seems inevitable. When Gatsby is shot dead by Wilson, who does not know that Daisy was driving Gatsby's yellow car when it killed his wife Myrtle, the only surprise is Fitzgerald's skill in thus engineering the resolution of his plot without melodramatic distortion. Appalled by the realisation that Tom and Daisy have drawn closer to each other out of defensive self-interest, Nick Carraway has already sensed that Gatsby, as an idealist, is doomed. The underworld associations have ceased to matter; Gatsby is 'worth the whole damn bunch put together'.

Myrtle Wilson dies under the blank gaze of Doctor T. J. Eckleburg, whose yard-high retinas and enormous yellow spectacles recur as a motif throughout the book. 'God sees everything', says the bereaved Wilson, but this is an unseeing god, overlooking a valley of ashes. Technically Fitzgerald is a traditionalist rather than an innovator; here his realism – the doctor is, after all, only an optician's advertisement – is combined with a modernist appreciation of the uses of imagery and an Eliotesque view of the world as a godless desert.

7

Modernisms

WALT Whitman's confident, declamatory style makes him precursor of a line in modern American poetry that runs through Ezra Pound (1885–1972) and Carl Sandburg to the Allen Ginsberg (*b.* 1926) of *Howl* (1956) and other 'Beat Generation' poets of the 1950s. In the formal proportions of his verse, its promotion of himself and its ebullient optimism, Whitman is a foil to the reserve of Frederick Goddard Tuckerman (1821–73), the miniaturist poetry of Emily Dickinson (1830–86), and the dark prophecies of Henry Adams. If by 'modern' is meant a historical period lasting from about 1910 to 1940, Emily Dickinson's withdrawal and her highly individual use of imagery, off-rhyme and unconventional syntax give a foretaste of modernist emphases on impersonality and language. Henry Adams evinces a modernist sense of the massive, alienating power of science.

Swinging through the variety of America, chanting his happy catalogues, Whitman makes his utterance and expects the reader to 'yawp' back at him in joyful accord. 'I must have the love of all men and women', he says. 'If there is one left in any country who has no faith in me, I will go to that one.' Tuckerman in his sonnets, and Emily Dickinson in most of her nearly two thousand poems, are different. They draw the world into themselves, model their perceptions into verse, and move on to their next act in a theatre empty, so far as they know or care, but for themselves.

Emily Dickinson

Emily Dickinson loves words: 'A Word made Flesh is seldom/And tremblingly partook', she begins one poem, although 'seldom' reflects her reverence for language rather than her practice of it. Apart from a year at Mount Holyoake Female Seminary, visits to Washington and Philadelphia and eye treatment in Boston, she lived her life in Amherst, the village of her birth. Withdrawn, she was possessed by the 'Glee' of an art as 'full as Opera' (no. 326) that kept her buoyant in obscurity:

> I'm Nobody! Who are you?
> Are you – Nobody – Too?
> Then there's a pair of us?
> Don't tell! they'd advertise – you know!
>
> How dreary – to be – Somebody!
> How public – like a Frog –
> To tell one's name – the livelong June –
> To an admiring Bog!

She settled for anonymity in 1862 when an impressed but bewildered T. W. Higginson, critic for *The Atlantic Monthly*, replied to her request for an assessment of her work with the advice that she should correct the 'irregularity' of her writing. The correspondence with Higginson continued, but she kept her individual syntactical rhythms and forbore to publish. Of the seven poems published during her lifetime, only 'Success' (no. 67) appeared in print with her reluctant permission. Publication of her works began in 1890, but a full text was not available until T. H. Johnson's three-volume edition of *The Poems of Emily Dickinson* in 1955.

Emily Dickinson has little time for the 'Menagerie' (no. 290; no. 1206) of things merely entertaining or showy. An exception is the 'docile and omnipotent' iron horse of the Amherst–Belchertown railroad in 'I like to see it lap the Miles – /And lick the Valleys up' (no. 585). Usually she finds her subject in nature, her relation to God, or her perception of death. An addict of nature – 'Inebriate of Air', 'Debauchee of Dew' (no. 214) – she masters the rising sun in the imagery of 'The Day Came slow' (no. 304) which startlingly juxtaposes rubies and topaz with 'the Light/A Sudden Musket – spills –' to create 'The Parlour – of the Day –'. In another mood she appreciates the impersonality of the natural world. 'The Grass so little has to do' (no. 333) and the death-life rhythm of God-ordained frost and sun in 'Apparently with no surprise' (no. 1624) accept the inexorable processes of nature. In yet another mood she laments the lapsing of summer 'As imperceptibly as Grief' (no. 1540). She displays her skill with association, ambiguity, simile and pun in 'There's a certain slant of light' (no. 258), which analyses the inner and outer effects of winter light. The first stanza measures the afternoon light by converting it into weight which, in turn, is measured by sound. The simile, 'like the Heft/Of Cathedral Tunes –', brings a wealth of implication into the poem by one organ-like chord of associations. The 'Hurt' of such moments is sent from Heaven – therefore, 'An imperial affliction' – and also 'Heavenly' in the sense that it is gravely pleasurable, received with thanks. By another daring conversion in the last stanza, the departure of the sombre light and mood of oppression becomes 'the Distance/On the look of Death –'. The splendours of the aurora borealis in 'Of Bronze – and Blaze –' (no. 290) include an 'Unconcern so sovereign' that she is tempted to emulation until, strutting on her 'stem' she grows conscious of her mortal insignificance. The heavenly spectacle will 'entertain the Centuries' when she is 'An Island in dishonoured Grass', known only to beetles. Nature brings primeval intimations in 'A narrow Fellow in the Grass' (no. 986). The poem begins by recording appearances exactly: the 'Grass divides as with a Comb', and the snake is like a 'Whip lash' until it 'wrinkled, and was gone', but not before reminding the poet of its special power to induce a feeling of 'Zero at the Bone –'.

Mirroring her own withdrawal from society, Emily Dickinson writes of the soul that 'selects her own Society' (no. 303). Her inner life was intense. 'Wild Nights' (no. 249) may have been inspired by her love for the Reverend Charles Wadsworth with whom she was in correspondence when he moved from Philadelphia to San Francisco in 1862, but it hardly matters now. The passion of imagined 'luxury' is accentuated by her selection and control of imagery and the harrowingly conditional 'Were' and 'Might' of the first and last stanzas. 'Mine – by the Right of the White Election' (no. 528) envisages an unconditional heavenly betrothal more cryptically but with comparable fervour.

Emily Dickinson declined to join the church but she sometimes attended services, and was continually preoccupied with God's majesty, his presence in nature and his elusiveness. She asserts her faith in 'The Love a Life can show Below' (no. 673) and her certainty of Heaven in 'I never saw a Moor' (no. 1052), but the confidence of 'I know that He exists' (no. 338) is eroded by the thought that the search for a hidden God might lead only to the grave, and she longs for an answer to prayer in 'At least – to pray' (no. 502). The pomp of death commands her in 'One dignity delays for all' (no. 98), and she meditates on its absolute repose in 'Safe in their Alabaster Chambers' (no. 216). Welcoming death as 'the securest Fold' (no. 1065), she later asks that her own be postponed (no. 1111). The experience of dying is brilliantly imagined in 'Because I could not stop for Death' (no. 712). Written from the point of view of someone who has been dead for centuries, the poem looks back on the unexpected arrival of Death as a kindly coachman. His 'Horses' Heads . . . towards Eternity', Death graciously conducts the speaker out of life to her final home, 'A Swelling of the Ground'. The tone of acceptance implies faith in 'Immortality', her companion on the journey; the memory of mild surprise adds pathos.

Although she characteristically uses the first person singular, the impression given by Emily Dickinson's work is less one of self-exhibition, than of moods, perspectives, intuitions and questions crafted into particular poems. In *The Poetry of Emily Dickinson* (1968) Ruth Miller suggests that each of the forty sewn fascicles, into which the poet gathered some nine hundred of her works, should be seen as a poem of assemblage portraying aspects of a unified experience. The impact of individual poems, however, is largely attributable to Emily Dickinson's ability to make each clipping from her intensely personal life into a poetic object that spins in its own orbit, drawing the reader into the drama of its language, rather than towards the personality from which it emanates. In this she is a modern.

Henry Adams and the dynamics of the modern world

The modernism of Henry Adams is a matter not of technique but of temperament and vision. The Adams family is one of the most considerable dynasties in American history. Henry (1838–1918) was descended from the second President and grandson of John Quincy Adams (1767–1848), sixth President of the United States. Educated at Harvard and in Europe, he served as private secretary to his father, Charles Francis Adams, the American diplomatic representative in London during the Civil War. After two years of political journalism in Washington, he became an assistant professor of medieval history at Harvard and editor of the *North American Review*. Disillusioned with politics he wrote *Democracy: An American Novel* (1880) which portrays the Washington of the 1870s as a corrupt system of fixed elections and cynical graft. His most significant contribution to formal history is the *History of the United States During the Administrations of Thomas Jefferson and James Madison* (1889–91) which follows the evolution of American political life through the war of 1812 to the advent of James Monroe as fifth President. The chapter on 'American Ideals' recalls the early

Jeffersonian belief in human perfectibility, and makes Adams's history a lesson in the tragic sequence by which lofty principles have been displaced by materialistic goals.

In *Mont-Saint-Michel and Chartres* (privately printed in 1904, published 1913), Adams's search for historical causality takes him to twelfth-century France. The architecture of Chartres Cathedral and the Abbey of Mont-Saint-Michel seems to him an expression of ideological unity achieved in response to 'the purity, the beauty, the grace, and the infinite loftiness of Mary's nature, among the things of Earth, and above the clamour of Kings'. Adoration of the Virgin Mary impelled medieval sensibility into a unifying ideal which held life and art in a lucid harmony of sex, love, energy and benevolence. Adams's Mariolatry is historically suspect – clerical monopoly of power in the twelfth century did not promote the Utopia he chooses to imagine – but the symbol of the Virgin remains valid as an expression of his own ideal. By comparison with the directed, purposeful lives of the century 1150–1250, modern people merely exist, prey to blind forces and chance events. The Virgin has been replaced by the dynamo, a symbol of mechanistic force which compels people into a worship fatal to their own well-being.

Henry Adams visited the Paris Exhibition of 1900. Describing his reactions in the third person in *The Education of Henry Adams* (privately printed in 1906, published 1918), he records that to him:

> the dynamo became a symbol of infinity. As he grew accustomed to the great gallery of machines, he began to feel the forty-foot dynamos as a moral force, much as the early Christians felt the Cross . . . one began to pray to it; inherited instinct taught the natural expression of man before silent and infinite force . . . he could see only an absolute *fiat* in electricity as in faith.

Although Adams's guide, the aeronautics pioneer Samuel P. Langley, seems enthusiastic about the power of modern motors, even he is worried by the anarchical character of newly discovered forces. Adams is unequivocal and calls the automobile a 'nightmare'. The discovery of radioactivity by Pierre and Marie Curie had shown that physical matter contained its own potential for disintegration, and Radium 'denied its God'. By reducing all matter to molecules that collide with each other at intervals varying up to 17,750,000 times per second, the kinetic theory of gas establishes Adams's belief that nature is without system:

> The kinetic theory of gas is an assertion of ultimate chaos. In plain words, Chaos was the law of nature; Order was the dream of man.

In his attempt to impose order on the flux of his existence, man seems to Adams like a spider snaring the forces of nature that 'dance like flies before the net' of its web. This image reappears in T. S. Eliot's (1888–1965) poem 'Gerontion' (1920), originally intended as a prelude to *The Waste Land* (1922), the modern period's most celebrated image of a world in disorder. Eliot considers the possibility that the spider might 'suspend its operations', thus consigning the poem's oddly named characters to disintegration in space:

> De Bailhache, Fresca, Mrs Cammel, whirled
> Beyond the circuit of the shuddering Bear
> In fractured atoms.

Unlike Henry Adams or Eliot's old man in 'Gerontion', most Americans hailed the twentieth-century as the next chapter of an infinite, bright future. The breach of President Monroe's isolationist 'Doctrine' of 1823, by which Woodrow Wilson took his country into the First World War, was hotly debated, but the war burden was light. America's decisive contribution to the allied victory brought new international respect which President Wilson compounded by supporting the League of Nations at the Paris Peace Conference in 1919. In the same year the Eighteenth Amendment prohibited 'the manufacture, sale, or transportation of intoxicating liquors' in the United States. (The Eighteenth Amendment was not repealed until the Twenty-first Amendment in 1933). Besides adding the savour of illegality to the vast quantities of drink actually consumed in the 1920s, Prohibition created boot-legging on a national scale and encouraged smuggling across the Mexican and Canadian borders. It promoted the gang warfare that made legendary figures of John Dillinger and Al Capone, 'Public Enemy Number One', and provided J. Edgar Hoover's Federal Bureau of Investigation with the opportunity to become a universal symbol of rigorous law enforcement. The social effects of Prohibition were pernicious, but for the majority of people the 1920s were years of progress and prosperity until 24 October 1929, when panic on the New York Stock Exchange led to the selling in one day of some thirteen million shares. The 'Crash' of American finance was the biggest national trauma since the Civil War: capitalist exploitation of the American technological miracle had contrived a chaos that was felt by every ordinary citizen.

With their fuel cut off, people in Los Angeles cooked over wood fires in back lots. Others died of hunger. 'Hobos' wandered, looking for employment and servants often worked for only board and lodging.

Banks foreclosed on mortgages and landlords evicted tenants who lived together in shanty towns called 'Hoovervilles' in honour of Herbert Hoover, the President who had failed them. Oklahoma farmers (Okies), like the Joad family in John Steinbeck's *The Grapes of Wrath* (1939), migrated to California from the starved soil of the 'Dust Bowl'. At Christmas 1931 a couple were found starving in a cottage near Anwana Lake, Sullivan County, New York. The *New York Times* reported that after 'three days without food, the wife, who is 23 years old, was hardly able to walk'. An Ohio newspaper bore the headline 'FATHER OF TEN DROWNS SELF', and told the story of a steel worker, unemployed for two years, who thus abandoned the family he could no longer support. There were fourteen million people out of work in 1932 when Franklin D. Roosevelt's campaign promise of 'a new deal for the American people' secured his election as President. By 1941 when America entered the Second World War, he had repaired the economy, made social welfare a reality and devised an administrative agency for regulating virtually every aspect of public life. Manipulating, conspiring and blackmailing, he mended America but could not put the clock back.

Advances in technology had been accompanied in America, as in Europe, by the decline of traditional institutions like the church, the state and the family. The Depression years simultaneously shook confidence in the institution of money and elevated it to the status of a supreme but fickle power. It was not necessary to share Henry Adams's knowledge of the kinetic theory of gas, or his lament for the lost Virgin, to see that the world had changed. It was no longer a static, created world, a home to man, but a world in process, a kinetic world of becoming. New methods had to be found to deal with it, new terminologies to describe and explain it. Modernism is, therefore, volatile, uncertain, assertive and experimental. Alert to the fallibility of social mechanisms, and aware of Sigmund Freud's theories of psycho-analysis, it focuses on individual experience both at conscious and unconscious levels. It has difficulty with moral concepts, partly because psychology has invalidated overt behaviour as a reliable index of human volition. When it is determined, like Ezra Pound, to 'Make It New', it often does so by seeking contact with the past. Modern literature is typically obsessed with doubt, alienation, and with its own 'technology', the form and language of its own medium.

Native voices in poetry

A connoisseur of unhappiness and alienation, Edwin Arlington Robinson (1869–1935) describes his life as a 'living hell' until 1905 when President Theodore Roosevelt, admiring his poetry, gave him a clerking position in the New York Custom House. The pessimism of his work was bred in him by an unsympathetic, afflicted family. His mother died of black diphtheria and his ailing father turned spiritualist; one brother became a drug addict and alcoholic, another died of tuberculosis. Intimate with the hopelessness of living 'Like a dry fish flung inland from the shore' ('Lost Anchors'), he recreates the place of his youth, Gardiner in Maine, as 'Tilbury Town'. Like the characters in Edgar Lee Masters's *Spoon River Anthology*, the people of Tilbury are beset by frustration, grief and loneliness. The rich, envied gentleman of 'Richard Cory' unaccountably 'went home and put a bullet through his head'; others, like the solitary Eben Flood of 'Mr Flood's Party', endure 'to the end/A valiant armour of scarred hopes outworn'. The most anthologised of Robinson's lives of quiet desperation, set in New England 'where the wind is always north-north-east/And children learn to walk on frozen toes', is that of the nostalgic 'Miniver Cheevy'. Born too late for Thebes and Camelot,

> Miniver coughed, and called it fate
> And kept on drinking.

Like Robert Frost, Robinson 'stayed with the old-fashioned way to be new', using the old forms of the sonnet, the ballad, the villanelle, for shorter poems in *The Children of the Night* (1897), and blank verse for the longer narratives of *Captain Craig* (1902). His most ambitious project attempts to re-tell the legend of King Arthur as a parable that speaks to the twentieth century in *Merlin* (1917), *Lancelot* (1920) and *Tristram* (1927). The collection published as *The Man Against the Sky* (1916) was well received critically and established him as a substantial poet with a distinctive voice. The volume includes 'Hillcrest' in tribute to the MacDowell colony, a writers' and artists' residence established by the widow of the composer, Edward MacDowell. Robinson spent his summers there from 1911 until his death. 'Ben Jonson Entertains a man from Stratford', is a clever dramatic monologue in which the tough-minded Jonson talks of his admiration for his friend Shakespeare's imaginative independence. 'Eros Turannos' portrays the hurt and betrayal of a marriage between a philanderer and an infatuated woman of 'blurred sagacity', who understands him perfectly but cannot live without him. The long title poem of the book pictures the emblematic figure of a man on a hill-top backed by a flaming sunset. The poet wonders about the meaning of life and wrests positive implication from imagery of the utmost pessimism. If life were worthless, this man, and countless others, would surely have committed suicide:

> 'Twere sure but weaklings' vain distress
> To suffer dungeons where so many doors
> Will open on the cold eternal shores
> That look sheer down
> To the dark tideless floods of Nothingness
> Where all who know may drown.

Robinson's modernism is the irony with which he grains his pessimism. In Robert Frost, too, modernism is at a deeper level than the stylistic surface of his poetry. There is much to support the popular image of Frost as a cracker-barrel philosopher in verses that come to a New England poet–farmer as naturally as making hay, or resting after apple-picking. Frost played up to this inadequate picture of himself as the snow-haired rustic sage, became the Grand Old Man of American Letters and read 'The Gift Outright' at President Kennedy's Inaugural ceremony on 20 January 1961. The disturbing complexity of his work was long ignored, the invitation of 'The Pasture' accepted as the whole truth:

> I'm going out to clean the pasture spring;
> I'll only stop to rake the leaves away
> (And wait to watch the water clear, I may)
> I shan't be gone long. – You come too.

This is a poet who talks comfortably of life, a practical man speaking to men, the Robert Frost who left Harvard without a degree, married and farmed. True, he left America, but he was not long an expatriate. In England he published *A Boy's Will* (1913), and *North of Boston* (1914), but he did not succumb to Ezra Pound's urgent modernism. He returned to America in 1915, when those whom Gertrude Stein called the 'lost generation' of writers, such as Hemingway, Fitzgerald, T. S. Eliot and John Dos Passos, were going off to Europe to be self-consciously artistic in London or on the Left Bank of the River Seine in Paris.

There is nothing aloof or *outré* about this Frost. He speaks directly in 'a language absolutely unliterary' without need of the formal strangeness and elusiveness practised by Pound and Eliot, or the elliptical private diction of Wallace Stevens. His early 'Mending Wall' ruminates so easily towards its famous apothegm, 'Good fences make good neighbours', that the poem's ironising of the sentiment is easily missed. Frost retained the aphoristic pose until his last, sadly geriatric volume, *In The Clearing* (1962): 'Forgive, O Lord, my little jokes on Thee/And I'll forgive Thy great big one on me'. 'The Death of the Hired Man' dramatises the universal need for self-respect without overplaying the difference of opinion between Mary and Warren. 'After Apple-Picking' evokes a season in terms of the harmony between man and nature. 'The Road Not Taken' perfectly catches the sense of loss that can accompany an act of choice. 'Fire and Ice' symbolically expresses life's paradoxes with a rhythmic wit that simultaneously defines and dispels the tension of opposites. In 'Stopping by Woods on a Snowy Evening', Frost's most famous poem, the horse's thinking it 'queer/To stop without a farmhouse near' draws attention to the speaker's unproprietory enjoyment of the atmosphere of the woods as they 'fill up with snow'. The repetition of the line 'And miles to go before I sleep' effects a clever key-change of meaning, whereby the suggestion that the speaker is simply far from home becomes a statement about the duties that must be discharged throughout life before the peace of this moment may be repeated or amplified.

A popular Frost exists; he is not merely a figment of public imagination, but darker, subtler elements were also visible in his poetry long before his death in 1963 allowed his biographer, Lawrance Thompson, to reveal domestic tensions, professional jealousies and other aspects of a nervous egotism. 'I'd like to get away from earth awhile/And then come back to it and begin over', he says in 'Birches'. Climbing the trees brings a taste of heaven, but confirms his preference for the exhilarating swing back to earth: 'Earth's the right place for love:/I don't know where it's likely to go better'. The formulation is refreshingly modest but it is also ambiguous. It chooses earthly before spiritual love, and carries a hint of Andrew Marvell's lines in 'To His Coy Mistress': 'The grave's a fine and private place,/But none I think do there embrace'. It states a conviction with a plain man's realism about what he does not know, and because he *is* a plain man, what he knows has authority. Yet his restraint is provocative. Does 'I don't know where it's likely to go better' mean much more than 'I'll settle for what I can get'? Do his weariness of 'considerations', the image of life like 'a pathless wood', and his one weeping eye imply that he would 'like to get away from earth awhile' because his own love is not going as well as it might? There is a suggestion of suppressed pain in this reverie which credibly associates its speaker with the ineptly loving husband of 'Home Burial', who is baffled by the emotional distance between himself and his wife.

Pain lies in ambush to become agony and death in 'Out, Out –'. The poem takes its title from the soliloquy in which Macbeth calls life 'a tale/Told by an idiot, full of sound and fury,/Signifying nothing' (*Macbeth*, V,v, 17 ff.). A buzz-saw snarls and rattles matter-of-factly in the yard; the sister comes out to announce, 'Supper', and suddenly there is horror when the saw, 'As if to prove saws knew what supper meant', leaps out at the boy's hand. 'All spoiled' by the amputation, the boy dies, and routine closes over the shocking incident as the living return 'to their affairs'. Similar incongruity between conversational tone and violent incident intensifies the impression of madness and suppressed guilt in 'The Witch of Coös'. Such eruptions from the ordinary surfaces of things add to the obscurity of the world Frost symbolises by the city in 'Acquainted with the Night' which makes expert use of the traditional Italian verse form, *terza rima*, to convey a rich complex of modern anxieties. There is no communication in Frost's city where a single 'luminary' clock proclaims 'the time was neither wrong nor right'. The poet's alienation is complete in a world without human assurances or moral standards. In the sonnet 'Design' he finds a fat, white spider on a white flower clasping a dead white moth. The colour of innocence contrasts shockingly with these 'assorted characters of death and blight'. The poet accepts that the insects, 'Mixed ready to begin the morning right', reflect truth, but the ultimate question remains unanswered. Is the design of things malevolent, or non-existent?

In 'The Figure a Poem Makes' (1939) Frost says that poetry, while offering no 'great clarification', can provide at least a 'momentary stay against confusion'. By this definition poetry is scarce in the work of Carl Sandburg and Robinson Jeffers (1887–1962). In Sandburg's 'Chicago', a Whitmanesque tribute to the brawny city of his adoption, in the six lines of 'Fog', and in short poems like 'Grass', 'Pennsylvania' and 'Limited', his tendency towards an overblown, cataloguing style is restrained by attention to image or by the controlling economy of simple irony. The isolating poverty of the rich man's social spirit is expressed in 'The Fence' by the security he needs to make his 'stone house on the lake front' safe. Workmen begin on the fence:

The palings are made of iron bars with steel points that
    can stab the life out of any man who falls on them.
As a fence, it is a masterpiece, and will shut off the rabble
    and all vagabonds and hungry men and all wandering
    children looking for a place to play.
Passing through the bars and over the steel points will go
        nothing except
Death and the Rain and To-morrow.

Here detail, though copious, is selected to develop a simple theme. But the affirmations of *The People, Yes* (1936) are undermined by a confusing excess of detail. The long, packed, incantatory lines become cluttered and monotonous. As a character Sandburg appeals, deserves to be liked, but sympathy for his democratic patriotism cannot make him more than a minor poet in the Whitman tradition. His most remarkable work remains the monumental biography of *Abraham Lincoln* (1926; 1936) in which the challenges of nineteenth-century America are dramatised by Lincoln's progress from self-taught wrestler, weight-lifter and rail-splitter to sixteenth President during the most agonising years of his country's history.

Sandburg and Jeffers are thoroughly American writers. If Sandburg is a latter-day Whitman *manqué*, Jeffers is a travesty of Emersonian individualism. Patches of poetry are occasionally to be found in the welter of his bombast and prosaic didacticism. The first half of 'The Purse-Seine' vivifies the lives of Pacific Coast sardine fisherman who 'circle the gleaming shoal', each fish a 'comet's tail wake of clear yellow flame', while the 'vast walls of night' stand 'erect to the stars'. The exact and sympathetic response to a proud creature in defeat in 'Hurt Hawks' nearly justifies the poet's assertion 'I'd almost, except the penalties, kill a man than a hawk'; but the pretentious use of classical myth in such poems as 'Tamar' and 'Roan Stallion' cannot dignify or poeticise Jeffers's laborious and perverse celebration of incest, violence and sexual cruelty. 'Humanity is the mold to break away from', he writes in 'Tamar'. The resolute independence he exemplified by building his home, Tor House at Carmel Bay near Monterey on the California coast, he vitiated by a strident literature of disgust. As he says in 'Thurso's Landing', so it might be said of him: 'Give him a blood-trail to follow,/That's all he wants for Christmas'.

Making it new

Most American poets of the early twentieth century were more influenced than Frost, Sandburg or Jeffers by Ezra Pound's mission-ary zeal on behalf of new poetic styles and standards. Many poets were first published through Pound's connection with the Chicago magazine *Poetry* which Harriet Monroe (1860–1936) founded in 1912 as a platform for contemporary verse. Miss Monroe's editorial policy was to open her pages 'to all sorts of experimental and unconventional work without neglecting the traditional forms'. Accordingly she extended the hospitality of her magazine to the rhythms of Vachel Lindsay (1879–1931), the lyricism of Edna St Vincent Millay (1892–1950) and the elegant intensities of Elinor Wylie (1885–1928) as well as to early modernist poems by Ezra Pound, T. S. Eliot, Wallace Stevens and William Carlos Williams.

In *Hugh Selwyn Mauberley* (1920) Ezra Pound says of his hero, an imaginary aesthete, that 'He strove to resuscitate the dead art/Of poetry'. This was Pound's own enterprise. He began by exiling himself from America when the Presbyterian administration of Wabash College at Crawfordsville in central Indiana encouraged him to resign from his post as instructor in Romance Languages. Pound had provided a stranded chorus girl with tea and lodging in his room, thus confirming the College's view that he was, in his own phrase, too much 'the Latin Quarter type'. In February 1908 he sailed from New York for Europe and landed at Gibraltar with eighty dollars and a handful of poems. He visited Italy, published his poems under the title *A Lume Spento* (1908) and settled in London where he lived until 1920, establishing himself as the belligerent founding father of literary modernism in English. Among the artists he helped and encouraged were T. S. Eliot, W. B. Yeats, James Joyce, Wyndham Lewis, the sculptor Henri Gaudier-Brzeska, and the musician George Antheil. In 1909 the title of *Personae* proclaimed his intention to 'mask' his verse in the voices and styles of other, earlier poets. Later in the same year *Exultations* included 'Ballad of the Goodly Fere', 'Ballad for Gloom', and 'Sestina: Altaforte'. Written in a manner derived from Robert Browning, the 'Sestina' is based on a war-song by the twelfth-century Provencal troubadour, Bertran de Born. It shows Pound's interest in the past and his relish for metrical experiment. Except for two minor lapses (11.21–2; 37–9) from the sestina's rotating set of six rhyme-words, the poem adroitly follows the permutations required by the form and conveys an appropriate flavour of antiquity without pulling any punches:

> Hell grant soon we hear again the swords clash!
> Hell blot for alway the thought 'Peace'!

While writing the poems for short volumes later absorbed into an enlarged *Personae* (1926), Pound joined the English writer, T. E. Hulme, in advancing the theory and practice of imagism as a reaction against the outworn forms and diction of Georgian verse. American poets who gathered round Hulme and Pound to form the *Imagistes* included H. D. (Hilda Doolittle, 1886–1961), John Gould Fletcher (1886–1950), William Carlos Williams and Amy Lowell (1874–1925), a lady of small talent and much aggressive energy, who smoked cigars and once provoked Carl Sandburg to say that arguing with her was 'like arguing with a big blue wave'. Pound edited the first imagist anthology *Some Imagiste Poets* in 1912, but, under the onslaught of what he called 'Amy-gism' he abandoned the movement in favour of Wyndham Lewis's Vorticism. In their short-lived journal *Blast* the Vorticists brought art and literature together in a call for the destruction of 'politeness, standardisation, and academic, that is civilised vision'. It was Pound, however, who formulated the principles of imagism, providing a crisp rationale for the most influential development in modern poetry. His 'recapitulation and retrospect' of the 'new fashion in poetry' is readily accessible in T. S. Eliot's edition of *Literary Essays of Ezra Pound* (1954):

1. Direct treatment of the 'thing' whether subjective or objective.
2. To use absolutely no word that does not contribute to the presentation.
3. As regarding rhythm: to compose in the sequence of the musical phrase, not in the sequence of a metronome.

The poems collected in *Ripostes* (1912) and *Lustra* (1916) proved that imagist rigour heightened feeling by controlling it. 'A Girl' images the female body inhabited by a tree, combining the classical idea of Daphne, the tree nymph, with the suggestion of premature sexual experience in a world sensitive to innocence. In 'The Seafarer' Pound feels his way into the stark utterances of the anonymous Anglo-Saxon poet, respects the elemental imagery of the original and recomposes the verse in phrases that live in his modern rendering by recalling the music of Old English. 'The Garden' begins with the image of a bored, directionless woman, 'Like a skein of loose silk blown against the wall', and moves on to satirical social comment and a wicked pun: 'In her is the end of breeding'. Acquisition of the American orientalist, Ernest Fenellosa's (1853–1908) notes on Japanese and Chinese language and literature led to Pound's imitations of Chinese 'imagistic' poetry in *Cathay* (1915) and to a deservedly famous emulation of the Japanese 'haiku' (or 'hokku'), 'In a Station of the Metro':

> The apparition of these faces in the crowd;
> Petals on a wet, black bough.

These two lines perfectly illustrate the Poundian image as 'an intellectual and emotional complex in an instant of time' by depicting the faces of people in the Paris underground in terms that convey the pathos of frailty and transience.

The elaborate 'Homage to Sextus Propertius' (1919) was at first received as a flashy perversion of its source in the Roman elegist, Sextus Aurelius Propertius (born *c.* 50 BC). A more rewarding approach to the poem is to allow Pound his latitude in attempting 'to bring a dead man to life', and to recognise the rhythmic virtuosity as well as the partisan elevation of poetic above political concerns. The poem's exemplary function is unfortunately diminished by its allusiveness, a trait which grew from Pound's uncompromising determination to be as lean in statement as he was learned in the older literatures. This is, perhaps, as much a compliment as a challenge to his reader, but the result in *Hugh Selwyn Mauberley* is a self-defeatingly cryptic style which in later sections of *The Cantos* (1975) becomes a sequence of elliptical polymath gestures. A multi-cultural blend of Greek myth, Dante, Chinese ideogram, medieval and American history, economic theory and personal circumstance, this most monumental of modern poems is incomprehensible to most, and as difficult to elucidate as the punning night language of James Joyce's *Finnegan's Wake*. In 'Canto CXVI' Pound confesses, 'I cannot make it cohere'. Critical opinion is still divided.

After three years in Paris, Pound made his home at Rapallo, near Genoa on the Italian coast, and became an active supporter of Mussolini's Fascism. During the Second World War he made regular pro-Axis broadcasts from Rome Radio attacking Roosevelt and denigrating Jews. It is clear now that these often rambling and disorganised talks arose from a simple-minded, essentially romantic longing for a better world by a man whose grasp of economic theory was weak and amateurish and whose anti-Semitism was not racial prejudice but hatred of the 'usura' defined as unnatural ('Contra Natura') in 'Canto XLV'. At the time, however, his views could only be treason. In May 1945 he was arrested by the occupying American Army and taken to a 'Disciplinary Training Centre' near Pisa where, after a period of solitary confinement in a cage, he suffered a physical and mental breakdown and was moved to a tent. Between May and November 1945 permission to use the typewriter in the camp's medical dispensary enabled him to work at night on *The Pisan Cantos* (LXXIV–LXXXIV; 1948), typing from notes he had made in Italian school exercise books during the day. Regarding the war as part of a long conflict between usurers and peasants, his sympathy with those he took to be the losers is movingly expressed in the opening line of 'Canto LXXIV': 'The enormous tragedy of the dream in the peasant's bent shoulders'. In the section of 'Canto LXXXI' beginning, 'The ant's a centaur in his dragon world', Pound recognises the ignominy of his position, his limitations and his ineffectuality:

> Pull down thy vanity
> Thou art a beaten dog beneath the hail,
> A swollen magpie in a fitful sun,
> Half black, half white
> Nor knowst 'ou wing from tail
> Pull down thy vanity
> How mean thy hates
> Fostered in falsity,
> Pull down thy vanity,
> Rathe to destroy, niggard in charity,
> Pull down thy vanity,
> I say pull down.

Ezra Pound was taken back to America, indicted for treason but pronounced mentally unfit to stand trial and committed to St Elizabeth's Hospital in Washington, where he remained for twelve years. The indictment was dismissed in 1958 after representations from Archibald MacLeish (1892–1982), Robert Frost, Ernest Hemingway, T. S. Eliot and others. Pound returned to Italy where he spent the remainder of his life at Schloss Brunnenberg, near Merano, at Rapallo and at Venice, where he died, a heroic, flawed figure who continues to disturb, tease, inspire and astonish.

In 1967 Pound said to Allen Ginsberg, 'I should have been able to do better'; but the power of his influence is indisputable. The voices of *The Cantos* and its cinematic method of cutting from one thought, image or scene to another, are present to varying degrees in *The Waste Land* – which owes its final form to Pound's editing of Eliot's manuscript – Hart Crane's (1899–1932) *The Bridge* (1930), Archibald MacLeish's (1892–1982) *Conquistador* (1932) and William

Carlos Williams's *Paterson* (1946–58). Poems look different after Pound. Punctuation becomes irregular and conventional sentence structure gives way to exclamatory techniques like Hart Crane's in 'Cutty Sark' (*The Bridge*, III), or e. e. cummings's (1894–1962) in the majority of *Poems 1923–54* (1954) and *95 Poems* (1958). Instead of traditional metres and rhyme many poets, more conservative than cummings, prefer free verse (*vers libre*) in which the poetic line is felt as a unit whose rhythm and cadence are freshly devised for the subject in hand. Familiar metres are sometimes used for special effect, like the iambic pentameter at the beginning of Eliot's 'A Game of Chess' (*The Waste Land*, II), or to provide a counterpointing norm for lines to pull against, as in Wallace Stevens's 'The Idea of Order at Key West'. Marianne Moore's (1887–1972) scrupulously 'literalist' poetry employs an intricate verse line that counts syllables rather than feet. W. H. Auden (1907–73) uses a variety of metres; in *The Age of Anxiety* (1947) he experiments with the epic effects of Anglo-Saxon alliteration and stress:

> Untalkative and tense, we took off
> Anxious into air; instruments glowed,
> Dials in darkness, for dawn was not yet.

Although Auden settled in the United States in 1939 and became an American citizen, his blend of socialism, Anglicanism and elliptical wit remained essentially Anglo-European. America was a welcome but intermittent convenience for him, not a spiritual home.

T. S. Eliot: alienation and language

In his role as one-man 'Ezuversity' Pound issued guidebooks with misleadingly approachable titles – *ABC of Reading* (1934), *Make It New* (1934), *Guide to Kulchur* (1938; 1952) – which disguise the allusive difficulty of their content. Even at his most openly didactic, Pound makes little effort to accommodate the ordinary reader without his own special interests. Eliot is not so uncompromising. A popular image of Eliot is of a man clerically grim, prim, precise – 'How unpleasant to meet Mr Eliot!' – and, if not actually unpleasant, at least austere. His reputation as bloodless exponent of a theory of impersonal poetry dates back to 1919, when the essay 'Tradition and the Individual Talent' came out in two instalments printed in *The Egoist*. At the end of the first instalment Eliot invites his readers:

to consider, as a suggestive analogy, the action which takes place when a bit of finely filiated platinum is introduced into a chamber containing oxygen and sulphur dioxide.

'At this moment', Hugh Kenner says in *The Invisible Poet: T. S. Eliot* (1960), 'the bell rang; and the readers of *The Egoist* were left to knaw their knuckles for two months.' Today readers of Eliot's *Selected Essays* (1932; 1951) can proceed without such suspense to the second instalment of the essay, where it is revealed that the analogy is that of the catalyst. The mind of the poet is likened to the shred of platinum, necessary for the poetic reaction, but distanced; promoting change, but remaining itself unchanged. 'The more perfect the artist', Eliot says, 'the more completely separate in him will be the man who suffers and the mind which creates.' The poet's personality is, in James Joyce's phrase, 'refined out of existence' while the creative act is performed. In the language of *Old Possum's Book of Practical Cats* (1939), the artist is like Macavity, the Mystery Cat:

> He always has an alibi, and one or two to spare:
> At whatever time the deed took place – MACAVITY WASN'T THERE!

Eliot's distinction between suffering man and creating mind has had a valuable corrective influence on the misuses of biography and poet psychology in literary criticism. Like Pound's theorising, it focused attention on the literary object and thus prepared the way for the objectivist methods of so-called 'New Critics'. John Crowe Ransom's (1888–1974) book *The New Criticism* (1941) belatedly gave a name to practices that had been followed for at least a decade and were already diverging away from the close textual scrutiny of Cleanth Brooks (*b*. 1906) into the symbolic and rhetorical approaches of Kenneth Burke (*b*. 1897), the neo-Aristotelian bias of R. S. Crane (*b*. 1886), the moralistic criteria of Yvor Winters (1900–68) and the liberal humanism of Lionel Trilling (1905–75). Eliot broadened his own critical position in 1940 when he wrote of W. B. Yeats's poetic development:

> to have accomplished what Yeats did in the middle and later years is a great and permanent example . . . of what I have called Character of the Artist: a kind of moral, as well as intellectual, excellence.

Here Eliot implies that a poet's developing personal force has a great deal to do with the work he produces, and that 'Character' is not only a legitimate concern of criticism, but possibly the ultimate test. The gap between suffering and creation is narrowing. Eliot's character declares itself from *Prufrock and Other Observations* (1917) to 'Little Gidding' (1942), the last of his *Four Quartets* (1943) and *The Elder Statesman* (1959), the last of his plays. The analogy of the catalyst is a useful way of thinking about the act of making or criticising poetry, but there is no more distinctive voice or personality in modern literature than Eliot's own.

Concern with language is evident early in Eliot's career. A 1920 essay on Swinburne urges respect for language that struggles 'to digest and express new objects, new groups of objects, new feelings, new aspects'; and in 1921 he admires the language of seventeenth-century English metaphysical poets for seeking 'the verbal equivalent for states of mind and feeling'. The spiritual effort of *Four Quartets* coincides with 'the intolerable wrestle/With words and meanings' ('East Coker', II). The poet is himself a J. Alfred Prufrock, admitting that 'It is impossible to say just what I mean'. Words 'strain', 'crack', 'sometimes break', 'decay', 'will not stay in place' ('Burnt Norton', V) and 'last year's words belong to last year's language' ('Little Gidding', II). In the last movement of the last Quartet, 'Little Gidding', Eliot reconciles the attempt to express the here-and-now with the ephemeral condition of truth. Truth is not static, the formulated phrase can be exact only for a moment, and every poem is, therefore, an epitaph; but 'we shall not cease from exploration' under the obligation to try continually for the ideal language:

> An easy commerce of the old and the new,
> The common word exact without vulgarity,
> The formal word precise but not pedantic,
> The complete consort dancing together.

As early as 'The Love Song of J. Alfred Prufrock' the problem of expression is associated in Eliot's work with the theme of alienation. Prufrock realises he is no prince, but the loneliness of his self-mocking soliloquy is as complete as Hamlet's. He neither fits into the genteel society of those whose eyes fix him, like a bug on a pin, 'with a formulated phrase', nor takes his place among the shirt-sleeved solitaries who lean from their windows. The mermaids will not communicate with him, though his own imagination has created them. 'Portrait of a Lady' is about the failure of communication between a woman and a man ironically trapped in his own 'self-possession'. The inhabitants of *The Waste Land* are, for the most part, like the old man of 'Gerontion', who says:

> I have lost my sight, smell, hearing, taste, and touch:
> How should I use them for your closer contact.

The mysterious, presumably sexual failure signified by the Hyacinth garden episode in 'The Burial of the Dead' is associated with an inability to speak. In 'A Game of Chess' failure to communicate underlies the futility of middle-class life. The thunder enjoins sympathy ('Dayadhvam') in Part V, but the outgoing movement of feeling is denied to men and women imprisoned within themselves. 'It isn't that I *want* to be alone', Celia Coplestone tells Sir Henry Harcourt-Reilly in Act II of *The Cocktail Party* (1950), but loneliness is the human condition when absence of shared belief means that speech, at best, is well-intentioned noise. Following Pound's example, Eliot's use of myth and his allusions to European as well as oriental culture are his way of dealing with the problem this poses the modern artist. In the notes for *The Waste Land* he refers the theme of communication to *Appearance and Reality* by the English philosopher, Francis Herbert Bradley, whose work Eliot studied as a graduate student at Harvard: 'my experience falls within my own circle, a circle closed on the outside; and, with all its elements alike, every sphere is opaque to the others which surround it'. Language is a way of attempting to break out of the enclosing circle, but there is no guarantee of success. Toward the end of 'Sweeney Agonistes', Sweeney expresses the dilemma with a comical acceptance that speaks for Eliot himself:

> I gotta use words when I talk to you
> But if you understand or if you don't
> That's nothing to me and nothing to you
> We all gotta do what we gotta do.

The Waste Land's epigraph from the *Satyricon* by the Roman writer Petronius (*d.* AD 66) introduces both Eliot's opening theme and his method for the poem. 'April is the cruellest month' for those who, like the Sibyl, desire death and resist spring. Like the Sibyl in her cave, the detached poet offers 'These fragments' (V), a sequence of scenes, allusions, legendary association, quotations from English, German, French, Italian and Sanskrit, which the reader is left to organise into meaning. The method did not impress Wyndham Lewis, who dismissed the poem as a 'cross word puzzle of synthetic literary chronology, of spurious verbal algebra'. The clue to Eliot's puzzle is that his 'algebra' is not spurious but symbolic in the manner of Laforgue, Mallarmé and other French *symbolistes*. It is also urban. Not only are the types and symbols those of Baudelaire's ghost-inhabited 'Fourmillante cité, cité pleine de rêves' ('Swarming city, city full of dreams'), but the cinematic technique of the poem answers exactly to Ezra Pound's idea of poetry that belongs to the city intellect. Pound defined this poetry in a review of Jean Cocteau's *Poésies, 1917–1920*, printed in the January 1921 issue of *The Dial*. 'The life of a village is narrative', Pound wrote, but, 'In a city the visual impressions succeed each other, overlap, overcross, they are cinematographic'. What Pound referred to as his 'Caesarean Operation' on Eliot's original manuscript both compressed the work and sharpened its features as a poem of the city intellect. It would be an act of violence against the final form of *The Waste Land* to attempt to press it into a narrative treatment of the ideas Eliot found in Jessie L. Weston's *From Ritual to Romance* or in Sir James Frazer's *The Golden Bough*. The Tarot pack, the Holy Grail and the myths of Frazer provide a polysemantic framework of resonances and motifs, but not, in any sense, a 'story'.

The quest for the Grail is an archetypal western expression of the search for value, self-knowledge and redemption. Modern man's alienation from his own nature and from spiritual value is related to his failure in this search by *The Waste Land*'s echoes, often parodic, of the Grail quester's journey. This is one motif by which Eliot convenes the poem's meanings in composite images and scenes. In 'The Burial of the Dead' the habit of escape, as well as insomnia, is implied by 'I read much of the night and go south in the winter'. The allusions to Wagner's *Tristan und Isolde* refer to several journeys associated with disunion, treachery and death, and, still in Part I, there is the routine, aimless journey of the crowd flowing over London Bridge. To the hysterical question of the anonymous woman in Part II, 'What shall we do tomorrow?' the speaker answers, at least in thought, 'The hot water at ten,/ And if it rains, a closed car at four', implying the customary wash and shave to be ready for a day whose only foreseeable activity is the purposeless journey of a drive in the rain. Journeys in Part III are connected with sexual futility. One leads to the seduction scene between the 'young man carbuncular' and the 'indifferent' typist (contrasted with Oliver Goldsmith's very different song of Olivia in *The Vicar of Wakefield*, sung when she returns to the place where she was seduced: 'Where lovely woman stoops to folly . . .'). Queen Elizabeth and Lord Robert Dudley, the Earl of Leicester, journey down the Thames in sterile magnificence (contrasted with the modern coupling in the canoe). The sea change of Phlebas the Phoenician in Part IV is a journey into decomposition without prospect of resurrection. In Part V the scene recalls the desert of Part I as the poem journeys through an arid, decayed land that expresses both natural and human hostility. Eliot quickly builds up tension through repetition: as nerves are ready to crack with heat and desperation, he modulates the verse to the softer anguish of exhaustion. By the way of the journey to Emmaus, to which Eliot's note refers, 'the third who walks always beside you' is Christ the risen God, the bloom from the corpse Stetson planted in his garden in Part I, the healed king. He remains unrecognised, unidentifiable by eyes not in a state of grace. The land, therefore, remains waste.

The alienation of man from religious and moral value is often expressed in Eliot's work by an ironic juxtaposition of past and present. At the beginning of 'The Fire Sermon' the line from Spenser's 'Prothalamion' – 'Sweet Thames run softly till I end my song' – makes an ironic comparison between Spenser's bridal ceremony and the promiscuity of modern sexual behaviour. The river is empty even of the trashy modern equivalents of bridal petals; there is nothing to indicate any genuine relationship between the twentieth-century 'nymphs' and the smart young 'heirs of city directors'. Any such encounter is as casual as the word 'loitering' suggests. The Thames still flows, but Spenser's world of ritual and married love is as directly opposed to the present scene as Sweeney and Mrs Porter are contrasted with Actaeon and Diana. Moments like this echo Pound's bark of contempt in 'Canto VII':

> 'Beer-bottle on the statue's pediment!
> 'That, Fritz, is the era, to-day against the past,
> 'Contemporary'.

More frequently, however, Eliot implies a continuity of past and present. Although Sweeney's sleaziness in 'Sweeney Among the Nightingales' is a contrast to the grandeur that tempered Agamemnon's crimes, the two men are aligned in the common shame of their abuse of women. (Sweeney is among prostitutes; Agamemnon nearly sacrificed his daughter Iphigenia to appease the wrath of Diana, whose stag he had killed.) The woman in the elaborate boudoir at the beginning of 'A Game of Chess' may contrast with the Cleopatra described by Enobarbus in *Antony and Cleopatra* (II, ii, 190 ff.), but she is also continuous with Cleopatra in her self-indulgence (as Prufrock is continuous with Hamlet in his excruciating self-awareness). 'All the women are one woman', Eliot says in his notes: the rape of Philomel is not today's news, but it is part of the present:

> And still she cried, and still the world pursues,
> 'Jug Jug' to dirty ears.

Those undone by death in 'The Burial of the Dead' are continuous with the damned in Cantos III and IV of Dante's *Inferno*. The land, therefore, is laid waste by a condition that has its roots in a past that displays symptoms of the modern situation, auguries of the 'beer bottle' as well as 'the statue's pediment'.

The affirmation of the triple blessing in Sanskrit with which *The Waste Land* ends suggests that 'the peace that passeth understanding' may be granted those who are willing to appraise themselves as meticulously as the poem diagnoses the *malaise* of the modern era. The benediction was prophetic, too. Peace awaited the expatriate Eliot himself, in the new dispensation of the Anglican church which he joined in 1927. In the same year he became a British citizen. Ahead lay his directorship of the publishing house of Faber & Faber, the measured affirmations of *Four Quartets*, the Nobel Prize for Literature in 1948, correspondence with Groucho Marx, and in 1957, ten years after the death of his first wife, a happy marriage to Valerie Fletcher.

Hart Crane

The paradox of Hart Crane is that he sought to affirm life in his poetry, but at the age of thirty-two found his own life intolerable and committed suicide. His candy-manufacturing father, hostile to poetry, was chiefly responsible for the unhappiness of Crane's Ohio childhood. Refusing to capitulate to his father's plans to make a businessman of him, Crane was permanently scarred both by the consequent breach with his father and by his parents' eventual separation. Travel showed him the exotic attractions of Cuba and the Caribbean, the lure of Paris and the excitement of New York where, after spells in an assortment of jobs – riveter, clerk, advertising copywriter, reporter – he settled in 1922. He came under the spell of T. S. Eliot's poetry, and studied Donne, the Elizabethans and contemporary continental poets, particularly Laforgue, Baudelaire and Rimbaud. His first collection of poems, *White Buildings* (1926), best-known for 'Black Tambourine', 'At Melville's Tomb' and the sequence of 'Voyages', earned the respect of fellow-poets, but it was the publication of *The Bridge* in 1930 which brought him wider recognition as a new voice in American poetry, leading to the award in 1931 of a Guggenheim Fellowship to Mexico, where he intended to write a long poem about Montezuma and the history of Mexico. Failing to produce the proposed epic, and apparently believing that sexual and alcoholic excesses had burned out his artistic powers, he vanished into the sea on 27 April 1932, from the stern of the ship on which he was returning from Mexico. The affirming hand of Walt Whitman had let go, despite the heartfelt apostrophe of 'Cape Hatteras' (*The Bridge*, IV):

> Yes, Walt
> Afoot again, and onward without halt, –
> Not soon, nor suddenly, – No never to let go
> My hand
> in yours
> Walt Whitman –
> so –

Repudiating the depersonalising aspects of mechanised modern society, Crane was simultaneously fascinated by the machine as symbol, technology as a form of poetry. His verse is best approached in terms of his love of music and of language. The epigraph for 'Atlantis', Part VIII of *The Bridge*, is taken from Plato: 'Music is then the knowledge of that which relates to love in harmony and system'. Crane's poetic enterprise is to harmonise the disparate elements of life in verse which often gives precedence to musical or textural effects over paraphrasable meaning. The opening lines of 'Atlantis', a hymn to the Brooklyn Bridge that provided his greatest inspiration, exemplify Crane's intense lyricism in its most lucid vein:

> Through the bound cable strands, the arching path
> Upward, veering with light, the flight of strings, –
> Taut miles of shuttling moonlight syncopate
> The whispered rush, telepathy of wires.
> Up the index of night, granite and steel –
> Transparent meshes – fleckless the gleaming staves –
> Sibylline voices flicker, waveringly stream
> As though a god were issue of the strings . . .

In the best-known of Crane's short poems, 'At Melville's Tomb', the sea is a symbol of reconciling peace and the implication is that it provides the state of rest earned by Melville's toil both as seaman and writer. There are portentous images of 'drowned men's bones' and 'wrecks . . . without sound of bells', but the time for Melville's ardent questing is over:

> Compass, quadrant and sextant contrive
> No further tides . . . High in the azure steeps
> Monody shall not awake the mariner.
> This fabulous shadow only the sea keeps.

The language of 'For the Marriage of Faustus and Helen' makes almost impossible demands on the reader. The poem assaults the mind with images in packed, clamorous lines that often seem connected only by the fact that they are printed in sequence. This is verse which assumes in the reader a capacity to enjoy sheer linguistic vigour. Its special energy of diction foreshadows the linguistic brilliance to be found, for example, in the earlier work of the contemporary poet, John Ashbery (*b*. 1927). The poem transposes into modern terms the marriage of Faust and Helen in the second part of Goethe's *Faust* and, like *The Bridge*, denies what Crane saw as the pessimism of Eliot's *The Waste Land* by discovering hope in twentieth-century urban life. Crane's *Letters* (ed. Brom Weber, 1965) reveal that Faustus is intended as 'the symbol of myself, the poetic or imaginative man' and Helen as a symbol of an 'abstract "sense of beauty . . ."'. Helen's beauty is fleshly and sensual – in phase with an age of materialism and commerce – and Crane wishes to suggest the possibility of its refinement towards the purely abstract and imaginative. In the first section of the poem Faustus imagines being 'lost yet poised in traffic', presumably in a streetcar, and finding Helen's 'eyes across an aisle'. Part II evokes an atmosphere of dance-hall jazz, suggesting a sensual union that lasts, presumably, until dawn:

> A thousand light shrugs balance us
> Through snarling hails of melody.
> White shadows slip across the floor
> Splayed like cards from a loose hand;
> Rhythmic ellipses lead into canters
> Until somewhere a rooster banters.

In Part III, which Crane called 'the ecstasy', the lovers are imagined as pilots who bring 'speediest destruction' on the everyday world beneath them, but who climb together to 'cities of the air'. Recognising the spiritual possibilities afforded by the imagination, Faust (or the poet) enjoins Helen, and the reader, to rejoice in the redemptive power of the mind:

> Distinctly praise the years, whose volatile
> Blamed bleeding hands extend and thresh the height
> The imagination spans beyond despair,
> Outpacing bargain, vocable, and prayer.

The Bridge is Crane's attempt to make a poem from 'the Myth of America'. Although it is no more a conventional narrative poem than *The Waste Land*, and therefore cannot be regarded as an epic in the traditional sense, it is, as Crane defined it, 'a symphony with an epic theme'. The complexities of the work are unified by the dominant symbol of Brooklyn Bridge, which is at once the triumphant actual structure that joins islands and permits the flow of humanity, and a symbol of human vision and aspiration. It is a miracle of creation whose meaning is far beyond utilitarian design or the labour of construction ('How could mere toil align the choiring strings!'). In Part VII, 'The Tunnel', the poet imagines meeting the ghost of Poe in a subway:

> And why do I often meet your visage here,
> Your eyes like agate lanterns – on and on
> Below the toothpaste and the dandruff ads?
> – And did their riding eyes light through your side,
> And did their eyes like unwashed platters ride?
> And Death, aloft, – gigantically down
> Probing through you – toward me, O evermore!

While the figure of Poe focuses Crane's awareness of the nightmare aspects of modern life and their pedigree in American culture, other sections of the poem also refer to negative forces, at work in history from Columbus's intimations of death, fear and cruelty even as he discovers the New World in 'Ave Maria', through the fog and morning racket of 'Harbour Dawn' and the brute 'whizz' of the train in 'The River' in Part II, to images of war in 'Cape Hatteras' ('War's fiery kennel'; 'rancorous grenades').

These concessions to a dark view of the evolution of modern America are no match for the irrepressibly affirming spirit symbolised by the bridge, a 'steeled cognizance' which mystically includes the wonder felt by Columbus (Part I), the beauty and innocence of Pocahontas (Part II), the drunk man's sense of past grandeur

(Part III), the creative genius and bravery of the Wright brothers (Part IV) and the sanctity that is to be found in a jaunty city secretary (Part V: 'Virginia'). If 'Quaker Hill' (Part VI) suggests that America may still be the 'Promised Land' only to the 'persuasive suburban land agent', 'The Tunnel' brings the subway train up from its dive under the River Hudson, and Part VIII, 'Atlantis', returns to the affirming majesty of that 'One Song, one Bridge of Fire' by which Crane has sought to encompass the history of his country and to assert a specifically modern promise of hope for the future, the union of Faust and Helen in the twentieth century.

e. e. cummings

The dramatic typography of e. e. cummings's indefatigably humorous poems is often so integral to their meaning that much of his poetry cannot be read aloud without substantial loss of sense. In the volume entitled & (1925), for example, a poem beginning 'i will be / M o ving in the Street of her / body' conveys the sense of a lover's excitement in terms of the flight of pigeons:

                    l oo k–
             pigeons fly ingand

   whee(:are,SpRiN,k,LiNg an in-stant with sunLight
   then)l–
   ing all go BlacK wh-eel-ing

The pictorial scattering of letters, with the mixture of upper and lower case printing, suggests the visual effect of the sun's rays on the birds. The parenthesis that separates 'whee' from the 'l' that completes the word indicates that the bracketed words are simultaneous with the birds' wheeling action. In 'here's a little mouse', from the collection *is 5* (1926), the poet contemplates a mouse 'gr(o o)ving the Room's Silence' until it disappears into its hole:

                 tail frisks)
                     (gonE)

Here the opposed curves of the first two brackets depict the movement of the frisking tail, the concluding pair of brackets suggests the enclosure of the mouse-hole, and the upper-case 'E' voices the departing mouse's squeak.

Some of cummings's early poems from *Tulips and Chimneys* (1923) are much anthologised, such as 'in Just –' with its whistling balloonman presiding over a 'mud-luscious' and 'puddle-wonderful' spring for children; 'Buffalo Bill's', which commemorates the death of a legend and sarcastically apostrophises death itself; 'the Cambridge ladies who live in furnished souls', a sonnet condemning the stereotyped, comfortable lives of conformists insensitive to the vitality that lies beyond their smug fulfilment in Christ, Longfellow and local gossip. 'O sweet spontaneous' rejoices in the earth's capacity to answer the abstractions of 'prurient philosophers' and the pressures of science and religion with the simple fact of spring. *50 poems* (1940) is best known for 'anyone lived in a pretty how town', which exemplifies the later style in which cummings solidifies language by using many parts of speech as nouns. The poem sets vital people ('anyone' and 'noone') against those who lead lives of plodding conformity ('they sowed their isn't they reaped their same') in a nursery-rhyme rhythm which implies that false 'adult' values as well as conventional syntax are healthily dislocated by this uncontaminated freshness of perception. Style and manner do, at times, result in sentimentality, but in many of his love poems cummings's language and angle of vision endow the erotic with the affecting innocence of tentative but delighted discovery, as in 'Sonnets-Actualities XXIV' from *&*:

> . . . i like kissing this and that of you,
> i like, slowly stroking the, shocking fuzz
> of your electric fur, and what-is-it comes
> over parting flesh . . . .And eyes big love-crumbs,
>
> and possibly i like the thrill
>
> of under me you so quite new

Cummings's romantic, even anarchic celebration of wonder from a childlike or unregenerately adolescent perspective alienated many, including the influential critics Yvor Winters and R. P. Blackmur (1904–65). Winters deplored cummings's 'infantile exhibitionism'; in his 'Notes on E. E. Cummings's Language' of 1930, Chapter 6 of *Language as Gesture* (1952), Blackmur judged his treatment of language 'a kind of baby-talk'. As a document against the perversions of totalitarianism, *The Enormous Room* (1922), a surrealistic novel based on cummings's experience of imprisonment in a French concentration camp during the First World War, has always been held in critical esteem, but recognition of his seriousness in poetry was a long time in coming. Few would now deny him his place among the innovative poets of the Modernist period. He is a lyric poet who celebrates love, spring, natural energy and the play of language with true passion, and, with passion just as true, expresses his loathing of death and the living death of conformity. He enjoyed painting as much as, if not more than, poetry, and wished to make poems that achieved the condition of graphic art, to exist as dynamic objects of beauty on the page and in the mind. In the 'Foreword' to *is 5* he suggests the context of things in which his poems should be seen:

> If a poet is anybody, he is somebody to whom things made matter very little – somebody who is obsessed by Making. Like all obsessions, the Making obsession has disadvantages; for instance, my only interest in making money would be to make it. Fortunately, however, I should prefer to make almost anything else, including locomotives and roses. It is with roses and locomotives (not to mention acrobats Spring electricity Coney Island the 4th of July the eyes of mice and Niagara Falls) that my "poems" are competing.

Reality and imagination

In his 'intolerable wrestle' with language Eliot says 'The poetry does not matter' ('East Coker', II). What matters is the organisation of the spirit, and the vision. For Wallace Stevens it is only the poetry that matters, and there is no vision without it. Ironically the special resistance to paraphrase of Steven's poetry has encouraged the impression that he is an unusually philosophical poet. The truth is that he is an unusually poetic one. He studied at Harvard and at the New York Law School, passed his bar examinations in 1904 and was admitted to practice. In 1915 Harriet Monroe's *Poetry* published the first version of 'Sunday Morning'. From 1916 until his death in 1955 he worked for the Hartford (Connecticut) Accident and Indemnity Company. He was a self-proclaimed 'domestic creature' for whom money was 'a kind of poetry', and poetry life's only sanction. The influence of the French symbolists is apparent in his first collection, *Harmonium* (1923), published when he was forty-four. Eight other volumes followed, culminating in *Collected Poems* (1954), and *Opus Posthumous* (1957) which includes two short, stiff plays, miscellaneous prose and 'Adagia', a selection of aphoristic jottings. *The Necessary*

Angel: Essays on Reality and the Imagination (1951) collects seven lectures given between 1942 and 1951.

Matthew Arnold, the nineteenth-century English poet and critic, prophesied a mounting reliance on poetry inversely proportionate to the decline in religion. Wallace Stevens's neo-Arnoldian belief in poetry as the 'Supreme Fiction' is clearly formulated in 'Adagia': 'After one has abandoned belief in god, poetry is that essence which takes its place as life's redemption'. The woman of 'Sunday Morning' is an arena in which the poem's imagery acts out the conflict between tangible secular pleasures that 'dissipate/The holy hush of ancient sacrifice', and the claims of 'that old catastrophe', Christ's crucifixion. The contest results in the conviction that 'Divinity must live within herself'. 'The imperishable bliss' she feels she needs can only be the pleasure in 'an old chaos of the sun' whereby mortal life is a cycle of rich, earthly particulars, endlessly renewed. In 'Asides on the Oboe', God is 'a mirror with a voice', a 'glass man' known without 'external reference'. Each human individual is a unique image in the mirror that 'sums us up' by the infinite facets of 'a million diamonds'. Poetry itself takes the place of 'empty heaven and its hymns', in 'The Man with the Blue Guitar', where green is the colour of the given world, blue the colour of things transmuted by imagination.

> The man bent over his guitar,
> A shearsman of sorts. The day was green.
>
> They said, 'You have a blue guitar,
> You do not play things as they are'.
>
> The man replied, 'Things as they are
> Are changed upon the blue guitar'.

Stevens is a clear case of the modern poet as post-romantic. In 'Tintern Abbey' Wordsworth writes of the 'mighty world of eye and ear' as a product co-operatively made by the objects of the external world and the human faculties of apprehension. Stevens takes the more extreme view of Coleridge's 'Dejection: An Ode':

> O Lady! we receive but what we give,
> And in our life alone does Nature live:
> Ours is her wedding garment, ours her shroud!

Life is what you make it, and the best thing to make it is metaphor. Caution is required, for metaphor, though brilliant, can be as forbidding as the world of 'No Possum, No Sop, No Taters' in which imaginative projection creates a sunless winter landscape in the likeness of human amputation and decay. 'Bad is final' in the light that displays broken stalks that have 'arms without hands' and 'trunks/Without legs, or, for that, without heads'. In the deep, hard January silence, 'Snow sparkles like eyesight falling to earth', and a rusty crow seals the ominous implications of the scene with the bright malice of his eye.

For the observer who does not have 'a mind of winter' ('The Snow Man') things need not be so austere. There is an infinite number of perspectives on the world; there are far more than merely 'Thirteen Ways of Looking at a Blackbird'. The imagination is always in danger of being dulled by 'The malady of the quotidian' as in 'The Man Whose Pharynx Was Bad'. In 'The Comedian as the Letter C' Crispin the mock-hero is left contemplating the 'insoluble lump' of the world, but the poem ends 'benignly' because Crispin's efforts have revealed that there is scope for illuminating, 'plain and common things' by 'fancy' and for making order out of the randomness of life ('Sequestering the fluster of the year'). 'Reality is a cliché from which we escape by metaphor', Stevens says in 'Adagia'. The poetic imagination's power of metaphor makes it 'the necessary angel of earth' ('Angel Surrounded by Paysans'), and the typically angelic act is to create order.

A jar placed in a Tennessee landscape ('Anecdote of the Jar') takes 'dominion everywhere' by virtue of its foreign character in such a context. The surrounding wilderness ceases to be 'slovenly' because it is visually compelled into order by the alien object to which the eye automatically refers other constituents of the scene. 'Earthy Anecdote' renders a forest fire as a 'firecat' that bristles in the way of stampeding buck, forcing them to swerve into symmetrical circles, 'to the right, to the left'. The poet's metaphor re-creates the reality of chaos and panic as a superior reality of balletic energy, perfect timing and simple geometry. 'The mind is the most powerful thing in the world', Stevens says ('Adagia') and adds, 'There is nothing in life except what one thinks of it'. In 'The Idea of Order at Key West' a woman singing by the sea becomes an image of the poet as maker in his 'Blessed rage for order'. For the woman, so for the poet as Wallace Stevens: 'there never was a world for her/Except the one she sang and, singing, made'.

Neither Wallace Stevens nor William Carlos Williams shares the reverence for the past felt by Pound and Eliot. 'The past is not part of the present', Stevens says ('Dutch Graves in Bucks County'), and history renders each era obsolete, 'like a stage-setting that . . . has been taken down and trucked away' ('The Irrational Element in Poetry', in *Opus Posthumous*). Williams is aware of 'The past above, the future below', but his allegiance, like Stevens's, is to 'the present pouring down:/the roar, the roar of the present' (*Paterson*, Book 3). The two poets have little else in common. 'The real is only the base', says Stevens in 'Adagia', 'But it is the base'. To be valuable, however, basic reality must be changed into the ordered sounds and shapes of poetry by the 'blue guitar' of imagination. In *Paterson*, Book 1 Williams explicitly accords objective reality a much higher status; for him it becomes not merely a source of opportunities for poetry, but the medium of thought itself:

> – Say it, no ideas but in things –
> nothing but the blank faces of the houses
> and cylindrical trees
> bent, forked by preconception and accident –
> split, furrowed, creased, mottled, stained –
> secret – into the body of the light!

Williams's determination to be distinctively American in language and mode of perception yields several short free-verse poems of startling clarity, like the famous 'red wheel/barrow' on which 'so much depends', 'Nantucket', 'Spring and All', 'Flowers by the Sea', 'The Yachts', 'The Motor-Barge', 'The Well Disciplined Bargeman' and most of the poems in *Pictures from Breughel* (1962). Attempting to 're-name the things seen', he analyses the special qualities of his own culture with lively insight in the essays of *In the American Grain* (1925). The extended collage of lyricism, vulgate American and dry fact in *Paterson* is less successful. The Black writer Jean Toomer (1894–1967) mixes verse and prose to more telling effect in his experimental *Cane* (1923) in which racial protest is absorbed into a celebration of fundamental human vitality. The verse sections are sometimes over-lush, but Toomer's emphasis on the exotic primitivism of Black sensibility is balanced by his assured control of a flowing prose style at once precise, intellectual and impressionistically free:

Face flowed into her eyes. Flowed in soft cream foam and plaintive ripples, in such a way that wherever your glance may momentarily have rested, it immediately thereafter wavered in the direction of her eyes. The soft suggestion of down slightly darkened, like the shadow of a bird's wing might, the creamy colour of her upper lip.

Williams's technique in *Paterson* is self-defeatingly gesticulant, drawing attention away from the 'things' of the poem; his vision of man as city is clouded by excessive detail. Similarly excesses of manner, sonority and rich language spoil the ruminative Conrad Aiken's (1889–1974) 'exploration of the fragmented ego' and urging of the creative mind in 'Preludes for Memnon' and 'Time in the Rock' (*Selected Poems*, 1961). Nevertheless the articles collected in *Reviewer's ABC* (1958) show Aiken's literary intelligence at work in some of the astutest American criticism of the twentieth century.

The rise of American drama

There was plenty of theatrical activity in America before the late nineteenth century, but little truly indigenous drama. The Hallams, a British acting company, stimulated theatrical interest in Virginia, South Carolina and New York. Calling themselves the 'American Company', they performed mainly English plays but also staged the American Thomas Godfrey's (1736–63) derivative blank-verse tragedy *The Prince of Parthia* (1763). America's first professional playwright William Dunlap (1766–1839) specialised in adapting continental plays for American audiences. James Nelson Barker's (1784–1858) *The Indian Princess*, produced in Philadelphia in 1808, is the first dramatic version of the legend of Pocahontas. John Howard Payne's (1791–1852) *Clari, or the Maid of Milan* (1823) is forgotten but for the heroine's song 'Home Sweet Home'. Romantic comedy and tragedy gave way to melodrama about 1850 when the Irish playwright Dion Boucicault (1820–90) won applause from American audiences with his adaptations of French plays and dramatisations of Dickens's novels as well as with *The Colleen Bawn* (1860), one of many comedies of Irish life.

In the 1920s David Belasco (1859–1931) attempted to develop a drama of social concern by using naturalistic methods of presentation, but the appearance on stage of a 'restaurant or boarding-house' could not disguise the sentimentality of his scripts. Belasco's enduring contribution to the theatre was the romanticised Orient of *Madame Butterfly* (1900), written in collaboration with John L. Long (1861–1927) who had published a story of the same title in the January 1898 issue of *Century* magazine. The Belasco–Long play provided Puccini's librettists with the basis for the famous opera. Musical immortality also awaited *Porgy* (1927), which DuBose

Heyward (1885–1940) with the assistance of his wife Dorothy adapted from his own novel (1925) of Negro life in Charleston, South Carolina. The play ran for 367 performances when the New York 'Theatre Guild' produced it in 1927, and Heyward later wrote the libretto for George Gershwin's (1898–1937) masterpiece, the folk-opera *Porgy and Bess* (1935). Gershwin's work has no equal either in its operatic use of jazz elements or its dramatic integration of ensemble singing, but the history of the American musical is a distinguished one principally because so many gifted practitioners have developed it into a form that combines melody and spectacle with humour and seriousness. Lynn Riggs's (1899–1954) historical 'cowboy' play *Green Grow the Lilacs* (1931) is almost buried under the tunes of the 1943 Rodgers and Hammerstein musical *Oklahoma!*; the vitality of Lerner and Lowe's *My Fair Lady* (1956) supersedes the text of Bernard Shaw's overrated *Pygmalion*. With brilliant choreography by Jerome Robbins, Leonard Bernstein's *West Side Story* (1957) provocatively transposes *Romeo and Juliet* to the context of ethnic gang rivalry in New York. The show's music, lyrics and social comment create a work of art that asserts its own standards of excellence. The sadness and resilience of the Russan Jew are celebrated with tenderness and wit in *Fiddler on the Roof* (1964) which Joseph Stein (*b.* 1912) based on stories by Sholem Aleichem (1859–1916). Stephen Sondheim (*b.* 1930) is incisive about love in *A Little Night Music* (1973) and about the price of progress in *Pacific Overtures* (1976) which uses Kabuki theatrical conventions to trace the history of Japan from the isolated screen-painting nation of 1853 to the present-day 'Floating Kingdom' of technology.

The Theatre Guild of New York became America's leading drama company in the 1920s. In 1931 some of its members followed the writer and director, Harold Clurman (*b.* 1901) and Lee Strasberg, to form The Group Theatre which concentrated on experimental drama of social content, notably Clifford Odets's (1906–63) propagandist *Waiting for Lefty* (1935) about a taxi-drivers' strike, and *Awake and Sing* (1935) about the contest between idealism and practicality in a New York Jewish family. The lively speech of Odets's characters compensates for mechanical plots and themes that now seem trite. Maxwell Anderson (1888–1959) had already succeeded with the realistic comedy of *Saturday's Children* (1927) and the blank-verse historical play *Elizabeth the Queen* (1930) when The Group Theatre staged his less effective *Night over Taos* (1932). Anderson's most impressive work is the verse play, *Winterset* (1935), based on the notorious Sacco–

Vanzetti murder case which provoked a world outcry against American legal procedures, prompted Edna St Vincent Millay to write her poem 'Justice Denied in Massachusetts' (1927), and Ben Shahn (1898–1969) to paint his series *The Passion of Sacco and Vanzetti* (1961). Anderson's last play *The Bad Seed* (1955) examines the phenomenon of evil in the character of a child. Like Anderson, Elmer Rice (1892–1967) experimented with styles. *The Adding Machine* (1923) uses expressionistic techniques of fantasy and symbolism to satirise the machine age's reduction of human individuals to 'waste product'. In *Street Scene* (1929) Rice's objective presentation of slum life, complete with realistic sound effects, culminates in a double murder. Thornton Wilder (1897–1975) had reached a wide public with his novel, *The Bridge of San Luis Rey* (1927), about people killed in a South American bridge disaster; he maintained his popularity with the play *Our Town* (1938) which dispenses with scenery and uses the Chinese theatrical convention of the property man as narrator. The play deftly evokes the life of Grover's Corners, a small town in New Hampshire. In the satirical fantasy *The Skin of Our Teeth* (1942) Wilder comments amusingly on man's ability to dodge ultimate catastrophe.

O'Neill

Eugene O'Neill (1888–1953), son of the actor James O'Neill, was the dominant American playwright during his own lifetime and remains a leading figure in the history of drama. When the production of *Bound East for Cardiff* (1916) took him into association with the Provincetown Players he had already been suspended from Princeton for 'general hell-raising', married and divorced, gone to sea, lived as a waterfront vagabond and spent a year in a tuberculosis sanatorium. 'Keep your eye on life', the drama critic Clayton Hamilton (1881–1946) told him in 1914, 'on life as you have seen it; and to hell with the rest.' The young playwright's already colourful career provided him with an abundance of life; but Ibsen, Shaw, Strindberg, Jack London and Joseph Conrad helped him to select and form its usable content for the theatre. The facts of O'Neill's life are deployed in the sanatorium of *The Straw* (1921), the symbolic sea of *Anna Christie* (1921) and the realistic atmosphere of Harry Hope's symbolic bar in *The Iceman Cometh* (1946). The 'four haunted Tyrones', whose recriminatory *Long Day's Journey into Night* (1956) proved O'Neill's masterpiece, are the playwright himself, his

father, mother and elder brother. There are elements of himself in
at least half of O'Neill's fifty-one surviving manuscripts, but his
work is only superficially autobiographical. Its recurrent project is
to find some connection between the self and mankind, between
man and God or the 'life force', and to express it in theatrical terms.
To this end O'Neill dissolved his life in his work as completely as
the identity of Edmund Tyrone is 'dissolved in the sea'.

O'Neill was a man of the theatre, committed to the medium.
Carlotta Monterey, his third wife, said he could feel 'real love' only
for his plays. His major subject matter is the tension-ridden family,
his major theme the power of illusion. They are both present in
Beyond the Horizon (1920), but it was by way of the theatrical vitality
and technical daring of *The Emperor Jones* (1920), *The Hairy Ape*
(1922) and *The Great God Brown* (1926) that he arrived at the
consummation of *Long Day's Journey into Night* in which the external
and internal facts of his own life are fused to create the greatest of
American confessionals. *The Hairy Ape* mixes realism and
expressionism contrapuntally. The two modes are implicit in the
first scene and give O'Neill the latitude he needs to penetrate to the
conclusion by way of a visual pun on Rodin's 'Thinker'. Yank's
descent from the illusion of his self-possession to caged, simian
bestiality implies that this is all the knowledge permitted him by his
fellow-man or fellow-ape. Man lives by illusion, dies by reality in
The Iceman Cometh. When Theodore Hickman (Hickey) is stripped
of his image as the gladhanding travelling salesman who has left
his wife with the iceman, and stands revealed as a murderer, the
iceman becomes death, life itself an illusion. Larry Slade sums up
the moral of the play:

> To hell with the truth! As the history of the world proves, the truth has
> no bearing on anything. It's irrelevant and immaterial, as the lawyers
> say. The lie of a pipe dream is what gives life to the whole misbegotten
> mad lot of us, drunk or sober.

A Moon for the Misbegotten was written in 1943, four years after
O'Neill completed the manuscript of *The Iceman Cometh*. The later
play answers Larry Slade by showing characters whose need for
truth is so intense that, in a good production, it even burns away
the sentimentality of O'Neill's plot. The virginal Josie Hogan passes
herself off as a slut to disguise her fear that no man could desire
her. Her act does not deceive the debauched James Tyrone, jun., a
part-time actor modelled on O'Neill's brother. He is drawn to Josie's

discernible innocence and, in a fervent, self-lacerating monologue, casts off his own image as the godless roisterer. He had accompanied his mother's coffin on a train journey across America. Neither liquor nor repeatedly making love to a fat woman 'with the face of a baby doll' in the compartment next to his dead mother could erase the pain of his loss. At the end of the play Josie, true to her nature, cradles Tyrone, absolving him of the failings that define him. If a plot like this seems to attract a Freudian approach to O'Neill's work, there is a caution in a letter from O'Neill to Barrett H. Clark, his first biographer, complaining about critics who saw his plays as Freudian case histories:

> . . . they read too damn much Freud into stuff that could very well have been written exactly as it is before psychoanalysis was ever heard of. Imagine the Freudian bias that would be read into Stendhal, Balzac, Strindberg, Dostoievsky, etc. if they were writing today! . . . Jung is the only one of the lot who interests me. Some of his suggestions I find extraordinarily illuminating in the light of my own experience with hidden human motives.

O'Neill experiments with a wide range of techniques from the symbolic jungle and silver bullet of *The Emperor Jones* to the use of masks in *Lazarus Laughed* (1927). The murder of Ezra Mannon by his wife Christine in *Mourning Becomes Electra* (1931) initiates a New England version of the fall of the house of Atreus as told by Aeschylus in the *Oresteia*. By exerting such innovative pressure on theatrical conventions, O'Neill advanced American dramatic consciousness by at least a generation and sustained his own interest in the possibilities of the stage. These were both considerable achievements even if much of his work now looks dated. Denunciation of American materialism in *The Great God Brown* becomes confused by the play's symbolic devices, and a similar theme is crowded out by oriental decoration in *Marco Millions* (1927). By the time he was ready for *Long Day's Journey into Night* O'Neill was sure-footed enough to pare technique down to his undoubted mastery of emotionally charged language. The Tyrones love and torture each other with only the sound of a foghorn outside to remind them that collision with truth can be fatal. In the final moments of the play it is Jamie's sobbing that breaks Tyrone, and it is Jamie who draws from him his only shows of violence and his most bitter sorrow. Over his drunk, unconscious son he says:

> A sweet spectacle for me! My first-born, who I hoped would bear my name in honour and dignity, who showed such brilliant promise!

The playwright's focus had finally swung away from the outer world of action, towards the inner world of intimate conflict. Fatal or not, willingness to impact with truth is the only assurance of honour and dignity.

Realism and protest in the novel

The novel soon emerged as the dominant literary form in twentieth-century America. The proletarian naturalism of James T. Farrell (1904–1979) doggedly charts the representative life and death of a young urban Irishman in the *Studs Lonigan* trilogy (1932–5). John Dos Passos's (1896–1970) ambitious trilogy *U.S.A.* (1930–6) offers a Marxist interpretation of American society by combining Theodore Dreiser's narrative realism with short biographies of contemporary public figures, impressions of current events, 'Newsreels' of news-paper headlines, advertisements, radio broadcasts and 'Camera Eye' views by the author.

John Steinbeck (1902–68) achieved his first popular success with *Tortilla Flat* (1935), a picaresque account of cheerful poverty among Californian *paisanos*. *In Dubious Battle* (1936) proclaims Steinbeck's keen interest in social conditions. While he recognises that capitalism and communism both exploit the individual, his sympathies are with the striking fruit-pickers of his fictitious Torgas Valley and with the men who try to organise them into effective action. The two tragic heroes in *Of Mice and Men* (1937) belong to the same migratory farm-working class. *The Grapes of Wrath* is an elegy for the American Dream, written out of Steinbeck's humanitarian response to the impact of the Depression on ordinary people. America is not God's country but the machine's, and the machine is as unreliable as the Joad's automobile. In a time of widespread hunger the big companies allow fruit to rot because there is insufficient profit to be gained from picking it. The novel's hero is the Joad family as a whole, and its theme is endurance. Driven from their home in the Oklahoma Dust Bowl, the Joads make the arduous trek to the promised land of California. Although the toll is heavy, the family gets through, triumphing over adversity as the turtle survives the truck in Chapter 3. The novel's symbolism is often obtrusive – especially in the resemblance of Jim Casy to Christ – but the lyric momentum gathers early in the story, pressing the narrative on through a single, genuinely epic movement. Given the obstacles set in the Joads' way by the police, strike violence and death, the novel's only implausibility is its optimism. Steinbeck asserts a pseudo-biological faith in the collective power of human organisms to make a sustaining ecology out of recalcitrant materials. None of Steinbeck's later books, including the confused *East of Eden* (1952), approaches the quality of this passionate novel of protest and hope. In 1940 *The Grapes of Wrath* was sensitively filmed by the director John Ford (1895–1973).

Hemingway

Ernest Hemingway (1899–1961) shares neither Steinbeck's optimism nor his social concern. Death is the only incontrovertible reality in Hemingway's world, where anything that might have been meant by 'God' has been replaced by 'nada', the nothingness to which the waiter prays in the short story 'A Clean, Well-Lighted Place':

> Our nada who art in nada, nada be thy name thy kingdom nada thy will be nada in nada as it is in nada . . . Hail nothing full of nothing, nothing is with thee.

Hemingway's nihilism permits an inverted sentimentality. The solitary hero, devoid of illusion, meeting the chaos of the twentieth century with understated bravery, assumes an essentially romantic posture. Frederic Henry in *A Farewell to Arms* (1929), Robert Jordan in *For Whom the Bell Tolls* (1940), Colonel Cantwell in *Across the River and into the Trees* (1950) are all male-chauvinist variations on the figure of the lone, tight-lipped cowboy, riding off into his uncompromising if sunset-tinted solitude. Yet few writers have been so closely identified with the modern age which, like Hemingway's books, is full of violence, death and disillusion, compelling man to devise a method of living significantly in a secular world. The first stage of Hemingway's method of heroism is reached when a man is strong enough to repudiate illusion, as Frederic Henry does in Chapter 27 of *A Farewell to Arms*, by rejecting the words commonly used to disguise the inglorious realities of war:

> There were many words that you could not stand to hear and finally only the names of places had dignity. Certain numbers were the same way and certain dates and these with the names of the places were all you could say and have them mean anything. Abstract words such as glory, honour, courage, or hallow were obscene beside the concrete names of villages, the numbers of roads, the names of rivers, the numbers of regiments, and the dates.

To achieve the second stage of heroism, a man must develop a style that makes him superior to death, life's inevitable 'dirty trick'. Style is the key to Hemingway's life and to the manner and meaning of his work.

In the 1920s, with some guidance from Gertrude Stein and Ezra Pound in Paris, Hemingway developed a spare, factual prose style from the practice of writing action journalism. (See William White's *By-Line: Ernest Hemingway. Selected Articles and Despatches of Four Decades*, 1967). Increasingly obsessed with death, he developed a style of living that made him a modern Byronic legend. He was an ambulance driver in the First World War, a war correspondent in both the Spanish Civil War and the Second World War. Four marriages, African safaris, deep-sea fishing, hunting, boxing and the bull-fighting extolled in *Death in the Afternoon* (1932) were all ways of proving his manhood. He asserted his immunity to death by flirting with it. When the obsession led to such paranoia that he could no longer believe his own act, he re-affirmed his mastery in a last stylistic flourish by killing himself.

The narrator of Hemingway's first novel *The Sun Also Rises* (1926) is Jake Barnes, an American newspaper correspondent. Before the action of the novel begins he has been emasculated by a war wound. His love for the hedonistic Lady Brett Ashley is therefore hopeless. The stoicism with which he confronts the waste land of his life makes him superior to Robert Cohn, a novelist boxer, and to Mike Campbell, a bankrupt alcoholic. He is also superior to the matador, Pedro Romero, whose ceremonial act of death in the bull-ring is fundamentally naïve. Jake's physical wound is less disabling than the spiritual deficiencies of the novel's other characters. Frederic Henry's stoicism in *A Farewell to Arms* is implicit in the style of his prose as it is explicit in his staccato protests against 'them', the faceless powers that kill Aymo 'gratuitously', give Rinaldi syphilis and destroy Catherine and her baby. Robert Jordan's is dramatised at the end of *For Whom the Bell Tolls* when he sacrifices love and life for the sake of the democratic principles which alone define him as an individual in the context of cynicism and chaos. In *The Old Man and the Sea* (1952) the Cuban fisherman Santiago loses his giant marlin to the sharks but is ennobled by the effort in which his gruelling three-day battle with the fish becomes a ritualised contest with the elemental forces of nature. Accepting the consequences of his error in going too far out to sea, the old man is beaten, but not destroyed. He survives, with style. When the boy comes to his shack and sees the upturned palms of the mutilated hands he starts to cry. Some find the book intolerably sentimental; others, moved by the image of an old man whose undefeat makes him commensurate with nature, gladly share the boy's weeping. In 1954 Hemingway was awarded the Nobel Prize for Literature.

The South

H. L. Mencken, author of *The American Language* (1919; *Supplements* in 1945 and 1948), was America's master of invective. His targets included the Ku Klux Klan, the 'booboisie', puritanism Prohibition, censorship and the cultural aridity of the South which he called 'the Sahara of the Bozart'. In 1917, when William Faulkner was twenty, Mencken wrote:

> Alas for the South! her books have grown fewer;
> She never was much given to Literature.

Several writers, born at the turn of the century, soon gave the lie to Mencken, but the literary situation in the South did not look promising in 1917. The shallow convictions and sickly opacities of Sidney Lanier's (1842–81) poetry are not redeemed by his theory, set out in *The Science of English Verse* (1880), that poetry is music. The novels of Thomas Nelson Page gave pleasure to conservative Southerners and their sympathisers. The mannered obscurities of James Branch Cabell's (1879–1958) laboured symbolic morality novels set in the mythical country of 'Poictesme' appealed to few in an era when the preference was for realism. The relative success of *Jurgen* (1919) was largely due to the charge of obscenity levelled against it for a sexual suggestiveness which today looks merely oblique. By the 1930s, however, the South had become the most productive literary region in America. In particular, the novels of William Faulkner and the critical and creative work of the Nashville 'Fugitives' brought about a literary renaissance which ensured the dominance of Southern letters well into the post-Second World War period.

The novels and stories of Ellen Glasgow (1873–1945) reject the 'sanctified fallacies' of the sentimental Southern tradition. In advertisements for her most celebrated novel *Barren Ground* (1925) her publisher used the slogan 'Realism crosses the Potomac'. The novel's heroine, Dorinda Oakley, would be determined, resourceful, 'Pensive, ironic, and infinitely wise' in any region. As Miss Glasgow says in her preface to the 1933 edition, 'Beneath the lights and shadows there is the brooding spirit of place there is the whole movement of life'. Thomas Wolfe (1900–38) writes with 'nakedness and directness' about his home town of Asheville, North Carolina. *Look Homeward, Angel* (1929), the first and best of Wolfe's sprawling autobiographical novels, began as a manuscript of some 800,000 words, but was reduced to a manageable size by Maxwell Perkins (1884–1947) of the publishing firm of Charles Scribners' Sons. Georgia's Erskine Caldwell (*b*. 1903) attracted a wide readership with stories in the mode of Southern 'grotesque', which is carried to a higher power by William Faulkner, Carson McCullers (1917–67) and Flannery O'Connor (1925–64). Caldwell's mixture of sex, violence and rural degeneracy became famous with *Tobacco Road* (1932) and *God's Little Acre* (1933). The dramatised version of *Tobacco Road* ran for seven and a half years on the New York stage. The South provides Eudora Welty (*b*. 1909) with a distinctive setting, but region does not obtrude in her stories of love, initiation and family life from *Delta Autumn* (1946) to *Losing Battles* (1970). Richard Wright (1908–60), the son of a plantation farm-hand, was born near Natchez, Mississippi, and moved to Chicago in 1934. *Native Son* (1940) describes the socially determined career of Bigger Thomas, a Black boy from the infested slums of Chicago's South Side. The book is protest as naturalistic art of harrowing power; as an indictment of white America's inhumanity to Blacks it stands with Faulkner's *Light in August* and Ralph Ellison's *Invisible Man*.

Faulkner

'Tell about the South', Shreve McCannon asks Quentin Compson in Chapter 6 of *Absalom, Absalom!* (1936), 'What's it like there. What do they do there. Why do they live there. Why do they live at all?' As the tragic story of Thomas Sutpen comes to an end in 1910, all that remains of his grand design to found a dynasty is an idiot Negro, Jim Bond, Sutpen's only living descendant, howling like a demented chorus in the ashes of a ruined mansion. The novel has shown what the South is like, what people do, but the only possible answer to Shreve's third question is that people live there because they belong. Belonging, they share Sutpen's enslavement to a hierarchy of values that prefers incest to miscegenation, and denies Blacks human status. Faulkner belonged, all his life, to the South. His works are an attempt to answer the questions he gave Shreve McCannon.

Born in New Albany, Mississippi, Faulkner was brought up in Oxford which, under the name of Jefferson, became the locale for much of his fiction. With his third novel *Sartoris* (1929) he discovered that his own 'little postage stamp of soil was worth writing about', and embarked on the creation of his mythical Yoknapatawpha County. *Sartoris* states, in embryo at least, most of the themes he would develop in a series of works which, thinking of the interconnected novels of Balzac or Proust, he often referred to as 'the book'. There is the influence of past on present, central to *Absalom, Absalom!*; the isolation of the individual, treated more focally in *The Sound and the Fury* (1929) and *Light in August* (1932); the moral decay of the old South, and the erosion of its traditions by the secular values of the modern age. In *Sartoris* modernism is represented by the car Bayard Sartoris drives recklessly along the dusty roads in a frantic effort to exorcise the ghosts of his recently killed twin brother and his long dead great-grandfather by courting what he sees as the redeeming violence of their deaths.

Another facet of modernism, more deadly than the automobile, is embodied in the Snopes family whose chronicle of avarice, perversion and murder occupies Faulkner in the trilogy, *The Hamlet* (1940), *The Town* (1957) and *The Mansion* (1959). (These are good works with which to begin reading Faulkner because of their comparative simplicity of style. 'Barn Burning' the first of *Collected Stories* (1950) functions as a preface to the trilogy.) The Snopeses are 'a seemingly inexhaustible family which for the last ten years had been moving into town in driblets from a small settlement known as Frenchman's Bend'. *Sartoris* refers to Flem, the first Snopes to move to Jefferson and, though sexually impotent, the spiritual father of them all. In the trilogy he cheats and manipulates his neighbours until he controls them all, marries the earth-goddess daughter of his chief victim, swindles a poor farmer with non-existent buried treasure thereby driving him insane, and moves on to Jefferson with his tribe of almost uniformly decadent relatives in tow to corrupt the town. Popeye, the gangster of *Sanctuary* (1931), and the Snopeses are the mechanistic anti-community forces that cause all modern alienations.

Faulkner's humour – in *As I Lay Dying* (1930), or *The Reivers* (1962) – is the joint product of his own shrewd eye and the folk tradition of the south-west. The violence in his work is explicable in terms of the apparent sources of his Southern myth. The poet and critic Allen Tate

(1899–1979) suggests that 'the Greco-Trojan myth (Northerners as the upstart Greeks, Southerners as the older, more civilised Trojans) presented Faulkner ... with a large semi-historical background' against which his characters 'could be projected in more than human dimensions'. The destruction of the old South released hitherto suppressed forces of disorder which were intensified by an army of occupation and the exploitations of the Carpetbaggers, those Northerners who tried to dominate Negro votes in their efforts to gain government positions. An old Southern order of dignity and principle was replaced by cynical materialism. It is not, however, a simple contest between good and evil. The aristocratic leaders of the old South are associated with nobility and bravery, and nearly all the Snopeses are amoral, but the Southern families are stained by the sin of slavery. This great sin, in Faulkner's not so very mystical reckoning, had to be expiated by defeat in the Civil War, the ordeal of Reconstruction and an anguished moral decadence that offers no effective resistance to the onslaught of Snopesism.

Many of Faulkner's fellow-Southerners thought him unacceptable in his attitude to the race problem, but there is nothing militant in the comment he made in 1956. Of the Negro's claim to equality he said: 'His equality is inevitable, an irresistible force, but as I see it you've got to take into consideration human nature, which at times has nothing to do with moral truths. Truth says this and the fact says that. A wise person says "Let's use this fact. Let's obliterate this fact first." To oppose a material fact with a moral truth is silly.' A loftier tone is taken in *Intruder in the Dust* (1948), his most didactic novel. Its hero, the boy Chick Mallison, is horrified by a society that sets law aside when the accused is Black. He is reconciled to his people in Chapter 7 by his uncle, Gavin Stevens, who associates the defence of the modern South against the North with what amounts to a policy of gradualism:

> Someday Lucas Beauchamp can shoot a white man in the back with the same impunity to lynch-rope or gasoline as a white man; in time he will vote anywhen and anywhere a white man can and send his children to the same school anywhere the white man's children go and travel anywhere the white man travels as the white man does it. But it won't be next Tuesday.

The Civil War failed to secure equality for the Negro and legislation is imposed from outside. The South must be converted from within, and man must work within his element, which is time: 'Yesterday and tomorrow are Is: Indivisible: One'.

Both Ike McCaslin in 'The Bear' (*Go Down, Moses*, 1942) and Chick

Mallison learn that they cannot repudiate their own. Ike realises that his pursuit of personal redemption for the sins of his forebears will be meaningless if it separates him from the people of the South who have given him identity, and Chick Mallison associates the same kind of belief with the notion that the South must cure itself. The final emphasis is dangerous in its implication that it might be better to sink together in shame than be forced by someone else to navigate differently, but the moral realism of Faulkner's position is its own defence, and must be seen in the context of his belief in the need for life in true community. The darkness of the tragedy in *Light in August* (1932) derives from the fact that the villain is the white community as a whole. Joe Christmas is racially ambiguous. He refuses to surrender his power of choice by actually choosing to be exclusively either Black or White. Others try to choose for him, and his life, including his killing of Joanna Burden, becomes a series of flights from categorisation. The murder of Miss Burden gives the community its way with him by satisfying the expected formula: a white woman has been raped and killed by a Negro. Definition is thus forced on Christmas after all as a consequence of the act by which he sought to escape it. As Melville's Ahab imposes the demonism of his own perception on the ambiguous white hump of Moby-Dick, so the white community of Jefferson forces Joe Christmas to become all Negro. A scapegoat for the communal racist fear, he is made to carry all the connotations of the word 'black', defined into evil by other people's imposition of evil upon him.

'The only folks in the South who are not lonesome', says the protagonist of Robert Penn Warren's novel *Flood* (1964), 'are the coloured folks . . . That is the heart of the race problem. It is not guilt . . . It is simply that your Southerner is deeply and ambiguously disturbed to have folks around him who are not as lonesome as he is. Especially if they are black folks'. Only the Black folks achieve true, specifically Christian community in *The Sound and the Fury* (1929). Entering, in the first three sections, the minds of the Compson brothers, Benjy the 'idiot', Quentin and Jason, the reader is trapped in three subjectivities which are sealed off from the objective world. In the fourth section Faulkner switches to third person narrative, presenting Dilsey the Negro cook who single-handedly has kept the Compson family precariously together by acting as a buffer to its warring factions. It is Dilsey who possesses the 'spirit capable of compassion and sacrifice and endurance', Faulkner's theme in his Nobel Prize acceptance speech (1950). Through Dilsey the novel reaches its climax. After the hermetic darkness of the brothers' monologues, Easter and the promise of Resurrection, 'the recollection and the blood of the Lamb', are discovered in a Negro church. The congregation's reiterated, ecstatic affirmation, 'Yes, Jesus', is pointed enough; and as they watch the 'worn small rock' of the preacher's body, eloquent in itself, the Negroes are consumed with him by his chanted expression of faith beyond reason, into a community that transcends the need for words.

Faulkner's style is a literary deployment of regional speech characteristics. He is a heightened version of the Southern raconteur sitting on his porch, saying either nothing at all over his bourbon and branch-water or saying everything, in one huge, measured, passionately monotonous and convoluted sentence. *Light in August*, for example, is divided into sentences, paragraphs and chapters, but it is a single expression. The voice begins, 'Sitting beside the road, watching the wagon mount the hill toward her, Lena thinks . . .,' and the voice does not stop, hardly even pauses, until the final return to Lena and her concluding, imperturbable, 'My, my. A body does get around. Here we ain't been coming from Alabama but two months, and now its already Tennessee'. These are the beginning and ending of the single, abundant image to which Faulkner gives the title *Light in August*. In between them there is all the detail, the clash of opposites, the fierce Calvinistic perversions, the violence which contrasts with Lena's pagan innocence, the changes of perspective, the flashbacks. Faulkner's method makes the same point as Eliot's form in *The Waste Land* or Pound's in *The Cantos*. Truth is not a simple case of 'once upon a time', not linear, and, therefore, not something that can be presented in traditional narrative form. It is a matter of cross-references, overlappings, fluidity. As V. K. Ratliff, the itinerant sewing-machine salesman says in *The Town*, 'if it ain't complicated up enough it ain't right'. No reader has understood this better than Conrad Aiken, who describes Faulkner's style as a way of keeping 'the form – and the idea – fluid and unfinished, still in motion, as it were, and unknown, until the dropping into place of the very last syllable'.

The Nashville Fugitives

In *The Fugitive Group, A Literary History* (1959), Louise Cowan describes the Fugitives as 'a quite tangible body of sixteen poets who, having no particular programme, met from 1915 to 1928 for the purpose of reading and discussing their own work'. The sixteen included John Crowe Ransom, Donald Davidson (1893–1967), Allen Tate and Robert Penn Warren. Public awareness of the group's existence was initiated by its magazine *The Fugitive* (1922–5), to which Laura Riding (now Laura [Riding] Jackson) (*b.* 1901) became a frequent contributor (then under the name of Laura Riding Gottschalk). Awarded the magazine's premier prize in 1924 as 'the discovery of the year', and praised for a distinctive idiom 'generally tense with emotion and concerned with profound issues', she was welcomed in March 1925 as 'a regular and participating member' of the group. While it would be wrong to associate Riding with the feminist movement of recent times, one of her poems of 1924, 'Mortal', anticipates the most sensitive aspects of the analytical self-consciousness found in women poets of the 1950s and 1960s. *The Fugitive* printed the poem as follows (Riding revised and shortened the text for her *Collected Poems* in 1938):

> There is a man of me that tills.
> There is a woman of me that reaps.
> One is true
> And one is fair.
> Scarce I know where either are.
>
> But I am seed the man should give
> And I am child the woman should bear
> And I am love
> That cannot find them anywhere.
>
> Father and mother and God and my shadowy ancestry—
> I think there's no way of making anything more than
>   a mortal of me.

Living at a distance from Nashville, Riding was not normally able to participate in the meetings, but took an active, though always independent, interest in the group's fortunes throughout her period as a contributor. The perceptiveness of *The Fugitive*'s estimate of her work may be judged by the review of her *Collected Poems* in *The Kenyon Review*: 'I hope, but hardly believe, that they will be assimilated soon into the general consciousness of literature. The authority, the dignity of truth telling, lost by poetry to science, may gradually be regained'. Although a definitive *Collected Poems* was published in 1980, Riding renounced poetry after 1940 because she believed it deficient in 'probity of word' and inadequate to the task of attaining 'that rightness of word that *is* truth'. She is co-author of

Safe in their Alabas-
ter Chambers -
Untouched by morning -
And untouched by noon -
Sleep the meek mem-
bers of the Resurrection
Rafter of Satin - and
Roof of Stone -

Grand go the Years.
In the Crescent - above
them -
Worlds scoop their Arcs.
And Firmaments - row -
Diadems - drop -
And Doges - surrender
Soundless as Dots,
On a Disc of Snow

1. Emily Dickinson. Facsimile of 'Safe in Their Alabaster Chambers'. (Boston Public
Library).

Leaves of Grass

Including

SANDS AT SEVENTY...*1st Annex*,
GOOD-BYE MY FANCY...*2d Annex*,
A BACKWARD GLANCE O'ER TRAVEL'D ROADS,
and Portrait from Life.

COME, said my Soul,
Such verses for my Body let us write, (for we are one,)
That should I after death invisibly return,
Or, long, long hence, in other spheres,
There to some group of mates the chants resuming,
(Tallying Earth's soil, trees, winds, tumultuous waves,)
Ever with pleas'd smile I may keep on,
Ever and ever yet the verses owning—as, first, I here and now,
Signing for Soul and Body, set to them my name,

Walt Whitman

PHILADELPHIA
DAVID McKAY, PUBLISHER
23 SOUTH NINTH STREET

2. Walt Whitman, *Leaves of Grass*. Facsimile of title page for the 1891–2 edition.

THE

CONFESSION

OF

JEREBOAM O. BEAUCHAMP.

WHO WAS EXECUTED AT FRANKFORT, KY

ON THE 7TH OF JULY, 1826.

FOR THE MURDER OF

Col. Solomon P. Sharp,

A member of the Legislature, and late Attorney General of Ky.

WRITTEN BY HIMSELF,

and containing the only authentic account of the murder, and
the causes which induced it.

TO WHICH IS ADDED,

SOME POETICAL PIECES,

WRITTEN BY

MRS. ANN BEAUCHAMP,

*Who voluntarily put an end to her existence, on the day of the ex-
ecution of her husband, and was buried in the same
grave with him.*

BLOOMFIELD, KY.
PRINTED FOR THE PUBLISHER

1826

3. *Beauchamp's Confession.* Facsimile of title page. Principal document of the
'Kentucky tragedy' — the murder of Sharp by Beauchamp — an incident utilised by
many writers.

4. Grant Wood. 'American Gothic', 1930. (Courtesy of the Art Institute of Chicago, Chicago, Illinois).

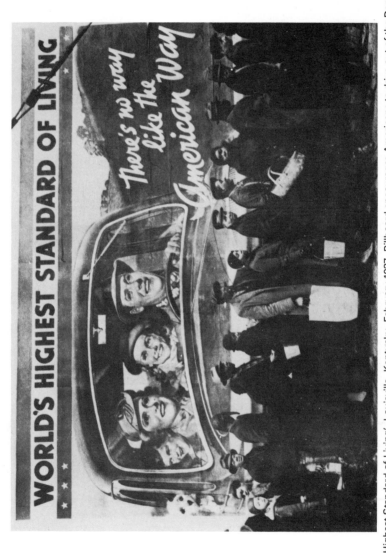

5. 'World's Highest Standard of Living'. Louisville, Kentucky, February 1937. Billboard encourages Americans to drive out of the Depression while blacks queue for flood relief. (Photo by Margaret Bourke-White. Courtesy of *Life*, Time Inc.).

6. 'Rowan Oak', William Faulkner's home near Oxford, Mississippi. (Marshall Walker).

7. 'This is a Pile of Junk'. A disappointed consumer makes his protest at a cross-roads in Georgia, August 1969. (Marshall Walker).

The sign in the image reads:

This is a Pile of Junk!

You Can Get One At Any Chrysler Dealer

8. Lipstick at the Beinecke Research Library. Protest, Ivy League style, by Yale undergraduates. Claes Oldenburg's giant vinyl lipstick signifies contempt for an administration that spent millions of dollars on a library dedicated to graduate research while young soldiers were still fighting in Vietnam. (Marshall Walker).

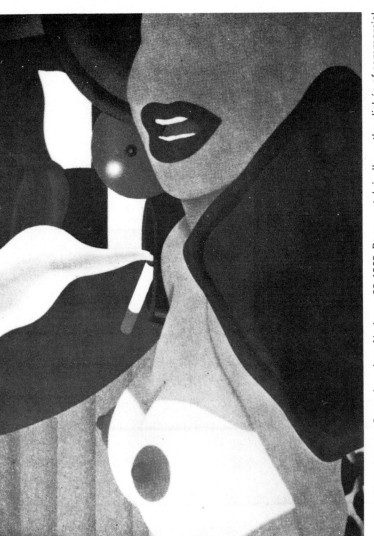

9. Tom Wesselmann, *Great American Nude no. 99*, 1968. Puns nostalgically on the clichés of commercial sex by referring to the soft-porn gloss of much advertising and of magazines like *Playboy*. (Collection Morton G. Newman, Chicago, Illinois).

10. Norman Rockwell. 'A Family Tree' *Saturday Evening Post* cover, October 24, 1959. Rockwell's 'Tree' represents the history of America. The artist perches on a branch at right centre as the prim, disapproving deacon. (Reprinted from *The Saturday Evening Post*, © 1959, The Curtis Publishing Company).

WALDEN;

OR,

LIFE IN THE WOODS.

By HENRY D. THOREAU,

AUTHOR OF "A WEEK ON THE CONCORD AND MERRIMACK RIVERS."

I do not propose to write an ode to dejection, but to brag as lustily as chanticleer in the morning, standing on his roost, if only to wake my neighbors up. — Page 92.

BOSTON:
TICKNOR AND FIELDS.
M DCCC LIV.

11. Thoreau. Title page of first edition, 'Walden'.

12. Frederick E. Church, 'Twilight in the Wilderness', 1860. (Courtesy of Cleveland Museum of Art, Cleveland, Ohio. Mr and Mrs William H. Marlatt Fund).

13. Albert Bierstadt, 'Lake Tahoe', 1868. (Courtesy of Fogg Art Museum, Harvard University, Cambridge, Mass. Gift of Mr and Mrs Frederick H. Curtiss).

14. Norman Rockwell, 'Breaking Home Ties', *Saturday Evening Post* cover, September 25, 1954. Captures the spirit of the early twentieth-century era of expanding opportunity. Father and son sit on the running board of the truck that has brought them from a western ranch to the train depot, where the son will take the train to the State University. The father's hunched position expresses his sense of the loss that already makes him forget the unlit cigarette in his mouth.

15. Birmingham, Alabama, May 1963. Martin Luther King's demonstrators are pressed to the wall by police fire hoses. (Charles Moore. Courtesy of Black Star).

16. The five principal Fugitives, at the Fugitive Reunion, Nashville, Tennessee, May 4, 1956. From left to right: Allen Tate, Merrill Moore, Robert Penn Warren, John Crowe Ransom, Donald Davidson. (Photograph by Rob Roy Purdy).

17. Atlanta, Georgia. Modern Atlanta rises from the red earth of Georgia. This vigorously expanding city illustrates the victory of new styles of architecture over the discredited traditions of the old south. (Marshall Walker).

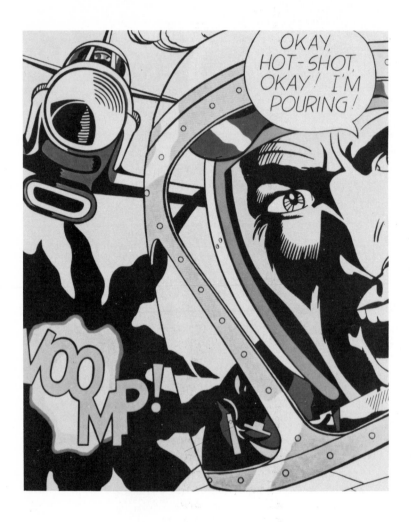

18. Roy Lichtenstein, 'Okay, Hot Shot, Okay', 1963. Comic strip imagery admits and satirises an exuberant fascination with popular images of violence. (Collection R. Morone, Turin, Italy).

A Survey of Modernist Poetry (London 1927; New York 1928) by Laura Riding and Robert Graves.

The first number of *The Fugitive* announced the Fugitives' defection from the cultural stagnation they attributed to 'the high-caste Brahmins of the Old South', but most writers in the group shared a keen sense of the Southern heritage and favoured literary regionalism. Deploring the sovereignty of materialism in modern American life and the alienation it imposed on the artist, they prized the securities of a tradition in an age of dissolving values. Many of the Fugitives became supporters of the Agrarian movement of the 1930s and contributed to the symposium, *I'll Take My Stand* (1930). Modern man's great hope was that he would ultimately enslave nature, but the Agrarians, with John Crowe Ransom in the lead, sought to re-endow nature with an element of terror and inscrutability. In *God Without Thunder: An Unorthodox Defence of Orthodoxy* (1930) Ransom argues that the myth of scientific perfectibility has replaced the mysterious God of the Old Testament by an amiable, understandable God who 'developed popularly out of the Christ of the Old Testament: the embodiment mostly of the principle of social benevolence and physical welfare'. The Nashville Agrarians resisted industrialisation; they sought to put man back into a quasi-Jeffersonian relation to the land, and to give God back his thunder.

As author of *The New Criticism* and editor of *The Kenyon Review* from 1939–59, Ransom became one of America's most respected literary men. The poems he published in *Chills and Fever* (1924) and *Two Gentlemen in Bonds* (1927) are, like 'Dead Boy' and 'Bells for John Whiteside's Daughter', typically short, ironic treatments of the theme of mortality. The influence of Thomas Hardy is clear, but the fastidious voice is Ransom's own. Donald Davidson's poetry is seldom more than competent, but he exerted a strong influence on the others by his personal integrity and devotion to letters as a Professor of English at Vanderbilt University, Alma Mater to several of the Fugitives and Agrarians. Allen Tate introduced the other Fugitives to the work of T. S. Eliot, and raised *The Sewanee Review* to international prominence. He wrote the magnificent poem, 'Ode to the Confederate Dead' (1926), a symbolic meditation on the modern Southerner's sense of emotional distance from his own past, and one spectral, overrated novel, *The Fathers* (1938). Tate's critical elegance and flair for personal mischief were unsurpassed by any of his colleagues, but the most versatile and vigorous of the Fugitives was Robert Penn Warren.

Robert Penn Warren

Warren (*b*. 1905) is a man of letters in the European sense of a writer involved with books and human kind, and at ease in a variety of genres. As a teacher and co-author of the influential textbooks *Understanding Poetry* (1938; fourth edition, 1976), *Understanding Fiction* (1943) and *Modern Rhetoric* (1949) he has been instrumental in raising standards of literary appreciation far beyond the United States. His *Selected Essays* (1958) is one of America's finest and most perennially useful collections of applied criticism. The vitality he has sustained throughout his life of writing is as evident in the energetic rhythms and forthright imagery of *Being Here: Poetry 1977–1980* (1980), as in the metaphysical control of *Eleven Poems on the Same Theme* (1942). Although he now lives in the North, dividing his time between Connecticut and Vermont, he has remained a Southerner revisiting the South to gather material for *Segregation* (1956) and *Who Speaks for the Negro?* (1965). The eternal return is as much a part of his own life as it is of the lives of his characters. Contrary to the message of Thomas Wolfe's *You Can't Go Home Again* (1940), Warren's work insists that you *must* go home again, even if, like the hero-victim of 'The Ballad of Billie Potts' (1944) it is only:

> To ask forgiveness and the patrimony of your crime;
> And kneel in the untutored night as to demand
> What gift-oh, father, father-from that dissevering hand?

At home 'the father waits for the son', and only from the father can the son receive forgiveness, the patrimony of his crime, and the gift of meaning. The Dantesque scheme of *At Heaven's Gate* (1959) projects a group of characters who violate nature. By denying his true father and taking Bogan Murdock as a false father, Jerry Calhoun commits a crucial impiety. Jack Burden, hero of *All the King's Men* (1946), adopts a series of false fathers, the most notable being the demagogue Willie Stark. In *A Place to Come To* (1977) Jed Tewksbury can achieve neither identity nor happiness until he comes to terms with his home town of Dugton, Alabama, and with the despair of the father who, born out of phase with his time, could not understand why the definition of man should be himself 'Setten in a wagon in the middle of the night with a bottle in his hand and looken at a mule's ass'. Invariably the true father is aligned with the truth of the situation. Warren concedes this in an interview of 1974 when he says that the perfect father will act as the reconciler of the world's great contraries, resolving the tension between the idea and the fact, the Emersonian and the Hawthornian. The point where fact and idea coincide is not, he conjectures, in our world: 'But we constantly want to have it in our world and we only find it by finding a new father, I guess, beyond us, beyond this world'. The human condition is one of perpetual quest.

A short poem in *New and Selected Poems: 1923–1985* (1985) begins with the observation that 'The stars are only a backdrop for / The human condition' ('Stargazing'). At the end of the poem Warren reneges against such a naturalistic astronomy:

> The stars
> Love me. I love them. I wish they
> Loved God, too. I truly wish that.

Although he has never subscribed to a religious orthodoxy, Warren early concerned himself with the conflict between naturalism and 'the religious sense'. The Agrarians' attempt to compile a religious, political and aesthetic programme that rejected the modern supremacy of reason was based on the conviction that science and rational philosophy, which flourish by generalisation and abstraction, are not true to the empirical facts of a mixed, mysterious world. Warren is an idealist who knows that he must be empirical in his approach to the 'doubleness of experience' especially as he finds it in 'the irony of history'. 'If poetry is the little myth we make, history is the big myth we live, and in our living, constantly remake' (*Brother to Dragons*, 1953; new version, 1979). Wallace Stevens believes that the past must be consigned to oblivion. Warren disagrees. 'What was *is* is now *was*', he says in 'Rattlesnake Country', and asks, 'But/Is *was* but a word for wisdom, its price?' The setting of *Brother to Dragons* is 'no place' and the time is 'any time', which, he says in the prefatory note, 'is but a whimsical way of saying that the issue that the characters here discuss is, in my view at least, a human constant'.

Of his ten novels, *World Enough and Time* (1950) is the most obviously 'historical'. Based on the 'Kentucky tragedy', (see plate 3) a celebrated murder case of 1825, it tells the story of Jeremiah Beaumont's discovery that, to be human, man cannot live exclusively either in the realm of ideals and abstractions or in the realm of nature. The idea for Warren's best-known novel *All the King's Men* was suggested by more recent history. The career of Willie Stark is based on the life of 'Kingfish' Huey P. Long. Elected Governor of

Louisiana in 1928, and elected to the U.S. Senate in 1930, Long continued to dominate the running of his state until his assassination in 1935. He won his reputation in the early 1920s by realistically addressing the needs of the common people; but by the end of his career he had established what amounted to a dictatorship that depended on a private army of storm troopers and a team of corrupt henchmen.

At the beginning of the novel, Willie Stark is the man of fact whose naturalistic view of life is imaged in Jack Burden's description of the highway to Mason City:

> You look up the highway and it is straight for miles, coming at you, with the black line down the centre coming at you and at you, black and slick and tarry-shining against the white of the slab, and the heat dazzles up from the white slab so that only the black line is clear.

Willie is a follower of the black line, acting according to his interpretation of life in terms of corruption: 'Man is conceived in sin and born in corruption and he passeth from the stink of the didie to the stench of the shroud'. He cannot see the white ground on which the black line is imposed, symbolic of other human possibilities. Mesmerised by his own black abstraction, he finally loses control. At the end he 'tries to turn off the ignition' by giving way to a fatal yearning for absolute good. He is shot and killed by Adam Stanton, the man of virtue who will not allow his moral preserve to be infected by the man of fact. Stanton, too, is killed: Beauty and the Beast are both destroyed by the same dream of simplified life.

In the book-length narrative poem *Brother to Dragons* the Beast is resurgent. Randall Jarrell (1914–65) thought this Warren's 'best book' when it was first published in 1953. The 'new version' of 1979 is better; tauter verse moves the story forward more efficiently and clarifies the poem's philosophical implications. The year 1811 became known as the *Annus Mirabilis* of the west because of a great comet which appeared in the northern sky, floods and earthquakes that shook the Mississippi Valley for months. Against this background Thomas Jefferson's nephew, Lilburne Lewis, aided by his brother Isham, murdered a young Negro slave named George on the Lewis plantation in Livingstone County, Kentucky. The issue which Warren's tormented characters are compelled to discuss, and from which they long to escape, arises when the idealistic Jefferson faces the 'inexpungable error' of being human and the fact of evil represented by the crime of his own nephew. Warren protects his Jefferson from the accusation of naïvety. Although he once thought

man, the 'master-monster', was innocent, Jefferson is allowed to put
the notion of innocence into a defining context:

> I scarcely held that meditation on the nurture of roses
> Is much comfort to a man who has just stepped in dung,
> And philosophy has never raised a crop of hair
> Where the scalping knife has done its scythe-work.

Realising the doubleness of life, Jefferson nevertheless clung to a
belief in man's essential innocence and in his power to redeem
nature according to the 'reserve and glorious frugality' symbolised
by the Maison Carrée ('that Square House') at Nîmes, which stood
in such contrast to the carved 'Beaked visage of unwordable evil' of
the Gothic imagination. Jefferson's first reaction to the bestiality of
his nephew is to lapse into a cynical view of all human ideals. The
purpose of the poem is to compel the imagined author of American
democracy to recognise his spiritual as well as his blood kinship to
Lilburne and to accept that ideal social vision must reach an
accommodation with intransigently messy reality.

Brother to Dragons demonstrates 'the irony of history'. In the shorter
Audubon: A Vision (1969) Warren uses the historical figure of the
great naturalist John James Audubon (1785–1851) to show how
the faculty of imagination enables life to be lived in a world so
characterised. The vision Warren offers is of a world of tension in
which 'human filth' is complemented by 'human hope', bestiality
by beauty, the anguish of self-uncertainty by the imaginative triumph
of self-realisation. This celebration of the imagination is Warren's
answer to 'this century, and moment, of mania'. In Audubon, as in
Brother to Dragons, he writes creative biography. He does so again in
the long narrative poem, Chief Joseph of the Nez Perce (1983), based
on the heroic life of Joseph, Chief of the much abused Nez Perce
Indians of Oregon. In each of these long poems Warren makes from
history – 'the big myth we live' – a story which becomes a 'little
myth' that may help us to live better.

In February 1986 the eighty-year-old Warren was designated
America's first official Poet Laureate. A new law of the previous
year authorised adding the new title to that of Consultant in Poetry
at the Library of Congress. Daniel J. Boorstin, the Librarian of
Congress, chose Warren after discussing the new position with
previous poetry consultants. Boorstin praised Warren for 'his feelings
for the promise and the frustration of American life' and for depicting
in his work 'the comic, the violent and the tawdry as well as the
grand and heroic'.

8

War and post-war

THE isolationism of the Monroe Doctrine, reaffirmed by simple-minded Neutrality Acts in the 1930s, became obsolete on 7 December 1941 when 353 Japanese carrier-borne aircraft made a surprise attack on America's Pacific base at Pearl Harbour, Hawaii. Congress declared war on Japan the following day; Germany and Italy, as Japan's allies, declared war on the United States on 11 December. America's history since then has been one of increasingly intricate global involvement and fluctuating national confidence.

The war strengthened America's influence and economy, but it was soon apparent that mutual distrust between the United States and the Soviet Union would prevent the United Nations Organisation's Security Council from acting as the world's policeman. Under President Harry S. Truman, an attempt was made to substitute economic for military involvement by the Marshall Aid plan for European economic recovery, devised in 1947 by Truman's Secretary of State, General George C. Marshall. When the Russian dominated countries of Eastern Europe rejected Marshall Aid and the Soviets blockaded Berlin in 1948, the lines of Cold War battle were drawn. The North Atlantic Treaty Organisation joined Britain, France, Belgium, the Netherlands, Luxembourg, Portugal, Italy, Denmark, Norway, Iceland, Canada and America in a defensive alliance against the Soviet bloc. The frustrations of the Korean War (1950–3) and America's quixotic support of Chiang Kai-shek were exacerbated by the anti-Communist witch hunts of Wisconsin's Senator Joseph McCarthy and the sabre-rattling of John Foster Dulles who became Secretary of State after General Dwight D. Eisenhower's election to the presidency in 1952.

In 1960 John F. Kennedy's election as the youngest, and first Roman Catholic, President in history ushered in a new period of hope for American liberals. His Civil Rights and social reform programmes were hobbled by opposition in Congress, but his foreign policy was spectacularly successful in reducing international tension. The feeling of disillusionment that followed his assassination in November 1963 was compounded by America's participation in the fifteen-year-long civil war in Vietnam. Some 56,500 American lives were lost in the Vietnam War (1965–73) which aroused greater resentment within the USA than any previous military undertaking in the nation's history. The cease-fire in 1973, American achievements in the exploration of space, and the skilful diplomacy of President Nixon's Secretary of State Henry Kissinger, which enabled the United States to recognise Communist China and promoted détente with the Soviets, helped to deflect attention from domestic problems.

Nixon's triumphant visit of 1972 to Mao Tse-tung in Peking and First Secretary Brezhnev in Moscow brought renewed hopes for world peace, but only two years later the Watergate scandal (1973–4) compelled Nixon to become the first American President to resign from office.

The war in fiction

The Second World War yielded its inevitable crop of novels about men in and out of combat. Although many were written out of direct war experience and with a great sense of urgency, they appear distinctly 'historical' in the nuclear world of today. There is still a terrible immediacy about John Hersey's *Hiroshima* (1946). A chillingly factual account of the first atomic devastation, Hersey's objective report concentrates on the lives of six citizens of Hiroshima to convey the horror of unparalleled human suffering. In *The Wall* (1950) Hersey portrays life in the Warsaw ghetto and the valiant attempt by the Jews to defend themselves against the relentless and well-equipped Nazis sent to destroy them. *The War Lover* (1959) considers the nature of violence by examining the character of an American bomber-pilot. Subtle treatment of human feelings as they are affected by the artificialities of army life makes James Gould Cozzens's (*b.* 1903) *Guard of Honour* (1948) more distinguished fiction than the popular but pretentious study of peace-time aspirations in *By Love Possessed* (1957).

Violence and explicitness account for the popular success of James Jones's (1921–77) long, raw display of undiluted maleness in *From*

Here to Eternity (1951), but the novel's depiction of army life in the months before the Japanese attack on Pearl Harbour is compellingly realistic. The chaos of war provides Jones with a context for a persuasively modern hero trapped in the confusions of a naturalistic world that he can neither 'stomach nor understand nor explain nor change'. None of Jones's subsequent war novels – *The Pistol* (1959), *The Thin Red Line* (1962) or *The Whistle* (1978) – achieves the rough grandeur of his first book although, in all of them, there is a raw note of authenticity in the portrayal of men processed by war into brutality, defeat or heroism. (Jones lived through many of the experiences upon which his novels are based. As an enlisted man in the Regular Army, he was at Pearl Harbour on 7 December 1941. As a corporal with the 25th – 'Tropic Lightning' – Division, he was hit by shrapnel at Guadalcanal, and remembered, to his pride, as he made his way to an aid station, 'to toss my full canteen of water to one of the men from headquarters lying there'.)

If Jones is a one-book writer, he is a phenomenon worth considering chiefly because his problem seems to have been a life-long ambition to model himself on Hemingway, thereby providing an object lesson in what the Hemingway cult of manly virtue has meant to American letters. (Would Norman Mailer (*b.* 1923), for example, have so assiduously courted notoriety and fostered his tough-guy image if Hemingway had not shown the way?) In *Go to the Widow-Maker* (1967) one of the characters, with the help of alcohol, sees himself as a heroic subject for comment by 'old Hemingway'. The book is a post-Hemingway dream in which muscular men couple with beautiful, boyish girls, in a male world of deep-sea diving, spear-fishing, shark-slaughter and basic rejection of the female. The precedent is evidently Hemingway's last, sadly self-parodying, Caribbean period. At the end of his novel, Jones attempts an analysis. The men in his story, in their feats of aggression, of risk and endurance, daring each other to exaggeratedly 'manly' exploits, are merely boys, competing with their fathers: 'It becomes important to be brave. It is more important to them to be brave than to be anything. Only by being brave can they be what they think – hope – is manly, a man'. Unfortunately this comes too late to redeem a book in which Jones's determination to write 'naturally', without an inhibiting regard for something as lonely and difficult as craftsmanship, is all too obvious.

Herman Wouk's most ambitious project is the Second World War story told in *The Winds of War* (1971) and its sequel, *War and*

Remembrance (1978), in which the Pacific theatre of war is set against vivid depictions of the Holocaust. Wouk, however, like Jones, will probably be remembered as a one-book writer. The book is *The Caine Mutiny* (1951) which won its author the Pulitzer prize for fiction. In Britain its reception was diminished by the popularity of *The Cruel Sea*, a novel by the British writer, Nicholas Monsarrat, which was published in the same year. Although *The Cruel Sea* deserved its success as a sensitive, graphic and panoramic account of the war at sea, it seems likely that Wouk's novel will prove with time to have been the more substantial achievement. The story of cruelty and cowardice on a minesweeper in the Pacific is given focus by the portrait of Captain Philip Queeg, the effects on the crew of his mental breakdown and the associated initiation and development of Midshipman Willie Keith. The film, produced by Stanley Kramer and released in 1954, gave Humphrey Bogart as the paranoid Queeg, an opportunity for one of his finest performances.

Norman Mailer's *The Naked and the Dead* (1948) is a more documentary account than Jones's of men living in the unnatural condition of war. Mailer's method is to create a microcosm of various representative American males. Conducting them through the war, he uses flashbacks to develop his characters and to expose the false sense of purpose the experience of war often imparts to inadequate lives. War is revealed as a grosser expression of peacetime futilities: a psychopathic American general sends thirteen soldiers on an attack which is bound to fail. Mailer's documentary style and sharp observation prevent the book from being merely depressing. As in Joseph Heller's *Catch-22*, where calculated glimpses of the dying Snowden break into the absurdist narrative like subliminal warnings of the horror only to be revealed some twenty pages before the end, there is a continual sense of the author's manipulative presence in Mailer's novel, urging the reader to reject stereotyped attitudes to war and to see it simply as waste. The American laureate of war's ironic and hideous detail is, however, the poet Randall Jarrell, who did not see active service. His much-anthologised 'The Death of the Ball Turret Gunner' takes only five lines to carry a man from the life-giving womb of his mother to the deadly one of war: 'When I died they washed me out of the turret with a hose'. The flat diction of 'Losses' is a wail of desolation:

> In bombers named for girls, we burned
> The cities we had learned about in school –

Till our lives were out; our bodies lay among
The people we had killed and never seen.

William Faulkner's *A Fable* (1954), set in France shortly before the end of the First World War, uses an allegory of the passion of Christ to reveal modern man's abandonment of individual moral responsibility in favour of submission to power and system. Despite brilliantly evocative passages, the book bogs down in its own wordiness. No more dauntingly prophetic fiction has emerged from the war than *The Cannibal* (1949) by the experimental novelist John Hawkes (*b*. 1925). The self-savouring, rather archaic style of Hawkes's more recent novels – *Second Skin* (1964), *The Blood Oranges* (1971), *The Passion Artist* (1980) and *Virginie: Her Two Lives* (1982) – has gained him a reputation for possessing a hyper-aesthetic imagination, but *The Cannibal* is an arresting, credible fable of the future in which the intellectual confusion of Western culture leaves a vacuum to be occupied by the political 'certitude' of a new Hitler and the nightmare of a third world war.

Civilian themes in the pre-war generation of novelists

Civilian themes of money, sex and social position occupy John O'Hara (1905–70) from his excellent, bitter first novel *Appointment in Samarra* (1934) to the attenuated realism of *Ten North Frederick* (1955) and *From the Terrace* (1958). O'Hara's writing benefits from the limitations imposed by the short story or novella as in the three stories included in *Sermons and Soda Water* (1961). *Pal Joey* (1940) follows the example of Damon Runyon (1884–1946) whose New York, suspended in the perpetual present tense of his gangsters, wise guys and curvaceous dolls, might well have included O'Hara's unscrupulous night-club entertainer.

Like O'Hara and the John P. Marquand (1893–1960) of *The Late George Apley* (1937), Louis Auchincloss (*b*. 1917) is fascinated by class. In short stories and novels of manners that benefit from his own experience of legal practice among the upper circles of New York, he ponders the neuroses of success and the absurdities of the very rich. His social atmospheres are like those of Henry James or Edith Wharton but his prose is plainer. *Powers of Attorney* (1963) and *The Partners* (1974) are both collections of interrelated stories about characters involved with the law. *The Rector of Justin* (1964) is a searching inquiry into the power exercised by a dominant New England headmaster. *The Dark Lady* (1977) coolly satirises the nationally worshipped trinity of wealth, fame and political power in an influential fashion editor's scheming on behalf of a protégée who beats her at her own game. Characteristic elegance of plot is the distinguishing feature of *The Book Class* (1984). Twelve women meet once a month between 1908 and 1972 to discuss a book. Besides books they value their names, their families and their own image of poise. When the architect Chester Bannard seems likely to abscond with the wife of a client, his wife, Justine, talks to the client. The strategy is simple and effective. 'Our job is to strip their fantasy of its glamour', Justine says, 'The first thing is to remove its illegality. They must feel free to marry'. The wayward spouses are accordingly offered freedom with allowances, decline the gambit, and, at least superficially, are re-absorbed into the cool, mannered world of middle-class respectability.

John Cheever

The world of John Cheever's fiction is the underside of middle-class respectability, invariably eccentric, sometimes comic, often dark. In *The Wapshot Scandal* (1964) a woman commits suicide when all her household appliances break down. John Cheever's satire is not only aimed at the twentieth-century's materialist allegiances. *The Wapshot Chronicle* (1957) depicts the once bustling Massachusetts port of St Botolph's as a wistful, enervated island of the past, except for the vigorous character of Cousin Honora who in *The Wapshot Scandal* nobly vanquishes the bureaucracy of the modern state by refusing to pay her income tax and by giving her fortune to charity. Suburbia is scrutinised in *The Stories of John Cheever* (1978), some of the best short fiction written in English this century. In the preface Cheever calls himself provincial, which, in his case, means that he does not mock the suburban way of life, but looks behind the commuters, the martinis, the golf, the adulteries and the curious children, with the eye of the narrator in 'The Death of Justina':

> There are some Americans who, although their fathers emigrated from the Old World three centuries ago, never seem to have quite completed the voyage and I am one of these. I stand, figuratively, with one wet foot on Plymouth Rock, looking with some delicacy, not into a formidable

and challenging wilderness but onto a half-finished civilisation embracing glass towers, oil derricks, suburban continents, and abandoned movie houses and wondering why, in this most prosperous, equitable, and accomplished world – where even the cleaning women practice the Chopin preludes in their spare time – everyone should seem to be disappointed.

It is the old theme of the American Dream and the mystery of its unfulfilment. Beneath the well-heeled suburban conformities, low-keyed domestic feuds, alcoholism, money troubles and love gone sour bear witness to Thoreau's observation that most men lead 'lives of quiet desperation'. In 'The Five-Forty-Eight' a suburban businessman commits an unexceptional adultery with a woman whose handwriting repels him, and fires her from employment in his office the day after that one encounter. She follows him on the commuter train with a gun, humiliates him and withdraws into her insanity. In 'The Housebreaker of Shady Hill' a man in financial trouble is horrified to find himself burgling his neighbours. Francis Weed survives a plane crash in 'The Country Husband'. He goes home to find that his family hardly seems to care, falls in love with a teenage babysitter and ends up doing therapeutic woodwork in the cellar of his house. Neddy Merrill in 'The Swimmer' goes home across the county through his neighbours' pools, where 'prosperous men and women gathered by the sapphire-coloured waters while caterer's men in white coats passed them cold gin'. Arriving home, he finds his house locked and empty.

Suburban innocence is almost fatal in *Bullet Park* (1969). Eliot Nailles is a monogamous, church-going chemist who loves his son Tony, and 'thought of pain and suffering as a principality lying somewhere beyond the legitimate borders of Western Europe'. Heedless of evil, he is vulnerable to the malevolent Hammer who nearly succeeds in immolating Tony on the altar of Bullet Park's Episcopalian Church. On the last page of the novel Cheever offers the assurance that 'everything was as wonderful, wonderful, wonderful, wonderful as it had been', but *Falconer*, Cheever's finest novel, proves otherwise. Ezekiel Farragut is a forty-eight-year-old college professor and an Episcopalian. A tender parent and uxorious husband he is also a drug addict and has, perhaps unintentionally, killed his brother. *Bullet Park* provides its version of Abraham and Isaac; Professor Farragut's suburbia offers Cain and Abel. With each new, appalling pressure of his confinement, Farragut's grace increases as he learns the meaning of freedom and compassion not only for his fellow inmates of 'Falconer Correctional Facility' but also for the people he watches from the prison window:

> They were free and yet they moved so casually through this precious element that it seemed wasted on them. There was no appreciation of freedom in the way they moved. A man stooped to pull up his socks. A woman rooted through her handbag to make sure she had the keys. A younger woman, glancing at the over-cast sky, put up a green umbrella. An old and very ugly woman dried her tears with a scrap of paper. These were their constraints, the signs of their confinement.

Entrapment, it seems, is universal. Escaping from Falconer in a bag designed to hold a dead convict, Farragut concludes that judgement is not man's but God's prerogative. As a man reborn, he is willing to 'settle for the stamina of love, a presence he felt like the beginnings of some stair'. It is the word 'stamina' that keeps sentimentality at bay and makes Farragut's hard-won moral victory an artistic one for Cheever.

Cheever's last book, *Oh What a Paradise It Seems* (1982) is both an elegy for the obsolete promises of the American dream and an affirmation of hope for the future. His publishers had wished for a big novel to consolidate the reputation he had gained with *The Stories*. According to his daughter's informative and touching memoir of her father, *Home Before Dark* (1984), Cheever himself had wanted to produce a novel on the grand scale. Instead, he ended his life of writing with a long short story, a novella about an old man called Lemuel Sears who tries to save the pond he loves to skate on from becoming a dumping site. When Sears discovers that Beasley's Pond is being used for a dump, the story shifts into the key of fable and the subject becomes the tension in American culture between mobility and permanence:

> Here was the discharge of a society that was inclined to nomadism without having lessened its passion for portables. Most wandering people evolve a culture of tents and saddles and migratory herds, but here was a wandering people with a passion for gigantic bedsteads and massive refrigerators. It was a clash between their mobility – their driftingness – and their love of permanence that had discharged its chaos into Beasley's Pond.

Like much of the book, this reads like preaching, but the tale is more song than sermon, and its endings are appropriately happy for 'a story to be read in bed in an old house on a rainy night'. Beasley's Pond is saved when a distraught housewife, whose lost baby son has been found and returned by an environmentalist,

poisons a bottle of sauce and leaves it in the 'Big Brite' supermarket
with the message: 'Stop poisoning Beasley's Pond or I will poison
the food in all 28 Big Brites'. Dumping stops at once. Lemuel Sears,
after two quirky love affairs, one of them homosexual, is moved by
the resurrected pond to recall the happiness of loving his late wife,
and to feel the pang of gratitude for life on earth:

> It was that most powerful sense of our being alive on the planet. It was
> that most powerful sense of how singular, in the vastness of creation, is
> the richness of our opportunity. The sense of that hour was an exquisite
> privilege, the great benefice of living here and renewing ourselves with
> love.
> What a paradise it seemed!

Other specialists

Wright Morris (*b*. 1910) and William Gass (*b*. 1924) examine Midwest love and community, notably in Morris's *Ceremony in Lone Tree*
(1960) and Gass's densely written *Omensetter's Luck* (1966). William
Gaddis (*b*. 1922) portrays states of extreme self-consciousness in *The
Recognitions* (1955), a long, virtuoso, satirical novel whose energy is
undermined by sheer prolixity, and *JR* (1975), in which realism is
carried to the point of becoming surrealism. The theme of *The
Recognitions* is falsity as it appears in art (an artist's originality yields
to his talent as a copier of old masters), the church, science, even in
death. It is about separations between people set in a world presented
as a degenerating waste land. Almost as protean in style as Joyce's
Ulysses, it is, like Joyce's novel, formidably difficult to read. Both *JR*
and *Carpenter's Gothic* (1985) are satirical works focused on ambition,
loss and the hunger for apocalypse in a world of competition, and
both choke on their author's cleverness. In small doses the super-
realism of speech in *Carpenter's Gothic* provides a lively black humour,
and Gaddis's association of evangelical religion, business interests
and government affords opportunities for the display of much
contemporary irony; but in cumulative effect the realism becomes
self-defeating, capriciously punctuated garrulity. Here, McCandless,
owner of the fake 'gothic' house referred to in the title – 'built to be
seen from the outside' – delivers a tirade about evangelism in Africa:

> . . . talk about a dark continent I'll tell you something, revelation's the
> last refuge ignorance finds from reason. Revealed truth is the one weapon
> stupidity's got against intelligence and that's what the whole damned

thing is all about . . . you've got enough sects slaughtering each other
from Londonderry to Chandigarh to wipe out the whole damned thing
. . . just try the Children's Crusade for a sideshow, thousands of kids led
into slavery and death by a twelve year old with a letter from Jesus . . .
all four horsemen riding across the hills of Africa with every damned
kind of war you could ask for . . . seven hundred languages they've all
been at each other's throats since the creation war, famine, pestilence,
death, they ask for food and water somebody hands them an AK47 . . .

In language of calculatedly incongruous flatness, James Purdy
(*b.* 1923) makes deviant behaviour a region of his own. *Malcolm*
(1959) is about a teenage boy's corruption by a Black undertaker;
The Nephew (1960) about a retired schoolteacher who abandons her
plan to write a memoir of her presumed dead soldier nephew when
she uncovers sordid aspects of his life; *Cabot Wright Begins* (1964)
about a well-mannered rapist; *Eustace Chisholm and the Works* (1967)
and *Narrow Rooms* (1978) about the disintegration of homosexual
lovers.

Novelists born between ten and twenty years before the war tend
towards realism, which proves again one of the most elastic terms
in the dictionary of literary typology, given that it can accommodate
the naturalism of Nelson Algren (1909–81), the memoir of a sixteen-
year-old boy in J. D. Salinger's *The Catcher in the Rye* and the drug-
inspired prose of William Burroughs. Among the novelists of the
pre-war generation, are several whose reputation depends either
upon a single novel with which they attracted an unusually large
readership in America and beyond – this would be true of Algren,
Salinger or Styron – or upon a combination of what they wrote and
what they seemed to be, as in the case of Jack Kerouac and William
Burroughs.

Nelson Algren, a writer of social protest novels, has earned his
niche in American literary history for two books. His best novel,
The Man with the Golden Arm (1949), tells the life of Frankie Machine
(the American–English version of his Polish family name, Majcinek),
trapped both in his marriage to a crippled wife and in his addiction
to morphine. The novel provided film director Otto Preminger with
an audacious script for the mid-fifties and an opportunity to portray
a 'cold turkey' withdrawal for the first time on the screen, and Frank
Sinatra with a vehicle in the character of Frankie. For the taste of
today there is an excess of melodrama and sentimentality, but Algren
deserves credit for addressing in fiction the increasing social problems
of drug addiction and urban claustrophobia. *A Walk on the Wild Side*

(1956) characterises the Depression underworld of New Orleans without illuminating its socio-moral implications sufficiently to forestall the suspicion that more than half an authorial eye was cocked on the prospect of lucrative film rights.

A greater regard for aesthetic values is to be found in the work of Gore Vidal (*b*. 1925). Like, for example, Hemingway, James Jones and Norman Mailer, he has cultivated a public image, and his posturing as an urbane iceberg ('I am exactly as I seem. Beneath my cold exterior, once you break the ice, you find cold water'.) has often deflected attention from his serious commitment to intellect in an age of feeling. His novels range from the early war novel, *Williwaw* (1946) to the historical novels, *Julian* (1964), *Burr* (1973), *1876* (1976), *Creation* (1981) and *Lincoln* (1984). His seventh novel, *The Judgement of Paris* (1952), an entertaining modernisation of the Trojan story, gave notice of interests extravagantly realised in the Hollywood novels *Myra Breckenridge* (1968) and *Myron* (1974). Myra, the same person as Myron but for a spectacularly successful sex-change, is the quintessential, dominant woman, a movie-style bitch-goddess, synthesised by the surgeon's artifice in the image of the stars of that '*blessed* celluloid upon which have been imprinted in our century all the dreams and shadows that have haunted the human race since man's harsh and turbulent origins (quote Lévi-Strauss)'. The popular appeal is pornographic: there are erotic clichés, sexual scenes and feelings are graphically described, and hermaphroditic fantasies amply catered for; yet these novels are essentially a parody of the cultural attitudes and concerns of the late 1960s. Myra/Myron's sexual ambiguity implies questions about the connections between sexuality and the forms society takes. Vidal scatters his text with allusions to the cultural gurus of the epoch – Lévi-Strauss, Marshall McLuhan, Robbe-Grillet – as if to emphasise the merely fashionable aspect of what may be mistaken, at any given moment, for eternal insight. It is fashion, collective whim, which makes the cult of youth, offers psychoanalysis as the new panacea, and develops theories of power and population. Vidal himself subscribes to some of these fashions, not to others. The glands are the real heart of it all, distorting human potential into eternal whores and lustful males, expressions of revenge and mindless tumescence, sadism and sterility – seldom love. Although 'put upon by women', the male is most to blame, and he is expendable. Love of a cool kind may still be a possibility, but only in a pan-sexual world of androgynes:

It is the wisdom of the male swinger to know what he is: a man who is socially and economically weak, as much put upon by women as by society. Accepting his situation, he is able to assert himself through a polymorphic sexual abandon in which the lines between the sexes dissolve, to the delight of all. I suspect that this may be the only workable pattern for the future, and it is a most healthy one.

This is Vidal's own voice being serious. His Myra/Myron novels are associated with his view that the male-female planet is insanely overpopulated to the stage where everyone feels merely part of a countless multitude without any power: 'So there is a sense of giving up, of being drowned in numbers, of being drowned in a system which nobody voted in but which just evolved'. From this point of view, although the androgynous Myra/Myron is a satirical construction she/he expresses a political position.

While *Myra Breckenridge* will doubtless continue to be Vidal's best-known novel, his more substantial work is in the genre of historical fiction. His most impressive exercises in historical imagination are *Burr* and *Lincoln*. Trusting Thomas Jefferson, Aaron Burr (1756–1836) killed the Federalist Alexander Hamilton in a duel in 1804. Burr died in obscurity, but Vidal's novel brings this man of style and energy back to life, especially in Burr's talk (to his fictional protégé, Charlie) about political events, the brittleness of the Constitution and his own sense of himself in relation to others. The inadequacies of Jeffersonian idealism were dramatically proved when Andrew Jackson's presidency let the people into the White House:

> Between the dishonest canting of Jefferson and the poisonous egotism of Hamilton this state has been no good from the beginning. Now it starts to change, with old Jackson . . . Unfortunately I was not able to be a King – though I very nearly was a president – but in my own way I have been very lucky, for I have always been able to indulge my true passion, which is to teach others . . . to make them *alive* . . .

One question raised by *Lincoln* is how Abraham Lincoln or anyone stayed alive in the White House of the day. The place was a rotting mansion, in a capital city erected on a malarial swamp, a home to flies, termites, rats and the enigmatic Mary Todd Lincoln, 'Hellcat' of the White House who was capable of buying one hundred pairs of French kid gloves in a single shopping expedition, and, treasonably, of selling Lincoln's messages to Congress to a newspaperman. Against a background of such details, Vidal's first triumph is to convey a sense of the complexity of his subject in the quality of Lincoln's political skills and the evolution of his attitudes towards all aspects of the slavery question. The second triumph of the book is the art that restrains art but cannot conceal a fidelity to the subject that lets the history speak precisely for itself, without the imposition of an artificial fictional form, and on the basis of scrupulously scholarly research.

William Styron won much acclaim with his first novel, *Lie Down in Darkness* (1951), a tragedy of love set in Virginia and influenced both by Faulkner's Gothic plots and, occasionally, by his poetic style of prose. As in Faulkner's *Light in August*, no one person is identifiable as the villain who causes the events that lead to Peyton Loftis's suicide. The forces of darkness are heredity and environment: the villain is the community. *The Long March* (1953) is a short novel, set in the Korean War, telling the gruesome story of a thirty-six-mile forced training march of Marines. The action centres on the mental and physical conflict between two officers, Colonel Templeton, a Regular who embodies the hard-line militarist view of life, and Captain Mannix, a sensitive Jewish Reservist, who struggles with his fury towards the enormities of the system in which he is caught. Stylistically the work is Styron at his painstaking best: the writing is both direct and expressive, avoiding the strained and clotted prose that mars his later works. The violent events of *Set This House on Fire* (1960) reverse the familiar pattern of American innocence and Old World corruption. The New World is represented by Mason Flagg, spoiled and dissolute son of a Hollywood producer, who corrupts the American painter, Cass Kinsolving, and rapes and presumably kills an Italian girl. Both *The Confessions of Nat Turner* and *Sophie's Choice* (1979) have provoked hostility from readers disposed to accuse Styron of ethnic trespass in appropriating materials reserved for Black or Jewish novelists. Looking back on the motivation to write *Nat Turner* with its challenge to enter the mind of the Black preacher who, in 1831, led the only carefully planned and effective slave uprising in American history, Styron said, 'All of a sudden I realised that all my work is predicated on revolt'. That some readers at least responded favourably to his account of this unique revolt is reflected in the award of the Pulitzer Prize and in James Baldwin's observation: 'He has begun the common history – *ours*'. What *is* hard to accept in *Nat Turner* is the language. It is surely an error of judgement to endow Nat with a flair for expressing complicated self-awareness in a mandarin prose that uses stylistic anachronisms like 'black militancy', and 'outward-going'. It is not the invasion of Jewish territory that gives cause for complaint in *Sophie's Choice*, a story about a Jewish girl who survives Nazi Germany at terrible cost, but the thick web of words which encloses the narrative. The disciplined writing of *The Long March* has given way to a prose that suggests a struggle to avoid Hemingwayese by means of long, indigestibly over-decorated sentences.

J. D. Salinger

Mastery of style is one reason for the success of Jerome David Salinger's prodigious best seller, *The Catcher in the Rye*. The novel brought Salinger an abrupt, worldwide prominence, and triggered what the British writer George Steiner resentfully called 'the Salinger industry' – hectic critical dismembering of the author's small corpus of work. Like *The Adventures of Huckleberry Finn*, the novel is about initiation – the impact of experience on a young sensibility tenacious of its innocence – and it is told in the vernacular. Holden Caulfield's immediate appeal, particularly for young people in the 1950s, is largely based on Salinger's impeccable ear for adolescent speech patterns: Holden's artless dialect is an artful ventriloquial trick by Salinger. A rebel against all the accepted forms of civilised life as he perceives them, Holden's continual flunking, his opting out is a modern replay of Huckleberry Finn's decision to choose hell in preference to a corrupt social system. On his picaresque journey from Pencey Prep (the third private school from which he has been dismissed), to his home in New York three days later, he moves into depression and identity crisis as he encounters people who seem to express the 'phoniness' of the world. (His headmaster is a 'phoney slob'; his fellow student, Stradlater, is a 'secret slob'; the Edmont hotel where he puts up after his departure from Pencey is 'lousy with perverts'; his trusted former teacher, Mr Antolini, turns out to be another phoney when he makes a homosexual approach, 'something perverty'.) Holden's need for human contact is repeatedly frustrated; it is only his young, unspoiled sister, Phoebe, who supplies the honesty and affection he craves and who, therefore, represents the possibility of life that is not phoney. To Phoebe he confides his ambition to be a 'catcher in the rye':

> I keep picturing all these little kids playing some game in this big field of rye and all. Thousands of little kids, and nobody's around – nobody big, I mean – except me. And I'm standing on the edge of some crazy cliff.

> What I have to do, I have to catch everybody if they start to go over the cliff – I mean if they're running and they don't look where they're going I have to come out from somewhere and *catch* them. That's all I'd do all day. I'd just be the catcher in the rye and all. I know it's crazy, but that's the only thing I'd really like to be. I know it's crazy.

Honest Phoebe thinks for a bit, but agrees that it's crazy: after all, brother Holden has run away from school, and that is no recipe for becoming a protector of the innocent. Dismissing the fantasy, all she says is: 'Daddy's going to kill you'. After seeing Phoebe for a last time, Holden decides to run away to the West, a latter-day Huck Finn in his rejection of civilisation, but a modern neurotic in his fantasy of withdrawal from the risk of human contact. In some sunny place, with a job at a filling station, he will complete his process of detachment from the treacherous world by pretending to be a deaf mute:

> . . . then I'd be through with having conversations for the rest of my life. Everybody'd think I was just a poor deaf mute bastard and they'd leave me alone. They'd let me put gas and oil in their stupid cars, and they'd pay me a salary for it, and I'd build me a little cabin somewhere with the dough I made and live there for the rest of my life.

The sentimentality of Salinger's work arises from an underlying scheme of exclusiveness, the implication in *The Catcher in the Rye* that Holden and Phoebe are two alone against an unredeemable America, rotten with phonies. In *Franny and Zooey* (1961) and *Raise High the Roof Beam, Carpenters* and *Seymour, An Introduction* (1963) the precocious children of the Glass family are custodians of goodness, love and enlightenment in a world otherwise made up of stupidity and falsity. The view of life implied, credible and affecting when centred in the adolescent sensitivities of Holden Caulfield, becomes disconcertingly arch and élitist when expressed more generally in terms of the numerous members of a model family. The Glass heroes are the seven brilliant children who have appeared on the radio quiz show, 'It's a Wise Child'. Now at various stages of adulthood (or dead) they are either making heavy weather of a disabling sense of superiority to the rest of humankind (truculent Buddy and perfectionist Franny), or they have despaired of bringing themselves into phase with a phoney world, like Seymour, who commits suicide in the story 'A Perfect Day for Bananafish', published in *Nine Stories* (1953) (British title, *For Esmé with Love and Squalor*). The Glass children love each other, their parents and their pets, and are expert in the detection of phonies, partly because they are all geniuses, partly because, thanks to the late Seymour, they derive strength from Zen and other mysticisms. Franny's nervous breakdown, as revealed by the two stories in *Franny and Zooey*, leads to the ultimate mysticism, the key to it all. In *Zooey* Franny is obsessed with an obscure, small green religious book entitled 'The Way of the Pilgrim' which teaches how to pray continuously. She is rescued from her semi-trance by Zooey who teaches her that Jesus is the 'Fat Lady', that is, ordinary, average humanity. The trouble is that ordinary humanity still excludes so many ordinary, fallible people, especially students, creative types and professors – people, it must be supposed, who are anathema to Salinger. *The Catcher in the Rye*, rooted in its era, is a small, durable masterpiece. Salinger's later works are the soap-box of a writer seeking to be his era's guru, to the detriment of his art. Salinger has not published since 19 June 1965, when *The New Yorker* printed a short story entitled 'Hapworth 16, 1924' about the seven-year-old Seymour Glass.

If Salinger's enduring place in American literature rests on his testimony to the pangs of adolescent isolation in *The Catcher in the Rye*, Jack Kerouac's name will surely be remembered for the shared isolation in which Dean Moriarty and Sal Paradise (a narrator-surrogate for the author) plunge into 'the ragged and ecstatic joy of pure being' in the novel *On the Road*. Kerouac's later novels, such as *The Dharma Bums* (1958), *The Subterraneans (1958)*, *Doctor Sax* (1959) and *Desolation Angels* (1965), are disappointingly little more than redecorated versions of the 'spontaneous prose' of *On the Road*. Man in motion is the hero, and the road itself is a more potent source of vitality than jazz, pot or poetry. *Desolation Angels* is a *roman à clef* for students of the Beat movement. The characters are real people: Duluoz is Kerouac himself: Irwin Garden is the poet, Allen Ginsberg; and Bull Hubbard is William Burroughs.

William Burroughs

Under the pseudonym 'William Lee', William Burroughs tells of his years as a drug addict in many parts of the world in *Junkie: Confessions of an Unredeemed Drug Addict* (1953). His next novel *The Naked Lunch* (1959, Paris; 1962, USA) made him a cult figure, as closely identified with drug experience as Salinger is with adolescence and Kerouac with freewheeling anti-establishment personal freedom. In *Junkie* Burroughs gives a hint about time as experienced by the drug addict, which foreshadows his treatment of time in subsequent works: 'A junkie runs on junk-time. When his junk is cut off, the clock runs down and stops . . . A sick junkie has no escape from eternal time'. In later novels simple chronology is displaced by time which is alternately frozen and syncopated (transitions between junk-time and normal time). The title of *The Naked Lunch* is the best clue to its method. According to Burroughs the title signifies 'a frozen moment when everyone sees what is on the end of every fork'. The book is a series of such moments, blocks of sexual and sadistic horror, a pageant of gruesome extremes, each panel representing the world 'on hold' as apprehended by a drugged consciousness. The strength of the novel is in its use of the drugged life as a metaphor for the conditioned existence fed to a person on a 'newspaper spoon'. For Norman Mailer it is 'a book of great beauty, great difficulty and maniacally exquisite insight', which proclaims Burroughs, perhaps 'the only living American novelist who may conceivably be possessed by genius'. Driven, like Mailer, by a compulsive loathing for American middle-class life, Burroughs attacks it by breaking all the conventions, literary as well as moral. Hallucinatory set-pieces take the place of plot, and there is an abundance of blood, sperm and excrement in sequences of such matter-of-fact obscenity that outrage gives way to a feeling of compassion towards such an appalling state of consciousness and anger towards the forces that have caused it. The episodes of the novel add up to a terrifying projection of the junkie's life, although there is humour among the ghouls who inhabit the extended nightmare of a mutating world, as in the case of the party prowler equipped with a sperm-filled water pistol for impregnating career women. Burroughs's prose is typically staccato and incisive, a style of writing well-suited to scenes of surrealist violence or panic. Here a naked man is trapped in a second-floor room of a hotel in Marrakesh with three murderous Arabs:

> . . . knives in hand . . . watching him . . . glints of metal and points of light in dark eyes . . . pieces of murder falling slow as opal chips through glycerine . . . Slower animal reactions allow him a full second to decide: straight through the window and down into the crowded street like a falling star and his wake of glass glittering in the sun . . . sustained a broken ankle and a chipped shoulder . . . clad in a diaphanous pink curtain, with a curtain-rod staff, hobbled away to the Commissariat de Police.

The three novels which followed soon after the publication of *The Naked Lunch* are all drawn or 'selected' from the same, original body of material, but *The Soft Machine* (1961), *The Ticket that Exploded* and *Nova Express* (1964) involve a new, controversial technique. Burroughs began experimenting with 'cut-up' and 'fold-in' methods of composition. Distrustful of logic and an enemy of all controls, he was attracted to the idea of liberating words from their captivity in the ordered sequences of a printed book and even from the constraints of whatever might be left of conventional usage in his own treatment of language. 'Words know where they belong better than you do', he writes in an article for the *Times Literary Supplement* (6 August 1964), 'I think of words as being alive like animals. They don't like to be kept in pages. Cut the pages and let the words out'. The 'cut-up' method involves cutting and rearranging a page of text to create surprising juxtapositions; in the 'fold-in' method the author folds a page of text lengthwise and places it on another page to create new connections, which subvert conventional language and the false reality it expresses. Burroughs uses these methods to heighten the sense of explosion suggested in the 'nova' of his title *Nova Express*; more commonly the result is an infuriating opacity, as in *The Ticket that Exploded*:

> I shut off the sound track on a shadow in the last words – Now dream flesh left no address for i see the images sharp and clear – so i press button in final ape of history.

Nova Express, *The Wild Boys: A Book of the Dead* (1971), *Cities of the Red Night* (1981) and *The Place of Dead Roads* (1984) are best approached as novels which use science-fiction methods to assert Burroughs's belief in 'the magical universe, a universe of many gods, often in conflict'. The world of drug addiction left behind, Burroughs's vision, still fantastic, becomes increasingly, if obscurely affirmative. 'My purpose in writing', he says 'has always been to express human potentials and purposes relevant to the Space Age'. In both *The Soft Machine* and *Nova Express* conflict between the forces of control and freedom takes the form of galactic war and the narrative action involves identity exchanges and interplanetary transit. *Cities of the Red Night* is his most successful novel so far: it retains the imaginative, often comic, energy of his earlier books, but employs a style closer to that of the title story in *Exterminator!* (1974), a short piece of lucid, hard-boiled narrative about the author's work for a Chicago fumigation company. *Cities of the Red Night* presents two coherent narratives – a detective story and the account of a sailor's adventures in 1702. Eventually the two stories converge: the young man from the eighteenth century exchanges identity with the missing boy from the present whom the detective, Clem Snide, has been hired to find, thereby expressing Burroughs's notion that the dead may be reincarnated by being fused with the living (here through a quasi-surgical swapping of heads). As a metaphor for history, the novel is provocative if far-fetched, the prose more vivid, precise and involving than that of *The Place of Dead Roads* in which the hero's predicament – 'sometimes he shifted his identity ten times in the course of a day' – leads to a degree of confusion which is compounded by the mixture of clipped and psychedelic prose styles. Undoubtedly Burroughs is an original writer, devoted to his craft and endowed with an experimental vigour that makes him a major presence in contemporary American letters. Access to his work is made relatively easy by *A William Burroughs Reader* (1982), introduced and expertly edited by the British publisher, John Calder.

Walker Percy and Truman Capote

Both Walker Percy, born in Alabama, and Truman Capote (1924–84) born in New Orleans, help, in their different ways, to carry the energies of the Southern literary renaissance well into the second half of the twentieth century. Neither relishes being classified as Southern. Percy is less indebted to Faulkner than to European existentialist philosophers like Kierkegaard, Sartre and Marcel, and to French and Russian novelists. The regionalism of Capote, who thought of himself as a Southerner only by accident, is incidental to his interests in innocence, loneliness, homosexuality and murder. Yet most of Percy's characters are recognisably Southern misfits, alienated people looking for salvation, and there is an unmistakable vein of Southern Gothic in Capote's earlier works. Percy thinks of himself as a Southern 'philosophical Catholic existentialist'; Capote thought of himself, simply, as a genius.

Underlying Percy's continual preoccupation with the existentialist view of man and the search for 'authenticity' is an almost agrarian dislike of the modern South as an amoral land of bankers and executives, dehumanised by science and economics. In *The Moviegoer* (1961) Binx Bolling manages a small brokerage firm in a suburb of New Orleans, but prefers the shadow world of movie fantasy which seems 'cleaner' than reality and more engaged with the search for meaning. Alienated from the world of numbing 'everydayness', Binx lives inwardly in terms of his surrogate reality, modelling his behaviour on that of film actors. Through his experience of variously demanding human relationships culminating in marriage, and in response to his Aunt Emily's question about his good in life, Binx achieves a balance between outer reality and his inner intensity – a touchingly credible if unspectacular measure of authenticity. By comparison with *The Moviegoer*, Percy's next novel, *The Last Gentleman* (1966) is disappointingly abstract. A picaresque story about an amnesiac Southerner, Williston Bibb Barrett, last representative of a deteriorating Delta family, the novel is about an outsider wondering rather vaguely how to get inside something. The problem is given a specifically Southern complexion:

> Southerners have trouble ruling out the possible. What happens to a man to whom all things seem possible and every course of action open? Nothing, of course.

Something does happen to Will Barrett, for in *The Second Coming* (1980) he has inherited a fortune from his late wife, 'about 50 or 60 million', he guesses. Even in such quantity, the almighty dollar cannot protect him either from a neurological affliction which causes him to black out on the golf course, or from a depression akin to the Kierkegaardian sickness unto death, brought on by the realisation that his father had tried to kill him. Firing his Luger pistol experimentally, he is kept from suicide by curiosity:

> He held the muzzle against his temple. Yes, that is possible, he thought smiling, that is one way to cure the great suck of self, but then I wouldn't find out would I? Find out what? Find out why things have come to such a pass, and a man so sucked down into himself that it takes a gunshot to knock him out of the suck – or a glimpse in a double mirror.

It is Allison, the girl in the greenhouse, who saves Will from suck, gun and double mirror. Something of a holy fool, she embodies true love, both human and divine, in contrast to the offer extended by a young minister who invites Will to an ecumenical retreat: 'A weekend with God in a wonderful setting . . . That's the bottom line'.

There is an attractive lightness of touch about Percy's style in *The Second Coming* which succeeds as a philosophical novel while keeping the reader in the company of flesh and blood. The apocalyptic novels, *Love in the Ruins* (1971) and *Lancelot* (1977), suggest that Percy should trust more in his gift for wry humour. *Lancelot*, although the powerful monologue of a man deranged by violence, sexual betrayal, the secularism of contemporary America and the need for

God, is too patently a quasi-allegorical thesis of the decline of the West. *Love in the Ruins* while admirably inventive in its imaginary picture of defunct Buicks, wolves in downtown Cleveland, and American politics stalemated between patriotic 'Knotheads' and radical 'Leftpapas', demonstrates that anti-Utopian satire is not the author's true métier.

Like that of William Styron, the early writing of Truman Capote is distinctively Southern. Success came early to Capote, when he was twenty-three with his first novel, *Other Voices, Other Rooms*, an essentially romantic story of alienation set in a portentous Southern atmosphere of decay and abnormality. The homosexual theme was audacious in its time. The supposition that Joel Knox's dependence on the transvestite Randolph was a projection of Capote's own insecurity and deviant sexuality made the author a celebrity. The stories in *A Tree of Night and Other Stories* (1949) develop Capote's vision of a fallen world in which maimed or despairing people realise that their cases are hopeless. In these works Capote displays an ability to write prose of striking delicacy and precision. In *The Grass Harp* (1951), the world of society and objective reality is still harsh and hostile, but an affirmation of hope and human continuity is sung out to the temporarily withdrawn characters of the story by the harp of grass which grows in the cemetery, 'a grass harp, gathering, telling, a harp of voices remembering a story'.

In the mid-fifties Capote became interested in the artistic possibilities of non-fiction. In 1955 he went to Russia with a company touring Gershwin's *Porgy and Bess*. His report of the experience in *The Muses are Heard* (1956) is an imaginative organising of facts and impressions that prefigures the method and aims of *In Cold Blood* (1966). *Breakfast at Tiffany's* (1958) takes its title from the heroine, Holly Golightly's dream of wallowing in the luxuries of New York City. The story of a Texas girl determined to live intensely and naturally, the book represents Capote's artistic touch at its lightest. Its portrayal of a naïve artist of life, determined to elevate everyday routine to the level of her imagination, seeks to combine the appeal of whimsy with the strength of fable but the writing is marred by archness. The controversial *In Cold Blood* solidified Capote's claim to literary fame. It took him six years to produce this detailed, painstakingly researched, chilling account of the 1959 murder of a Kansas farm family and the capture, trial and execution of the two killers. Capote's insistence that he had raised nonfiction to a new art form was vigorously debated. Some readers thought the narrative overmanipulated, some insisted that a work of fact could not presume to the status of art, and others found a profound statement about reality, a grave and reverend book committed to exposing the doubleness of American life. The book's title expresses an irony: as Capote presents it, the apparently cold-blooded murder of the Clutter family was a crime of passion, whereas the execution of the murderers, Hickock and Smith, was a killing carried out in the cold blood of protracted legal process. In June 1975 Capote allowed *Esquire* magazine to publish the first of four excerpts from his major work in progress, *Answered Prayers* (unfinished when he died), in which real people are portrayed as characters in a work that defiantly mixes fact and fiction. In the preface to *Music for Chameleons* (1980) – a collection of stories and journalistic experiments – Capote reaffirms his belief in an art form based on the combination of cinematic, reportorial and fictional techniques.

John Updike

Updike (*b.* 1932) has occupied a position never far from centre stage in American fiction since his first novel *The Poorhouse Fair* (1959), an affecting record of one day in an old people's home. 'What the writer most needs', he says, 'is an instinctive habit of honesty. He must instil his wrists with the refusal to write whatever is lazily assumed, or hastily perceived, or piously hoped.' In the late 1950s, when the permissive society was pitching its tent in suburbia and Dean Moriarty was exhilarating readers of Jack Kerouac's *On the Road* with his 'ragged and ecstatic joy of pure being', Updike's *Rabbit, Run* brought the honesty of a corrective anxiety back into the moral economy. Striving for the perfection he once knew on the basketball court, 'Rabbit' Harry Angstrom ('Angst' means 'anxiety' in German) may be partly the saint his feckless wife accuses him of trying to be. There is tawdriness in everything he runs away from, but his bid for pure experience hurts other people. When a garage man says, 'The only way to get somewhere, you know, is to figure out where you're going before you get there', Rabbit answers, 'I don't think so.' It is only the movement itself that seems to matter: 'the wandering thread of his feelings leads nowhere'. The pursuit of *being*, in opposition to society's injunctions to *become*, should require only heroism; but in the real middle-class world heroism and irresponsibility are the same thing.

In *The Centaur* (1964) Updike transplants the Greek myth of Chiron and Prometheus to a Pennsylvania high school where George Caldwell (Chiron, the centaur) teaches science, and his fifteen-year-old son (Prometheus) is a pupil. The novel is a heightened but apparently honest autobiography. When Updike was upbraided for the portrait of his father as George Caldwell, his father insisted, 'No, it's the truth. The kid got me right.' George Caldwell has no illusions, but sacrifices himself to the discouragements of his colitis and his pupils in order to help Peter toward a career in art. *Couples* (1968), based, Updike admits, on his own experience and that of his friends, uses the sexual interrelationships of ten well-to-do couples in a New England town called Tarbox to examine the connection between the idea of community and individual sensibilities with vaguely Rabbit-like aspirations. A best seller, the book shocked many less by its wife-swapping and oral sex than by its matter-of-factness, its tenderness and its comedy. Updike's lyrical descriptions of erotic emotion are sometimes overlush – the besetting defect of his prose is that of self-display – but they invalidate conventional moral judgements by suggesting that the sexual assumptions underlying the behaviour of his couples are normal, even commonplace. Worse still, such behaviour can be a substitute for religion as in Piet Hanema's love for the pregnant Foxy Whitman. This is the romanticism which Updike sees as 'a heresy, a secret church'. A churchgoing Congregationalist, he plotted most of *Couples* during sermons.

Of the Farm (1965) is about the aftermath of a divorce in which Joey Robinson tries not to be split between his lost past and uncertain present. The stories in *Your Lover Just Called* (1979) follow the marriage of Joan and Richard Maple through 'a million mundane moments' to the morning in the divorce court when the 'merry chitchat' of the lawyers makes the couple feel 'obsolete at their own ceremony'. It is, after all, continuity of love that directs them into a new present:

> Joan and Richard stepped back from the bench in unison and stood side by side, uncertain of how to turn, until Richard at last remembered what to do; he kissed her.

In *Rabbit Redux* (1971) and *Rabbit is Rich* (1981) Harry Angstrom is cut down from flight into voyeurism and a querulous compromise with the America of Black power, draft-dodging, marijuana and gloomily competitive consumerism. Sloppy Janice Angstrom turns the tables sexually on her would-be saintly husband in *Rabbit Redux*. She confides her thoughts of Harry to Stavros, her lover:

> Maybe he came back to me, to Nelson and me, for the old-fashioned reasons, and wants to live an old-fashioned life, but nobody does that any more and he feels it. He put his life into rules he feels melting away now.

The ironic truth of the matter is that the plaintive Rabbit has discovered his own woeful lack of originality: 'But all this fucking', he complains to Janice, 'everybody fucking, I don't know, it just makes me too sad. It's what makes everything so hard to run.' Perhaps, but the 'country club/of mankind's copulating swarm' ('Midpoint', the first of the poems collected in *Midpoint* [1969]) is the premise of most of Updike's books. *Buchanan Dying* (1973) is a fiction-drama about President James Buchanan. Half a world away from the territory of middle-class sexual mores, *The Coup* (1978) is about Kush, an imaginary African nation ruled by Colonel Hakim Félix Ellelloû for whom America is the 'fountainhead of obscenity and glut'. A broader canvas helps Updike to aerate his style. The polished voice is distinctively his but the expected blend of metaphorical surprises and *New Yorker* magazine 'purple' has developed into a prose both copious and lucid, which abundantly evokes a place and accommodates both seriousness and satire.

The poetic eloquence of Updike's best writing is based on exact observation and precision of expression. It is this combination of imaginative gift and technical skill which enables him to create a memorable short story from a mood, an irony or an image. In 'Wife-wooing' from *Pigeon Feathers* (1962) a husband realises, after seven years of marriage, that there is need for a new beginning in his relationship with his wife. In bed his 'ornate words' fail to woo her; she meets his desire with sleep which he judges 'cunning'. At breakfast the next morning, to the husband's relief, his wife appears ugly, drab and worn. In endorsement 'the toaster sticks' and the husband takes his vulnerability and energy away from the churning ambiguities of marriage towards his job in the hard, competitive city:

> The man, he arrows off to work, jousting for right-of-way, veering on the thin hard edge of the legal speed limit. Out of domestic muddle, softness, pallor, flaccidity: into the city. Stone is his province. The winning coin. The manoeuvring of abstractions, making heartless things run. Oh the inanimate, adamant joys of a job.

That evening, preoccupied with a professional problem, he is surprised when his wife comes to him with a promising 'kiss of toothpaste ... moist and girlish and quick'. Compactly, unforgettably, the story renders the rhythms of memory, domestic clutter, love, desire and dependence. The operation of memory and the impact of the past are central to 'When Everybody Was Pregnant' in *Museums and Women and Other Stories* (1972). Again, Updike's ability to portray a mood with economy and startling precision gives the story its power. A community stockbroker recalls the bygone, almost unimaginable time of young parenthood: 'Voluptuous wallpaper. Crazy kids. Sickening sensations of love. The trains slide forward. The decades slide seaward, taking us along'. Here it is the word 'slide', suggesting both the vertiginous force of circumstance and the irrevocable movement of time, that lifts simple memories into a unified, poignant image. In *Problems and Other Stories* (1979) a teenage family has been told of how their parents do not make each other happy enough. One son, on the edge of sleep, asks 'Why?'. The question gives Updike an opportunity to show that his acuity and his prose can rise to the measure of such a moment. They can and do: 'It was a whistle of wind in a crack, a knife thrust, a window thrown open on emptiness'.

The linked collection of short stories entitled *Bech: A Book* (1970) creates a comic portrait of Henry Bech, a *'recherché* but amiable' Jewish writer in the grip of writer's block, a condition he plans to conquer by writing a book called 'Think Big'. He becomes unblocked, and less interesting in *Bech is Back* (1982). The first volume of this pair, while sympathetic to Bech, is best enjoyed for its satire of the writer's situation in America:

> ... the silken mechanism whereby America reduces her writers to imbecility and cozenage. Envied like Negroes, disbelieved in like angels, we veer between the harlotry of the lecture platform and the torture of the writing desk, only to collapse, our five-and-dime Hallowe'en priests' robes a-rustle with economy-class jet-set tickets and honorary certificates from the Cunt-of-the-Month Club, amid a standing crowd of rueful, Lilliputian obituaries.

Satire is also the key of *The Witches of Eastwick* (1984). Each one of the coven of three divorcees is capable of very black magic by any suburban standard. It seems only metaphorical at first when Alexandra Spofford's former husband is said to rest 'on a high kitchen shelf in a jar, reduced to multi-coloured dust', and Jane Smart's 'ex', relegated to 'the cellar of her ranch house among the dried herbs and simples', is 'occasionally sprinkled, a pinch at a time, into a philtre, for piquancy'; but when reference is made to Sukie Rougemont's using her Monty as a place mat on which a cup of tarry coffee leaves a gritty ring, it begins to look like the real, impossible thing. There is an allegorically candid devil – Darryl Van Horne – who lures the three promiscuous witches to his hot tub and holds them in sexual thrall for as long as it suits – that is, until he prefers to marry a younger woman. The satire thus has a double focus: middle-class life is defective, but once in you can't get out without turning nasty or being made to look a fool. If you are an escaping woman with children, no magic can maintain your standards of housekeeping or prevent you from becoming a bad mother. In Updike's world divorce and decorum seem to need each other, secular modern replacements for love and marriage.

Humour and satire

If satire is the expression of amusement or disgust, American satire veers towards amusement, tending to interpret life in terms of folly rather than of vice. It invokes the laughter of acceptance associated with comedy rather than the bitter, sardonic laughter which can push beyond the wry pleasure of recognition to a deepened moral repugnance of the kind familiar in the writings of Pope or Swift.

Benjamin Franklin's Poor Richard Saunders, an uneducated but experienced countryman, could form the views of a nation that prized 'horse sense' above all forms of wisdom. His witty comments helped to shape political opinion. Mark Twain's vicious Pap Finn, lauding racial discrimination, is a device by which Twain attacks an abhorrent attitude and makes a political and moral point that assisted the cause of emancipation; but satire of this kind is an exception. Clarence Shepard Day's (1874–1935) popular books *God and My Father* (1932), *Life with Father* (1935) and *Life with Mother* (1937) depict a quaintly indignant, conservative figure whose ways of thinking are outmoded. It is true that public life is plagued by 'chuckle-headed talk and rascality in business and politics', but that is how things are, and to expect to change the way of the world is to be quixotically absurd, a figure of fun. The implication is that Father really ought to adapt – yet, if he did, the human race would be the poorer by one eccentric whose foibles are an enriching source of amusement.

Robert Benchley (1889–1945) assumes the role of 'a perfect neurotic' both in his writings and his work as a film actor. Whereas earlier humorists exaggerated the difficulties they had to overcome, Benchley exaggerates the smallness of his difficulties and his inability to cope with them in *From Bad to Worse* (1934), *My Ten Years in a Quandary* (1936), and *Inside Benchley* (1942). The character Benchley pretends to be is thwarted from doing simple things – pick flowers, smoke a cigarette, wear a white suit, leave a party. The resultant phobias reflect the frustrations of twentieth-century urban existence, but also make them ingratiating: who would wish to reform such a source of assuaging recognitions and, therefore, of entertainment? The appeal of Benchley's humour associates him with the view of humour held by James Thurber (1894–1961): 'I think humour is the best that lies closest to the familiar, to that part of the familiar which is humiliating, distressing, even tragic'. The drawings and prose writings of James Thurber expose the follies of America 'from the year Lindbergh flew the Atlantic to the year coffee was rationed', that is, the period between the wars. Thurber's targets include pseudo-scientific articles on sex in *Is Sex Necessary?* (1929, with E. B. White (*b*. 1899)), psychoanalysis in *Let Your Mind Alone* (1937) and other twentieth-century pretensions in *Fables for Our Times* (1940). The most accessible collection of his writings and drawings is *The Thurber Carnival* (1945). Thurber's cynicism is tempered by tenderness and whimsy and the delight he takes in 'emotional chaos'. Dorothy Parker (1893–1967) is the soul of acerbity. Both writers abjure sentimentality in their view of the relations between the sexes. In Thurber's drawings tyrannical wives snarl at feckless husbands; in Dorothy Parker's verse romance is out of the question. It is an 'Unfortunate Coincidence' that by the time the lady yields, the game is over:

> By the time you swear you're his,
> Shivering and sighing,
> And he vows his passion is
> Infinite, undying –
> Lady, make a note of this:
> One of you is lying.

Like Thurber, Mrs Parker frequently published in *The New Yorker* after being discharged as drama critic of *Vanity Fair* because her reviews were too caustic. (She once described the actress, Katherine Hepburn, as 'running the whole gamut of emotion from A to B').

The Portable Dorothy Parker (1973) is a good selection of Mrs Parker's poems, articles and reviews.

S. J. Perelman (1904–79) entitles one of his books *Keep it Crisp* (1946). American humorists are funniest when they obey his injunction and follow a national talent for the wisecrack. Dorothy Parker even made a wisecrack out of her own epitaph, 'Excuse my dust', and carried the principle of pith into epigrammatic verses about great literary figures. Charles Dickens is defended:

> Who call him spurious and shoddy
> Shall do it o'er my lifeless body
> I heartily invite such birds
> To come outside and say those words!

but Harriet Beecher Stowe has, perhaps, been idealised too much:

> The pure and worthy Mrs Stowe
> Is one we all are proud to know
> As mother, wife, and authoress –
> Thank God, I am content with less!

Ogden Nash (1902–71) taps language out of shape and into wisecrack, pointed by rhymes that are funnier the more strained they become, as in his 'Reflection on Babies': 'A bit of talcum / Is always walcum', or in 'The Parent': 'Children aren't happy with nothing to ignore, / And that's what parents were created for', or in his salute to the resourcefulness of 'The Turtle':

> The turtle lives 'twixt plated decks
> Which practically conceal its sex.
> I think it clever of the turtle
> In such a fix to be so fertile.

Thurber's whimsy and Dorothy Parker's wisecracking are combined and amplified in the humorous writing of S. J. Perelman. His humour depends partly on his pleasure in the self-mockery he achieves by adopting comically implausible personae, as he does in 'Nothing but the tooth':

> I am thirty-eight years old, have curly brown hair and blue eyes, own a uke and a yellow roadster, and am considered a snappy dresser in my crowd. But the thing I want most in the world for my birthday is a free subscription to *Oral Hygiene*, published by Merwin B. Massol, 1005 Liberty Avenue, Pittsburg, Pa.

or in 'And thou beside me, yacketing in the wilderness':

> If I ever sit down like a retired Scotland Yard inspector to write my memoirs, which I have provisionally entitled, 'Forty Years a Boob', one

of the episodes I plan to glaze over is the night of pub-crawling I spent in Hollywood last summer with a beautiful, Amazonian extra player named, for purposes of this indiscretion, Audrey Merridew.

Another striking feature of Perelman's writing is his feeling for the slapstick possibilities of language, as in 'Captain Future, Block that Kick' in *Crazy Like a Fox* (1944) and an associated gift for parody. His 'Farewell, My Lovely Appetizer' is aimed particularly at Raymond Chandler's detective, Philip Marlowe and the novel, *Farewell, My Lovely* (1940), but it also sends up the tough-guy stereotype familiar from innumerable Hollywood films, with or without Humphrey Bogart. An ash-blonde has entered the office of private detective, Mike Noonan, and hidden herself in the wardrobe where he keeps 'a change of bourbon'. When she emerges, with an implausible commission for Mr Noonan he naturally asks what there is in it for him:

> 'Anything you want'. The words were a whisper. I leaned over, poked open her handbag, counted off five grand.
> 'This'll hold me for a while', I said. 'If I need any more, I'll beat my spoon on the high chair' . . . She trailed past me in a cloud of scent that retailed at ninety rugs the ounce. I caught her wrist, pulled her up to me.
> 'I go for girls named Sigrid with opal eyes', I said.
> 'Where'd you learn my name?'
> 'I haven't been a private snoop for twelve years for nothing, sister'.
> 'It was nine last time'.
> 'It seemed like twelve till you came along'.
> I held the clinch until a faint wisp of smoke curled out of her ears, pushed her through the door. Then I slipped a pint of rye into my stomach and a heater into my kick and went looking for a bookdealer named Lloyd Thursday.

Perelman's work is most readily sampled in *The Most of S. J. Perelman* (1958).

Ring Lardner (1885–1933) was an established sports journalist before his *You Know Me Al* (1916) series of 'Jack Keefe' baseball letters for the Chicago *Tribune* brought him fame as an exponent of semi-literate speech in sardonically funny exposures of demotic vanity, self-deception and ineptitude. Lardner's work, including stories published in *The Saturday Evening Post* and selections from *The Love Nest and Other Stories* (1926) is most accessible in *The Collected Short Stories* (1941) and *The Portable Ring Lardner* (1946). His third son Ring Lardner, jun., (*b.* 1915) has also practised the art of satire in his screen writing for the popular anti-war movie *M*A*S*H* (1970) and in *The Ecstasy of Owen Muir* (1954), a tight-lipped attack on war, politics, big business, organised religion and penal servitude in the tradition of Nathaniel West (1904–40), though lacking West's stylistic agility and bite. In *Miss Lonelyhearts* (1933) West's pessimism is conveyed through the story of a newspaper agony-column writer whose attempts to evade or alleviate suffering are equally unsuccessful and end in his own bizarre death. *A Cool Million* (1934) satirises individual and political motivations by parodying the Horatio Alger rags-to-riches myth. The surrealism of *The Dream Life of Balso Snell* (1931) is intensified and broadened in West's most ambitious work, *The Day of the Locust* (1939), which carries a satirical portrayal of Hollywood towards an apocalyptic, self-destructive orgy that expresses the febrile vacuity West sees consuming American society. The symbolic potential of West's surrealist vein in satire is developed by Donald Barthelme (*b.* 1933) in short stories and novels which present life as an irrational dream, from *Come Back, Dr. Caligari* (1964) to *Guilty Pleasures* (1974) and *Sixty Stories* (1981).

De Vries and Condon

Like John Cheever and John Updike, Peter De Vries (*b.* 1910) finds in suburbia abundant scope for the analysis of a wide range of contemporary behaviour from sexual ethics to artistic and intellectual pretensions. *Comfort Me With Apples* (1956) introduces Chick Swallow, an aesthete in a quandary both about the morality of writing 'pepigrams' for the local paper and about the extent of his responsibility for a poetess whom he has encouraged in bohemian living. The adventures of Swallow are continued in *The Tents of Wickedness* (1959) which anticipates the Women's Liberation Movement by about a decade and includes admirable parodies of Thomas Wolfe, Ernest Hemingway and William Faulkner, as well as Proust, Joyce and Kafka. When he is being funny, De Vries is more comic than satirical. He enjoys the contemporary foibles burlesqued in *Tunnel of Love* (1954). Although Stewart Smackenfelt of *Forever Panting* (1972) is fatter than De Vries's previous heroes, he bears a clear resemblance to Chick Swallow, being a compulsive wisecracker endowed with a talent for entangling himself in marital and extra-marital situations of ludicrous complexity. The complexity of *Reuben, Reuben* (1964) derives from its ironic use of different perspectives in a comic yet fundamentally serious treatment of the shortcomings of Freudian interpretations of life and the post-Romantic claims of art as redemptive. *I Hear America Swinging* (1976) sends up the age of sexual liberation by anatomising its effects in a farming community in Iowa, and both *Into Your Tent I'll Creep* (1971) and *Sauce for the Goose* (1981) satirise women's liberation, the first in relation to marriage, the second in relation to career.

The new, scrupulously vague Christianity parodied in *The Mackerel Plaza* (1958) preaches that 'It is the final proof of God's omnipotence that he need not exist in order to save us'; but this will not do for De Vries himself. In *The Blood of the Lamb* (1962), a relatively sombre novel for De Vries, but perhaps his best, the harrowing death of Carol almost displaces comedy by Wanderhope's – and De Vries's – anger at the Almighty's inscrutable trifling. Almost, but not quite: De Vries's balance is impeccable. After a surprise infection has killed Carol in the hospital's children's ward, Wanderhope, drunk, finds himself outside a church. Removing from its box the cake he had taken to the hospital, he hurls it at the face of the crucified Jesus:

> Then through scalded eyes I seemed to see the hands free themselves of the nails and move slowly towards the soiled face. Very slowly, very deliberately, with infinite patience, the icing was wiped from the eyes and flung away.

Nathaniel West's wide range of targets and effects anticipates the synoptic fantasies of Richard Condon (*b.* 1915). The popular success of *The Manchurian Candidate* (1960), a tightly-made political thriller, and its excellent movie version (1962) may be partly responsible for the neglect of Condon as a serious writer. He is, certainly, guilty of potboilers, such as *The Star-Spangled Crunch* (1974), a spoof on the international oil crises of the 1970s; but his view of the world as a slapstick conspiracy, always on the edge of violence, his relish for factual data and for language itself, produce brilliantly funny, threatening projections of where the world may be going if it is not much more careful than Condon supposes it can ever be. *An Infinity of Mirrors* (1966), still his best book to date, uses the techniques of comedy in preference to those of analysis to attack the mass murders committed by the Nazis. Mixing clinical enumeration with farce, Condon exposes the nightmare's essential sleaziness without muting its horror. *Mile High* (1969) indicts the greed of American big business by way of a story about Prohibition. *The Vertical Smile* (1971), a staggeringly bravura satire, makes Nixon's America appear so hilarious that the reforming spirit is undermined by the feeling that even an appalling reality which can promote such comic virtuosity must have its own perverse value. The value, of course, is that of black comedy, with sudden eruptions of satirical horror. A preternaturally well-preserved elderly woman thinks she recognises a former lover of similar vintage on a New York bus. She tries to recall his name:

> While there was a sudden diversion in the street below – someone's viciously trained guard dog was savaging a passing woman's throat – his name flashed into her mind.

The man's name is Osgood Noon, hers Ada Clarke. Conversation gets going, but there are distractions:

> Noon stared out of the bus window at a mugging which was taking place on the far side of Park Avenue. The mugger held the elderly woman's head locked in his arm while he slammed a metal garbage can lid into her face repeatedly with his free hand. People hurried around them or reversed their directions casually.

As the bus creeps forward to Madison Avenue, 'a band of students were laying a dynamite charge into the facade of a religious articles shop', and Ada's 'piratically forward' advances on Noon are counterpointed by yet further atrocities:

> They were diverted as two city policemen caught a small group of Negro youths in a crossfire. As the young people fell in the gutters and on the pavement, the crowds in the evening streets suddenly vanished. But Ada was not to be diverted. 'Would you like to have a little more?' she asked breathily.

The effect of the two levels of action is to ask if the increasingly sexual ongoings between the two elderly people on the bus is more or less outrageous than the violence of the streets which is merely a norm of city life and, therefore, 'respectable'. Equally, the chaotic alienations of the city, as foil to the activity in the bus, confers a comic sanctity on the coming together (again) of two people who should, by 'respectable' standards, have no further capacity for sex, but who still know how to make contact and can still live in terms of simple pleasures that harm no-one.

Winter Kills (1974) shakes away all tidy explanations of President Kennedy's assassination. *Prizzi's Honour* (1982) is Mario Puzo's (*b*. 1920) best seller about life in the Mafia, *The Godfather* (1969), with the glamour and sentimentality replaced by irony, rapidity and wit. Charley Partanna has 'chrome eyes and brows like awnings' and comes over a telephone line 'like a talking brewery horse'. As chief enforcer for the Prizzi family he is the soul of reliability, having killed his first man ('made his bones') at the age of thirteen. 'Charley was solid. Nothing shook him up.' The exception that proves the rule is Irene Walker, a beautiful ex-prostitute now turned assassin, who shakes him up considerably when she still wants to marry him after he has shot her husband in the face, the chest and the throat. Unfortunately for Irene, Charley's love for her is transcended by his obligation to kill her on behalf of the family she has relieved of some $360,000. In the second last chapter she prepares to shoot him while he prepares for a night of love-making, but he has picked the same occasion for a showdown and beats her to the draw. In the last chapter he sends two of her blouses and one dress to the Brooklyn branch of the Salvation Army, and invites a former mistress to dinner. The intermittent comedy which Condon creates chiefly by his use of pace and language – parodying the hard-boiled style, and overgoing it in precision – may at times lull the moral sense, but the novel's remorseless point is that the Mafia world is irredeemably diseased, vicious and lethal.

Kurt Vonnegut

The vitality of Condon's best work deserves to outlast the generally overrated writing of Kurt Vonnegut, jun., (*b.* 1922) despite the latter's cult following in the 1960s and 1970s. Vonnegut's *Slaughterhouse-Five or The Children's Crusade* (1969), based on the author's experiences as a prisoner-of-war during the fire-bombing of Dresden in the Second World War, is justly admired for its mixture of informed compassion and satirical bite. The desiccation of Billy Pilgrim's spirit by the effects of a punitive air raid that burned to death more people than died at Hiroshima leads to his frustratingly pointless marriage and a life of affluent, deadpan hopelessness as a suburban optometrist. There are two atrocities in the novel: the Dresden bombing is one; the other is the heartlessness of American bourgeois standards. The double satire of reality is reinforced by Vonnegut's customary time-warp of fantasy. While plodding through his bleak middle age on earth, Billy is simultaneously alive and comfortable on the distant planet of Tralfamadore. Housed in a luxurious cage he is partnered by a pneumatic starlet called Montana Wildhack, between whose breasts hangs a locket bearing the words of the framed prayer on Billy's office wall on earth as an expression of 'his method for keeping going':

GOD GRANT ME
THE SERENITY TO ACCEPT
THE THINGS I CANNOT CHANGE,
COURAGE
TO CHANGE THE THINGS I CAN,
AND WISDOM ALWAYS
TO TELL THE
DIFFERENCE

Vonnegut disposes of the difference: 'Among the things Billy Pilgrim could not change were the past, the present, and the future'.

In Vonnegut's mechanistic and deterministic universe, no one is responsible for anything. Even on Tralfamadore, Montana Wildhack moves her baby from one breast to the other 'because the moment was so structured that she *had* to do so'. The Tralfamadorian who conducts Billy Pilgrim to his unearthly felicity remarks that he has visited thirty-one inhabited planets, studied reports on a hundred more, and found talk of free will only on earth. For Vonnegut it is only talk. All, everywhere, are at the mercy of indeterminate events and unpredictable systems like the giant corporation RAMJAC in *Jailbird* (1979) which envelops every major American enterprise from Kentucky Fried Chicken and the *New York Times* to Macdonald's Hamburgers, and even assimilates as its Vice-President, Walter F. Starbuck, recently released minor Watergate conspirator and the 'jailbird' of the title. In *Galapagos* (1985) the scene is set a million years back from the present occupied by its narrator, Mr Leon Trotsky Trout (son of Kilgore Trout, Vonnegut's ubiquitous and protean character – a writer, of course). The year is 1986, when human beings had absurdly big brains that weighed around three kilograms. 'There was no end', repines Trout, 'to the evil schemes that a thought machine that oversized couldn't imagine and execute'. It was time for 'A Second Noah's Ark'. In the wake of planetary catastrophe (economic chaos, famine, World War III) a group of ill-assorted representatives of the human race lands, as Darwin had done, on the Galapagos Islands where the colony of Santa Rosilia includes one sea captain and nine females. By luck, humanity has been diminished into a tiny point, and now, also by luck, it is permitted to expand again. There is a succinct definition of the human soul: 'It's the part of you that knows when your brain isn't working'. By evolution, and for survival, our brains shrank. (Early in the process the sea captain, on the last day of his life, throws the perfect pocket computer into the ocean 'As the new Adam, it might be said, his final act was to cast the Apple of Knowledge into the deep blue sea'.) We grew flippers and beaks – a distinct improvement on the old anatomy because even if people thus evolved 'found a grenade or a machine gun or a knife or whatever left over from olden times, how could they ever make use of it with just their flippers and their mouths'? Presumably, too, the smaller brains work well to dispose of the need for a monitoring, fallible soul. Survival is secular.

It is the lack of soul that vitiates much of Vonnegut's writing. The folksy cartoon inventions jell, at best, into a comic-book divertimento, and satirical purpose is undermined by determinist conviction. If life is inescapably a condition of nonsense, alternately poignant and hideous, what is the point of satire itself? 'So it goes', says Vonnegut repeatedly in *Slaughter-house Five*, to which the only possible response is: 'If so, so what?' There is brilliant invention in his work, but its cumulative effect is to commend detachment if not despair.

Despite their American citizenship, Vladimir Nabokov (1899–1977) and Jerzy Kosinski (*b.* 1933), immigrants from Russia and Poland are more appropriately considered European writers. Nabokov's *Pnin* (1957) is a short comic novel about an aging émigré professor of Russian in an American college. Although Nabokov denied that criticism of his adopted country was his intention in *Lolita* (1955, Paris; 1958, USA), satire of middle-class vulgarity and hypocrisy is contained in his story of the middle-aged Humbert Humbert's obsession with a teenage 'nymphet', Dolores Haze, known as Lolita. Aesthetics replaces morals for Humbert, the one respect in which he demonstrably resembles his author. 'One should notice and fondle details', Nabokov advises in *Lectures on Literature* (1980). Kosinski's books, beginning with *The Painted Bird* (1965) about a boy's fight for life and sanity among the brutalities of Nazi-ravaged Eastern Europe, are typically acrid fables of survival. In *Being There* (1971) a brain-damaged youth called Chance is compelled to leave the garden he has tended all his life when his employer dies. Out in the world he turns into a descendant of Voltaire's Candide. The readiness of others to interpret his simple remarks as profound metaphorical wisdom leads to his becoming a vice-presidential candidate and provides as much comedy as satire.

Science fiction

Kurt Vonnegut's popularity is partly explicable in terms of his odd relation to the fashionable mystique of science fiction, a kind of literature in which Americans have led the world since H. G. Wells. The appeal of science fiction today can be seen as a consequence of anxiety about the future of the planet. In *God Bless You, Mr Rosewater* (1965) Eliot Rosewater drunkenly addresses a convention of science-fiction writers:

> I love you sons of bitches . . . You're all I read any more. You're the only ones who'll talk about the really *terrific* changes going on . . . You're the only ones with guts enough to *really* care about the future, who *really* notice what machines do to us, what wars do to us, what cities do to us, what big, simple ideas do to us, what tremendous misunderstandings, mistakes, accidents, and catastrophes do to us.

Like H. G. Wells, the best modern American writers of science fiction use their genre realistically to make intelligent guesses about a future from whose vantage point a critical eye may be cast over the present. Vonnegut himself employs the conventions to create moral landscapes, like Lewis Carroll's Wonderland or Jonathan Swift's Lilliput and the country of the Houyhnhnms in *Gulliver's Travels*. The genre is not easy to define, but generally implies fantasy in which the imagination, unrestricted by mundane reality, operates within the limits of what might be scientifically possible.

H. P. Lovecraft (1890–1937) is best known for tales of Gothic terror which recall the imagination, if not the craft, of Poe, but his dislocation of time and space and the extraterrestrial origins of his horrific beings in the Cthulhu Mythos stories make him something of a pioneer in the area of science fiction in which fantasy predominates over science. His posthumously collected works include *The Outsider and Others* (1939), *Beyond the Wall of Sleep* (1943) and *The Lurker at the Threshold* (1945). Many of Lovecraft's stories appeared in the magazine *Weird Tales*. Further impetus was given to the development of science fiction in 1926 by the founding of *Amazing Stories* by Hugo Gernsback (1884–1967) and in 1937 by the founding of *Astounding Science Fiction* by John W. Campbell. Gernsback, an indomitable publisher of magazines committed to science and fantasy, approached science fiction from an enthusiasm for electricity (he designed batteries and radios). The impact on science fiction of his publishing ventures and his 'Baron Munchausen' stories ('Munchausen on the Moon', 1915; 'Munchausen Departs for the

Planet Mars', 1916) is commemorated annually by 'Hugo' awards for excellence in the genre. If Gernsback's efforts have earned him the title 'Father of Science Fiction', the 'Father of Space Opera' is Edward Elmer (E. E.) Smith (1890–1965), commonly known as 'Doc' Smith, and a best selling 'pulp' writer for some fifteen years prior to the Second World War. His 'Lensman' novels have come back into favour among aficionados in recent years. Despite doggedly amateurish writing he attracts readers and influences writers by a grandiose epic scheme in which the mighty opposites of good and evil act out their eternal conflict in terms of the war between the benign Arisians and the malign Eddorians, cowboys and Indians of a hazardous future. In order to defeat the absolute evil of the Eddorians, the Arisians resolve to develop a refined form of civilisation on selected planets by special breeding processes. The first three volumes of the 'Lensman' sequence are *Triplanetary* (1934; revised 1948), *First Lensman* (1950) and *Galactic Patrol* (1937–8; revised 1950). Certain members of the Galactic Patrol are endowed with telepathic and other special powers by wearing a 'Lens' or bracelet – 'a lenticular polychrome of writhing, almost fluid, radiance' – hence the word, 'Lensman' in so many of Smith's titles.

The scientific literalism of Gernsback and the operatic fantasies of E. E. Smith are combined, refined and amplified into a literature of ideas by the work of Robert A. Heinlein (*b.* 1907) and Frank Herbert (*b.* 1920). In 1956 Heinlein won a Hugo award for *Double Star* (1956), a novel about a failed actor who pretends to be a galactic politician, and in 1962 was awarded another Hugo for *Stranger in a Strange Land* (1961), about a messianic young American raised on Mars by Martians. By the Martian technique of 'grokking', Valentine Michael Smith apprehends people instantly and completely, and enjoys agreeably intense religious and sexual experiences. One young beauty, asked why she fainted after being kissed by Smith, replies 'When Mike kisses you he isn't doing anything else!' Heinlein's most popular work, *Stranger*, seduced the anti-establishment youth of the 1960s by its iconoclastic advocacy of individualism, mysticism and free love, yet for many Heinlein has remained a 'fascist' since the publication of *Starship Troopers* (1959), a violent novel about interstellar war. It is reasonable to fault his work for its tendency to sermonise, but while Heinlein is undoubtedly opinionated, his targets are not confined to one political extreme. Much of his writing functions as wide-ranging satire against social taboos as well as against fashionable but – to his mind – shallow trends in contemporary liberal attitudes: What's wrong with marriages that reject monogamy? Is not the Christian communion service a form of ritual cannibalism? Is there any reason why women should not serve as combat troops? Would not Blacks enjoy being slavemasters just as much as whites? Is there a better reason for killing a man than bad manners? A moralising maverick, with a fertile imagination and prodigious staying power, Heinlein's saving grace as demonstrated by *Job: A Comedy of Justice* (1984) and *The Cat Who Walks Through Walls* (1985) is an inability to take himself or his species too seriously for too long.

Paul Atreides, the messianic hero known as 'Maud'dib' of Frank Herbert's *Dune* series, is even more versatile than Heinlein's V. Michael Smith. Thought-hypnotist, swordsman and ecologist, he is descended from a line of space migrants whose religious faith, 'Thou shalt not disfigure the soul', pulls the human spirit back from the futuristic technological prodigies of Herbert's setting. *Dune* (1965) – the biggest-selling science fiction novel ever – is a complicated tale of political intrigue, mystical implication and ecological theory. It is outstandingly successful in its creation of an elaborate but plausible alien environment in which the human species is challenged to show its mettle against fearful odds. The plot is intricate and, besides the famous sandworms, involves discussions of social control, free will and destiny, and the relationship between man, technology and environment. The sequels – *Dune Messiah* (1969) and *Children of Dune* (1976) – explore the dangers of messianism as the universe explodes in 'jihad', holy war, Maud'dib's vision of truth is corrupted by a priestly bureaucracy, and the messiah enters the wilderness, leaving his children to inherit the burdens of destiny. 'We're locked into forms, of government, of belief and behaviour which doom us to keep repeating ourselves', Herbert says, 'That's one of the points I wanted to make in *Dune*'. As a sustained enquiry into the human condition by way of science fiction methods the *Dune* books are only equalled by the prolific Isaac Asimov's (*b.* 1920) consideration of the nature of human history in the *Foundation* trilogy (1951–2, 1953).

Ray Bradbury's (*b.* 1920) long, worldwide and just success as a writer of science fiction is based on his skilful use of the O. Henry short-story formula to moralising effect in futuristic settings in such collections as *The Silver Locusts* (1950; US title, *The Martian Chronicles*), *The Illustrated Man* (1951) and *The Golden Apples of the Sun* (1953). Bradbury's *Fahrenheit 451* (the title gives the temperature at which books are said to burn) is an Orwellian cautionary fable about a totalitarian state in which books are banned and thought is controlled by television. A more thorough-going fabulist is Ursula Le Guin (*b.* 1929) whose brand of fantasy alternates between science and magic, sometimes combining the two as in her early novels *Rocannon's World* (1966), *Planet of Exile* (1966) and *City of Illusions* (1967) which show less interest in technology than in anthropology and extrasensory perception. Her most ambitious work, the 'Earthsea' trilogy, seriously considers human problems in fairy-tale terms. Each volume presents an argument about the need to face truth. *A Wizard of Earthsea* (1968) shows the need to face the evil in one's self; *The Tombs of Atuan* (1971) is about the triumph of trust over suspicion; *The Farthest Shore* (1972) argues that life is meaningless unless the inescapable truth of death is accepted. In the introduction to her prize-winning *The Left Hand of Darkness* (1969) Le Guin says, 'Science fiction is not predictive; it is descriptive'. This highly original novel is an extended metaphor which 'describes' sexual prejudice and its consequences by creating a people who can be, at different times, male, female or neuter. An ordinary human who falls in love with a member of this trisexual society is compelled to examine the meaning of sexual roles. Le Guin's purpose is to show what it may mean to be merely human, living through situations freely, that is without the determining factor of a given sexual identity.

The novels of Philip K. Dick (1928–82) are much concerned with perception and the problem of distinguishing between reality and illusion. *The Three Stigmata of Palmer Eldritch* (1964) considers the arguments for and against the use of drugs in terms of space colonists who can only tolerate life on Mars with the help of the superdrug, 'Can D' (government controlled, but illegal) until the sinister Palmer Eldritch appears with 'Chew Z', the ultimate hallucinogen. In *A Scanner Darkly* (1977), Dick finally condemns hallucinogenic drugs because they damage consciousness by distorting natural perception. Mechanical simulacra are agents of illusion in *Do Androids Dream of Electric Sheep?* (1968) in which android animals are marketed to atone for the guilt people feel because real ones have been almost exterminated. The opening pages of the novel illustrate Dick's unsurpassed ability to set a credible and engaging scene in a plausible future setting with speed and economy. Rick Deckard, a hunter of renegade androids, has awakened to the sound of the 'mood organ' beside his bed and is immediately involved in an argument with his wife who accuses him of being a hired murderer.

'I've never killed a human being in my life.' His irritability had risen, now; had become outright hostility.

Iran said, 'Just those poor andys.'

'I notice you've never had any hesitation as to spending the bounty money I bring home on whatever momentarily attracts your attention.' He rose, strode to the console of his mood organ. 'Instead of saving,' he said, 'so we could buy a real sheep, to replace that fake electric one upstairs. A mere electric animal, and me earning all that I've worked my way up to through the years.' At his console he hesitated between dialling for a thalamic suppressant (which would abolish his mood of rage) or a thalamic stimulant (which would make him irked enough to win the argument).

'If you dial,' Iran said, eyes open and watching, 'for greater venom, then I'll dial the same. I'll dial the maximum and you'll see a fight that makes every argument we've had up to now seem like nothing. Dial and see; just try me.' She rose swiftly, loped to the console of her own mood organ, stood glaring at him, waiting.

The work of Samuel R. Delany (*b.* 1942) is even more complex than Dick's and richer in style. *The Einstein Intersection* (1967) is an ambitious, but only partly successful, attempt to satirise patterns of human life by science fiction methods. *Nova* (1968) is an extraordinarily dense transposition into futuristic terms of the myths of Prometheus and the Holy Grail in which cryptic narrative information alternates with passages of lyrical rhetoric and characterisation is consistently bizarre. The dazzling energy of Delany's work commands attention, nowhere more so than in the nearly nine-hundred-page *tour de force*, *Dhalgren* (1975). Joycean in its fullness – a 'book about many things', as the author says, somewhat unnecessarily – and in its linguistic ebullience, it presents the violent city of Bellona which has suffered a disaster so cataclysmic that the space-time continuum has been distorted. When the haze clears from the sky two moons appear. Buildings burn endlessly, but are not consumed. A powerful image of a society in chaos, the novel seems to imply that order may be restored through a combination of youth and art.

Drama after 1940 – Williams and Miller

In the mode of domestic melodrama Lillian Hellman (*b.* 1905) portrays Southern moral turpitude, avarice and neurosis in *The Little Foxes* (1939) and *Toys in the Attic* (1960). Her *Watch on the Rhine* (1940) is an attempt to alert liberal-minded Americans to the threat of Fascism. To protect his work from exposure, Kurt Müller, a German anti-Nazi, murders a guest at his mother-in-law's home. The American mother-in-law suggests to Müller, 'Perhaps we have private definitions. We are all anti-fascists, for example', to which her daughter Sara replies that Kurt, at least, works at being one. It was time, Lillian Hellman believed, for America to work at being one too, by taking sides against the European dictatorships. Many of William Inge's (1913–73) popular, realistic Mid-western plays of middle-class sentiment rapidly found their way into film: *Come Back, Little Sheba* (1950), *Picnic* (1953), *Bus Stop* (1955) and the more symbolic *The Dark at the Top of the Stairs* (1957) in which the staircase leading to a darkened hall represents each character's fear of the unknown.

During the 1940s and 1950s, the strongest presences in American drama were those of Tennessee Williams (1911–83) and Arthur Miller (*b*. 1915). They complemented each other as inheritors of Eugene O'Neill's pioneering achievements in American drama. Tennessee Williams's more poetic theatrical style refined O'Neill's modernist experiments with symbolism: the result was a group of plays which, while superficially and psychologically realistic, derive their power from a high degree of formal integration. Arthur Miller developed O'Neill's interest in the status of the individual into a theatre of social concern. Although the 'Modern' period is still commonly thought to have yielded to the 'contemporary' about the year 1940 – or with the end of the Second World War – these two writers illustrate the inevitability of changing perspectives in matters of literary history. It would be difficult to argue that forty-year-old works – older than the Vietnam war, older than the first moon-landing, older than the nuclear near-disaster of Three Mile Island and the Russian reactor accident at Chernobyl – were in any useful sense 'contemporary', even if their themes, like Poe's, Melville's or Dickinson's, remain commandingly 'relevant'. The framework of social values and concerns has changed on a global scale since Williams achieved his first major success with *The Glass Menagerie* in 1945 and Miller his in 1947 with *All My Sons*. Intrinsically, Williams and Miller belong more to the modern than to the contemporary because of their styles and preoccupations. Williams's ritualistic, operatic style combines the influences of Eugene O'Neill, Maurice Maeterlinck and August Strindberg; and Arthur Miller earnestly follows in the footsteps of the moralising Henrik Ibsen and the reforming Bernard Shaw.

After *Suddenly Last Summer* (1958) Tennessee Williams failed to produce a major play with a coherence of symbol and character to raise it from what he calls 'the singular to the plural concern'. *The Milk Train Doesn't Stop Here Any More* (1962) makes a laboured pantomime from an earlier short story 'Man Bring This Up Road' (included in *The Knightly Quest*, 1966). *Sweet Bird of Youth* (1959) jumbles its symbolism, confusing the plight of the Princess Kosmonopolis and her sketchily portrayed gigolo-companion, Chance Wayne, with a crude account of Southern bigotry. If symbols are planted as they are in *Period of Adjustment* (1960), they must justify themselves by informing the texture of their play: here they remain hangers-on to the generally unfunny comedy. The final crack as the Bates's house sinks further into the cavern over which it is built is an embarrassingly obvious ironic comment on their prospects of marital success. *The Night of the Iguana* (1961) is Williams's most disappointing play since 1958 simply because it is his nearest miss. There are the characteristic themes – loneliness, mendacity, nausea, a god of wrath who permits corruption – and, in the tethered iguana, a central symbol to which all the values of the play are related; but the diverse guests who come to Mrs Faulk's Costa Verde Hotel remain a random collection, and the iguana is never more than a symbolic prop, dragged on too late in the action, to make the facile observation that all the main characters are at the ends of their ropes.

In the last phase of his career, from *Slapstick Tragedy* (1965), which includes *The Mutilated* and *The Gnädiges Fräulein*, to *Clothes for a Summer Hotel* (1980), a 'ghost play' about Scott and Zelda Fitzgerald, Williams's work became increasingly pessimistic as he pared his style down towards the monologue as prolonged, neurotic aria. Death, confinement and deprivation are recurrent themes alleviated only by a quality of grotesque comedy in the self-exposing speeches of frustrated, bitter characters who, although pitiably vulnerable in their isolations, typically alienate an audience or a reader by sheer querulousness. This quality of compulsive neurotic shrillness mars *In the Bar of a Tokyo Hotel* (1969). Based on the life of the painter, Jackson Pollock, and obviously a work in which its author invested much of himself, the play tries to dramatise the theme of artistic impotence (is the painter thwarted by himself or by his alternately bitchy and plaintive wife?), but succeeds only in conveying the monotony of sustained hysteria.

The plays which earn Williams a permanent place in dramatic

literature are *The Glass Menagerie, A Streetcar Named Desire* (1947), *Cat on a Hot Tin Roof* (1955) and *Suddenly Last Summer* (1958). Their success depends on Williams's organisation of meanings in terms of a central symbol which he animates theatrically, and on his ability to achieve poetic effects with the spoken language.

The title of *The Glass Menagerie* names the play's symbolic centre, the collection of glass animals signifying the fragile Laura Wingfield, withdrawn from reality into illusion, on the shelf. Through the translucent medium of this symbol the humours of the diverse characters drawn together to share a desperate evening are, in a fashion, reconciled, seen to make a sad harmony. Below superficial differences all four have their fragilities and are revealed subject to illusion. Even the sociologically 'average' Jim, through whose normality Amanda hopes Laura may re-enter reality, needs the wholesome ideal of Betty, the American Dream girl, to bolster his illusion of imminent success. Amanda escapes from the severities of the present into the illusory Blue Mountain of her youth which symbolises, as Belle Reve is to symbolise for her descendant, Blanche Du Bois, the traditional values of the 'genteel South', no longer recognised in a world 'lit by lightning'. Tom, absconding like his father, soon finds his feet dragging when he has 'skipped the light fantastic' out of town: for him escape is the illusion:

> Perhaps I am walking along a street at night, in some strange city, before I have found companions. I pass the lighted window of a shop where perfume is sold. The window is filled with pieces of coloured glass, tiny transparent bottles in delicate colours, like bits of a shattered rainbow.
>
> Then all at once my sister touches my shoulder. I turn around and look into her eyes . . . Oh, Laura, Laura, I tried to leave you behind me, but I am more faithful than I intended to be!

'A little woman of great but confused vitality clinging frantically to another time and place', Amanda Wingfield suffers tragic reincarnation in *A Streetcar Named Desire*'s Blanche Du Bois whose fragility and incongruity with her surroundings are immediately apparent: 'her delicate beauty must avoid a strong light. There is something about her uncertain manner as well as her white clothes that suggests a moth'. Blanche's disintegration, begun with the suicide of her young homosexual husband as a result of her taunts, is nearing its end. Lonely and frightened she has tried to fill her empty life with sex, but death was winning, no matter what she did to buy it off:

How in hell do you think that all that sickness and dying was paid for?
Death is expensive, Miss Stella! And old Cousin Jessie's right after
Margaret's, hers! Why, the Grim Reaper had put up his tent on our
doorstep! . . . Stella. Belle Reve was his headquarters! Honey – that's
how it slipped through my fingers! Which of them left us a fortune?
Which of them left a cent of insurance even? Only poor Jessie – one
hundred to pay for her coffin. That was all Stella! And I with my pitiful
salary at the school. Yes, accuse me! Sit there and stare at me, thinking
I let the place go!

Although Blanche has supervised the collapse of Belle Reve, her
own symbolic extension, she clings with pathetic determination to
the passé airs and dubious graces of the Southern gentlewoman and
to the mirage of a life she knows has ceased to exist. In the Kowalski
household she is an anachronism, alien and doomed. A supporting
cast of expository symbols forms a texture of implication rich enough
even to bear the allegorical, if actual, streetcars and the irony of
'Elysian Fields', the vulnerable paper lanterns and the aristocratic
Shep Huntleigh. For Mitch, Blanche is exposed as no more than an
illusion of beauty, a *belle rêve*.

In *Cat on a Hot Tin Roof* the inner malignancy of Big Daddy
Pollitt's cancer symbolises the erosion of the individual by loneliness,
guilt or greed for 'twenty-eight thousand acres of the richest land
this side of the Valley Nile'. The World of *Cat* is one of multiple
disease: mendacity, avarice and hypocrisy are proliferated through
the play like cancer cells, as ubiquitous as Gooper and Mae's
obnoxious brood of no-neck monsters. Her honesty makes Maggie,
the 'Cat', a symbolic antibody to Big Daddy's cancer, the only
means whereby the body of corruption displayed in the play may
eliminate its poisons. The original ending holds out minimal hope;
as revived by Williams for the Broadway production, on the advice
of the director, Elia Kazan, there is a little more, but Williams's
vision as a whole is pessimistic.

'Nothing but pitiless nature', says the dramatised D. H. Lawrence
in *I Rise in Flame Cried the Phoenix* (1952). *Suddenly Last Summer* has
many affinities with this wordy little play about the English novelist
whose hands 'gripped the terrible stuff of life and made it plastic'.
Mrs Venable is a rich version of Lawrence's Gertrude Morel in *Sons
and Lovers*, wife-mother and more to Sebastian whose insistence that
he 'handle this situation' at Cabeza de Lobo echoes the stage
Lawrence's determination to die without help, 'fiercely and cleanly
with nothing but anger and fear and other hard things like that'.

Lawrence's obsession with the voracious side of the earth's 'obscene, corrupting love' as Nonno calls it in *Night of the Iguana*, anticipates the symbolic core of *Suddenly Last Summer*, the Venus fly trap, a devouring organism aptly named after the goddess of Love, and the most livid hieroglyph in the Williams collection.

Arthur Miller studies the relation between society and the individual in terms of three clearly identifiable themes, all of which are developed in his first, Ibsenesque success, *All My Sons* (1947): the impact of the past on the present, personal idealism and responsibility. The plot of *All My Sons* emerges from the past which contains Joe Keller's dishonour. The effect of his moral dereliction on the other characters creates the present action of the play in which the principled Larry's suicide teaches Joe about the moral superiority of communal responsibility to the materialistic ideal of production-line success. 'Sure he was my son', he says, moving into the tragic awareness that leads him to take his own life, 'But I think to him they were all my sons. And I guess they were, I guess they were.' Two kinds of past invade the present in *Death of a Salesman* (1949). Uncle Ben's air of frontier self-reliance is a reproach to the exhausted Willy Loman, and Willy's actual past ebbs and flows around him in the memory sequences which Miller heightens by expressionistic use of lighting, music and an open, semi-realistic set. Willy's death is a final effort to realise his own ideal of being a good husband and provider; a good salesman, too, for his life is worth $20,000.

John Proctor's and Eddie Carbone's conceptions of themselves draw Miller's themes together in *The Crucible* (1953) and *A View from the Bridge* (1955). By going to his execution in defiance of the sin of mass hatred, Proctor transcends his own minor fault and achieves heroic stature; but this situation is only made possible for him when he realises that he cannot bring himself to surrender his name by associating it with the lie that is demanded of him if he is to save his own life. As Alfieri says at the end of *A View from the Bridge*, Eddie Carbone was 'himself purely, for he allowed himself to be wholly known'; but it is only by the act which undoes him that Eddie learns how much he needs his name as the point where his conception of himself merges with the idea others have of him. The fusion of personal and social identities is perfectly caught in his last, fatal contact with Marco. Victor's problem in Act I of *The Price* (1968) is that he has no conception of himself. He confesses to Esther:

> I'll be frank with you, kid – I look at my life and the whole thing is incomprehensible to me. I know all the reasons and all the reasons and all the reasons, and it ends up – nothing.

Victor finds himself by facing the past, acknowledging the truth about his former behaviour and his love for his father.

For many admirers of Miller's plays *The Price* was a momentary recovery from the excessive wordiness that has spoiled his work since 1964. Prolixity and an uneasy vaudeville archness undermine any potential dramatic vitality in *The Creation of the World and Other Business* (1972), Miller's least characteristic play. When Cain, rejecting both the Devil and God, bears the Fall with him into his exile, an audience can only rejoice that an evening of strained effects, forced humour and embarrassing cuteness, is over. *The Archbishop's Ceiling* (1977) is less of a play than an argument about freedom. *Incident at Vichy* (1965), a short play about Frenchmen caught by German Nazis in 1942, deserves a more enduring place in the story of American drama. If it is theatrically lean, a play of words rather than of action, it does succeed in making the analysis of a situation something that is felt dramatically as a process involving genuine moral passion.

After the Fall (1964) was particularly disliked as an embarrassing confession of Miller's personal failures, a case of the playwright's need for retributive judgement in order to earn back his own good name. The hero of the play, Quentin, a lawyer, has failed to appreciate his father and his first wife. He has been unworthy of his own professed liberal beliefs during the McCarthy era, and has failed to sustain his second marriage to Maggie, a celebrated popular singer suspiciously like the film star Marilyn Monroe (Miller's second wife). Quentin is certainly full of self-accusation, his mind 'questing over its own surfaces and into its depths'; but the other characters are flawed too. It is by Miller's orchestration of their flaws that Quentin's speech before the final curtain reconciles all the fallen in an unillusioned vision of new possibility for the ruined garden of the American Dream. The speech is a kind of reaction to the death of the American myth portrayed in the film *The Misfits* (1961):

> I wake each morning like a boy – even now, even now! I swear to you, I could love the world again! Is the knowing all? To know, and even happily, that we meet unblessed; not in some garden of wax fruit and painted trees, that lie of Eden, but after, after the Fall, after many, many deaths. Is the knowing all? And the wish to kill is never killed, but with

some gift of courage one may look into its face when it appears, and with a stroke of love – as to an idiot in the house – forgive it; again and again . . . for ever?

Poetry, personality and politics

The era of Pound and Eliot favoured impersonality in the poet and a view of the poem as a self-contained organism, a space-wandering monad held together by the inter-animation of its parts. The fastidious, craftsmanly poetry of Richard Wilbur (*b.* 1921) belongs to this modernist tradition as does the precision of statement by which Elizabeth Bishop (1911–79) conveys her sense of 'the surrealism of everyday life'. In syntax, like Marianne Moore's, almost indistinguishable from that of prose, Bishop speaks directly to the reader, but the first person singular in her poems is a device: she remains detached, and the 'I' of the poet affords no access to the person beyond the text. 'The Fish' begins:

> I caught a tremendous fish
> and held him beside the boat
> half out of water, with my hook
> fast in a corner of his mouth.

The poem's simple narrative tells how the poet 'thought of the coarse white flesh' of the fish? 'looked into his eyes', 'admired his sullen face', 'stared and stared', and finally 'let the fish go'; but the evolution of the poet's response only serves to focus attention on the actuality of the fish. Bishop's 'I' is not autobiographical but a lens through which objects are seen or an antenna for catching impressions worth writing down because of their intrinsic appeal. In assessing the significance of things the poet is like a map-maker whose province is the whole of present reality and who is therefore superior to the historian whose view of the world is inhibited by chronology and distorted by relations in time. 'The Map' is a defence of poetry:

> Topography displays no favourites; North's as near as West.
> More delicate than the historians' are the map-makers' colours.

Like the map-maker, the poet displays no favourites: the material of poetry is present everywhere and a fish is as good as a monument or an aunt emitting an '*oh*' of pain in the dentist's chair ('In the Waiting Room'). In 'The Monument' Bishop suggests that the process of responding to an artifact – in this case an apparently arbitrary pile of wooden boxes, but it could just as easily be a painting or a poem – is only an intense version of the way in which we unavoidably respond to the world itself. The curious structure with its 'sort of fleur-de-lys of weathered wood' on top, its 'odd holes', 'warped poles' and 'vaguely whittled ornament' demands a response from the resisting spectator ('Why did you bring me here to see it?'). The monument means something, says 'commemorate', and offers readier coherence than the random constituent parts of the natural world which the human imagination constantly tries to compose into order:

> It is an artifact
> of wood. Wood holds together better
> than sea or cloud or sand could by itself,
> Much better than real sea or sand or cloud.

Wearying of his vulnerabilities, Theodore Roethke (1908–63) yearns in his last book *The Far Field* (1964) for 'the imperishable quiet at the heart of form' ('The Longing'), but he will be remembered for his personal world of plants, play and elegy. The 'COMPOSITION BY FIELD' theory of 'Projective Verse' advanced by Charles Olson (1910–70), instructor and, from 1951–56, rector of the experimental Black Mountain College in North Carolina, only looks like a set of purely formal prescriptions. Olson's argument for freedom of lay-out and his emphasis on the writer's 'breath' are in the interest of the individual poet's instinctive expression of personality in the rhythms of his verse. Drawing his terminology from modern physics, Olson argues that a poem is a 'high-energy construct' in which 'the perception must immediately and directly lead to a further perception'. Olson's achievement in poetry rests on 'The Kingfishers' (1949) and his magnum opus, *The Maximus Poems* (1953–75). In its feeling for the past, its mixture of colloquial and formal language and its aggressiveness, *The Kingfishers* anticipates *The Maximus Poems*, a diffuse mosaic sequence of more than three hundred letters and songs in which the poet appears at first as Maximus, but reveals himself as Olson engaged in exploring the meaning of America by cutting through the veneers of civilisation particularly as they may be found in the fishing town of Gloucester, Massachusetts, where he grew up. Owing much to Ezra Pound's *Cantos* for form and William Carlos Williams's *Paterson* for focus, the poet's search for 'the primal features of those founders who lie buried in us' is best understood as an archaeological dig into the social, historical and geological features of his place: 'An American/is a complex of occasions,/themselves a geometry/of spatial nature'. As he says at the end of 'The Kingfishers':

> ... if I have any taste
> it is only because I have interested myself
> in what was slain in the sun
>
> I pose you your question:
>
> shall you uncover honey/where maggots
> are?
> I hunt among stones

The avant-garde artists Olson brought together at Black Mountain College included the musician John Cage, the choreographer and dancer Merce Cunningham, the painters Robert Rauschenberg and Franz Kline, and the architect and futurist Buckminster Fuller. Denise Levertov (*b.* 1923) became associated with the Black Mountain community through its journals, *Black Mountain Review* and *Origin*. Poets who studied at the College included Robert Duncan (*b.* 1919), Robert Creeley (*b.* 1926) and Edward Dorn (*b.* 1929), who proclaims his allegiance in the title of his volume *From Gloucester Out* (1964). Dorn's best work is in the *Gunslinger* books – collected as *Slinger* in 1975 – which question the values of American culture by parodying the cowboy epic.

In 'Maximus to Gloucester, Letter 27', Olson says:

> I have this sense,
> that I am one
> with my skin
>   Plus this – plus this:
> that forever the geography
> which leans in
> on me I compell
> backwards I compell Gloucester
> to yield, to
> change
>   Polis
> is this

The majority of modern American poets from Richard Eberhart (*b.* 1904) and Karl Shapiro (*b.* 1913) to younger writers of today move between these poles – sense of themselves and engagement with 'Polis', the social and political attributes of the American superstate.

Beat poets

While the Black Mountain group of artists reacted against established conventions in the arts, San Francisco became Mecca for writers of the so-called 'Beat Generation'. Jack Kerouac is said to have invented the term 'Beat' to describe his friends who were drop-outs, beaten by society. There may also be references to freedom as in the beat of jazz rhythms and to the beatitude of innocence. The most famous and flamboyant Beat poet is Allen Ginsberg, but the movement derived much of its sustenance from Lawrence Ferlinghetti's (*b.* 1919) City Lights Bookshop in San Francisco where the emerging poets could meet, read their work to each other and be published by the bookshop's press. Other poets who figured prominently in the San Francisco renaissance are Robert Duncan, Gary Snyder, Jack Spicer (1925–65), Gregory Corso (*b.* 1930) and Richard Brautigan (*b.* 1935).

In *A Coney Island of the Mind* (1958) Ferlinghetti portrays the poet as a public performer, an acrobat given to risk:

> Constantly risking absurdity
> 　　　　　　and death
> Whenever he performs
> 　　　　　above the heads
> 　　　　　　　of his audience
> The poet like an acrobat
> 　　　　climbs on rime
> 　　　　　　to a high wire of his own making
> And balances on eyebeams
> 　　　　　above a sea of faces

Few of the Beat poets do 'climb on rime', but the element of performance is strong in their work. Ginsberg's 'Howl' needs to be declaimed aloud to achieve its impact as a diatribe against the corruptions of American society and politics – the system he calls 'Moloch'. At this stage of his career – the mid-fifties – Ginsberg's vague solution to the perversions of his country was a reliance on drugs, sex and pseudo-Zen buddhist spontaneity:

> I saw the best minds of my generation destroyed by madness,
> 　　　　　starving hysterical naked,
> dragging themselves through the negro streets at dawn
> 　　　　　looking for an angry fix,
>
> angelheaded hipsters burning for the ancient heavenly connection to the
> 　　starry dynamo in the machinery of night . . .

who passed through universities with radiant cool eyes hallucinating
   Arkansas and Blake-light tragedy among the scholars of war,

who were expelled from the academies for crazy & publishing obscene
   odes on the windows of the skull———

If Ginsberg's bardic style derives in part from a Hebraic tradition
of denunciation and prophecy, it also owes much to Olson's ideas
about the poetic line as a unit of breath and to the long-lined
cataloguing verse of Walt Whitman. In 'A Supermarket in
California', Whitman is a 'lonely old grubber, poking among the
meats in the refrigerator and eyeing the grocery boys'. Ginsberg
acknowledges his spiritual kinship:

Where are we going, Walt Whitman? The doors close in an hour.
Which way does your beard point tonight?
(I touch your book and dream of our odyssey in the supermarket and
feel absurd.)
Will we walk all night through solitary streets? The trees add shade to
shade, lights out in the houses, we'll both be lonely.

At its best, Ginsberg's verse can be enjoyed for its energy, its pace
and the abundance of its imagery; at its worst it becomes rant. His
most successful work is the long poem 'Kaddish for Naomi Ginsberg
1894–1956', an elegy for his mother ('Kaddish' in Judaism is a
mourning prayer) who was hospitalised several times and finally
died of a stroke in a mental hospital. Deep feeling keeps Ginsberg's
focus steadily on his subject and prevents his jagged exclamatory
style from descending to anarchy. The poem opens with the poet in
New York, beginning to come to terms with his loss:

Strange now to think of you, gone without corsets & eyes, while I
   walk on the sunny pavement of Greenwich Village.
downtown Manhattan, clear winter noon, and I've been up all
   night, talking, talking, reading the Kaddish aloud, listening to
   Ray Charles blues shout blind on the phonograph . . .

It ends with an incantatory evocation of crows crying out a salute
to the dead as they fly over the cemetery where his mother is buried:

Caw caw caw crows shriek in the white sun over grave stones
   in Long Island
Lord Lord Lord Naomi underneath this grass my halflife
   and my own as hers

Berryman and Lowell

John Berryman (1914–72) says that his major work *The Dream Songs* (*77 Dream Songs*, 1964; *His Toy, His Dream, His Rest* [Nos 78–385], 1968) 'is essentially about an imaginary character (not the poet, not me) named Henry'; but Henry – or 'Mr Bones' as his unnamed interlocutor calls him – is clearly a mask for an evolving poet engaged in a programme of self-exposition. The evolution continued from 1968 until Berryman's death by suicide in 1972, enabling John Haffenden to gather another forty-five 'Dream Songs' for *Henry's Fate and Other Poems* (1977). The work as a whole records 'the warring state' (No. 367) of Henry's moods and opinions in a kaleidoscopic vaudeville of dream situations, emotional reversals and speech idioms from formal literary diction to movie 'tough' talk and a parody of minstrel 'coon' language. Henry is huffy, careful, ill, drunk, libidinous, parental, old, horrible, happy, gross and 'at odds wif de world & its god' (No. 5).

Although Berryman is by far the funniest of the so-called 'confessional' poets, connection with Henry, especially for women, 'seemed to be an acre in hell' (No. 303). His guilt often focuses on women. Lust for the 'compact and delicious body' of 'the hottest one for years of night' leads to an endorsement of Henry's self-reproach by his unnamed friend: 'There ought to be a law against Henry,/–Mr Bones: there is' (No. 4). In No. 29 guilt makes him wonder how destructive he has been. The possibilities are comically ghoulish, but the mundane truth is a gnawing insecurity that cannot be explained away by simple cause and effect:

> But never did Henry, as he thought he did,
> end anyone and hacks her body up
> and hide the pieces, where they may be found.
> He knows: he went over everyone & nobody's missing.
> Often he reckons, in the dawn, them up.
> Nobody is ever missing.

Self-mocking and 'headed for the night' (No. 309), Henry can nevertheless make merry with his own boredom, as in 'Dream Song' No. 14:

> Life, friends, is boring. We must not say so.
> After all, the sky flashes, the great sea yearns,
> we ourselves flash and yearn,
> and moreover my mother told me as a boy
> (repeatedly) 'Ever to confess you're bored
> means you have no

> Inner Resources'. I conclude now I have no
> inner resources, because I am heavy bored.
> Peoples bore me,
> literature bores me, especially great literature,
> Henry bores me, with his plights and gripes.

Henry may have bored Berryman quite literally to death, but Berryman does not permit him to bore the reader. This volatile poetry of neurotic discovery and surprise emanates from 'a very useful mind' (No. 380) whose antics in verse are among the century's most original utterances. It remains to be seen how many 'assistant professors become associates/by working on his works' (No. 378).

Robert Lowell's English versions of other poets from Homer to Pasternak in *Imitations* (1961), his trio of plays *The Old Glory* (1965), based on stories by Hawthorne and Melville, and his free translations of Racine's *Phaedra* (1960) and Aeschylus's *Prometheus Unbound* (1967) are the work of a learned writer with a gift for re-creation. Lowell was, however, like Berryman, torn by conflicts which he shares with his readers. Self-confessed 'screwball' in 'Waking in the Blue' (*Life Studies*, 1959), he evokes a morning in the mental hospital where he sought to stabilise the anxieties of his hyperactive mind:

> Cock of the walk,
> I strut in my turtle-necked French sailor's jersey
> before the metal shaving mirrors,
> and see the shaky future grow familiar
> in the pinched, indigenous faces
> of these thoroughbred mental cases,
> twice my age and half my weight.
> We are all old-timers,
> each of us holds a locked razor.

Despite the irony of this self-excoriating narcissism, the strutting 'Cock of the walk' can continue to vex the response to Lowell's poetry. Any subject is fair game for poetry, but there is a relish of extremity here, as there is masochism in John Berryman's view that 'The artist is extremely lucky who is presented with the worst possible ordeal which will not actually kill him'.

There has been no disputing Lowell's mastery of the poetic line and the arresting image, or his strategies of symbolism and association since 'The Quaker Grave at Nantucket' (*Poems 1938–1949*, 1950) combined a sense of his own New England ancestry with allusions to Ahab's *Pequod* 'packing off to hell' and the 'expressionless' expression of God on the face of the Virgin Mary. An elegy for

Lowell's cousin, lost at sea in the Second World War, the poem ends in tolling ambiguity. The final cadence is one of resignation but the subservience to God in which man must acquiesce is reflected in God's power to renege on his own promise:

> . . . the Lord God formed man from the sea's slime
> And breathed into his face the breath of life,
> And blue-lung'd combers lumbered to the kill.
> The Lord survives the rainbow of his will.

In *Life Studies* the condemned murderer, Louis Lepke, is embalmed for ever 'in his air of lost connections' in 'Memories of West Street and Lepke', and the wife of 'To Speak of Woe That Is in Marriage' is unforgettably frozen in her submission to a 'whiskey-blind' husband: 'Gored by the climacteric of his want,/he stalls above me like an elephant'. The barbarism of commerce is summed up by the commercial photographer who 'shows Hiroshima boiling/over a Mosler Safe, the "Rock of Ages"/that survived the blast' in the title poem of *For the Union Dead* (1964). Lowell's public spirit marched in protest against the Vietnam War, and the mood of his first person singular moves compassionately into the plural concern in 'Waking Early Sunday Morning' (*Near the Ocean*, 1967):

> Pity the planet, all joy gone
> from this sweet volcanic cone;
> peace to our children when they fall
> in small war on the heels of small
> war – until the end of time
> to police the earth, a ghost
> orbiting forever lost
> in our monotonous sublime.

In the 'Afterthought' to *Notebook* (1970) Lowell cautions his reader not to regard the work as his 'private lash or confession, or a puritan's too literal pornographic honesty'. He protests a little too much. Originally published in the United States as *Notebook 1967– 1968* (1969) and further developed in the 1973 volumes, *History, For Lizzie and Harriet* and *The Dolphin*, the poems connect the personal experience of their author to public events from the Six Day War between Israel and Egypt in 1967 to the murders of Che Guevara, Martin Luther King and Robert Kennedy, and the Russian occupation of Czechoslovakia. Yet the confessional impulse is still strongly felt; 'Cock of the walk' of his own awareness, Lowell compels his 'geography' inwards, absorbing outer events into the centre of himself.

9

Diversity

AFTER President Richard Nixon's resignation in 1974 and the lacklustre administration of his successor, Gerald Ford, liberal Americans looked to the Democrat, Jimmy Carter, for leadership of integrity and intelligence. Despite President Carter's success in defusing the political crisis in the Middle East by bringing Israel's Prime Minister, Menachem Begin and Egypt's President Sadat into conversation at Camp David and overseeing the signing of the Egyptian-Israeli Peace Treaty of 1979, the general ineffectuality of his single-term administration favoured a more hawkish successor. In November 1980 the sixty-nine-year-old Republican, Ronald Reagan, an ex-movie-actor and former Governor of California, was swept to the White House by one of the biggest election landslides in American history.

During his first term President Reagan cut income taxes, reduced government spending, created a large budget deficit, induced a severe recession and ended the high inflation of the late 1970s. He also carried out an extensive military build-up to counter the Soviet accumulation of arms. In foreign affairs Reagan adopted a hard-line policy toward the USSR. His administration deployed US nuclear missiles in Britain, Italy and West Germany despite strong European and Soviet opposition, overcame the national reluctance to use force overseas by invading and liberating Grenada, helped to place the Soviets on the defensive and restored national pride with his assertive foreign policy. Re-elected by a huge majority in 1984, Reagan saw his popularity plummet and his credibility almost vanish when the nation learned in late 1986 that his administration had sold arms to terrorist-supporting Iran and had provided illegal aid to the Contra guerrillas in Nicaragua.

Until the mid 1960s American literary history is a sequence of dominations by particular regions. In the 1820s and 1830s the literary capital was New York City with William Cullen Bryant,

Washington Irving and James Fenimore Cooper, but by the middle of the century leadership had passed to New England and Boston had become the literary centre. New England remained the dominant region until the end of the nineteenth century, through the period of Emerson, Thoreau, Hawthorne and Melville to the pre-modern works of Emily Dickinson and Henry Adams. In the twentieth century the literary centre of the United States has moved twice. First came new leadership in the Middle West with Theodore Dreiser, Vachel Lindsay, Sherwood Anderson and Carl Sandburg; then, about 1925, it became evident that the country's major literary energies were in the South. The Southern literary renaissance is the last definable grouping of talents in terms of region. Since the 1960s groupings of literary talent have broken from regional boundaries and it has become increasingly more appropriate to consider American literature in terms of ethnic and other groupings, like Black writers, women writers and Jewish writers.

Social minorities asserted themselves with new vigour after the war, especially in the 1950s and 1960s. A new emphasis on individuality is reflected in the phrase, 'the "me" generation', used in reference to the 1960s and 1970s. In 1961 and 1962 American publication of Henry Miller's (1891–1980) long-banned *Tropic of Cancer* (1934) and *Tropic of Capricorn* (1939) made widely available the scatological exuberance of a rampant individualist who believed that 'Civilisation is the arterio-sclerosis of culture'. Continuing sexual discrimination, the imposition of the military draft and Federal incompetence in Civil Rights encouraged women, homosexuals, lesbians, Indians and, most of all, Blacks to believe that they would win their rightful status only by energetic campaigning.

Civil Rights and Black writing

A Supreme Court ruling of 1896 held that distinctions based on colour were constitutionally permissible if the accommodations separately provided for 'white' and 'coloured' persons were of equal amenity. The erosion of 'separate but equal' began in 1938 when the Supreme Court ruled that equal protection of law had been denied a Negro applicant who had been refused admission to the University of Missouri Law School. He had been offered instead a money grant allegedly sufficient to pay his tuition at a university outside the state. In 1954 a unanimous Supreme Court decision in the case of 'Brown v. Board of Education of Topeka (Kansas)' asserted that segregation deprived Negroes of the 'equal protection of the laws' guaranteed by the Fourteenth Amendment to the Constitution, and that 'in the field of public education, the doctrine of "separate but equal" has no place'.

The violence of Southern white reaction to Federal enforcement of this decision and subsequent desegregation rulings led to 'sit-ins' and protest marches which culminated in the 'March on Washington' on 28 August 1963, when some 250,000 Blacks led and controlled by Martin Luther King demonstrated peacefully in support of their rights under the Constitution. Although President Lyndon B. Johnson's administration responded by passing the Civil Rights Act (1964) and the Voting Rights Act (1965), Black protest grew more militant. Anarchist elements were indicated by violent outbursts in New York's Harlem (July 1964) and the Watts district of Los Angeles (August 1965). With the assassination of Martin Luther King at Memphis, Tennessee, on 4 April 1968 the Black movement lost both its solidarity and much of its effectiveness. Commenting 'After the Los Angeles riots' in his 'Letter from America' (The Listener, 26 August 1965) Alistair Cooke (b. 1908) said:

> We are just beginning to realise that the chances of open violence are greater where the Negro has more legal and social equality, but still does not have the money or the jobs or the housing he would like.

A century after the Civil War the law had achieved colour blindness, but the provision of opportunity remained a challenge to the resources of American society.

Proper understanding of the Black struggle requires not only a reading of history, but also of such Black testimony as the anti-slavery orator, Frederick Douglass's (c. 1817–95) Narrative of the Life of Frederick Douglass, An American Slave (1845), and the great educator, Booker T. Washington's (1856–1915) autobiography Up From Slavery (1901). William E. B. DuBois' (1868–1963) plea for greater understanding of his race in The Souls of Black Folks (1903) begins with the forethought that 'the problem of the Twentieth Century is the problem of the colour line'. It ends with a prayer to God as 'The Reader':

> Hear my cry, O God the Reader; vouchsafe that this book fall not still-born into the world wilderness. Let there spring, Gentle One, from out its leaves vigour of thought and thoughtful deed to reap the harvest wonderful. Let the ears of a guilty people tingle with truth, and seventy

millions sigh for the righteousness which exalteth nations, in this drear day when human brotherhood is mockery and a snare. Thus in thy good time may infinite reason turn the tangle straight, and these crooked marks on a fragile leaf be not indeed THE END.

First published anonymously, James Weldon Johnson's (1871–1938) novel *The Autobiography of an Ex-Coloured Man* (1912), written in the first person of a Black whose nerve repeatedly fails him, purports to be a genuine autobiography and was read as such even when Johnson revealed his authorship. Johnson published a real autobiography *Along this Way* in 1933. Richard Wright says in his autobiography *Black Boy* (1945) that 'All my life had shaped me for the realism, the naturalism of the modern novel'. *Native Son* superbly endorses the claim, and strengthens its realism with well-judged symbolic effects. Wright speaks directly about racial injustice in his lecture *White Man, Listen!* (1957) and returns to fiction in the short stories published as *Eight Men* (1961).

Since the early 1960s spokesmen for Black writers have often argued that Black literature is necessarily a separatist art and Black experience a province to be defined only by and for Blacks. This understandable if regrettable parochialism is in part politically motivated, and in part a delayed reaction to earlier periods in the history of Black literature in America. The first definable period of Black American writing, from the last years of the nineteenth century until the 1920s, was characterised by an 'integrationist' view of Black ambitions. Black writers still professed belief in the possibility of assimilation to white culture, and the usually unspoken goal was white approval. Early Black writers knew how whites preferred to see Blacks in literature. As the poet, Sterling A. Brown (*b.* 1901) says, 'the Negro has met with as great injustice in American literature as he has in American life. The majority of books about Negroes merely stereotype Negro character'. The stereotypes which, Brown suggests, confirm the Black man's acceptance of his inferior status and perpetuate the myth of 'nigger' include those of the contented slave, the local colour Negro or the exotic primitive, the wretched freeman and the tragic mulatto. Unfortunately for the Black cause, Black writers often reinforce these stereotypes. Paul Lawrence Dunbar (1872–1906) writes dialect poetry in the conventional plantation tradition because with such material he could gain, as he said, 'a hearing', even though he recognises the artificiality of the image he is reinforcing in the minds of white people:

> We wear the mask that grins and lies,
> It hides our cheeks and shades our eyes,
> This debt we pay to human guile;
> With torn and bleeding hearts we smile,
> And mouth with myriad subtleties

The fiction of Charles W. Chestnutt (1858–1932) deals with racial tension, but often confirms the myth of white superiority. In the story 'A Matter of Principle' the principle in question is whiteness when a Black merchant insists that his daughter maintain her social standing by marrying a 'light' and therefore socially acceptable Black.

In the 1920s the so-called 'Harlem Renaissance' seemed to replace an acceptance of stereotypes with a new affirmation of racial pride among Blacks. In *The New Negro* (1925) the sociologist and art critic Alain Locke (1886–1954) argued that 'the old Negro . . . a creature of moral debate and historical controversy . . . has been more of a formula than a human being'. The migration of Blacks to the cities, with the resultant economic and intellectual opportunities available to them, was creating a new kind of Black who rejoiced in the special energy of his race and believed in the development of American society by 'race co-operation'. Despite Black celebration of the exotic and primitive, however, the new Negro only succeeded in becoming another formula, an Uncle Tom of the arts; he still had to convince his white countryman that he was a person. The poet Langston Hughes (1902–67) had few illusions about the Harlem Renaissance; as he recalls in his autobiography, *The Big Sea* (1940):

> . . . I was there. I had a swell time while it lasted. But I thought it wouldn't last long. For how could a large and enthusiastic number of people be crazy about Negroes for ever? But some Harlemites thought the millenium had come . . . They were sure the New Negro would lead a new life from then on in green pastures of tolerance created by Countee Cullen, Ethel Waters, Claude McKay, Duke Ellington, Bojangles and Alain Locke.

However deficient in gaining Blacks the status they sought, the Harlem Renaissance did draw white attention to the creative energies of Black people and was a period of energy and accomplishment that deepened Black self-consciousness and increased the momentum of Black aspiration towards the Civil Rights movement across the country.

The ingredients of Black feeling during the Civil Rights years of effort and anguish are especially accessible in autobiographical writings such as *The Autobiography of Malcom X* (1965), Eldridge Cleaver's (*b.* 1935) scathingly confessional *Soul on Ice* (1968), *Seize the Time* (1970) by Bobby Seale (*b.* 1936), Chairman of the Black Panther movement, and Angela Davis's (*b.* 1944) autobiography (1974). If these more recent Black voices already seem unwarrantably strident, their claims and frustrations may quickly be seen in context by a reading of *The Algiers Motel Incident* (1969) by John Hersey (*b.* 1914). On the night of 26 July 1967 armed police and members of the Michigan National Guard broke into the annexe of a motel in the Black ghetto of Detroit, rounded up ten Black youths and two white girls and demanded information about snipers who had been reported in the vicinity. The girls were beaten, had their clothes torn off and were exposed to sexual insult; three of the Blacks were taken separately into bedrooms and shot dead at point-blank range. Hersey sees the incident as an episode of white racism with pathological sexual overtones. The law enforcers behaved as they did because they could get away with it. There were, apparently, no snipers at the Algiers Motel that night.

Ralph Ellison's *Invisible Man* is the most comprehensive treatment in fiction of the twentieth-century Black predicament. 'That invisibility to which I refer', explains the anonymous narrator, 'occurs because of a peculiar disposition of the eyes of those with whom I come in contact.' Invisibility is the absence of social identity felt by a Black whose colour prevents him from being 'seen' by others – even by those of his own race – as an individual. The novel sees through the heartlessness that can vitiate social protest. When the narrator's talent for oratory wins him a political role with the communists, he realises that he is being used as a symbol of the Negro and that he remains invisible as a man. A Harlem riot shows him that he must contend against both whites and Blacks who seek to exploit him for their own political ends. The Negro in *Invisible Man* thus becomes a Black American Everyman. Ellison paraphrases the moral of his story in 'Some Questions and Some Answers' in Part III of *Shadow and Act* (1964). His definition of the values of Black people opposes the Black Muslim movement's militant refusal to be assimilated into the mainstream of American life:

> the values of my own people are neither 'white' nor 'black', they are American. Nor can I see how they could be anything else, since we are a people who are involved in the texture of the American experience.

The Street (1946) by Ann Petry (*b*. 1911) is an eloquent novel about a coloured woman's fight to defend her middle-class values and her son from sabotage by the influence of the Harlem streets. *If He Hollers Let Him Go* (1945) by Chester Himes (*b*. 1909) is the most raucous of Black protest novels, a violent wartime story of racial discrimination in a California shipyard. Later books show Himes moving towards a position from which he can satirise both sides of the colour line. In *Pinktoes* (1965) sex is so prominently the leveller that there is hardly room for further implication. The violent comedy of *Cotton Comes to Harlem* (1965) introduces Himes's careening detectives, Coffin Ed and Grave Digger. Their quarry is the Reverend Deke O'Malley whose Back-to-Africa movement offers a passage to the homeland for $1,000 per family. The hijacking by white bandits of the $87,000 O'Malley has collected leads Coffin Ed and Grave Digger down a trail of caricatured tarts, pimps, gangsters, churches, clubs and brothels. They also encounter Colonel L. Calhoun who is mounting a Back-to-the-Southland campaign, advertised by pictures of Congolese tribal war and famine in contrast to others of fat, happy, Black Southerners driving cars as long as the street. Himes checks his tendency toward mere sarcasm in *The Heat's On* (1966), a Harlem detective story, and *Blind Man with a Pistol* (1969).

In the popular mind of the time, the writer most closely identified with the Civil Rights period was James Baldwin (*b*. 1924). His first novel *Go Tell it on the Mountain* (1953) analyses the compulsions and frustrations of Black culture in Johnny Grimes's relation to the rabid fundamentalism of the 'Temple of the Fire Baptized'. *Giovanni's Room* (1956) reads like an unfinished sketch for *Another Country* (1962) in which Baldwin queries racial barriers by juxtaposing the problem of sexual ones. Unfortunately the themes collide instead of meshing to illuminate each other. Later novels, from *Tell Me How Long the Train's Been Gone* (1968) to *Just Above My Head* (1978), are looser in form, repetitive in effect and surprisingly prolix, although there is invariably a sense of the author's striving to use fiction as a means of clarifying experience. In *The Fire Next Time* (1963) Baldwin says: 'For the horrors of the American Negro's life there has been almost no language'. After *Go Tell it on the Mountain* his own language has been most eloquent in the essays of *Notes of a Native Son* (1955), *Nobody Knows My Name* (1961) and *The Fire Next Time* which ends with a call to arms that is also a warning:

Everything now, we must assume, is in our hands; we have no right to assume otherwise. If we – and now I mean the relatively conscious whites and the relatively conscious blacks, who must, like lovers, insist on, or create, the consciousness of the others – do not falter in our duty now, we may be able, handful that we are, to end the racial nightmare, and achieve our country, and change the history of the world. If we do not now dare everything, the fulfillment of that prophecy, recreated from the Bible in song by a slave, is upon us: *God gave Noah the rainbow sign, No more water, the fire next time!*

In recent years much of the best Black writing has been by women, several of whom show the influence of Zora Neale Hurston (1901–60), one of the most vivid personalities of the Harlem Renaissance. Langston Hughes said of her: 'Only to reach a wider audience, need she ever write books – she is a perfect book of entertainment in herself'. Despite her personality, her books and much acclaim especially for her autobiography *Dust Tracks on a Road* (1942), by 1950 Hurston was reduced to working as a maid, and in 1960 died penniless in a welfare home in Florida. One reason for the obscurity of her later years is that her work was not liked by her influential male contemporaries. Sterling A. Brown, Richard Wright and Ralph Ellison condemned her work as 'socially unconscious'. The lush style in which she captures the subtlety and rhythm of Southern Black vernacular speech was seen as reactionary by the proponents of social realism. She even had the temerity to publish *Moses: Man of the Mountain* (1939), an allegory which translates the Moses myth into the Black tradition and satirises divisions between Black classes – upper class, bourgeoisie and proletariat. It is both Hurston's vitality and her lyrical style of writing which lead Alice Walker (*b.* 1944) to say: 'In my mind, Zora Neale Hurston, Billie Holliday, and Bessie Smith form a sort of unholy trinity. Zora *belongs* in the tradition of black women singers, rather than among "the literati," at least to me' (*In Search of Our Mother's Gardens*, [1983]). Under her lyrical manner, Zora Neale Hurston's novels portray the realities of Black life as she sees them. She rejects the Black party-line in literary fashion as in politics and is not inhibited by the fear of pandering to white expectations of Black violence, fecklessness or bigotry. Her candour is her moral eminence, implying that anything less than the truth would be a diminution of Black people. This is what first attracted Alice Walker: '. . . the quality I feel is most characteristic of Zora's work: racial health; a sense of black people as complete, complex, *undiminished* human beings, a sense that is lacking in so much black writing and literature'. In most Black American literature there has been an underlying desire to present positive images of Blacks. In preferring the complexity of truth to political expediency, Toni Morrison (*b*. 1931), Alice Walker, Gayl Jones (*b*. 1949), Carlene Hatcher Polite (*b*. 1932) and Toni Cade Bambara (*b*. 1939) are all inheritors of Zora Neal Hurston. These writers share a concern for those who are oppressed both as Blacks and as women, and agree that the Black aesthetic means commitment to the betterment of Black life.

Of Toni Morrison's four novels the most critically acclaimed is *Song of Solomon* (1977), an elaborate account of a young Black man's search for his roots. The book appeals by its Dickensian exuberance, but ends in an ambiguously sensational mixture of history and fantasy. *Tar Baby* (1980) is a near surrealist, symbolic story of freakish love and motherhood which explores the underlying relationships between white masters and Black servants in a Caribbean setting. Morrison's most satisfying novel to date is *Sula* (1973) which traces the friendship of two Black girls in a Black community called the Bottom in Ohio. The power of the novel comes less from Morrison's considerable skill in evoking the relationship between the girls or the sense of life's vicissitudes in a Black township, than from Sula's strength of character. When Sula returns to the Bottom after an absence of ten years she earns general disapproval by putting her grandmother in a home and proceeding to sleep with most of the married men in the neighbourhood, including her friend Nel's husband, Jude. Three years later, Sula dies, possibly by suicide. The irony of the novel becomes apparent when it emerges that Sula's role was to keep the community in a condition of moral order, by giving people something to react against:

> . . . mothers who had defended their positions as mothers from Sula's malevolence (or who had defended their positions as mothers from Sula's scorn for the role) now had nothing to rub up against. The tension was gone and so was the reason for the effort they had made. Without her mockery, affection for others sunk into flaccid disrepair. Daughters who had complained bitterly about the responsibilities of taking care of their aged mothers-in-law had altered when Sula locked Eva away, and they began cleaning the old women's spittoons without a murmur. Now that Sula was dead and done with, they returned to a steeping resentment of the burdens of old people. Wives uncoddled their husbands; there seemed no further need to reinforce their vanity.

Black women novelists often seem to suggest that sexism is more oppressive than racism and portray Black men as smooth, brutal or masochistic. In Toni Morrison's first novel *The Bluest Eye* (1970), the young heroine is raped by her drunken father on the kitchen floor. In Toni Cade Bambara's short story 'Talkin Bout Sonny' (in the collection, *Gorilla, My Love* [1972]) the distraught, bewildered male protagonist attacks his wife with an axe. Gayl Jones's novel *Corregidora* (1975) begins with the pregnant heroine being pushed down a flight of stairs by her jealous husband. The abuse of women by men is not a universal obsession of Black women writers: the fact that the position of Black women can now be fully discussed in fiction is one of the signs that Black writing has reached new and impressive maturity. A persuasive analysis of male aggression and inadequacy is given in Carlene Hatcher Polite's novel *The Flagellants* (1967). After breaking with her lover, a Black poet, she delivers an indictment in which his defects are scathingly attributed to Black masochism:

> Denounce the slave nature, the reactionary stigma. Who is enslaving you? . . . Change your mythical virility into courage, your commendable knowledge into spirit; disavow your history of being the mangy, flea-bitten, unvalued, black underdog. Go on out there . . . if I were a man, Jimson, I would give you the beating you desire. This is your thrill, your kick. You would like a man to beat you down, especially a white one. You have come to expect it, anticipate it. Once, so violated, you will feel delivered, free of the calling of your manhood.

Alice Walker's recurrent subject in fiction is the struggle of ordinary people for self-survival in hostile environments. In *Meridian* (1976), and more starkly in *The Colour Purple* (1982), the hostility is largely male. An epistolary novel, *The Colour Purple* consists of a girl's letters to God then to her absent sister Nettie. In a small town in Georgia in the early years of the twentieth century, Celie, hardly more than a child herself, gives birth to two children, fathered by the man she calls 'Pa' who takes the infants from her at birth and will tell her no more about their fate. Abused first by Pa then by the man she calls 'Mr', a widower with four children to whom Pa has 'given' her, Celie lives in isolated misery until 1921 when a blues singer, Shug Avery, the preacher's daughter and Mr's lover, begins to encourage her to be aware of her own worth. Her effort towards self-esteem is rewarded when Shug brings her dozens of letters withheld by Mr for years, written to her by Nettie, now a missionary in Africa. A happy ending provides a reunion between the sisters. Celie's progress towards possession of her own identity is dramatised by language as her letters become increasingly articulate. Alice Walker's artistic judgement in controlling this mirror of developing self assurance is impeccable. Celie's last letter is to God reporting the reunion, and it is the authenticity of untutored idiomatic Black speech which protects the moment from sentimentality:

> When Nettie's foot come down on the porch I almost die. I stand swaying ... Nettie stand swaying ... Then us both start to moan and cry. Us totter toward one nother like us use to do when us was babies. Then us feel so weak when us touch, us knock each other down. But what us care? Us sit and lay there on the porch inside each other's arms.
> After while, she say *Celie.*
> I say *Nettie.*

Black poets

The cultural movement of the 1920s known as the Harlem Renaissance brought to prominence the poetry of Countee Cullen (1903–46) and Langston Hughes. Cullen's poems, collected in *On These I Stand* (1947), are about being Black but are conventional in form, with Keats an acknowledged influence. In 'A Song of Praise' he reproaches 'one who praised his lady's being fair':

> My love is dark as yours is fair,
> Yet lovelier I hold her
> Than listless maids with pallid hair,
> And blood that's thin and colder.

In 'Yet Do I Marvel' Cullen ponders the mystery of a God who could 'make a poet black and bid him sing!' Most recent Black poets have chosen to sing in less orthodoxly literary accents, preferring to mix techniques derived from Langston Hughes and the colloquial poems of Sterling A. Brown with the Whitmanesque manner of Beat generation poets like Allen Ginsberg and Lawrence Ferlinghetti. Hughes experiments with free verse, jazz and blues rhythms in a large body of poetry from *The Weary Blues* (1926) to *Selected Poems* (1965) and *The Panther and the Lash; Poems of Our Times* (1967). In his cycle of Harlem poems *Montage of a Dream Deferred* (1951) Hughes moves from the simple statement of 'Dream Variations' where a dance throughout the 'white day' ends as night comes, tenderly, 'Black like me', to the jazzy insinuations of 'Dream Boogie':

> Good morning, daddy!
> Ain't you heard
> The boogie-woogie rumble
> Of a dream deferred?

Listen closely:
You'll hear their feet
Beating out and beating out a –

> *You think*
> *It's a happy beat?*

Listen to it closely:
Ain't you heard
something underneath
like a –

> *What did I say?*

Sure
I'm happy!
Take it away!

> *Hey, pop!*
> *Re-bop!*
> *Mop!*

> *Y-e-a-h!*

Social circumstances and Black American history bring Charles
Olson's two poles together for Black poets: the sense of their own
skin commits them to changing the geography that leans in on them.
An articulate Black is by definition political. Gwendolyn Brooks
(*b*. 1917), whose *Annie Allen* (1949) made her the first Black poet to
win the Pulitzer Prize, is less obviously militant than some of the
younger voices heard in recent years. She concedes the racial element
in her work, but adds, 'It is my privilege to present Negroes not as
curios but as people'. In 'The Chicago Defender Sends a Man to
Little Rock', she writes from the point of view of a reporter sent to
Little Rock, Arkansas in 1957 to cover the disturbances that resulted
from Federal enforcement of desegregation rulings. The townspeople
are ordinary, churchgoing, sensitive, kindly, yet now 'they are
hurling spittle, rock,/Garbage and fruit'. The speaker's hatred
modulates to sadness:

> I scratch my head, massage the hate-I-had.
> I blink across my prim and pencilled pad.
> The saga I was sent for is not down,
> Because there is a puzzle in this town.
> The biggest News I do not dare
> Telegraph to the Editor's chair:
> 'They are like people everywhere'.

In more recent poetry Gwendolyn Brooks has engaged more directly with the anger of Black revolutionary feeling, developing the satirical quality of 'The Lovers of the Poor' which ends an account of a visit to ghetto flats by members of the Ladies' Betterment League with a contemptuous description of the do-gooders' departure:

> Keeping their scented bodies in the centre
> Of the hall as they walk down the hysterical hall,
> They allow their lovely skirts to graze no wall,
> Are off at what they manage of a canter,
> And, resuming all the clues of what they were,
> Try to avoid inhaling the laden air.

Younger Black poets, many of them women, usually write more aggressive verse than this. Imamu Amiri Baraka (LeRoi Jones, *b*. 1934) writes verse which uses Black vernacular according to the method of writing poetry advocated by Jack Kerouac who defined the act of creation in terms of the popular Beat image of the poet as musician uttering an 'undisturbed flow from the mind of personal secret idea-words, *blowing* (as per jazz musician) on subject of image'. Baraka writes out of the same cultural pressures as Ralph Ellison's 'invisible' hero when, in 'Hymn for Lanie Poo', he represents the values of all-powerful white America by

> the huge & loveless
> white anglo-sun/of
> benevolent step
> mother America

and when he says in 'Numbers, Letters' (*Black Magic: Poetry 1961–1967*, 1967), 'I can't say who I am/unless you agree I'm real'. The posture of dependence, however, is just one strategy in an increasingly militant campaign. 'We want "poems that kill"', he declares in 'Black Art', and in *Home: Social Essays* (1966) says that 'The Black Artist's role in America is to aid in the destruction of America as he knows it'. Haki R. Mahubuti (Don L. Lee, *b*. 1942) agrees; but wonders how the art of poetry can help the cause:

> i an't seen no poems stop a .38
> i an't seen no stanzas break a honkie's head
> i an't seen no metaphors stop a tank.

In the volume *Don't Cry Scream* (1973) Mahubuti settles for poetry as a means of raising and directing the consciousness of his fellow Blacks in the street dialect that can often exclude white readers:

```
cool-cool so cool
he didn't know,
after detroit, newark, chicago &c.
we had to hip
            cool-cool/super-cool/real cool
        that
    to be black
    is
    to be
    very-hot
```

Sonia Sanchez (b. 1935) relocates the American pioneering tradition in a violent Black future in 'Right on: white America' (*We a BaddDD People*, 1973):

```
        this country might have
        been a pion
                eer land.          once.
                and it still is.

                check out the falling
        gun/shells        on our blk/tomorrows.
```

In *Black Women Writers (1950–1980)* (ed. Mari Evans, 1984), Sonia Sanchez writes: 'The most fundamental truth to be told in any art form, as far as Blacks are concerned, is that America is killing us'. Mari Evans (b. 1923) shows two moods of Black defiance in her *I Am a Black Woman* (1970). In 'Vive Noir!' she is vengeful:

```
                i'm
        gonna make it a
            crime
                to be anything BUT black
        gonna make white
        a twenty-four hour
        lifetime
        J.O.B.
```

In her title poem Evans is proud of being 'a black woman/tall as a cypress/strong beyond all definition'. Superior in her blackness, she commands: 'Look on me and be/renewed'. A different kind of pride leads Nikki Giovanni (b. 1943) to reject the sentimentality of white liberal patronage in 'Nikki-Rosa' (*Black Judgement*, 1973):

I really hope no white person ever has cause to write about me because they never understand Black love is Black wealth and they'll probably talk about my hard childhood and never understand that all the while I was quite happy.

It would be the kind of sentimental distortion which Nikki Giovanni resents not to admit that much Black poetry of the 1960s and 1970s is little more than rage expressed in lines of varying length, 'stanzas to beat a honkie's head'. The best work is fresh, direct and illuminating. It draws its energy not only from sociologically verifiable attitudes, but also from a wish to 'make it new' in a language that goes back, through Hughes, from the city street 'jive' of contemporary America to the cry and holler and changing pitch of the blues, and the work-songs of the old plantations.

Fiction by women

Shortly before her death in 1979 Elizabeth Bishop explained why she refused to be included in women's anthologies: 'Undoubtedly gender does play an important part in the making of any art, but art is art and to separate writings, paintings, musical compositions, etc., into two sexes is to emphasize values in them that are *not* art'. In the large volume of writing by women in the twentieth century, there is work in which 'values that are not art' – female patterns of living, feeling, and perceiving – are made into art, just as there is 'feminist' work which fails to rise above the level of 'anti-phallocratic' revolt or propaganda. Opinions will differ as vigorously about the intentions and qualities of women's writing as they do about literature produced by men. That the century has yielded an abundance of artistic writing by women is beyond dispute.

Mary McCarthy (*b*. 1912) anatomises the manners and pretensions of intellectuals in short stories and novels from *The Company She Keeps* (1942), which includes 'The Man in the Brooks Brothers Shirt' about a middle-aged businessman's seduction of an intellectual young woman, to *The Groves of Academe* (1952), *A Charmed Life* (1955) and the stories collected in *Cast a Cold Eye* (1952). In *Birds of America* (1971) Mary McCarthy filters through the mind of a nineteen-year-old American boy samples of those migratory people who spend parts of their lives in the United States and parts in Europe. *Cannibals and Missionaries* (1980) is set in 1975 when an international committee – six Americans, a Dutchman and a Scot – are sent to investigate allegations of torture in Iran. Between Paris and Teheran their plane is hijacked and it is revealed that the passenger list includes a party of rich art collectors on a package tour to view Iran's art and archaeology. In their Dutch farmhouse hide-out the terrorists ignore their original prey, 'the liberal cat's paws of the energy interests', and negotiate for the exchange of art collectors for art collections. The agility of Mary McCarthy's irony is not sufficient to the task of providing this topical novel of ideas with a clear focus; it is never dull but remains a clever patchwork of unrealised possibilities.

According to Mary McCarthy, her Danish translator 'was the only one who spotted that *The Group* (1963) was written from the point of view of each girl in turn, like a pastiche'. The novel traces the lives of eight educated young women from their graduation from Vassar College in 1933 to the end of the decade and the Second World War. Under McCarthy's clinical but not cruel eye they respond in different ways to the loss of virginity, marriage, arguments for and against breast-feeding, the claims of psychoanalysis and the obligations the Spanish Civil War imposes on caring leftists. The real theme of the novel is progress. 'No first-rate mind can accept the concept of progress any more', the opportunistic Norinne tells Priss near the end. Norinne's mind, as McCarthy makes clear, is second-rate – she is not one of 'the group'. Progress is not bad, but even for bright Vassar girls, difficult to distinguish from the trends, postures and easy formulae in which men particularly specialise. The book is about the inevitability of disillusion and the need for compromise. Only a woman – this woman – could have written *The Group*; but the book goes beyond the scope of what is currently regarded as 'feminist' fiction. Nevertheless it is still one of the most intelligent twentieth-century novels about specifically female experience.

Marilyn French's best-selling story of Mira Ward, 'wife of the Fifties . . . woman of the Seventies' in *The Women's Room* (1977) is trendily shrill and turgid by comparison, and *Beyond Power* (1985) a hectoring diatribe against partriarchy based on a perverse reading of history, the equation of fatherhood with tyranny, and a vague belief that feminism is 'blessed'. Among contemporary treatments of woman's situation in the modern world, the most concentratedly painful is Joan Didion's (*b*. 1934) *Play It As It Lays* (1970), the most incisively satirical is Alison Lurie's (*b*. 1926) *The War Between the Tates* (1974), and the most straightforwardly touching, Mary Gordon's (*b*. 1950) first novel *Final Payments* (1978). Gail Godwin (*b*. 1937) writes in the tradition of 'the realistic novel which deals with people trying to understand their lives and live them fully'. *Violent Clay* (1978) is an incisive study of the relationship between an artist's life and her work. In *A Mother and Two Daughters* the death of a gentle, cultivated North Carolina lawyer offers the challenge of freedom to his widow, Nell, and their daughters Cate, an idealist, and Lydia who, opting for risk, has just walked out of what appeared to be the ideal marriage. If the plan of the novel seems thematically diagrammatic, its development holds the attention because of Gail Godwin's eye for psychological detail and her ability to create attractive characters with whom it is easy to become involved. After forty years of comfortable marriage, Nell Strickland doubts her competence to live alone without her husband: 'He protected me from so much . . . from my harshest judgements of myself as well as of others'. The plot of *The Finishing School* (1984) is also initiated by the death of a protecting husband and father. Godwin's stake in the women she launches on the world is expressed by Ursula de Vane whose influence on the young Justine Stokes is the latter's 'finishing school' in education for life: 'She's a clean slate. When she meets new people or new challenges, she is free to respond to the unique demands of the moment'. There is nothing doctrinaire about Godwin's work: she succeeds as a novelist whose special interest is in the use to which women put their opportunities for freedom and self-realisation.

The stories of Joyce Carol Oates (*b.* 1938) are full of marital disaffection, and insights that proclaim a woman's point of view, but the typical concern of her fiction, as in *Expensive People* (1968) – a crafty subversion of the type of the holy adolescent recurrent in American fiction from Twain to Salinger – and *Do With Me What You Will* (1973), is with the alienations of power and money, and the discontinuity of personal identity in a fragmenting world. The tendency to melodrama which spoils *Angel of Light* (1981) is a strength in *Bellefleur* a Gothic family saga, *A Bloodsmoor Romance* (1982) and *Mysteries of Winterthurn* (1984), a sequence of turbulent novels dealing with nineteenth-century and early twentieth-century America in an abundant, Dickensian style which combines the appeal of soap opera with shrewd and humorous recreations of the era and its *grand guignol* vitality. Oates's parody of nineteenth-century popular fiction is particularly clear – and entertaining – in *A Bloodsmoor Romance*:

> Having no capability, and, indeed, no desire, so far as graphic descriptions of 'love embraces' are concerned, I shall make no attempt to sketch for the repelled reader precisely how The Beast (sexual desire) emerged to make a loathsome mockery of the love declarations, kisses, caresses, and

other amorous indulgences which transpired between Malvinia and Mr. Twain, in Malvinia's sumptuously appointed bedchamber.

The novel *Them* (1969), is a study of violence in terms of the race riots in Detroit in 1967. Although Oates considered then that 'War, rape, murder and the more colourful minor crimes evidently fall within the exclusive province of male action', she rejects any attempt to define her as a feminist, remarking 'I learned long ago that being Lewis Carroll was infinitely more exciting than being Alice'. Like the work of Joyce Carol Oates, Anne Tyler's (*b.* 1941) novels including *Morgan's Passing* (1980) and *Dinner at the Homesick Restaurant* (1982) and *The Accidental Tourist* (1985) earn distinction not by way of a feminist perspective, but by the quality of sustained creative effort. Anne Tyler's strengths are her moral wisdom, her analytical eye and her ability to write lucid, witty prose which continuously illuminates her samples of American life. Her plotting, too, is exemplary.

Less prolific than Oates or Tyler, Eleanor Clark (*b.* 1913) is more variously experimental through a range of genres. *The Bitter Box* (1947) is set with commendable precision in the Depression years, and Clark's ability to combine imagination and exactness yields a justly celebrated work of non-fiction in *Rome and a Villa* (1952; revised edition 1975) which mixes past and present in a personal account of a great city, its architecture and the culture it expresses. Set in Brittany, *The Oysters of Locmariaquer* (1964) tells the story of the oysters grown on the Breton coast. The novel *Baldur's Gate* (1970) and *Dr Heart: A Novella and Other Stories* (1974) demonstrate Eleanor Clark's advances in fiction, partly due to her ability to make a place seem solid, and her strong sense of nature. *Eyes, Etc.* (1977) sets down her response to the loss of sight caused by 'retinal hemorrhages beyond laser treatment, leaving permanent scar tissue and known by the bleary name of macular degeneration'. Writing with felt-tip marking pens on drawing pads, she considers and adjusts to her impairment in a memoir which pungently examines the meaning of suffering and cross examines the liberal hypocrisies by which the fact of pain is suppressed by people less honest than herself. ('Loss of sight far from total. Job must have looked pretty lucky too to some of the neighbours.') Twentieth-century violence in all its forms is the theme of the novel *Gloria Mundi* (1979); in *Camping Out* (1986) specifically male violence both defiles and illuminates the unexpected and tender loving of decorous Dennie Hensley and lesbian Marilyn

Groves in a novel which bristles with contemporary awareness without being trendy and expands into a parable of our time by the use of flashback parallels from Dennie's and Europe's past.

Southern women have contributed handsomely to twentieth-century American fiction. The theme of isolation, clearly implied by the title of Carson McCullers's first novel *The Heart is a Lonely Hunter* (1940), is the common factor among writers as different in other respects as Katherine Anne Porter (1890–1980), Flannery O'Connor, Harper Lee (*b.* 1926) and Shirley Ann Grau (*b.* 1929). Katherine Anne Porter contended all her life with writer's block, produced one novel which made her famous – *Ship of Fools* (1962), an only partially successful fable about the decline of the West – and two impeccable stories, 'Flowering Judas' and 'Pale Horse, Pale Rider'. Harper Lee's reputation is based on *To Kill a Mockingbird* (1960), a sensitive and morally trenchant story about a lawyer's daughter in an Alabama town in the 1930s whose father defends a Negro accused of raping a white woman. Shirley Ann Grau's strength, her feeling for Southern atmosphere, is most evident in her third and fourth novels, *The Keepers of the House* (1964) and *The Condor Passes* (1971). Among these writers the outstanding creativity is the Gothic, devotedly religious imagination of Georgia's Flannery O'Connor. Like Carson McCullers, O'Connor specialises in the grotesque.

The term 'Gothic' suggests extravagance combined with violence. Flannery O'Connor's work is full of eccentric characters, bizarre situations, violent behaviour and macabre death. Her satire can provoke laughter at the beginning of a story, as in the title piece of *Everything That Rises Must Converge* (1965), and end it with panic and a heart attack. As a Roman Catholic she finds 'the centre of existence' in the Holy Ghost. In one of the letters published in 1979 as *The Habit of Being* she writes:

> One of the awful things about writing when you are a Christian is that for you the ultimate reality is the Incarnation, the present reality is the Incarnation, and nobody believes in the Incarnation; that is, nobody in your audience. My audience are the people who think God is dead. At least these are the people I am conscious of writing for.

Avowedly 'not interested in abnormal psychology', Flannery O'Connor uses grotesque characters partly because the most enduring childhood influence on her was a volume called *The Humerous Tales of E. A. Poe*, partly because she wants to delight in sheer originality, and particularly because she wants to show people

who think God is dead that the Holy Ghost infuses grace into the
most improbable poor white souls of the Southern Bible belt. The
title of *Wise Blood* (1952) refers to Enoch Emery's claim that he has
'wise blood'. Hazel Motes proclaims a religion of self-sufficiency in
his 'Church of Christ Without Christ', but blinding himself with
lime, wearing barbed wire next to his skin and walking with broken
glass in his shoes are as much acts of penitential self-immolation as
of perverted pride. The stolen mummy Emery gives Motes as a new
'Jesus' signifies the dust to which man is reduced in a world without
God. In *The Violent Bear It Away* (1960) the atheistic Rayber resists
the religious indoctrination of the fanatical Mason Tarwater, but is
powerless to prevent his son's baptism and death at the hands of
Tarwater's grandnephew, Francis. At the end of the novel Francis
smears himself with dirt from old Tarwater's grave, assumes his
mission, and moves 'toward the dark city where the children of God
lay sleeping'. For O'Connor all her characters in the stories of *A
Good Man is Hard to Find and Other Stories* (1955) and *Everything That
Rises Must Converge* are children of God, whether they like it or not.

Poetry by women

The belief that poetry is by definition genderless is naïve. Equally,
the idea that a poem written by a woman must necessarily be read
and evaluated according to standards and expectations different
from those appropriate to a poem by a man is critically preposterous.
When Sylvia Plath (1932–63) says in 'Lady Lazarus' '. . . I a smiling
woman./I am only thirty./And like the cat I have nine times to
die', she explicitly presents herself as a woman in a particular
circumstance with a defined preoccupation. When she goes on to a
furious, sarcastic protest against the medical skill that brings her
back from the edge of death she uses imagery which compactly
exemplifies the male prejudices that have suppressed female
individuality by a system of possessive and dismissive labels:

> So, so, Herr Doktor.
> So, Herr Enemy
> I am your opus,
> I am your valuable,
> The pure gold baby
>
> That melts to a shriek.

'Lady Lazarus' is a poem about a woman's death wish and it is full of gender. The act of reading and analysing it must involve judgement about the quality of imagery used to express specifically female experience, and such judgement will contribute to the final evaluation of the poem as a work of art. But when Mary Oliver (*b*. 1935) conveys the exhilaration of climbing a tree ('The Honey Tree') into an ecstatic sense of self and of the world, there is no evidence of gender:

> And so at last I climbed
> the honey tree, ate
> chunks of pure light, ate
> the bodies of bees that could not
> get out of my way, ate
> the dark hair of the leaves,
> the rippling bark,
> the heartwood. Such
> frenzy! But joy does that,
> I'm told, in the beginning.

There is nothing in Mary Oliver's thought or imagery to insist that her poem be considered in a different way from, for instance, Robert Frost's 'Birches', in which tree-climbing is also exhilarating. Frost, of course, does say that when he sees his birches bent he 'likes to think some boy's been swinging them' and imagines the trees subdued not by ice-storms but by 'some boy too far from town to learn baseball', but such references to male activity are incidental to the poem's overall intention and effect. Plath's poem is the only one in which experience is 'gendered', and each of the three poems must, in the end, stand or fall by purely aesthetic criteria. Doctrinaire considerations of gender are dangerous in so far as they threaten to impose a double standard in aesthetics. What is beyond doubt, however, as in the case of fiction, is that progress towards social equalising of the sexes in the twentieth century has helped to promote the publication of fine poetry by an unprecedentedly large number of women.

The influences that shaped Denise Levertov include Wallace Stevens as well as William Carlos Williams and the Black Mountain poets Charles Olson, Robert Duncan and Robert Creeley (*b*. 1926). 'Form is never more than *revelation* of content', she says, modifying Creeley's assertion that form is only an extension of content. She shares with Creeley a miniaturist's attention to fleeting moments of awareness but her moments range more widely than

Creeley's. Her poetry is justly known for directness of utterance and symbolic originality, but it is her skill in making an act of perception carry a point that ensures her place among the most effective protégées of the Black Mountain movement. Wallace Stevens's interest in the relation of reality to metaphor is evident in 'The Cat as Cat':

> The cat on my bosom
> sleeping and purring
> – fur-petalled chrysanthemum,
> squirrel-killer –
>
> is a metaphor only if I
> force him to be one . . .

In 'Living' the theme of transience is lightly developed in a succession of simple images, with a brief final comment that assures poignancy by clinching the point:

> The fire in leaf and grass
> so green it seems
> each summer the last summer.
>
> The wind blowing, the leaves
> shivering in the sun,
> each day the last day.
>
> A red salamander
> so cold and so
> easy to catch dreamily
> moves his delicate feet
> and long tail. I hold
> my hand open for him to go.
>
> Each minute the last minute.

Polemics mar Levertov's social protext and anti-Vietnam poems in *The Sorrow Dance* (1967) and *Releasing the Alphabet* (1970), but the sequence of 'Olga Poems' about the death of her sister is distinguished by accurate observation and sparely, precisely rendered feeling.

A contemporary of Denise Levertov's, Adrienne Rich (*b.* 1929) has moved from decorously formalist verse in *A Change of World* (1951) and *The Diamond Cutters* (1955) to a more autobiographical mode of writing and to feminist themes in *Necessities of Life* (1966) and subsequent volumes until *Diving into the Wreck* (1973). With directness of statement her poetic line and formal organisation become looser. In *Diving into the Wreck* she asks:

> why do the administrators
>
> lack solicitude, the government
> refuse protection,
>
> why should the wild child
> weep for the scientists
>
> why

In *Snapshots of a Daughter-in-Law* (1963) Adrienne Rich offers glimpses of women, including Mary Shelley, Fanny Burney and Emily Dickinson, which show them as figures of high achievement in spite of unpropitious circumstances. Emily Dickinson, for example, is 'shot' in the context of those domestic chores to which a woman of her time and position was doomed. Yet she triumphs:

> Reading while waiting
> for the iron to heat,
> writing, *My Life had stood – a Loaded Gun –*
> in that Amherst pantry while the jellies boil and scum,
> or, more often,
> iron-eyed and beaked and purposed as a bird,
> dusting everything on the whatnot every day of life.

In her most recent poetry Adrienne Rich's interest in the alienations and connections of female circumstance has been refined towards a focus on the nature of language in contemporary society. In *The Dream of a Common Language* (1978) she acknowledges her dependence on language – 'writing words like these, I'm also living' – but admits that in the harsh world of Olson's 'Polis' metaphoric language can be a soft option too easily preferred to the task of dealing directly and unambiguously with the problem of achieving freedom for women in a patriarchal society:

> And how have I used rivers, how have I used words
> to escape writing of the worst thing of all –
> not the crimes of others, not even our own death,
> but the failure to want our freedom passionately enough
> so that blighted elms, sick rivers, massacres would seem
> mere emblems of that desecration of ourselves?

Anne Sexton and Sylvia Plath

Before her first suicide attempt when she was twenty, Sylvia Plath grasped her mother's hand and cried, 'Oh, Mother, the

world is so rotten! I want to die! Let's die together!' Both Sylvia
Plath and her friend, Anne Sexton (1928–74) were confessional
poets, much possessed by death. In a memoir published soon after
Plath's death in 1963, Anne Sexton recalls: 'We talked death with
burned-up intensity, both of us drawn to it like moths to an electric
light bulb. Sucking on it'. Sexton's own tragedy was that life was
never vivid enough to be her element, and writing became a method
of confronting the resultant pain. 'Creative people must not avoid
the pain that they get dealt', she wrote to an editor. 'I say to myself,
sometimes repeatedly "I've got to get the hell out of this hurt" . . .
But no. Hurt must be examined like a plague'. A student of Robert
Lowell and W. D. Snodgrass (*b.* 1926) whose volume *Heart's Needle*
(1959) contains some of the most candid verse in the confessional
mode, Anne Sexton published her first collection of poems *To Bedlam
and Part Way Back* (1960) a year after the appearance of Snodgrass's
book and outdid her mentor in the extravagance of her own
confessional idiom. The epigraph to *Selected Poems* (1964) is taken
from a letter of Franz Kafka: '. . . the books we need are the kind
that act upon us like a misfortune, that make us suffer like the death
of someone we love more than ourselves, that make us feel as though
we were on the verge of suicide, or lost in a forest remote from all
human habitation – a book should serve as the axe for the
frozen sea within us'. With the exception of *Transformations* (1971),
reworkings of German fairy tales, Anne Sexton's poems convey
misfortune, suffering and isolation, and most of them are written on
the verge of suicide by a woman who only made it 'part way back'
from the mental hospital where she was 'queen of this summer
hotel/or the laughing bee on a stalk/of death' ('You, Doctor Martin').
All My Pretty Ones (1962) and *Live or Die* (1966) speak with searing
candour about a life of unremitting self-exacerbation in a world 'full
of enemies' ('Noon Walk on the Asylum Lawn') where 'the odour
of death hung in the air/like rotting potatoes' ('For Johnny Pole on
the Forgotten Beach'). In 'With Mercy for the Greedy' Anne Sexton
sums up her destiny and gives her definition of poetry:

> My friend, my friend, I was born
> doing reference work in sin, and born
> confessing it. This is what poems are:
> with mercy
> for the greedy,
> they are the tongue's wrangle,
> the world's pottage, the rat's star.

The poetry of Anne Sexton and Sylvia Plath often implies an equation of poetry to styles of personal distress. In 'Elm' the tree speaks for Plath herself:

> I am inhabited by a cry;
> Nightly it flaps out
> Looking, with its hooks, for something to love.
>
> I am terrified by this dark thing
> That sleeps in me;
> All day I feel its soft, feathery turnings, its malignity.

This inner malignity is projected outwards, even in an early poem, 'Mushrooms', from *The Colossus* (1960), the only collection of poems published in Plath's lifetime: 'We shall by morning/inherit the earth./Our foot's in the door.'; and in 'Moonrise':

> Lucina, bony mother, labouring
> Among the socketed white stars, your face
> Of candour pares white flesh to the white bone . . .

The neurotic, elemental power of Plath's poetry is to be found in the posthumously published volumes *Ariel* (1965), *Crossing the Water* (1971), which collects poems written in the transitional period between *The Colossus* and *Ariel*, and *Winter Trees* (1971) which prints poetry written during the nine months before her suicide. Like Anne Sexton, Plath writes about madness, loneliness and the longing for annihilation. She writes with fierce intensity about the experience of giving birth in 'Morning Song', about a woman's 'barricade of barb and check' to keep love out in 'Spinster', about her several attempts at suicide in 'Lady Lazarus', and in 'Daddy' about her need to kill her father in paradoxical revenge for his dying when she was ten. The recreation of her father as a Fascist ('a man in black with a Meinkampf look') is a violent act of the imagination which expresses the love-hate relationship and the speaker's concept of herself as possibly Jewish enables her to mythologise her suffering by reference to the history of Nazi oppression. The speaker's sense of her own frustration and immaturity is dramatised by the nursery-rhyme rhythm and the repeated rhyming on one word through the poem ('you do not do, you do not do . . . I thought every German was you . . . Daddy, daddy, you bastard, I'm through'.). The style of Sylvia Plath's anguish is more controlled than Anne Sexton's and her best poems map out a territory which, while harrowing, is ordered by the aesthetic sense displayed in 'Winter Trees':

The wet dawn inks are doing their blue dissolve.
On their blotter of fog the trees
Seem a botanical drawing –
Memories growing, ring on ring,
A series of weddings.

In *The Bell Jar* (1963), Sylvia Plath's only novel, the heroine struggles with mental illness, despair and suicide and chooses, in the end, to live; but a month after the book was published and accorded an enthusiastic critical reception, Sylvia Plath chose to die. Whether this was victory or defeat is likely to remain the unsolved mystery of her life.

Mary Oliver

Among more recently successful women poets, Mary Oliver commands attention by a lyric voice that is distinctive without being shrill and a sensibility that is thoughtful, tender and wise without being either brashly intellectual or soft. Her three consistently substantial and individual volumes of poetry are *Twelve Moons* (1979), *American Primitive* (1983) and *Dream Work* (1986). Her themes are the sanctity of life and the possibility of joy through connection with nature's 'country of original fire' ('Humpbacks'). In 'Entering the Kingdom' she says:

> The dream of my life
> Is to lie down by a slow river
> And stare at the light in the trees –
> To learn something by being nothing
> A little while but the rich
> Lens of attention.

What her lens discovers makes her advocate union of the human and the natural, and she does it by example. She sleeps in a forest ('Sleeping in the Forest') and awakes to find that she 'had vanished at least a dozen times/into something better'; she wades into a pond and joins the frogs ('Pink Moon–The Pond'); she eats the flesh of a bear and absorbs its life; and swimming in 'The Sea' almost makes her turn fish:

> Stroke by
>   stroke my
>   body remembers that life and cries for
>   the lost parts of itself –

fins, gills
> opening like flowers into
> the flesh – my legs
> want to lock and become
one muscle, I swear I know
> just what the blue-gray scales
> shingling
> the rest of me would
feel like!

Mary Oliver's poetry is full of such testimony to the joy of sensual experience: 'What a holy and sensual splashing', she cries in 'Postcard from Flamingo'. Climbing, in 'The Honey Tree', she eats 'chunks of pure light' and is aware of 'the cords/of my body stretching/and singing in the/heaven of appetite'. She writes like a contemporary William Wordsworth unconstrained by any nineteenth-century obligation to provide philosophical comment on what Wordsworth calls his 'glad animal movements', but her joy in nature is never facile and she reckons directly and responsibly with natural violence, ugliness and the fact of death. 'What blazes the trail', she notes in 'Skunk Cabbage', 'is not necessarily pretty', and in 'Blossom', a key poem in *American Primitive*, observes: 'What/we know: that time/chops at us all like an iron/hoe, that death/is a state of paralysis. What/we long for: joy/before death, nights/in the swale–everything else/can wait but not/this thrust/from the root/of the body'.

If Mary Oliver's great gift is her ability to commend her own conviction about the possibility of sensual fulfilment in nature, her effectiveness is partly owing to her buttonholing knack of drawing the reader into the poem by direct, personal comment, often in an aside. 'This is not a pleasant story', she warns in 'Something'; and 'You know what I mean', she says in 'Humpbacks'. For Wallace Stevens reality was a cliché from which we might attempt to escape by metaphor, but for Mary Oliver, in love with the reality of mussels, snakes, fish, bears, turtles, the sea, sharks, whales, trees and moons, reality is something to embrace and enter, and the only source of symbols adequate for explaining itself. In 'The Bobcat' one half of reality is the bobcat who 'leaped/like a quick/clawed/whirlwind of light/from the pines/beside the road', and the other half is the lynx who 'wanders like silk/on the deep/hillsides of snow–/blazing,/it lounges in trees/as thick as castles,/as cold as iron'. As though in a dream 'we drive toward/the white forest', the poem concludes,

implying that our search is for a destination in which the two halves
are joined and the world unified.

In her most recent volume, *Dream Work*, Mary Oliver continues
to write of joyous participation in nature, but there is a new caution
in 'One or Two Things':

> For years and years I struggled
> just to love my life. And then
>
> the butterfly
> rose, weightless, in the wind.
> 'Don't love your life
> too much', it said,
>
> and vanished
> into the world.

The poems in this book still offer evidence of 'The Chance to Love
Everything', but the poet earns her credo by coming courageously
to terms with the uncompromising realities of the world that lies
beyond her beloved sea, woods and ponds. In 'Acid' she sees an
injured boy begging in the streets of Jakarta and stores the image
'like a bead of acid/to remember how,/once in a while,/you can
creep out of your own life/and become someone else'. In '1945–
1985; Poem for the Anniversary' she humbly connects her personal
ambition to 'go on living in this world' in a way that 'wouldn't hurt
anything' with the horrors of the Holocaust:

> In the films of Dachau and Auschwitz and Bergen-Belsen
> the dead rise from the earth
> and are piled in front of us, the starved
> stare across forty years,
> and lush, green, musical Germany
> shows again its iron claw, which won't
>
> ever be forgotten, which won't
> ever be understood, but which did,
> slowly, for years, scrape across Europe
>
> while the rest of the world
> did nothing.

Jewish novelists

In the 1950s, according to Leslie Fiedler (*b.* 1917) in *No! in Thunder*
(1960), Zion became Main Street:

we live at a moment when, everywhere in the realm of prose, Jewish writers have discovered their Jewishness to be an eminently marketable commodity, their much vaunted alienation to be their passport into the heart of Gentile American culture.

Many Jewish writers found a common theme in that variation of the economic law attributed in the nineteenth century to Sir Thomas Gresham ('bad money drives out good') by which public life drives out private life and the individual is reduced to his dislocation or to his method of coping with it. J. D. Salinger's Holden Caulfield bolts from the fakeries of American society in *The Catcher in the Rye*; the Glass children in *Franny and Zooey* and *Raise High the Roof Beam, Carpenters* seek refuge in precocity. Joseph Heller shows man as the victim of mad, conspiratorial military and political systems in *Catch-22* and *Good as Gold* (1979), and offers a more realistic study of impotence in *Something Happened* (1974). Saul Bellow's Henderson and Herzog make their bids for freedom from the homogenising rule-book of society, and Bernard Malamud's (*b.* 1914) Yakov Bok in *The Fixer* (1966), a fact-based fable about anti-Semitism, is a lonely, valiant speck against the dark, determining backcloth of history.

It is not surprising that such novelists commanded a wide, appreciative audience. Two world wars had proved that individuals were manipulated, even into losing their lives, by cynical forces beyond their control or comprehension. The nuclear age was shaped by the conspiracies of politicians and business corporations. Bureaucracy dictated that, like W. H. Auden's 'Unknown Citizen', the individual was at best a case, more commonly just a number. Man had dispossessed himself of his own world. Jews knew about dispossession. Long before the American Adam found himself beyond the ruined garden with his lost innocence, the Jew had been expelled from his Promised Land and become habituated to the ways of the travelling ghetto. 'Nobody lived in Eden any more', thinks Malamud's 'Fixer':

> Once you leave [the *shtetl*, i.e. village] you're out in the open; it rains and it snows. It snows history, which means that what happens to somebody starts in a web of events outside the personal. It starts of course before he gets there. We're all in history, that's sure, but some are more than others, Jews more than some. If it snows not everybody is out in it getting wet.

Most thinking people today, irrespective of their origins, feel wet with the snow of history; as Sandor Himmelstein says in Bellow's *Herzog*, 'We're on the same identical network' as the Jew.

Jewish novels of the mid-twentieth century often provide brilliant diagnoses of the era. They are psychologically persuasive, sociologically apposite, linguistically beguiling. Too often, however, they compound the alienations they deplore by authenticating the gap between their anti-heroes and the world, and going no further. Bellow, Malamud and Roth seem to imply not merely that awareness alone is certain good, but that awareness alone is possible. The awareness of the novelist becomes an end in itself, his book an exhibition of intellectual self-sufficiency in which a rendered, recognisable world matters less and less. It is less a matter of *Making It* (1967), as in Norman Podhoretz's (*b*. 1930) memoir of that name, than of 'knowing it' in a slippery world from which the protections of the *shtetlach* have long gone. The writer becomes the fiddler on his own roof.

The tendency is exemplified by the work of Isaac Bashevis Singer (*b*. 1904). Clearly Singer's huge output is full of import for the real world, but one response to his work is surprise that, as Irving Howe (*b*. 1920) says, 'Here is a man living in New York City, a sophisticated and clever writer, who composes stories about Frampol, Bilgoray, Kreshev *as if they were still there.*' The impression is of a writer who locks himself in the past because it suits his mind. Stanley Elkin (*b*. 1930) positively cavorts with his own pessimisms in *The Franchiser* (1976), *The Living End* (1979) and *George Mills* (1982), a surreal, complicated, dynastic novel whose energy derives largely from Elkin's acrid gift for parody and wisecrack. Elkin writes allegories of life in modern America, setting them in an all-night radio station (*The Dick Gibson Show* [1971]), and heaven and hell (*The Living End* [1979]). In *A Bad Man* (1967) the setting is the basement of a department store where Leo Feldman proves that he has inherited his father's mercantile wisdom – 'Nothing for something' – by rising to ownership of the store, transformed into a prince in a legend by the ringing of a cash register. If enthralled by his success, he is also nauseated by his own wilderness of product, and becomes a symbol of America choking on its fat: 'He knew there was nothing he could buy, except his comfort, that would please him. He knew more: there was nothing he could give'. The merchant discovers that the almighty dollar is a fiction after all and comfort an unmarketed commodity, so he gets by on 'joyless *joie de vivre* and forced life force', yet knowing his life ultimately futile. Feldman is sentenced to a year in the penitentiary because in the basement of his store he has supplied the names of judges who can be bribed, the addresses of abortionists and catered to the needs of homosexuals and drug addicts. His crime is twofold: by servicing subterranean needs in the American temple of his store, Feldman is subverting the formal, symmetrical shape of civilised morality (dark needs must be met in dark places), and by participating happily in the perverted lives of his clients he is guilty of exploitation. Here Elkin is persuasively satirical, implying that the man who caters to needs is more culpable than the man who creates them because the latter operates in terms of recognised forms under the aegis of the dollar sign. In jail Feldman is rigorously schooled in the warden's theorem of virtue as system, grace as 'a contract and codicils'. Solitary confinement, 'the old wilderness routine', teaches Feldman that man cannot live by self alone: he needs forms and he needs other people. Yet Feldman contrives to remain himself, unprocessed by the system, and as he is beaten up by the convicts who have tried him and, under the Warden's direction, apparently found him guilty, he feels innocent, thinks he may live. The reader is left wondering why. Elkin's satirical allegory is often brilliantly original, but as novels his books typically end without any clear resolution of their serious moral conflicts and useful questions.

No contemporary novelist has a better ear for the spoken language or writes with greater intelligence about the problems of spiritual poverty and the need for love than Bernard Malamud. Yet Malamud's imagination somehow commits what it selects to a realm of detachment. William Dubin of *Dubin's Lives* (1979) is a biographer in his late fifties working on the life of D. H. Lawrence. Although he knows that 'One writes lives he can't live', the appearance of Fanny Bick, a girl in her early twenties, plunges him into an attempt to deny the axiom. Despite his best efforts, his marriage to Kitty survives because he is, after all, 'an odd inward man held together by an ordered life'. Malamud's books since *A New Life* (1961) are like Dubin: they comprise an odd, inward world sealed into itself by wise yet eccentric moralising. Artistically, Malamud seems most comfortable with the medium of the short story, and his best work is included in *The Stories of Bernard Malamud* (1983).

After the early *Goodbye, Columbus* (1959), Philip Roth's irresistible humour of catastrophe, obviously in *The Breast* (1972), but also in *My Life as a Man* (1974) and *The Professor of Desire* (1977), illuminates chiefly itself. 'Literature got me into this and literature is gonna have to get me out', says Peter Tarnopol in *My Life as a Man*; but literature keeps Roth in. Roth's most impressive achievement is the comic trilogy of novels about Nathan Zuckerman, a writer whose hilarious progress from earnestness, through fame and wealth (and alienation from his father whose dying word to him is 'Bastard') to neurosis and hypochondria is told in *The Ghost Writer* (1979), *Zuckerman Unbound* (1981) and *The Anatomy Lesson* (1983). The three volumes are reprinted in the omnibus *Zuckerman Bound* (1985) with a novella called 'The Prague Orgy' in which Zuckerman, trying to be serious in Czechoslovakia, is thwarted by writers and artists who are coping with government repression of their works by being as Rabelaisian as possible.

Norman Mailer's novels of ideas – *Barbary Shore* (1951), *The Deer Park* (1955), *An American Dream* (1965) and *Tough Guys Don't Dance* (1984) – are less convincing works than *The Armies of the Night* (1968) or *A Fire on the Moon* (1970), which project the author as a reporting guru of modern culture, committed to 'the disturbance of complacent notions'. *The Executioner's Song* (1979) is a minutely detailed account of events surrounding the execution for double murder of Gary Gilmore in January 1977, written in the documentary style of Truman Capote's non-fiction novel *In Cold Blood* (1966). Mailer almost completely excludes himself from the narrative, yet his very self-effacement is felt as a controlling device, a kind of presence in the display of fact and in the prompting of questions about Gilmore's right to die, and the evident failure of the penal system either to protect his victims or to do anything for him during a total of eighteen years in prison. Mailer's most ambitious novel is *Ancient Evenings* (1983). Set in the Egypt of 1100 BC, the novel has a double hero. There is Menenhetet (ex-general and royal charioteer, master of the Pharaoh's harem, priest) and his six-year-old great-grandson. This comes about because of the ancient Egyptian's capacity to inhabit the consciousness of several people at once, a disconcerting feature of life under the Pharaohs and calculated to induce identity crisis. The great-grandson wonders:

> For if Menenhetet could die, yet become himself once more, so did I wonder if I was supposed to have been the fifth appearance – could it be said? – of Menenhetet the First. Or was I intended to become Menenhetet the Second, his true son, not his own continuation? Might I, either way, have been given his power to father oneself?

Reincarnation is as painful as it is bewildering and involves prickly memories of the embalming process:

A hook went into my nose, battered through the gate at the foot of the nostril, and plunged into my brain. Pieces, gobbets, and whole parts of the dead flesh of my mind were now brought out through one aperture of my nose, then the other.

In the early stages of young Menenhetet's recycling, Mailer's prose has a dark intensity at times reminiscent of the British author William Golding's writing in his novel *Pincher Martin*, but the vitality becomes strained as the consciousness of great-grandfather Menenhetet takes over for an account of the battle of Kadesh, followed by interminable descriptions of the sexual variations available to an Egyptian of his time, and a listing of the assorted difficulties of getting on with a Pharaoh whose claims run to sodomy and whose concubines (especially one called 'Honey-Ball') make strenuous demands. The moral of this gigantic misfire of a novel seems to be 'Don't cuckold your Pharaoh'. Menenhetet does and is soon 'crawling with ants in the hot baked desert of my heart'. Mailer has characterised himself 'the gadfly to complacency, institution, and the dead weight of public taste'. In this book the gadfly has leaden wings. Since *The Naked and the Dead*, a high achievement in realism in its time, he has been a man of 'faction' rather than fiction. He is much better at projecting himself as the shaman of his tribe than he is at producing the great American novel.

Saul Bellow

In *Dangling Man* (1944) Bellow (*b*. 1915) questions the meaning of freedom. Both *The Victim* (1947) and *Seize the Day* (1956) are about identity. *The Adventures of Augie March* (1953) uses the tradition of the picaresque for a prolonged cadenza of Bellow's prodigious knowingness. The planet in *Mr Sammler's Planet* (1970) is painfully Mr Sammler's, but too *outré* to be shared: the world is turned curiously word by an extreme, self-scrutinising sensibility. Based on the sad, chaotic life of the poet Delmore Schwartz (1913–66), *Humboldt's Gift* (1975), though warmer and more animated, is a new projection of moods familiar from Bellow's earlier novels. Bellow's *persona* in *The Dean's December* (1982) is Albert Corde, Professor of Journalism and Dean of Students at a university in Chicago. He is dislocated from the urban ugliness he knows because his mother-in-law is lying semi-conscious in a state hospital in Bucharest. Corde and Minna his wife – beautiful, and a distinguished enough astronomer to book sessions on the Mount Palomar telescope – have gone East to attend the old lady. Corde is a backward-looking Orpheus, flight imposed on him, constantly surveying over his liberal-humanist shoulder the Chicago he has left behind and the career from which he is momentarily suspended. Corde's method of dealing with life is to have 'topics':

> Oh, he had lots of topics: the crazy state of the U.S., the outlook and psychology of officialdom in the Communist world, the peculiar psychoses of penitentiary societies like this one.

The novel becomes a comparative meditation on Western enormities and Eastern tawdriness. It is crammed with awareness. Bellow knows the fashionable liberal stances, and how readily they provide fulcra for all persuasions. Militants at Corde's university hammer the ideological aspects of a case in which a Black pimp is accused of killing a white student with help from a Black prostitute who lives by servicing the campus:

> the college was trying to restrict black housing in the neighbourhood, it refused to divest itself of South African investments, it was slow on Affirmative Action. Himself a campus radical forty years ago, the Dean saw how little things had changed.

A 'hungry observer', and 'temperamentally an image man', Corde vivifies the irony of East–West *hauteurs*. In the golden West is the Chicago where ugly nights are filled with the rotten music of summer, and autumn sounds the same in a cooler key. The oppressive socialist wonderland provides taps that go dry from 8 a.m. till evening, devices behind the draperies and an inscrutable black market of favours and supplies – capitalist music in a Gothic key. Watching, collecting his images, pondering his wife's situation, his alienations, his friend Dewey Spangler and nagging at news from home, Corde vibrates away, a clever man, no doubt. Bellow's Corde is plangently intellectual, dislocated yet never really lost; but the resonances die away rather quickly. Intelligence however keen, flashed too knowingly, can be so forgettable. Corde observes to Minna that although people talk to themselves all the time, nobody really knows what racket he is in – 'his *real* racket'. Bellow's real racket is knowing, and it is the sort of knowing that Ezra Pound once objected to in the work of Pope: 'Knowledge is to know man; Mr Alexander Pope rubs it a bit too smooth'.

Herzog, however, still stands as the most inclusive novel of awareness, in which the theme of alienation gets its most thorough workout since Dostoevsky. Moses Herzog attempts a 'five-cent synthesis' of modern man, his mind focusing on himself before panning across the general condition:

> His own individual character cut off at times both from facts and from values. But modern character is inconstant, divided, vacillating, lacking the stone-like certitude of archaic man, also deprived of the firm ideas of the seventeenth century, clear hard theorems.

In *Herzog* modern man is doubly a Jew: first by birth, secondly by virtue or by defect of being an academic, always the Jew among Gentiles. The story of Herzog is that of a professional systematiser, a man of syntheses who becomes disenchanted with intellectual constructs and the modern reality systems represented by Himmelstein, Aunt Zelda, Valentine Gersbach, Madeleine and the flower-power of Ramona. Like Augie March before him, he resists the attempts of others to reduce him to their idea of what he should be; like Joseph in *Dangling Man* he at once seeks to know and to escape from himself, narcissistic, masochistic, anachronistic character as he is by his own confession. The Herzog who follows Ramona's instructions and shops for clothes that will proclaim a brighter, still virile personality, is an absurd Solomon in his off-the-peg glory, although his precise, humane response to the salesman's skin, breath and boredom makes him endearing too. The episode is clearly an experiment in becoming, the process that is to be replaced at the end of the novel – as in *Henderson the Rain King* – by the state of being: it is part of the man's attempt to come to himself. 'Not to be one's self is *despair*'? Not merely that: for Herzog it is inconceivable. Who else would assume the burden of such a mystery?

Wry acceptance of his predicament is remote from the militant philosophy of selfhood propounded by Nachman, derelict author of 'New Psalms to the Self'. The contrast emphasises the modernity and responsibility of Herzog's awareness. As he lies waiting for the return of Ramona – she is decking herself for love – his mind moves outward to survey the epoch:

> he let the entire world press upon him. For instance? Well, for instance, what it means to be a man. In a city. In a century. In transition. In a mass. Transformed by science. Under organised power. Subject to tremendous controls. In a condition caused by mechanisation. After the late failure of radical hopes. In a society that was no community and devalued the person. Owing to the multiplied power of numbers which made the self negligible. Which spent military billions against foreign enemies but would not pay for order at home. Which permitted savagery

and barbarism in its own great cities. At the same time, the pressure of human millions who have discovered what concerted efforts and thoughts can do. As megatons of water shape organisms on the ocean floor. As tides polish stones. As winds hollow cliffs. The beautiful super-machinery opening a new life for innumerable mankind. Would you deny them the right to exist? Would you ask them to labour and go hungry while you enjoyed delicious old-fashioned Values? You – you yourself are a child of this mass and a brother to all the rest. Or else an ingrate, dilettante, idiot.

Herzog's self-concern is simultaneous with concern for the world. This is not a typical anti-Utopian protest, despite familiar allusions to the dark aspects of the modern democratic state. It would be wrong to think of Bellow's novel along with the admonitory visions of George Orwell's *1984* or Aldous Huxley's *Brave New World*. The world needs warnings of their kind but – and it is precisely because they were so right – it also needs a balancing recognition of the positive aspects of life in the twentieth century, the benefits of Alphaville. Herzog's is surely meant to be taken straight: 'The beautiful super-machinery opening a life for innumerable mankind . . . Would you ask them to labour and go hungry while you enjoyed delicious old-fashioned Values?' It is this generous sense of the world in the context of his self-preoccupation that gives Herzog his moral eminence.

Instruction in reality comes to Herzog not only from the people around him but also from Hegel, Nietzsche, Heidegger, Kierkegaard – philosophers who have shaped contemporary ideas of man. The novel is as much the story of his emancipation from them as of his parallel escape from the coercions of American society. According to Herzog, these philosophers have encouraged modern descent into crisis, corruption and despair. Their ideas have become the canned goods of intellectuals, a standardised pedantry of gloom, the staple of fashionable magazines. Herzog finally repudiates the contemporary *Angst* philosophy of 'apocalypses', 'crisis ethics and florid extremism' and asserts his own humanity. Alone with nature in the Berkshires at the end of the novel, like Joyce's Leopold Bloom, 'He rests. He has travelled.' In his jotted lines to God he notes, 'Everything of intensest significance. Especially if divested of me'. He rejoices in a condition that might be paraphrased by the last line of Theodore Roethke's poem 'The Abyss': 'Being, not doing, is my first joy'. He has blessed his water-snakes ('Dear Madeleine . . . Bless you . . . And you, Gersbach . . .') and 'is pretty well satisfied to be, just as it is willed'. What is the reader to make of Herzog's being? Is it any worthier than the chimera Harry Angstrom pursues in Updike's *Rabbit, Run?*

In an interview for *The Paris Review* in 1966 Bellow says:

> I feel that art has something to do with the achievement of stillness in the midst of chaos. A stillness which characterises prayer, too, and the eye of the storm. I think that art has something to do with the arrest of attention in the midst of distraction.

'A stillness which characterises prayer' would not be an inappropriate description of Herzog in his last few pages; but this is still vague. His progress is from authorship of a dissertation about nature to life in nature, sharing his bread with the rats like a latter-day Thoreau. Is he not, in his fashion, a drop-out, a one-man egghead hippie hegira? In a few minutes, it seems, he intends to call out to Mrs Tuttle, 'Damp it down, Mrs Tuttle. There's water in the sink'; but the emphasis falls on the negatives that follow: 'But not just yet. At this time he had no messages for anyone. Nothing. Not a single word.' The American hippie movement of the 1960s was a collective drop-out from a society whose 'Reality instruction' is in the primacies of work, status, money and power. Does Herzog's final state imply kinship with the indiscriminate, all-embracing, fluid love of the hippie? Supine as he is, when the dust has been dampened down, might he be disposed to 'Superzap them all with the love'? 'Not a single word', he says; yet it is precisely here that his old verbosity is needed to carry him, and the reader, back into society to enact that disproof of the waste-land mentality which Bellow repeatedly demands. The novel prompts the desire to see a regenerate Herzog reconnected to the world. A *shtetl* of one is not enough. Bellow shows him 'knowing it', but the reader wants to see him 'making it' too.

In *Him With His Foot in His Mouth and Other Stories* (1984) Bellow further develops ideas that have continued to interest him since the publication of *Herzog*. The five stories – or 'exercises in memory' – are connected by two common themes. The first is that they are all about people whose lives have reached a point at which they feel compelled to undergo what one character calls 'my self-examination'. The second is the problem of the conflict between the world of power and wealth and the world of intellect and art. Predictably, Bellow's characters opt for intellect and art, but in so doing fail to show how the gap between the two worlds may be closed.

Jonathan Penner (*b.* 1940) is a younger writer whose work swings away from the mind of the writer towards connection with the world. His novel *Going Blind* (1975) is about survival in the modern age. Penner yields nothing in awareness to his peers. He has an acute sense of his era but transmits it with splendid economy. His narrative line uncoils cleanly, a spring wound tight in the opening chapters, stretched to full length by the last. Paul Held believes that his blindness will ruin his chances with the widow of his friend and bar him from tenure at the college where he teaches English. Concealing his plight requires ingenuity and continuous vigilance. The feel of this is conveyed by precisions that contribute greatly to the novel's distinction, from 'the soft ding of elevators, the cushioned rumble of their doors' as Paul's sense dominance shifts from sight to sound, to his discovery of facial vision, a new typing technique and how to get to work safely in New York. Penner's control is such that he can let a Braille Bible take his hero into the light of a new Genesis without lapsing into sentimentality. The dead friend's last remains are 'a pale fallout' of dust blown from the heads of his electric shaver. The static of rivalry that crackles in the cut-throat atmosphere of a Modern Languages Association meeting charges the air of academe with the hostility of a world where 'knowing it' is one thing, but respect for persons is something else again. *Going Blind* is a compact novel of extraordinary wit, compassion and accuracy. Without a trace of exhibitionism it tells of the world and a man's efforts to stay in it. It is first-rate as a love story, as an academic novel, as a novel of the contemporary city or as a tale of resolution and independence.

Among Jewish women writers Cynthia Ozick's (*b.* 1928) treatment of specifically Jewish subjects has brought distinction to the modern American short story in *The Pagan Rabbi and Other Stories* (1971), *Bloodshed and Three Novellas* (1976) and *Levitation: Five Fictions* (1982). In the essays of *Art and Ardour* (1983) she is an energetic proponent of 'a new Yiddish' by which she means a culturally Jewish-American literature. The relation between Jewish heritage and gentile culture in America provides the theme of her novel *The Cannibal Galaxy* (1983) in which the cannibal of the title is Europe seen as devouring its Jewish people. The novel's protagonist is Joseph Brill, Principal of the Edmond Fleg Primary School, a survivor of Nazi-occupied France and a devotee of European culture, since his days as a serious student who 'felt it his obligation to keep it from his parents that Western Civilization was sometimes not serious'. Brill cannot be faulted for not taking his job seriously:

. . . he felt himself not so much a schoolmaster as a man of almost sacral power. He knew what lay in his hands: the miraculous ascent of lives, the future implicit in the present, the very goodness of humankind. *The world rests on the breath of the children in the schoolhouses* – this fragment of Talmud feathered his spirit like a frond from a tree in deep warmth.

Despite Principal Brill's best intentions, the message of Cynthia Ozick's novel seems to be that Gentile American culture cannot absorb the Jewish heritage without damaging it. Brill's efforts to follow the Talmudic injunction by providing a unifying education is thwarted by 'middling parents and their middling offspring'.

E. L. Doctorow

E. L. Doctorow is best known for the highly successful novel *Ragtime* (1975), a kaleidoscopic fictionalised slice of early twentieth-century social history. Its episodes include appearances by such figures as Emma Goldman, Harry Houdini and J. P. Morgan. *Welcome to Hard Times* was described by the *Times Literary Supplement* as a 'taut, blood-thirsty read', but it is also a skilful demythologising of the romantic western and a dramatic but credible display of the need for a community, a *shtetl* of a kind, at almost any cost. The novel is a fable which never seems less than real. *The Book of Daniel* is based on the case of Julius and Ethel Rosenberg who were put to death as convicted spies on 19 June 1953. The book encloses the reader in the mind of Daniel Isaacson whose parents have been executed for conspiring to steal atomic secrets. In the silence of the library at Columbia University Daniel is supposedly working on a Ph.D. thesis. Instead he writes a memoir which poses questions about guilt and innocence, sincerity and social justice. If the subjectivity of Doctorow's hero approaches opacity at times, his mind jamming with the complexity of events, it is not paralysed by self-absorption. Taking his bearings from the fact of his parents' death, Daniel moves erratically out into the ambiguous real world of relations, questioning its values. He is sceptical and perplexed, but remains connected. *Loon Lake* (1980) reconstructs the mid-1930s world of organised crime and capitalism in a disjointed sequence of autobiographical sections and 'poetic' interludes, ending with a CIA computer printout report in 'Who's Who' jargon. Like the 'Pyramid Club' in *Ragtime*, Loon Lake is an exclusive haven of the super-rich. The owner of Loon Lake, F. W. Bennett, who also owns the Bennett

Autobody Works, hires a servant, Joe Korzeniowski. The use of Joseph Conrad's Polish family name suggests that Joe is an artist of a kind, and a solitary, struggling to survive in what a character in Conrad's novel *Lord Jim* calls 'the destructive element' of life. The novel is an elaborate and often fascinating experiment in mixed styles and perspectives and an indictment of capitalism as a system of vested interests that maintains itself by the aggressive and ubiquitous exercise of power. *Lives of the Poets* (1984) consists of six short stories and a novella in which Jonathan, the imagined writer of the stories, reveals his state of mind and the circumstances of his life. Doctorow's method raises questions about the possibility of art in a disintegrating world. Marriages are falling apart, including Jonathan's own. 'Let's make some useful distinctions here', Jonathan says. 'On the one side are the traditionally married, battling, shrieking, and occupying each other's brains like some terrible tumour until one of them dies ... on the other hand are more marriages that need to be severed instantly', and there is also 'the phenomenon of the neither married nor divorced but no longer entirely together'. Collapsing human relationships are the centre of an urban chaos which includes muggings, murders and the apartment doorman who eyes Jonathan's new coat and hints that the gift of it could guarantee a degree of protection. The anarchy of city life is met by the chaos of remedies offered in Greenwich Village. Doctorow satirises the ineffective capriciousness of contemporary trends in self-fulfilment when Jonathan considers the available options:

> On the other hand, this is the Village, whatever can be tried to stem disaster is tried here, so I'm ready for action. A free paper found in the lobby tells all about it: I can begin with lessons in the Alexander technique, a proven method for attaining awareness and physical reeducation and postural alignment, and then I can go buy the Bach Flower Remedies, look in on the Breathing Center, stop awhile at the Center for Jewish Meditation and Healing, sign up for some t'ai chi exercise in flowing motion for vitality and health, and if things still don't work out, I can submit myself to some deep-tissue manipulation by a qualified Rolfer. The Gurdjieff discussion group might come in handy, and if I need some companionship the Loving Brotherhood is there making "the planet a place where it is safe for people to love each other." Can't knock that. ... I feel better already.

Jonathan himself is allowed to give the edge to Doctorow's social comment when he further reflects: 'But as I make my way along these various paths to fulfillment, maybe I ought to take some martial-arts training so I can kick the shit out of anyone who tries to stop me'.

Barth, Pynchon, Kennedy and Gardner

The most flamboyantly erudite among contemporary American novelists, John Barth and Thomas Pynchon (*b*. 1937) are both devotees of words, complicated structures and surrealist situations. Barth is an optimist for whom the world, though often painful, is more often gratifyingly absurd; he enjoys its energies. Pynchon savours doom and, as his early story 'Entropy' suggests, sees energy as fatal. Both make large demands of their readers, although Barth's two early novels are relatively straightforward companion pieces about the elusiveness of definition in a world morally blank. Todd Andrews in *The Floating Opera* (1956) and Jacob Horner in *The End of the Road* (1958) anticipate Henry Burlingame's remark to Ebenezer Cooke in *The Sot-Weed Factor*: 'I know of naught immutable and sure'. Andrews decides not to commit suicide because 'There's no final reason for living (or for suicide)'; Horner, bound like the bust of Laacoön on his mantelpiece by 'the serpents Knowledge and Imagination', ends his story not knowing what to do and taking a taxi to a metaphysically implausible 'Terminal'. Abandoning conventional form, *The Sot-Weed Factor* is an extravagant parody of eighteenth-century English picaresque fiction and an irreverent spoof of American colonial history. Ebenezer Cooke's career is an education in the meaning of Henry Burlingame who, for ubiquity and doubleness, outdoes even Moby-Dick as 'an ungraspable phantom of life'.

Barth's least self-justifying assault on the orthodoxies of novel form, *Giles Goat-Boy, or The Revised New Syllabus* (1966), allegorically satirises education and computer programming in a world of perpetual mutability. *Lost in the Funhouse* (1968) is a series of short fictions for print, tape and live voice in which the status of narrative itself is questioned. *Chimera* (1972) brilliantly exploits the possibilities of the 'frame-tale' as exemplified by *The Thousand and One Nights*, bringing down the classical myths of Perseus and Bellerophon to the level of the hilarious mundane. The book's first section, the 'Dunyazadiad', is about the plight of Scheherazade as told by her younger sister, Dunyazade, who sat at the foot of the royal bed while the Shah was held spellbound by the famous combination of love and storytelling. As a bald genie with queer lenses, Barth enters the scene to discuss narrative art with the sisters. 'Making love and telling stories both take more than good technique – but it's only the technique that we can *talk* about', says Scheherazade, displaying a shrewd sense of the limits of criticism. A little earlier, Barth as genie provides a gloss on Barth the novelist's next production: 'My project is to learn where to go by discovering where I am by reviewing where I've been – where we've *all* been'. The 'project' becomes the epistolary novel *Letters* (1979), in which Barth reviews his own literary past, reintroducing old characters and adding new ones over a time span of some 200 years. The method affords the 'Author' an opportunity to reconsider America's past as well as 'the rise and fall and rise of the novel' and 'the sundry passions of the human breast'.

In *The Sot-Weed Factor* Burlingame describes himself as 'Suitor of Totality, Embracer of Contradictories, Husband to all Creation, the Cosmic Lover!' So saying, Burlingame defines his maker, for Barth's playful embrace of the world in art bespeaks just such a craving for the wholeness of 'the seamless universe'. His narrative games may irritate and repel some for others there is much to be said for getting lost in the Joycean jocoseriousness of the funhouse. There is still fun in *Sabbatical: A Romance* (1982) but seriousness supervenes. Set in Chesapeake Bay in 1980, the question shadowing the narrative is whether the world will end before the novel does. 'The world *is* a seamless web', the heroine declares, echoing both Burlingame and Barth, but this could mean that, given the Big Bang, we all go together when we go.

Thomas Pynchon's first novel *V* (1963) supplies alligator hunts in the sewers of New York and tenuous narrative footholds through two heroes. Benny Profane's quest for identity is paralleled by the activities of a brainy, neurotic group called The Whole Sick Crew; Stencil's search for the secret meaning of his father's memoirs involves diverse excursions into Maltese history and German colonialism. The novel seems to insist on the individual's involvement even in history apparently remote, and to suggest that the world's energies are disintegrative. *The Crying of Lot 49* (1966) is a short, still complex satirical novel about the problem of communication in a society arranged in patterns of conspiracy that relate back to the Tristero System, a sixteenth-century postal service believed to be operating in twentieth-century America.

Gravity's Rainbow (1973) elaborates the world-as-conspiracy theory with help from quantum mechanics, probability theory and assorted engineering lore. Lieutenant Tyrone Slothrop seems to be the key to the German V-2 rocket attacks on England late in the Second World War. Whenever Slothrop has an erection a rocket is sure to follow within two to ten days. At the centre of an intricate code of bizarre characters, obscure allusions and enigmatic obscenities, the rocket symbolises sex, paranoia and the inevitable angel of death human energy must bring down on mankind in an apocalypse of the ultimate absurd. In Chapter 2 Katje urges Slothrop to respect the mysterious, five-minute life of the rocket:

> it is a curve each of them feels unmistakably. It is the parabola. They must have guessed, once or twice – guessed and refused to believe – that everything, always, collectively, had been moving toward that purified shape latent in the sky, that shape of no surprise, no second chances, no return. Yet they do move forever under it, reserved for its own black-and-white bad news certainly as if it were the Rainbow, and they its children.

Two novelists born before the Second World War whose works have come recently to prominence are William Kennedy (*b.* 1928) and John Gardner (1933–82). The 'Albany' novels of William Kennedy began to be widely known when the publication of *Ironweed* (1983) drew attention to *Legs* (1975), *Billy Phelan's Greatest Game* (1978) and *The Ink Truck* (1969). As an outsider and dreamer, the journalist Bailey in *The Ink Truck*, Kennedy's first novel, is a forerunner of the heroes of the later books. *Legs* mixes fact and fiction about the gangster Jack (Legs) Diamond whose lawyer in the novel calls him 'the underside of everybody's life'. Kennedy was drawn to the popularly mythologised hoodlum as subject for a novel because Diamond 'was a character who had galvanized the imagination of America. Legs is another version of the American dream – that you can grow up and shoot your way to fame and fortune'. The gangster also gave an opportunity to consider simple human qualities in an implausible combination. After all, as Kennedy says, 'the people that live this kind of life are human beings like you and me. People did love Legs Diamond'. People also love Billy Phelan, pool hustler, poker player and small-time bookie amply endowed with Irish resilience, a chip off the old block of his father, Francis, the hobo hero of *Ironweed*.

Kennedy's novels are rooted in his native city. Albany, in the state of New York, is to him what Mississippi is to Faulkner or Dublin to James Joyce. The city provides what Kennedy calls 'the verifying elements . . . a verification that life was lived in a specific way'. *Ironweed* verifies the human spirit as indomitable, even when the ex-ball-player Francis is simply running in the manner of John Updike's Rabbit Angstrom:

> Francis began to run, and in so doing, reconstituted a condition that was as pleasurable to his being as it was natural: the running of bases after the crack of the bat, the running from accusation, the running from the calumny of men and women, the running from family, from bondage, from destitution of spirit through ritualistic straightenings, the running, finally, in a quest for pure flight as a fulfilling mannerism of the spirit.

After a series of appalling accidents, including his killing of a scab during a trolley-workers' strike and dropping and killing his baby son while changing a nappy, Francis Phelan abandons his family. Wandering the streets of Albany during the Depression, he talks to the dead, speculates about the past, looks for food and shelter and cares for an ageing tramp called Helen. He likes helping her, and besides it's 'easier than working'. In a meditation about the meaning of his own struggle to exist, Francis joins the growing ranks of non-conformist outsiders from Melville's Ishmael and Twain's Huck Finn to Heller's Yossarian and John Irving's Homer Wells in *The Cider House Rules* (1985) 'The trick was to live'. Francis thinks, 'to beat the bastards, survive the mob . . . and show them all what a man can do to set things right, once he sets his mind to it'. A warrior himself, 'a warrior, he was certain, was not a victim. Never a victim'.

John Gardner is a philosophical novelist whose consistent purpose is to affirm the value of life through the medium of fiction. 'Art leads, it doesn't follow', he says in a 1977 interview in *The Atlantic Monthly*. 'Art doesn't imitate life, art makes people do things . . . if we celebrate bad values in our arts we're going to have a bad society; if we celebrate values which make you healthier, which make life better, we're going to have a better world'. *October Light* (1976) comprises two interwoven stories. One story is the framing narrative about James Page who locks his 'puffy, widowed' sister, Sally Abbott, in her bedroom for bringing into his house with her television set 'the filth of hell made visible in the world'. Disgusted by the television's 'endless simpering advertising, and, worse yet, its monstrously obscene games of greed', James takes his shotgun and blows 'the TV screen to hell, right back where it come from'. The other, subsidiary story comes from a dog-eared paperback called 'The Smugglers of Lost Souls' Rock', which Sally finds on the floor of her room and is a burlesque of the fashionable contemporary novel of nihilism, entropy and alienation.

> 'Snuff it, baby', he'd hissed at the world, but the world dragged on.
>
> After thirty-three years of insipid debauchery – balling and whiskey and dreary books (poetry and novels, philosophy and science), more foreign ports than he could now remember and, between them, endless weeks at sea, where he shoveled his head fuller yet with books – Peter Wagner had come to the end of his rope or, rather (this time), the centre of his bridge. All life, he had come to understand, was a boring novel. Death would be boring too, no doubt, but you weren't required to pay attention.

A cover blurb for 'The Smugglers of Lost Souls' Rock' commends it as 'A sick book, as sick and evil as life in America', and critical reactions are given in extracts from reviews, one of which calls it 'Deeply disturbing' and another, 'Hilarious'. As burlesque it is hilarious, but in relation to the main narrative it is disturbing: running the two stories parallel implies that the real world in which the incensed, principled, James Page has incarcerated his sister is at best as ridiculous and at worst as poisoned as the pulp world of the paperback fiction. Gardner's final point is made when Page realises that he has damaged the people around him and is reconciled to his sister. The difference between the absurd, sensationalist, trendy world of the paperback novel and the actual one of human relationship is that in the real world redemption is possible through self-knowledge and love.

There is nothing facile about Gardner's affirmations. The real, random world is absurd because it is governed by accident. *The Sunlight Dialogues* (1972) opposes Fred Clumly, a chief of police possessed by a manic obsession with law and order, to an 'irregular outlaw' called The Sunlight Man, a 'lunatic magician' who asks, 'What is there in this world but accident?' and unnerves Clumly with his pragmatic view of life:

> ... all your grand American responsibility is trash: what will happen will happen ... Hate as freely as you love, by inclination. Wait and let progress happen when it can, because it will, if the gods will it, and if not, then it will not ... You ask me what my answer is to America's problems – psychological, social, political. I have none ... I doubt that anything in all our system is in tune with, keyed to, reality.

Giving a final laugh 'at the childish credulity of man', the Sunlight Man is shot dead shortly before the end of the novel. Clumly is humanised. His involvement with the Sunlight Man does not deprive him of his belief in order, but it teaches him that the principle of order is too mysterious and individual to be exppressed adequately in laws and police regulations. In an entropic world the order in a person's life may be invisible until the life is over: 'That's what it's all about, you know. Order. Correct. It's a beautiful thing, the order in a man's life, and sometimes you wonder if that's not the only time it's visible, after he's dead and it's there beside his grave'.

Accident, much of it violent, rules the world of *Nickel Mountain* (1977) which Gardner subtitles 'A Pastoral Novel', but life is affirmed in the story of Henry Soames who rises above the shabbiness and disappointment of his past, his fear of death and the guilt he feels about causing the death of Simon Bale. Henry is obsessed by a vision of 'people as meaningless motion, a stream of humanity down through time, no more significant than rocks in a mountain slide. It was different in the country, where a man's life or a family's past was not so quickly swallowed up, where the ordinariness of thinking creatures was obvious only when you thought a minute, not an inescapable conclusion that crushed the soul the way a pavement shattered men's arches'. Henry achieves significance in the country, against the press of absurdity, through his love for Callie Wells and finally wins through to the serenity of a belief in the natural order of continuing life. Gardner's message that 'life goes on' is most densely considered in *Freddy's Book* (1980) but most succinctly and eloquently expressed in *Grendel*, a novel which tells the story of the Old English epic poem 'Beowulf' from the monster's point of view. Just as Clumly and the Sunlight Man are shown to need each other – after all, where would order be without anarchy to work on? – so the brutishness of Grendel is revealed as necessary for the civilising forces of science and the arts. A dragon almost pities Grendel for being the brute existence on which humans depend for their definition of themselves:

> You stimulate them! You make them think and scheme. You drive them to poetry, science, religion, all that makes them what they are for as long as they last. You are, so to speak, the brute existent by which they learn to define themselves. The exile, captivity, death they shrink from – the blunt facts of their mortality, their abandonment – that's what you make them recognize, embrace! You *are* mankind, or man's condition: inseparable as the mountain-climber and the mountain. If you withdraw, you'll instantly be replaced.

Grendel's tragedy – to be a brute and to be destroyed – is an expression of life's triumphant continuance. As the hero Beowulf twists the monster's arm he whispers: 'Believe it or not. Though you murder the world, turn plains into stone, transmogrify life into I and it, strong searching roots will crack your cave and rain will cleanse it: The world will burn green, sperm build again. My promise. Time is the mind, the hand that makes . . . By that I kill you'.

Recent American theatre: Albee and after

His first full-length play *Who's Afraid of Virginia Woolf?* (1962) established Edward Albee (*b*. 1928) in the public mind as the successor to Tennessee Williams and Arthur Miller. Albee had already shown a less hopeful view than Miller's of the American Dream's potential for salvage. Personified as the empty Young Man in *The American Dream* (1959–60), the Dream confesses its hollowness:

> I have no emotions. I have been drained, torn asunder . . . disembowelled. I have, now, only my person . . . my body, my face. I use what I have . . . I let people love me . . . I accept the syntax around me, for while I know I cannot relate . . . I know I must be related *to*. I let people love me . . . I let people touch me . . . I let them draw pleasure from my groin . . . from my presence . . . from the fact of me . . . but, that is all it comes to . . . And it will always be thus.

Mommy and Daddy have sacrificed their adopted son to the American way; the Young Man is next in line. The 'wish to kill', which Miller's Quentin says 'is never killed', figures prominently in Albee's terrifyingly funny, ritualistic plays, although it may be muted by 'a stroke of love' or the doubtful forgiveness of truce by exhaustion.

In *The Zoo Story* (1958) death provides the only means of communication. Jerry has failed to establish a relationship with his landlady's dog and his visit to the zoo has taught him that all lives are caged in isolation. His aggression towards Peter in trying to take the whole Central Park bench for himself is an attempt to make contact with someone, 'to make a beginning . . . to understand and just possibly be understood'. Rather than endure Peter's recoil from him, Jerry engineers the irrevocable moment of contact in which he impales himself on his own knife held by the reluctantly self-defending Peter. In *The Sandbox* (1959) the Young Man reappears as a vacuous Angel of Death who watches indifferently as Mommy and Daddy bury Grandma in a child's sandbox. In *The Death of Bessie Smith* (1959) the great blues singer bleeds to death, murdered by the racial prejudices of the divided South. In *Who's Afraid of Virginia Woolf?* George kills the imaginary son on whom he and Martha have based the illusions of their marriage. The death of their crucial fiction brings a little hope: although Martha is 'afraid of Virginia Woolf' – that is, of consciousness – the play ends with husband and wife touching each other, albeit tentatively, in a moment of painful truth which both manage with weary tenderness.

Albee is nothing if not articulate. The language of *Tiny Alice* (1964) is almost hypnotic enough to deflect irritation with its metaphysical pretentiousness. The relationship between reality and the tiny scale model of Miss Alice's mansion in which Brother Julian eventually yields to temptation is never made clear, although the play urges its significance. If it is simply that of greater to lesser reality, presumably Julian is guilty of succumbing to illusion, but his final soliloquy does little to clarify things either for him or the audience. *A Delicate Balance* (1966) wordily develops the themes of cruelty and illusion in a high-caste suburban version of the American nightmare. *Box-Mao-Box* (1968) is theatrically experimental, thematically fragile. In *All Over* (1971) a dying man's wife, daughter, mistress, son, lawyer, physician and nurse are put through assorted self-revelations as they await the moment when death will terminate the network of relations in which his life has held them. The characters are sketchy, each a gathering of attitudes instead of a person, and the play is ruinously static, an exercise in the aesthetics of unpleasantness. Characterisation remains sketchy in *The Lady from Dubuque* (1980), a play more like *Who's Afraid of Virginia Woolf?* in language and theatrical style, but lacking the imaginative energy that comes, in the earlier play, from commitment to a genuinely tense and difficult human problem. The play makes the unexceptional point that a person can be defined by the needs of surrounding people. *Lolita* (1981), an inexplicably clumsy attempt to put Nabokov's novel on the stage, merely demonstrates the extent to which the effectiveness of the novel depends on Nabokov's use of language, a commodity for which Albee's work offers no adequate substitute.

Jack Gelber (*b*. 1932) employs audience participation and improvisation to dramatise the life of drug addiction with innovative immediacy in *The Connection* (1950). Kenneth H. Brown (*b*. 1936) powerfully exploits the latent theatricality of prison routine in *The Brig* (1963). The success of Michael McClure's (*b*. 1932) meretricious *The Beard* (1965) demonstrates how talk of 'ritual drama' and support from Norman Mailer can disarm criticism even in the presence of tedium. James Baldwin's *Blues for Mister Charlie* (1965) projects the ideas about Black-white relations discussed in *The Fire Next Time*. Also propagandist, but more vigorously theatrical are three plays by LeRoi Jones (later known as Imamu Amiri Baraka): *Dutchman*, *The Slave* and *The Toilet* (1964). Both Preston Jones (1936–79) and David Mamet (*b.* 1947) have been justly praised for their ear for American speech, but Jones's *Texas Trilogy* (1973–5) is in the regional tradition of Thornton Wilder's *Our Town* and it is Mamet who has developed the vernacular into a truly theatrical idiom of impassioned realism especially in his Pulitzer prize-winning two-act play *Glengarry Glen Ross* (1984).

The thirty-one short scenes of Mamet's *Sexual Perversity in Chicago* (1974) are apparently little more than a set of clever variations on material more sensitively treated in Jules Feiffer's (*b.* 1929) screenplay for Mike Nichols's film *Carnal Knowledge* (1971), but Mamet takes his subject seriously. The play's portrayal of nine weeks in the life and loves of Bernard Litko and his protégé, Danny Shapiro, is intended to make a solemn point, according to the comment Mamet makes on the play for the *National Playwrights Directory* (ed. Phyllis Johnson Kaye, 1977): 'The human organism perceives the passage of time because of its limited understanding of the essential immortality of the germ plasm. We are restricted in our understanding because we reproduce bi-sexually and the individual organism is not complete unto itself. This is why we refer to sexual experimentation as "making time"'. The play hardly betrays any such portentousness of theme, and remains a show of undergraduate verbal slapstick whose chief merits are fast talk and rapid changes of scene. *Edmond* (1982) also employs revue-style scenes to dramatise the hero's frantic search for identity amid the hazards of violent urban America, but fails to convince because Edmond's exit from middle-class conservatism into the risks of street life seems gratuitous. *American Buffalo* (1975), like *Glengarry Glen Ross* is about people caught in the heartless processes of American business. ('Mine eyes have seen the glory of the coming of the Lord. He is peeling down the alley in a Black and Yellow Ford'.) In *American Buffalo* Donny Dubrow runs a junkshop in Chicago as a cover for his operations as a small-time fence. In *Glengarry Glen Ross* Mamet's characters are real-estate salesmen selling tracts of land in Florida and the romantic lilt of the Scottish title refers to the wish-fulfilment fantasy names of the bits of worthless swampland they are trying to sell. In both plays a robbery is planned, the implication of which is that the difference between robbery and salesmanship tends to be only one of method. The distinction of the play is in its revelation of the desperation and perverse resourcefulness of the salesmen who, to earn a living, must combine the cynicism becoming to their fraudulent trade with a belief in the value of their virtuoso sales techniques. In Act Two, Shelly Levene, whose sales performance has been slipping to such an extent that he fears for his job, makes a comeback. He has sold property to a Jewish couple by a craftily graduated approach and by keeping his nerve. The full horror of the incident does not depend on the irony that his customers' cheques habitually bounce; it inheres in the image of a man who has become a travesty of human decency, and who is proud of the fact. Levene recounts his success in concluding the sale:

LEVENE: ... I locked on them. All on them, nothing on me. All my thoughts are on them. I'm holding the last thought that I spoke: 'NOW is the time'. (*Pause.*) They signed, Ricky, It was *great*. It was fucking great. It was like they wilted all at once. No *gesture* . . . nothing. Like together. They, I swear to God, they both kind of *imperceptibly slumped*. And he reaches and takes the pen and signs, he passes it to her, she signs. It was so fucking solemn. I just let it sit. I nod like this. I nod again. I grasp his hands. I shake his hands. I grasp *her* hands. I nod at her like this. 'Bruce . . . Harriett . . .'. I'm beaming at them. I'm nodding like this. I point back in the living room, back to the sideboard. (*Pause.*) *I didn't fucking know there was a sideboard there*!! He goes back, he brings us a drink. Little short glasses. A pattern in 'em. And we toast. In silence. (*Pause.*)

ROMA: That was a great sale, Shelly.

Sam Shepard

In a prodigiously large output of plays from *Cowboys* (1964) to *A Lie of the Mind* (1985) Sam Shepard (*b.* 1943) converts questions about the connection between American reality and myth into strikingly inventive dramatic imagery whose theatrical vividness is often greater than its philosophical weight. Shepard's aims are consciously theatrical rather than literary. (He now dislikes most of *Buried Child* (1979): '. . . it just seems verbose and overblown. It seems unnecessarily complicated'.) His last three major plays – *Curse of the*

Starving Class (1977), *Buried Child* and *A Lie of the Mind* (1985) – all deal with the capacity of people to wound each other within the context of family relationships. The subject matter is fundamentally the same as Eugene O'Neill's in *Long Day's Journey into Night*, but Shepard's expressionistic methods explode a theme on stage where O'Neill's realism merely unfolds it. In *Action* (1975) the play ends as a character called Jeep describes the moment when he was arrested and his life changed:

JEEP: The second I got arrested I understood something. I remember the phrase 'getting in trouble', I remember the word 'trouble'. I remember the feeling of being in trouble. It wasn't until I got in trouble that I found out my true position . . . I was up for grabs. I was being taken away by something bigger . . . I had no idea what the world was. I had no idea how I got there or why or who did it. I had no references for this.

Shepard's plays make the world strange – 'something bigger' – and violent in order to show the need to find new moral reference points. Unexamined conventions cannot prevent family life from becoming debris in *Curse of the Starving Class*. The father is continually drunk, the son abuses his mother for calling the police when his father broke down a door, the daughter decides to become a criminal, and everyone screams. The use of food in the action of the play provides the simple pivotal symbolism on which all the family relationships turn. 'WE DON'T BELONG TO THE STARVING CLASS', Emma the daughter shouts at her mother who has boiled the chicken Emma has raised for a 4-H Club project; but, of course, they are all starving emotionally, connected to each other not by love but by a network of betrayals. In *Buried Child* the family atmosphere arises from drunkenness, mental derangement and incest. A nephew throws his uncle's wooden leg from the house and makes the cripple crawl out after it. A son enters, carrying the disinterred and decomposing body of the child his mother had borne him years ago. Each primary human relationship is poisoned by aberration or cruelty, yet Shepard's vision, if bleak, is not hopeless. There is a miraculous reference point in the backyard where corn is growing, although it has not been planted there for years. Hailie, the mother, marvels at the crop she sees through the window:

HAILIE'S VOICE: . . . I've never seen such corn. Have you taken a look at it lately? Tall as a man already. This early in the year. Carrots too. Potatoes. Peas. It's like a Paradise out there

... A miracle. I've never seen it like this. Maybe the rain
did something. Maybe it was the rain ... You can't force
a thing to grow. You can't interfere with it. It's all hidden.
It's all unseen. You just gotta wait till it pops up out of
the ground. I've never seen a crop like this in my whole
life. Maybe it's the sun. Maybe that's it. Maybe it's the
sun.

Unknown to her, Hailie's husband, Dodge, has just died, but life, it
seems, goes elementally on. In *A Lie of the Mind*, however, Shepard
makes it clear that while 'you can't force a thing to grow', neither
can everything be left to nature. Human propensities to cruelty and
violence can be overcome or redeemed only by strenuous, even
heroic effort.

Shepard's early plays (collected in *The Unseen Hand and Other Plays*,
1986) are multi-faceted theatrical images made up of fragmentary
characters, syncopated plots and disjointed dialogue. The playwright
thinks of these early works as 'a series of impulsive chronicles
representing a chaotic, subjective world', written at a time – the
mid-sixties – when 'experimentation was the life-blood not only of
the playwright but also of actors, directors, and even of producers
and critics', and 'the moment ... was seething with a radical shift
of the American psyche'. In *La Turista* (1967), *The Unseen Hand*
(1969) and *Operation Sidewinder* (1970) he uses surrealistic visual and
verbal effects to floodlight the familiar. *Operation Sidewinder*, about
an experimental computer, draws on Shepard's talents as poet,
musician and dramatist in a satirical play whose targets include
Indian folklore, Black power and UFO's as well as the clichés of
attitude and language bred by the computer age. Shepard's most
cogent assault on trendiness, however, is *The Tooth of Crime* (1973)
in which Hoss, a rock-and-roll hero, struggles to choose his own
destiny in the game of the 'Great Killer Race' whose principal
challenge to him is the rivalry of Crow, a younger musician who
represents the force of the latest popular trend. The title of the play
comes from a line in a sonnet by the French poet, Mallarmé: 'A
heart that the tooth of crime cannot wound'. The poem contrasts a
vulnerable figure with an invulnerable one, and in Shepard's play
the outmoded Hoss loses to Crow, the new man of the media. There
is true pathos in the spectacle of Hoss as the fading superstar who
cannot keep pace with the pressures of changing fashion and the
code of current taste. Shepard brilliantly exposes the heartlessness
of media-dominated values when he brings the two pop antagonists

face to face and reduces Hoss to the shame of admitting defeat and appealing to his adversary for help:

HOSS: How did this happen? This ain't the way it's supposed to happen . . . Look at me. Everything was going so good. I had everything at my finger-tips. Now I'm outa' control. I'm pulled and pushed around from one image to another. Nothin' takes a solid form. Nothin' sure and final. Where do I stand! Where the fuck do I stand!

CROW: Alone, Leathers.

HOSS: Yeah, well I guess I don't got your smarts. That's for sure. You played me just right. Sucked me right into it. There's nothin' to do but call ya'. All right. The turf's yours. The whole shot. Now show me how to be a man.

Once again the cry is for a reference point, and the question asked by the play is where one may be found in a volatile world in which what is right depends on the fickle processes of image-projection. The turf may be Crow's now, but for how long? Hoss finally succeeds in choosing his fate and living by his own code, but to do so, protecting his life and identity from the pressures of commercial expediency, he has to resort to suicide. 'It's my life and my death in one clean shot', he says as he puts the gun in his mouth. 'Perfect, Leathers, Perfect', says Crow admiringly, 'A genius mark . . . you slid right home'. As the curtain falls the audience is prompted to wonder when Crow will be compelled to slide home by the same route.

Mind and language in recent poetry

James Dickey's (*b.* 1923) novel *Deliverance* (1970) is a violent fable of the senses. In the best of his poetry in *Poems 1957–1967* (1968) intensely sensual awareness is the source of a clamorous poetic diction in lines that seem to gasp with amazement at themselves. Rhythm, sometimes over-insistent, is typically imparted to simple declarative lines by a basic anapaestic pattern in poems which fuse inner and outer states to create a higher reality through the blending of fact and fantasy. In 'The Lifeguard' a man working as a lifeguard at a summer camp fails to rescue a boy from drowning. He hides in a boathouse and in the extremity of his grief comes to believe, for a while, that he can walk on the lake where the child drowned and raise him up to life. He steps 'outward from earth onto water/In quest of the miracle', intent on being the 'saviour of one/who has already died in my care', and for a moment seems to be granted the resurrection he seeks as the child's voice answers his call and a body rises through the water before reality supervenes:

> I wash the black mud from my hands.
> On a light given off by the grave
> I kneel in the quick of the moon
> At the heart of a distant forest
> And hold in my arms a child
> Of water, water, water.

Dickey sees a strong connection between the extremes of joy and ruin, as in the concluding image of the speaker in 'Cherrylog Road' who departs from his girl on a motorbike 'fleshed/with power . . . wild to be wreckage for ever', or the terrible, erotic descent of the airline stewardess in 'Falling'. In 'The Firebombing' Dickey's use of what he calls 'the split line, in which spaces . . . take the place of punctuation' succeeds in achieving the 'presentational immediacy' the poet aims for, especially when the poem depicts the feelings of a wartime pilot at night as he flies over Japan, the enemy's home country:

> Enemy rivers and trees
> Sliding off me like snakeskin,
> Strips of vapour spooled from the engines
> Going   invisible   passing   over   on
> Over   bridges   roads for nigh-walkers
> Sunday night is the enemy's country   absolute
> Calm   the moon's face   coming   slowly
>
> About
>   the inland sea
> Slants   is woven with wire thread
> Levels out   holds together like a quilt
> Off the starboard wing

James Dickey has always distrusted artificiality in poetry. At his best he is remarkably successful in presenting the matter of a poem with a 'compulsiveness' designed to 'cause the reader to forget literary judgements entirely, and simply experience'. Galway Kinnell (*b*. 1927) too has a gift for immediacy. The influences of W. B. Yeats, Hart Crane and Pablo Neruda are noticeable in *The Book of Nightmares* (1971), a set of ten related poems characterised by tense utterance and bombarding imagery modelled on Rilke's *Divine*

Elegies. Kinnell believes that poetry is a shedding of those inhibitions that keep us from expressing our most intimate feelings. In *What a Kingdom It Was* (1960) and *Flower Herding on Mount Monadnock* (1964) his feelings are chiefly for nature. 'I know I live half alive in the world', he says in 'The Middle of the Way'. Half of his life 'belongs to the wild darkness' which he confronts in *Body Rags* (1968). In 'The Bear' he imagines himself becoming one with the non-human realm by entering the body of a bear he has killed:

> I hack
> a ravine in his thigh and eat and drink,
> and tear him down his whole length
> and open him and climb in
> and close him up after me, against the wind,
> and sleep.

Kinnell's often elegiac poetry is kept steady by anecdotal fact and it is rich in landscapes from which meanings rise without strain. Like James Joyce's Stephen Dedalus in the 'Proteus' chapter of *Ulysses*, Kinnell reads the 'signatures' of things, but even when the discovered significance is highly personal, the thing remains itself, enhanced by the poet's imagination, not distorted by a forcing hand. In *The Past* (1986), Kinnell's masterly poems of reminiscence include 'The Old Life', in which personal feeling and natural setting match and interpenetrate perfectly:

> The waves collapsed into themselves
> with heavy rumbles in the darkness
> and the soprano shingle whistled
> gravely its way back into the sea.
> When the moon came from behind clouds
> its white full-moon's light
> lightly oiled the little beach stones
> back into silence. We stood
> among shatterings, glitterings,
> the brilliance. For some reason
> to love does not seem ever
> to hurt any less. Now it happens
> another lifetime is up for us,
> another life is upon us.

Robert Creeley's poetry can seem to preen over its brevities. Influenced by Olson's theory of 'projective verse', Creeley believes that a line of verse must be a breathing of the person who writes. The poet, as Olson puts it, 'thinks not *before* but *with* his poem'. Although there is, Creeley allows, a rhythm in the world 'which projects/from itself continuity/bending all to its force' ('The Rhythm'), a poem should be like a Jackson Pollock 'action painting', expressing the responsive and creative energies of the poet as they are at the ephemeral moment of writing. The poet deals with 'the grit of things' in terms of a particular action, a specific place, but 'no/one ever/quite the same' ('Song'). Creeley's short lyrics, mainly about personal relationships, often suffer from intellectual cuteness, but at their best they convey an affectingly tentative sense of wonder about love, memory and his own acts of perception. In 'Somewhere' he recalls an evening when he walked into a house, a 'galloping collection of boards':

> From outside it must have seemed
> a wonder that it was
> the inside *he* as *me* saw
> in the dark there.

The poems of James Wright (1927–80) and W. S. Merwin (*b*. 1927) often appear less occupied with a subject than with a startling effect or with the aesthetic satisfactions of using language intensely and unexpectedly. Merwin writes about birth, death and the continuance of life in collections of poems from *A Mask for Janus* (1952) to *Green with Beasts* (1956). His concern with language is explicit in 'Dictum: a Masque of Deluge' where he says 'We shall find/Dictions for rising, words for departure'. His poetry has been more open and colloquial since the publication of *The Moving Target* (1963). A colloquial tone of voice is the most immediately appealing quality of A. R. Ammons's verse. The Wordsworthian manner of 'a man speaking to men' draws the reader into poems that marvel at the fluid abundance of a world in flux which the poet tries to apprehend as fully as he can, but upon which he imposes no restraining order ('I have reached no conclusions, have erected no boundaries ... I have drawn no lines'). Ammons is most widely admired for the shorter poems gathered in *Collected Poems 1951–1971* (1972) but he is nowhere more eloquent in a style of writing and a quality of open-pored response worthy of Walt Whitman than in 'Corson's Inlet'

> I see narrow orders, limited tightness, but will
> not run to that easy victory:
> still around the looser, wider forces work:
> I will try
> to fasten into order enlarging grasps of disorder, widening
> scope, but enjoying the freedom that

Scope eludes my grasp, that there is no finality of vision,
that I have perceived nothing completely,
     that tomorrow a new walk is a new walk.

For John Ashbery 'Nothing is too "unimportant"' ('The Explanation'). The impenetrability of Ashbery's earlier work in which brilliant, fragmented surfaces alternate with equally enigmatic prosaic fullness, has given way to more consistently accessible verse in *Houseboat Days* (1977) where attention to particular words and phrases does not preclude a detectable flow of thought. He is still more direct – even Whitmanesque – in the poems of *A Wave* (1984), 'democratising' his language to the address of 'Just walking around':

You always seemed to be
    traveling in a circle.
And now that the end is near

The segments of the trip
    swing open like an orange.
There is light in there, and
    mystery and food.
Come see it. Come not for
    me but it.
But if I am still there, grant
    that we may see each other.

It is a humble, supplicatory use of the poet's art in the service of love, Ashbery's theme throughout the volume. Much possessed by the idiom of dream, the poet begins the title poem, 'The Wave', with three dreamlike, ominous lines:

To pass through pain and not know it,
A car door slamming in the night.
To emerge on an invisible terrain.

In the poem 'When the Sun Went Down' Ashbery makes the terrain visible, announcing the concern of his book:

To have been loved once by someone – surely
There is a permanent good in that,
Even if we don't know all the circumstances
Or if it happened too long ago to make any difference.

Like the work of Berryman and Lowell, the poetry of James Merrill (*b.* 1926) since *Water Street* (1962) is an autobiographical project 'to make some kind of house/Out of the life lived, out of the love spent' ('An Urban Convalescence'). Landscapes are states of his witty, probing mind in *Braving the Elements* (1972). In 'The Book of Ephraim' (*Divine Comedies*, 1977), *Mirabell: Books of Numbers* (1978) and *Scripts for the Pageant* (1980) Merrill enlarges his house of poetic fiction and the scope of his relations. Seances with an Ouija board bring messages from W. H. Auden, Albert Einstein, his mother and other inhabitants of the ether whose views of God ('Biology'), myth, history, the significance of the atom and the state of humanity comprise an energetic, allusive, humorous, ultimately sobering but always engaging meditation on the 'greenhouse' world and its purposes. Merrill is an outstandingly complete writer. Thrall to no fashion, he displays technical virtuosity in poetic forms from the sonnet and the ode to terza rima and an unobtrusive iambic pentameter. As his work has progressed, self-concern has become simultaneous with an expanding concern for the world he illuminates and warns. His chief informant in *Mirabell: Books of Numbers* is agitated in Book 2 by 'increasing human smog' which has cut the spirits' customary long vision to the sight of 'CONCERTED USE OF ATOMIC/WEAPONRY NOW FALLING INTO HANDS OF ANIMAL SOULS'.

The truest art is news of life, not exercises in aesthetics, although aesthetics are always part of the news. The medium must be understood for the message to be received. Moving the cup among the letters of the Ouija board in *Mirabell*, Book 1, James Merrill's conjured spirits spell out their requirement: 'FIND US BETTER PHRASES FOR THESE HISTORIES WE POUR FORTH/HOPING AGAINST HOPE THAT MAN WILL LOVE HIS MIND & LANGUAGE'. Bearing witness to the rewards as well as the perils of consciousness, the arts of literature, in America as elsewhere, teach love of mind and language. Thus they offer their own potent motivations towards the maintenance of peace in a blood-stained world.

Chronological table

Abbreviations: (D) = drama, (P) = prose, (V) = verse

DATE	AUTHOR AND TITLE	EVENT
1492		Christopher Columbus discovers West Indies, landing at San Salvador
1502		Amerigo Vespucci sails down eastern seaboard of S. America
1513		Florida discovered for Spain by Ponce de Leon
1585		Attempt under Sir Walter Raleigh to found colony in North Carolina; abandoned 1586
1588	Harriot, Thomas (*c.* 1560–1621): *A Brief and True Report of the New Found Land of Virginia* (P)	Defeat of Spanish Armada by English fleet
1607		Colony of Virginia inaugurated at Jamestown by John Smith
1608	Smith, John (1580–1631): *A True Relation* (P)	
1611		King James Version of the Bible is published
1616	Smith, John: *A Description of New England* (P)	
1620	*The Mayflower Compact*	Voyage of the *Mayflower*; settlement of Plymouth by Separatist Pilgrims
1624	Smith, John: *The Generall History of Virginia, New England, and the Summer Isles* (P)	

DATE	AUTHOR AND TITLE	EVENT
1626		Dutch colony of New Amsterdam founded on Hudson River. *Manhattan Island purchased from Indians for about 60 guilders' worth of cloth and trinkets
1629		Colony of Massachusetts founded
1636		Harvard, first American university founded; so-named in 1639
1637	Morton, Thomas (*c.* 1575–*c.* 1647): *New English Canaan* (P)	
1638		First printing press in America established at Cambridge, Mass.
1640	*The Bay Psalm Book* (V) printed at Cambridge, Mass. In use until 1773	
1641	Cotton, John, (1584–1652): *The Way of Life* (P)	
1643		Colonies of New England formed New England Federation
1644	Cotton, John: *The Keyes of the Kingdom of Heaven* (P) Williams, Roger (1603–83): *The Bloudy Tenent of Persecution, for Cause of Conscience* (P)	
1649	Mather, Richard (1596–1669): *A Platform of Church Discipline* (P) Winthrop, John (1588–1649): *History of New England* (P) completed [published 1825–6]	Trial and execution of Charles I
1650	Bradford, William (1590–1657): *History of Plymouth Plantation* (P) completed [published 1856] Bradstreet, Anne (*c.* 1612–72): *The Tenth Muse Lately Sprung up in America* (V)	
1652	Williams, Roger: *The Bloudy Tenent Yet More Bloudy* (P)	
1659	Hooker, Thomas (1586–1647): 'A True Sight of Sin' (P)	
1660		Restoration of Charles II to English throne

DATE	AUTHOR AND TITLE	EVENT
1662	Wigglesworth, Michael (1631–1705): *The Day of Doom* (V)	
1664		English seize New Amsterdam, later renamed New York
1676		War against Indians in New England ended Destruction of Jamestown by Bacon and followers
1678	Bradstreet, Anne: *Severall Poems* (V)	
1682	Rowlandson, Mary (*c.* 1635–78): *The Soveraignty and Goodness of God . . . Being a Narrative of the Captivity and Restauration of Mrs Mary Rowlandson* (P)	
1691		Plymouth Colony absorbed by Massachusetts
1692		Witchcraft trials at Salem, Mass.
1693	Mather, Increase (1639–1723): *Cases of Conscience Concerning Evil Spirits* (P)	
1700	Sewall, Samuel (1652–1730): *The Selling of Joseph* (P)	
1701		Foundation of Collegiate School of America, later Yale University
1702	Mather, Cotton (1663–1728): *Magnalia Christi Americana* (P)	Asiento Guinea Co. formed to develop slave trade between Africa and America
1704		The *News-Letter*, first continuously published weekly paper founded by John Campbell of Boston
1708	Cook, Ebenezer (*c.* 1672–1732): *The Sot-Weed Factor* (V)	
1725	Franklin, Benjamin (1706–90): *Dissertation on Liberty and Necessity, Pleasure and Pain* (P)	
1728	Byrd, William (1674–1744): *A History of the Dividing Line Run in the Year 1728* [Between Virginia and North Carolina] (P) [published 1841]	Vitus Bering discovers Straits between Asia and North America

DATE	AUTHOR AND TITLE	EVENT
1729	Sewall, Samuel completed his *Diary* (P) [published in 3 vols 1878–82]	
1731		Building (to 1751) of State House, Philadelphia, later Independence Hall, designed by Alexander Hamilton
		Benjamin Franklin founds free public library at Philadelphia
1732	Franklin, Benjamin: first issue of *Poor Richard's Almanack* (P)	Founding of Georgia, last British colony in America
1733	Byrd, William: *A Journey to the Land of Eden, A.D. 1733* (P) [published 1841]	Molasses Act: American trade with West Indies forbidden
1740	Edwards, Jonathan (1703–58): *Personal Narrative* (P)	
1741		Edwards preaches sermon, 'Sinners in the Hands of an Angry God' at Enfield, Conn.
1745		Foundation of Philadelphia Academy, later Pennsylvania University (1789)
1746		Princeton University and Library founded
1754		Anglo-French War in North America, George Washington defeated at Great Meadows
		George II founds King's College, New York (Columbia University)
1756		Start of Seven Years War
1763		Peace of Paris ending Seven Years War
1764		Sugar Act levied
1765		Stamp Act; Patrick Henry's speech to Virginia House of Burgesses
1766		Stamp Act repealed; withdrawal of British troops from Boston
		Mason–Dixon Line marks boundaries between Pennsylvania and Maryland, separating free and slave regions

DATE	AUTHOR AND TITLE	EVENT
1767	Dickinson, John (1732–1808): *Letters from a Farmer in Pennsylvania to the Inhabitants of the British Colonies* (P). First letters printed in Pennsylvania newspapers	
1770		Boston 'Massacre'
		Repeal of American Import Duties except for that on tea
1773		Boston Tea Party
1774	Woolman, John (1720–72): *Journal* (P)	Parliamentary suppression of opposition to tea duty First meeting of Continental Congress at Philadelphia
1775		War of American Independence; Battle of Bunker's Hill; Paul Revere's ride; Battle of Lexington
1776	Paine, Thomas (1737–1809): first of thirteen pamphlets in *American Crisis* series (P) Paine, Thomas: *Common Sense* (P) Trumbull, John (1750–1831): *McFingal: A Modern Epic Poem* (V) Jefferson, Thomas (1743–1826): *Declaration of Independence* (P)	Declaration of Independence from Britain
1780	Freneau, Philip (1752–1832): 'The British Prison Ship' (V)	American Academy of Sciences founded at Boston
1781		British under Cornwallis surrender to Washington at Yorktown
1782	Crèvecoeur, Hector St John de (1735–1813): *Letters from an American Farmer* (P)	Bank of America established at Philadelphia
1783		Treaty of Paris ends War of American Independence
1785	Dwight, Timothy (1752–1817): *The Conquest of Canaan* (V)	Dollar established as official US currency
1786	Barlow, Joel (1754–1812), Lemuel Hopkins (1750–1801), David Humphreys (1752–1818), *et al.*, *The Anarchiad* (V) [concluded 1787]	Daniel Shays's Rebellion in Massachusetts

DATE	AUTHOR AND TITLE	EVENT
1789	Brown, William Hill (1765–93): *The Power of Sympathy* (P)	Adoption of the American Constitution George Washington elected first President of USA
1791	Bartram, William (1739–1823): *Travels through North and South Carolina, Georgia, East and West Florida* (P) Franklin, Benjamin: *Autobiography* (P)	Bill of Rights becomes law
1792	Brackenridge, Hugh (1748–1816): *Modern Chivalry* (P) [completed 1815]	Invention of the cotton gin by Eli Whitney US Mint established
1798	Brown, Charles Brockden (1771–1810): *Wieland* (P)	
1799	Brown, Charles Brockden: *Edgar Huntly* (P), *Ormond* (P), *Arthur Mervyn* (P) [publication completed 1800]	Death of George Washington
1800	Weems, Mason Locke (1759–1825): *The Life and Memorable Actions of George Washington* (P)	Library of Congress established
1803		Purchase of Louisiana territory from France
1804		Alexander Hamilton killed in duel with Aaron Burr
1808		Importing of slaves forbidden by Federal Government
1809	Irving, Washington (1783–1859): *A History of New York* (P)	Sequoya (*c.* 1760–1843) begins to develop writing system for Cherokees
1812		Naval war between USA and Britain
1814	Key, Francis Scott (1779–1843): 'The Star-Spangled Banner'	Washington, DC burned by British troops
1820	Irving, Washington: *The Sketch Book of Geoffrey Crayon, Gent.* (P) Cooper, James Fenimore (1789–1851): *Precaution* (P)	Founding of Liberian Republic for freed slaves Missouri Compromise
1821	Bryant, William Cullen (1794–1878): *Poems* (P) Cooper, James Fenimore: *The Spy* (P)	*Saturday Evening Post* begins publication

DATE	AUTHOR AND TITLE	EVENT
1823	Cooper, James Fenimore: *The Pilot* (P), *The Pioneers* (P)	Monroe Doctrine
1826	Cooper, James Fenimore: *The Last of the Mohicans* (P)	
1827	Cooper, James Fenimore: *The Prairie* (P) Poe, Edgar Allan (1809–49): *Tamerlane and Other Poems* (V) Audubon, John James (1785–1851): first sections of *The Birds of America* [completed 1838]	Disciples of Christ founded by Alexander Campbell
1828	Webster, Noah (1758–1843): *An American Dictionary of the English Language*	Washington Square Park created in New York
1829		Andrew Jackson inaugurated President
1830	Smith, Joseph (1805–44): *Book of Mormon* (P)	Debate in Congress between Daniel Webster and Robert Y. Hayne on the nature of the Union
1831	Poe, Edgar Allan: *Poems* (V) Bird, Robert Montgomery (1806–54): *The Gladiator* (D)	Nat Turner's rebellion
1832	Irving, Washington: *The Legends of the Alhambra* (P)	Anti-slavery Abolitionist Party, Boston
1835	Tocqueville, Alexis de (1805–59) [French]: *Democracy in America*, Vol. 1 (P) [Vol. 2, 1840]	New York *Herald* founded; Samuel Colt patents his revolver
1836	Emerson, Ralph Waldo (1803–82): *Nature* (P)	
1837	Emerson, Ralph Waldo: 'The American Scholar', Phi Betta Kappa address at Harvard Hawthorne, Nathaniel (1804–64): *Twice-Told Tales* (P)	
1838	Poe, Edgar Allan: *The Narrative of Arthur Gordon Pym* (P)	'Underground railway' organised by abolitionists
1839	Longfellow, Henry Wadsworth (1807–82): *Voices of the Night* (V) Audubon, John James: *Ornithological Biography* (P) [1831–9]	10,000 Mormons settle at Nauvoo, Illinois (formerly Commerce)

DATE	AUTHOR AND TITLE	EVENT
1840	Cooper, James Fenimore: *The Pathfinder* (P) Poe, Edgar Allan: *Tales of the Grotesque and Arabesque* (P)	Transcendentalist magazine, *The Dial* founded under editorship of Margaret Fuller (1810–50)
1841	Cooper, James Fenimore: *The Deerslayer* (P) Emerson, Ralph Waldo: *Essays* (P)	New York *Tribune* founded by Horace Greeley
1843	Prescott, William Hickling (1796–1859): *History of the Conquest of Mexico* (P)	John Smith authorises Mormon polygamy
1845	Mowatt, Anna Cora (1819–70): *Fashion; or, Life in New York* (D) Poe, Edgar Allan: *Tales* (P) *The Raven and Other Poems* (V)	USA annexes Texas *Scientific American* begins publication
1846	Hawthorne, Nathaniel: *Mosses from an Old Manse* (P) Melville, Herman (1819–91): *Typee* (P) Whittier, John Greenleaf (1807–92): *Voices of Freedom* (V)	US War with Mexico Mormons under Brigham Young set out for Utah Smithsonian Institute, Washington, is founded
1847	Emerson, Ralph Waldo: *Poems* (V) Longfellow, Henry Wadsworth: *Evangeline* (V) Melville, Herman: *Omoo* (P) Prescott, William Hickling: *History of the Conquest of Peru* (P)	US troops capture Mexico City Salt Lake City founded by Mormons Gold discovered in California More than 200,000 leave Ireland, many bound for USA
1848	Lowell, James Russell (1819–91): *The Biglow Papers* [First series] (V/P)	American Association for the Advancement of Science End of Mexican War
1849	Packman, Francis (1823–93): *The California and the Oregon Trail* (P) Thoreau, Henry David (1817–62): 'Civil Disobedience' (P); *A Week on the Concord and Merrimack Rivers* (P)	William Hunt invents safety pin 'Bloomers' introduced by Amelia Jenks Bloomer
1850	Emerson, Ralph Waldo: *Representative Men* (P) Hawthorne, Nathaniel: *The Scarlet Letter* (P) Melville, Herman: *White-Jacket* (P)	*Harper's New Monthly Magazine* founded Slave trade forbidden in District of Columbia 'Raftsmen Playing Cards' (painting) completed by George Caleb Bingham Building of St Patrick's Cathedral, New York [completed 1879] by James Renwick

DATE	AUTHOR AND TITLE	EVENT
1851	Hawthorne, Nathaniel: *The House of the Seven Gables* (P) Melville, Herman: *Moby-Dick* (P) Packman, Francis: *The Conspiracy of Pontiac* (P)	First US State prohibition law voted in Maine
1852	Hawthorne, Nathaniel: *The Blithedale Romance* (P) Melville, Herman: *Pierre, or the Ambiguities* (P) Stowe, Harriet Beecher (1811–96): *Uncle Tom's Cabin* (P)	Wells, Fargo stagecoach company founded at New York Governor of California seeks land grants to encourage further Chinese immigration
1854	Thoreau, Henry David: *Walden* (P)	Republican Party formally established
1855	Boker, George Henry (1823–90): *Francesca da Rimini* (D) Longfellow, Henry Wadsworth: *The Song of Hiawatha* (V) Whitman, Walt (1819–92): *Leaves of Grass* (V)	John Bartlett publishes his own compilation, *Familiar Quotations*
1856	Melville, Herman: *The Piazza Tales* (P)	Pottawatomie Creek Massacre by John Brown
1857		*Atlantic Monthly* begins publication
1858	Holmes, Oliver Wendell (1809–94): *The Autocrat of the Breakfast Table* (P)	Central Park, New York, opened to public
1859	Thoreau, Henry David: 'A Plea for Captain John Brown' (P) Boucicault, Dion (1820–90): *The Octoroon, or, Life in Louisiana* (D)	'Thunderstorm with Rocky Mountains' (painting) by Albert Bierstadt, 'Old Kentucky Home' (painting) by Eastman Johnson After raid on federal arsenal at Harper's Ferry, John Brown hanged; song 'John Brown's Body' attributed to T. B. Bishop (1835–1905)
1860	Boucicault, Dion: *The Colleen Bawn* (D) Emerson, Ralph Waldo: *The Conduct of Life* (P)	Abraham Lincoln elected President South Carolina secedes from Union
1861	Holmes, Oliver Wendell: *Elsie Venner* (P)	Outbreak of American Civil War
1862	Whittier, John Greenleaf: *Snow-Bound* (V)	Battles of Shiloh, second Bull Run, Antietam, Fredericksburg Sioux rising in Minnesota suppressed

DATE	AUTHOR AND TITLE	EVENT
1863	Longfellow, Henry Wadsworth: *Tales of a Wayside Inn* (V)	'Symphony in White' (painting) by James McNeill Whistler Lincoln proclaims emancipation of slaves from 1 Jan. Battles of Gettysburg, Vicksburg, Chattanooga
1864		Sherman's march through Georgia Ku Klux Klan organised at Pulaski, Tennessee
1865	Whitman, Walt: *Drum-Taps* (V) and *Sequel to Drum-Taps* including 'Where Lilacs Last in the Dooryard Bloom'd' (V)	Abraham Lincoln assassinated by John Wilkes Booth End of Civil War. 'Prisoners from the Front' (painting) by Winslow Homer
1866	Melville, Herman: *Battle Pieces* (V)	American Equal Rights Association founded
1867	Alger, Horatio (1834–99): *Ragged Dick* (P)	Alaska ceded by Russia to USA
1868	Alcott, Louisa May (1832–88): *Little Women* (P) [completed 1869]	Fourteenth Amendment to Constitution ratified
1869	Harte, Francis Bret (1836–1902): *The Outcasts of Poker Flat* (P) Twain, Mark (1835–1910): *The Innocents Abroad* (P)	Ulysses S. Grant inaugurated President Union Pacific and Central Pacific Railroads join in Utah American Woman's Suffrage Association started by Susan B. Anthony
1871	Whitman, Walt: *Democratic Vistas* (P)	
1873	Twain, Mark: *The Gilded Age* (P)	Financial panic in USA caused by speculation, over-production Remington Company produces typewriter
1875	Eddy, Mary Baker (1821–1910): *Science and Health* (P)	'The Gross Clinic' (painting) by Thomas Eakins
1876	James, Henry (1843–1916): *Roderick Hudson* (P) Lanier, Sidney (1842–81): 'The Symphony' (V) Twain, Mark: *The Adventures of Tom Sawyer* (P)	Telephone patented by Alexander Graham Bell Phonograph invented by Thomas Edison 'Breezing Up' (painting) by Winslow Homer
1881	James, Henry: *The Portrait of a Lady* (P)	Boston Symphony Orchestra founded President Garfield mortally wounded by assassin

DATE	AUTHOR AND TITLE	EVENT
1883	Twain, Mark: *Life on the Mississippi* (P) Wilcox, Ella Wheeler (1850–1919): *Poems of Passion* (V)	New York Metropolitan Opera founded Northern Pacific Railroad constructed *Life* magazine begins publication
1884	Twain, Mark: *The Adventures of Huckleberry Finn* (London) (P)	The Mergenthaler Linotype machine patented
1885	Howells, William Dean (1837–1920): *The Rise of Silas Lapham* (P) Riley, James Whitcomb (1849–1916): *Little Orphant Annie* (V)	
1886	Carnegie, Andrew (1835–1919): *Triumphant Democracy* (P) James, Henry: *The Bostonians* (P); *The Princess Casamassima* (P)	Statue of Liberty, New York, cast in copper, gift from France, designed by Frederick Auguste Bartholdi American Federation of Labour founded to replace federation of Unions
1888	Bellamy, Edward (1850–98): *Looking Backward: 2000–1887* (P)	'Kodak' box camera invented by George Eastman
1890	Dickinson, Emily (1830–86): *Poems*(V) James, William (1842–1910): *The Principles of Psychology* (P) Whittier, John Greenleaf: *At Sundown* (V)	Anti-trust law enacted Mississippi legislature institutes poll tax, literacy tests, etc. designed to restrict voting by Blacks; other Southern States follow this example
1892	Whitman, Walt: *Leaves of Grass* (V) ['Death-bed' edition]	California earthquake disaster Antonin Dvorak [Czech] accepts directorship of National Conservatory of Music, New York
1893	Crane, Stephen (1871–1900): *Maggie A Girl of the Streets* (P) [privately printed; published 1896]	Chicago World Exhibition 'Struggle of the Two Natures of Man' (sculpture) by George Gray Barnard Symphony No. 9 ('From the New World') by Dvorak
1895	Crane, Stephen: *The Red Badge of Courage: An Episode of the American Civil War* (P)	'Coca-Cola is now sold in every state of the Union'
1896	Jewett, Sarah Orne (1849–1909): *The Country of the Pointed Firs* (P) Robinson, Edwin Arlington (1869–1935): *The Torrent and the Night Before* (V) [revised edn 1897 as *The Children of the Night*]	Louisiana 'Jim Crow car law' upheld by Supreme Court
1898	James, Henry: *'The Turn of the Screw'* (P)	Spanish–American War

DATE	AUTHOR AND TITLE	EVENT
1899	Norris, Frank (1870–1902): *McTeague* (P) Dewey, John (1859–1952): *The School and Society* (P)	Scott Joplin's 'Original Rag' and 'Maple Leaf Rag' are first ragtime piano pieces published in sheet music form
1900	Dreiser, Theodore (1871–1945): *Sister Carrie* (P) Baum, Lyman Frank (1856–1919): *The Wizard of Oz* (P)	Philadelphia Orchestra organised 'The Sitwell Family' (painting) by John Singer Sargent
1902	James, Henry: *The Wings of the Dove* (P) James, William: *Varieties of Religious Experience* (P) Keller, Helen (1880–1968): *The Story of My Life* (P) Robinson, Edwin Arlington: *Captain Craig* (V)	US coal strike (May–Oct.)
1903	James, Henry: *The Ambassadors* (P) London, Jack (1876–1916): *The Call of the Wild* (P)	New York Stock Exchange building completed
1905	Santayana, George (1863–1952): *The Life of Reason* (P) Wharton, Edith (1862–1937): *The House of Mirth* (P)	Big oil strike at 'Tulsey Town', in Oklahoma, a prelude to 'Tulsa' as 'Oil Capital of the World' 'Wrestlers' (painting) by George Benjamin Luks
1906	Henry, O. (1862–1910): *The Four Million* (P) London, Jack: *White Fang* (P) Sinclair, Upton (1878–1968): *The Jungle* (P)	Pure Food and Drugs Act passed as result of Upton Sinclair's exposure in *The Jungle* of conditions in Chicago stockyards San Francisco earthquake
1907	Adams, Henry (1838–1918): *The Education of Henry Adams* (P) [private printing] James, William: *Pragmatism* (P)	*The North American Indian*, Vol. 1, published by photographer Edward S. Curtis
1909	Pound, Ezra (1885–1972): *Personae* (V) James, William: *A Pluralistic Universe* (P)	Henry Ford's Model 'T' car Sigmund Freud lectures in US on psychoanalysis Frank Lloyd Wright's prairie style 'Robie House' completed in Chicago
1912	Dreiser, Theodore: *The Financier* (P) Grey, Zane (1875–1939): *Riders of the Purple Sage* (P)	*Poetry* (Chicago) founded by Harriet Monroe F. W. Woolworth Company incorporated by Frank Woolworth

DATE	AUTHOR AND TITLE	EVENT
	Johnson, James Weldon (1871–1938): *The Autobiography of an Ex-Coloured Man* (P) Pound, Ezra (ed.): *Some Imagiste Poets* (V)	
1913	Cather, Willa (1873–1947): *O Pioneers!* (P) Frost, Robert (1874–1963): *A Boy's Will* (V) Glasgow, Ellen (1874–1945): *Virginia* (P) Lindsay, Vachel (1879–1931): *General William Booth Enters Heaven* (V) Williams, William Carlos (1883–1963): *The Tempers* (V)	Armoury Show of post-Impressionist paintings in New York and Chicago Charlie Chaplin signs contract with film-maker, Mack Sennett Henry Ford pioneers use of conveyor belt
1914	Frost, Robert: *North of Boston* (V)	
1915	Masters, Edgar Lee (1868–1950): *Spoon River Anthology* (V) Pound, Ezra: *Cathay* (V)	D. W. Griffith's film, *Birth of a Nation*
1916	Aiken, Conrad (1889–1974): *The Jig of Forslen* (V) Doolittle, Hilda [H. D.] (1886–1961]: *Sea Garden* (V) O'Neill, Eugene (1888–1953): *Bound East for Cardiff* (D) Robinson, Edwin Arlington: *The Man Against the Sky* (V) Sandburg, Carl (1878–1967): *Chicago Poems* (V)	*Saturday Evening Post* buys its first Norman Rockwell illustration Coca-Cola adopts distinctively shaped bottle
1917	Eliot, Thomas Stearns (1888–1965): *Prufrock and Other Observations* (V)	USA declares war on Germany and Austria-Hungary 'The Darktown Strutters' Ball' recorded as first jazz record
1918	Cather, Willa: *My Antonia* (P)	Charlie Chaplin's *Shoulder Arms* (film) End of First World War President Wilson's Fourteen Points
1919	Anderson, Sherwood (1876–1941): *Winesburg, Ohio* (P) Cabell, James Branch (1879–1958): *Jurgen* (P) Mencken, Henry Louis (1880–1956): *The American Language* (P)	New York's 'Commodore' opened – the world's largest hotel
1920	Fitzgerald, F. Scott (1896–1940): *This Side of Paradise* (P)	Prohibition of sales of alcoholic beverages (Eighteenth Amendment)

DATE	AUTHOR AND TITLE	EVENT
	Lewis, Sinclair (1885–1951): *Main Street* (P)	League of Nations comes into being
	O'Neill, Eugene: *The Emperor Jones* (D)	
	Millay, Edna St Vincent (1892–1950): *A Few Figs from Thistles* (V)	
1922	Eliot, Thomas Stearns: *The Waste Land* (V)	First issue of *The Fugitive*
	Lewis, Sinclair: *Babbitt* (P)	
1923	Millay, Edna St Vincent: *The Harp-Weaver and Other Poems* (V)	First issue of *Time* magazine
	Rice, Elmer (1892–1967): *The Adding Machine* (D)	
	Stevens, Wallace (1879–1955): *Harmonium* (V)	
1924	Melville, Herman: *Billy Budd, Sailor* (P)	First performance of 'Rhapsody in Blue for Jazz Band and Piano' by George Gershwin
	Jeffers, Robinson (1887–1962): *Tamar and Other Poems* (V)	
	Ransom, John Crowe (1888–1974): *Chills and Fever* (V)	
1925	Dreiser, Theodore: *An American Tragedy* (P)	State of Tennessee forbids teaching of human evolution in schools 'Monkey Trial' of John D. Scopes
	Dos Passos, John (1896–1970): *Manhattan Transfer* (P)	
	e. e. cummings: *&*	
	Fitzgerald, F. Scott: *The Great Gatsby* (P)	
	Glasgow, Ellen: *Barren Ground* (P)	
	Pound, Ezra: *Cantos I–XVI* (V)	
1926	e. e. cummings: *Ls 5*	Dancer Martha Graham makes first solo appearance in New York
	Hemingway, Ernest (1899–1961): *The Sun Also Rises* (P)	Chicago bootlegger Al Capone's hotel headquarters sprayed with machine-gun fire by rival gang; execution of Sacco and Vanzetti
	Hughes, Langston (1902–67): *The Weary Blues* (V)	
	Parker, Dorothy (1893–1967): *Enough Rope* (V)	
1929	Faulkner, William (1897–1962): *Sartoris* (P); *The Sound and the Fury* (P)	Collapse of US Stock Exchange begins world economic crisis
	Hemingway, Ernest: *A Farewell to Arms* (P)	
	Wolfe, Thomas (1900–38): *Look Homeward, Angel* (P)	
1930	Crane, Hart (1899–1932): *The Bridge* (V)	More than four million unemployed in USA
	Hammett, Dashiell (1894–1961): *The Maltese Falcon* (P)	'American Gothic' (painting) by Grant Wood

DATE	AUTHOR AND TITLE	EVENT
1933	Caldwell, Erskine, (*b.* 1903): *God's Little Acre* (P) Stein, Gertrude (1874–1946): *The Autobiography of Alice B. Toklas* (P) West, Nathaniel (1904–40): *Miss Lonelyhearts* (P)	Financial crisis continues; newly inaugurated President Roosevelt says 'We have nothing to fear but fear itself' James Joyce's *Ulysses* ruled acceptable for US publication End of Prohibition 'Calderberry Bush', early mobile by Alexander Calder
1934	O'Hara, John (1905–70): *Appointment in Samarra* (P) Saroyan, William (*b.* 1908): *The Daring Young Man on the Flying Trapeze* (P)	*Partisan Review* begins publication First performance of 'Symphony: 1933' by Roy Harris Gangster John Dillinger shot dead by FBI agents
1935	Anderson, Maxwell (1888–1959): *Winterset* (D) Odets, Clifford (1906–63): *Waiting for Lefty* (D) *Awake and Sing* (D) Santayana, George: *The Last Puritan* (P) Steinbeck, John (1902–68): *Tortilla Flat* (P)	New Deal social security legislation *Porgy and Bess* (opera) by Du Bose Heyward and George Gershwin
1936	Dos Passos, John: *U.S.A.* [trilogy completed] (P) Faulkner, William: *Absalom, Absalom!* (P) Mitchell, Margaret (1900–49): *Gone With the Wind* (P) Sandburg, Carl: *The People, Yes* (V)	Ford Foundation established Frank Lloyd Wright's 'Kauffmann House', Bear Run, Penn.
1937	Marquand, John Phillips (1893–1960): *The Late George Apley* (P) Stevens, Wallace: *The Man with the Blue Guitar* (V)	*Newsweek* magazine begins publication *Popular Photography* magazine begins publication
1938	cummings, edward estlin (1894–1962): *Collected Poems* (V) Schwartz, Delmore (1913–66): *In Dreams Begin Responsibilities* (V) Wilder, Thornton (1897–1975): *Our Town* (D)	*Snow White and the Seven Dwarfs*, film by Walt Disney *Billy the Kid*, ballet by Aaron Copland
1939	Chandler, Raymond (1888–1959): *The Big Sleep* (P) Steinbeck, John: *The Grapes of Wrath* (P) Thurber, James (1894–1961): *The Cream of Thurber* (P) Warren, Robert Penn (*b.* 1905): *Night Rider* (P)	'Grandma Moses' (Anna M. Robertson) becomes famous in Unknown American Painters Exhibition

DATE	AUTHOR AND TITLE	EVENT
1940	Hemingway, Ernest: *For Whom the Bell Tolls* (P) McCullers, Carson Smith (1917–67): *The Heart is a Lonely Hunter* (P) Wilson, Edmund (1895–1972): *To the Finland Station* (P) Wright, Richard (1908–60): *Native Son* (P)	US unemployment over eight million First Social Security payments made
1941	Agee, James (1909–55): *Let Us Now Praise Famous Men* (P) with photographs by Walker Evans Ferber, Edna (1887–1968): *Saratoga Trunk* (P) Zukofsky, Louis (1904–78): *55 Poems* (V)	Japanese bomb Pearl Harbor and USA enters Second World War *Citizen Kane*, film by Orson Welles
1944	Bellow, Saul (*b.* 1915): *Dangling Man* (P)	Supreme Court rules an American cannot be denied right to vote because of colour
1945	Williams, Tennessee (*b.* 1911): *The Glass Menagerie* (D) Winsor, Kathleen (*b.* 1919): *Forever Amber* (P) Wright, Richard: *Black Boy* (P)	Second World War ends in Europe Franklin D. Roosevelt dies and is succeeded as President by Harry S. Truman USA drops atomic bombs on Hiroshima and Nagasaki; Japan surrenders
1946	Hersey, John (*b.* 1914): *Hiroshima* (P) Lowell, Robert (1917–77): *Lord Weary's Castle* (V) Merrill, James (*b.* 1926): *The Black Swan and Other Poems* (V) Warren, Robert Penn: *All the King's Men* (P)	Returning veterans swell US college enrolments to over two million
1947	Miller, Arthur (*b.* 1915): *All My Sons* (D) Williams, Tennessee: *A Streetcar Named Desire* (D)	Truman Doctrine of aid to countries threatened by communism
1948	Mailer, Norman (*b.* 1923): *The Naked and the Dead* (P) Pound, Ezra: *The Pisan Cantos* (V)	President Truman recognises the State of Israel 'Number One' (painting) by Jackson Pollock
1949	Miller, Arthur: *Death of a Salesman* (D)	
1950	Olson, Charles (1910–70): 'Projective Verse' (P)	Korean War begins United Nations Building, New York, completed

DATE	AUTHOR AND TITLE	EVENT
1951	Hughes, Langston: *Montage of A Dream Deferred* (V) Jones, James (1921–77): *From Here to Eternity* (P) Lowell, Robert: *The Mills of the Kavanaughs* (V) Salinger, Jerome David (*b.* 1919): *The Catcher in the Rye* (P) Wouk, Herman (*b.* 1915): *The Caine Mutiny* (P)	First performance of Symphony No. 2 by Charles Ives CBS broadcasts colour television US Atomic Energy Commission builds first power-producing nuclear reactor
1952	Hemingway, Ernest: *The Old Man and the Sea* (P) McCarthy, Mary (*b.* 1912): *The Groves of Academe* (P) Malamud, Bernard (*b.* 1914): *The Natural* (P) Merwin, William Stanley (*b.* 1927): *A Mask for Janus* (V) O'Connor, Flannery (1925–64): *Wise Blood* (P)	General Dwight David Eisenhower nominated by Republicans to run for presidency against Democratic nominee, Governor Adlai Stevenson; Eisenhower wins election
1953	Baldwin, James (*b.* 1924): *Go Tell It on the Mountain* (P) Bellow, Saul: *The Adventures of Augie March* (P) Ellison, Ralph (*b.* 1914): *Invisible Man* (P) Miller, Arthur: *The Crucible* (D) Olson, Charles: *The Maximus Poems (1–10)* (V) Roethke, Theodore (1908–63): *The Waking* (V) Shapiro, Karl (*b.* 1913): *Poems: 1940–1953* (V) Warren, Robert Penn: *Brother to Dragons* (V) [new version, 1979]	Ethel and Julius Rosenberg executed for passing atomic secrets to Soviet agents Eisenhower proposes 'Atoms for Peace' programme Korean War ends *Playboy* magazine begins publication
1954	De Vries, Peter (*b.* 1910): *Tunnel of Love* (P) Stevens, Wallace: *Collected Poems* (V) Welty, Eudora (*b.* 1909): *The Ponder Heart* (P)	Vietnam divided into North and South Lolita Lebron and associates injure congressmen in 'Free Puerto Rico' demonstration
1955	Donleavy, James Patrick (*b.* 1926): *The Ginger Man* (P) Nabokov, Vladimir (1899–1977): *Lolita* (P)	Rosa Parks of Montgomery, Alabama, refuses to give up her seat on bus to a white man
1956	Barth, John (*b.* 1930): *The Floating Opera* (P)	Lerner and Lowe's *My Fair Lady*

DATE	AUTHOR AND TITLE	EVENT

Ginsberg, Allen (*b*. 1926):
Howl and Other Poems (V)
O'Neill, Eugene: *Long Day's
Journey Into Night* (D)

1957　Cheever, John (1912–82):
The Wapshot Chronicle (P)
Kerouac, Jack (1922–69):
On the Road (P)
Singer, Isaac Bashevis (*b*. 1904):
Gimpel the Fool (P)
Stevens, Wallace: *Opus
Posthumous* (V/D/P)

School integration disturbances at
Little Rock, Arkansas
Civil Rights Commission established
Roger Sessions's Symphony No. 3
first performed
Leonard Bernstein's *West Side Story*

1958　Albee, Edward (*b*. 1928):
The Zoo Story (D)
Capote, Truman (*b*. 1924):
Breakfast at Tiffany's (P)
Kunitz, Stanley (*b*. 1905):
Selected Poems 1928–1958 (V)

John Birch Society founded
First US Earth Satellite launched

1959　Bellow, Saul: *Henderson the Rain
King* (P)
Burroughs, William (*b*. 1914):
The Naked Lunch (P)
Faulkner, William: *The Mansion* (P)
Gelber, Jack (*b*. 1932):
The Connection (D)
Purdy, James (*b*. 1923): *Malcolm* (P)
Roth, Philip Milton (*b*. 1933):
Goodbye, Columbus (P)
Snodgrass, William De Witt
(*b*. 1926): *Heart's Needle* (V)
Updike, John (*b*. 1932):
The Poorhouse Fair (P)

Alaska and Hawaii admitted to the
USA as the 49th and 50th States
Eisenhower says nation's economy
is 'on a curve of rising prosperity'
Completion of Frank Lloyd Wright's
'Solomon R. Guggenheim Museum',
New York (1943–59)

1960　Barth, John: *The Sot-Weed Factor* (P)
Hellman, Lillian (*b*. 1905): *Toys in
the Attic* (D)
Kinnell, Galway (*b*. 1927): *What a
Kingdom it Was* (V)
O'Connor, Flannery: *The Violent
Bear It Away* (P)
Plath, Sylvia (1932–63):
The Colossus (V)
Sexton, Anne (1928–74): *To Bedlam
and Part Way Back* (V)
Singer, Isaac Bashevis: *The
Magician of Lublin* (P)
Updike, John: *Rabbit, Run* (P)

John Fitzgerald Kennedy wins election
to the presidency by defeating
Republican Vice-President
Richard Milhous Nixon

DATE	AUTHOR AND TITLE	EVENT
1961	Baldwin, James: *Nobody Knows My Name* (P) Heller, Joseph (*b.* 1923): *Catch-22* (P) Malamud, Bernard: *A New Life* (P) Percy, Walker (*b.* 1916): *The Moviegoer* (P) Salinger, J. D.: *Franny and Zooey* (P)	USA severs relations with Fidel Castro's Cuba Bay of Pigs invasion; Khrushchev supports Cuba Berlin Wall erected First US manned space expedition by Commander Alan B. Shephard
1962	Albee, Edward: *Who's Afraid of Virginia Woolf?* (D) Baldwin, James: *Another Country* (P) Bly, Robert (*b.* 1926): *Silence in a Snowy Field* (V) Porter, Katherine Anne (1890–1980): *Ship of Fools* (P)	Cuban missile crisis brings nuclear confrontation with USSR USA aids South Vietnamese against Vietcong guerrillas
1963	Friedan, Betty (*b.* 1921): *The Feminine Mystique* (P) Pynchon, Thomas (*b.* 1937): *V* (P) Vonnegut, Kurt (*b.* 1922): *Cat's Cradle* (P) Williams, William Carlos: *Paterson, Books I–V* (V)	Assassination of President Kennedy at Dallas, Texas Lyndon Baines Johnson sworn in as successor Martin Luther King makes speech, 'I have a dream' at Emancipation centennial ceremony Civil Rights march on Washington
1964	Baraka, Imamu Amiri (LeRoi Jones, *b.* 1934): *Dutchman* (D) Bellow, Saul: *Herzog* (P) Berger, Thomas (*b.* 1924): *Little Big Man* (P) Berryman, John (1914–72): *77 Dream Songs* (V) Lowell, Robert: *For the Union Dead* (V) Selby, Hubert (*b.* 1926): *Last Exit to Brooklyn* (P) Shepard, Sam (*b.* 1943): *Cowboys* (D)	USA bomb North Vietnamese bases President Johnson re-elected Race riots in Harlem and Philadelphia Student 'Free Speech' demonstration at University of California
1965	Kosinski, Jerzy (*b.* 1933): *The Painted Bird* (P) Malcolm X (original name Malcolm Little, 1925–65) [with Alex Haley]: *The Autobiography of Malcolm X* (P) Plath, Sylvia: *Ariel* (V) Warren, Robert Penn: *Who Speaks for the Negro?* (P) Wolfe, Tom (*b.* 1931): *The Kandy-Kolored Tangerine-Flake Streamline Baby* (P)	USA formally allies with South Vietnam Civil Rights demonstrations at Selma, Alabama and Chicago Race riots in Watts district of Los Angeles Malcolm X shot dead 'Early Bird' put into orbit as world's first commercial satellite Painting of a giant Campbell's Tomato Soup Can by Andy Warhol

DATE	AUTHOR AND TITLE	EVENT
	Zukofsky, Louis: *All: The Collected Short Poems 1923–1958* (V)	
1966	Baraka, Imamu Amiri: *Home: Social Essays* (P) Capote, Truman: *In Cold Blood* (P) Condon, Richard (*b.* 1915): *An Infinity of Mirrors* (P)	James Meredith, University of Mississippi's first Black graduate shot from ambush Race riots in Cleveland, Chicago and Atlanta
1967	Baraka, Imamu Amiri: *Black Magic: Poetry 1961–1967* (V) Bly, Robert: *The Light Around the Body* (V) Brautigan, Richard (*b.* 1935): *Trout Fishing in America* (P) Styron, William (*b.* 1925): *The Confessions of Nat Turner* (P) Vidal, Gore (*b.* 1925): *Washington, D.C.* (P)	Anti-Vietnam War demonstrations, notably at New York, San Francisco and Washington Race riots throughout country, worst at Newark and Detroit; Stokely Carmichael urges 'Black Power' movement to be more militant
1968	Cleaver, Eldridge (*b.* 1935): *Soul on Ice* (P) Dickey, James (*b.* 1923): *Poems 1957–1967* (V) Mailer, Norman: *The Armies of the Night* (P) Updike, John: *Couples* (P) Vidal, Gore: *Myra Breckenridge* (P) Wolfe, Tom: *The Electric Kool-Aid Acid Test* (P)	My Lai Village massacre in South Vietnam Senator Robert Kennedy assassinated Martin Luther King assassinated Demonstrations and riots in Chicago, Boston, Kansas and other cities Students for a Democratic Society (SDS) promote strike action on many campuses Richard Milhous Nixon wins presidential election
1969	Cheever, John: *Bullet Park* (P) Jarrell, Randall (1914–65): *The Complete Poems* (V) Nabokov, Vladimir: *Ada* (P) Roth, Philip: *Portnoy's Complaint* (P) Vonnegut, Kurt: *Slaughterhouse Five, or The Children's Crusade* (P)	US moon landing Death of Mary Jo Kopechne at Chappaquiddick Island damages reputation of Senator Edward M. Kennedy US economic boom Woodstock Music and Art Festival, New York *Saturday Evening Post* ceases publication
1970	Brown, Dee (*b.* 1908): *Bury My Heart at Wounded Knee* (P) Didion, Joan (*b.* 1934): *Play It As It Lays* (P) Lowell, Robert: *Notebook* (V) Millett, Kate [Katherine Murray, *b.* 1934]: *Sexual Politics* (P) Toffler, Alvin (*b.* 1928): *Future Shock* (P) Welty, Eudora: *Losing Battles* (P)	National Guardsmen open fire on protesting students at Kent State University (Ohio), killing four Arabs blame USA for Israel's refusal to give up territory occupied since Six Day War (1967)

DATE	AUTHOR AND TITLE	EVENT
1971	Condon, Richard: *The Vertical Smile* (P) Doctorow, Edgar Lawrence (*b.* 1931): *The Book of Daniel* (P) O'Hara, Frank (1926–66): *Collected Poems* (V)	Vietnam War increases rate of inflation Excerpts from Pentagon Papers published in the *New York Times*
1972	Ammons, A.R. (*b.* 1926): *Collected Poems 1951–1971* (V) Barth, John: *Chimera* (P) Wright, James (1927–80): *Collected Poems* (V)	Watergate affair begins; *Washington Post* investigates
1973	Giovanni, Nikki (*b.* 1943): *Black Judgement* (V) Jong, Erica (*b.* 1942): *Fear of Flying* (P) Oates, Joyce Carol (*b.* 1938): *Do With Me What You Will* (P) Pynchon, Thomas: *Gravity's Rainbow* (P) Vidal, Gore: *Burr* (P)	Cease-fire in Vietnam, but bombing of Cambodia continues *Skylab* astronauts photograph Comet 'Kohoutek'
1974	Heller, Joseph: *Something Happened* (P) Lurie, Alison (*b.* 1926): *The War Between the Tates* (P) Mamet, David (*b.* 1947): *Sexual Perversity in Chicago* (D) Roth, Philip: *My Life as a Man* (P)	World energy crisis deepens President Nixon resigns as a result of Watergate; he is pardoned by successor, President Gerald Ford
1975	Ashbery, John (*b.* 1927): *Self-Portrait in a Convex Mirror* (V) Doctorow, Edgar Lawrence: *Ragtime* (P) Gaddis, William (*b.* 1922): *JR* (P) Penner, Jonathan (*b.* 1940): *Going Blind* (P) Wolfe, Tom: *The Painted Word* (P)	Watergate cover-up trial continues Puerto Rican militants explode bombs in New York America's *Apollo 16* spacecraft docks in space with Russia's *Soyuz 19*
1976	Gardner, John (*b.* 1933): *October Light* (P) Haley, Alex (*b.* 1921): *Roots*(P) Warren, Robert Penn: *Selected Poems: 1923–1975* (V)	Bi-centennial celebrations Patricia Hearst found guilty of armed robbery *Viking II* spacecraft lands on Mars
1977	Ashbery, John: *Houseboat Days* (V) Cheever, John: *Falconer* (P) Coover, Robert (*b.* 1932): *The Public Burning* (P) Merrill, James: *Divine Comedies* (V)	Jimmy Carter inaugurated as President Gary Gilmore executed by firing squad President Carter pardons draft-dodgers and supports production of neutron bomb

DATE	AUTHOR AND TITLE	EVENT
	Miller, Arthur: *The Archbishop's Ceiling* (D) Percy, Walker: *Lancelot* (P) Warren, Robert Penn: *A Place To Come To* (P)	Department of Energy created USA yields control of Panama to the Panamanians
1978	Cheever, John: *The Stories of John Cheever* (P) Gordon, Mary (*b.* 1950): *Final Payments* (P) Irving, John (*b.* 1942): *The World According to Garp* (P) Merrill, James: *Mirabell: Books of Numbers* (V) Updike, John: *The Coup* (P) Williams, Tennessee: *A Lovely Sunday for Creve Coeur* (D)	Settlement of 110-day coal miners' strike which has led to violence in Ohio, Kentucky, Indiana, West Virginia Striking firemen in Memphis, Tenn. blamed for starting over 200 fires Over 1,000 Indians walk 3,000 miles from California to Washington to protest against legislation hostile to their treaty rights US announces intention to end diplomatic relations with Taiwan
1979	Barth, John: *Letters* (P) Heller, Joseph: *Good as Gold* (P) Mailer, Norman: *The Executioner's Song* (P) Malamud, Bernard: *Dubin's Lives* (P) Roth, Philip: *The Ghost Writer* (P)	USA recognises new government in Iran Severe winter weather paralyses north-east President Carter supports production of new MX super-missile Sioux Indians awarded $17,500,000 compensation for Black Hills of Dakota, confiscated in 1877, and judged entitled to interest of $105,000,000
1980	Doctorow, Edgar Lawrence: *Loon Lake* (P) Levin, Harry Tuchman (*b.* 1912): *Memories of the Moderns* (P) Toole, John Kennedy (1937–69): *A Confederacy of Dunces* (P)	Ronald Reagan elected to presidency winning 44 States US hostages held in Iran
1981	De Vries, Peter: *Sauce for the Goose* (P) Irving, John: *The Hotel New Hampshire* (P) Robinson, Marilynne (*b.* 1943): *Housekeeping* (P)	US hostages freed by Iranians President Reagan hit by shot from would-be assassin *Columbia* space shuttle into orbit Mrs Sandra O'Connor appointed first woman member of Supreme Court
1982	Bellow, Saul: *The Dean's December* (P) Forché, Carolyn (*b.* 1951): *The Country Between Us* (V) Kosinski, Jerzy: *Pinball* (P) Mamet, David (*b.* 1947): *Edmond* (D) Merrill, James: *The Changing Light at Sandover* (V) Walker, Alice (*b.* 1944): *The Colour Purple* (P)	In his first State of the Union address on 26 January, President Reagan says: 'Don't let anyone tell you that America's best days are behind her – that the American spirit has been vanquished. We've seen it triumph too often in our lives to stop believing in it now.'

1983   Adler, Renata (*b.* 1938): *Pitch Dark* (P)
Clampitt, Amy (*b.* 1920): *The Kingfisher* (V)
Kennedy, William (*b.* 1928): *Ironweed* (P)
Mailer, Norman: *Ancient Evenings* (P)
Malamud, Bernard: *The Stories of Bernard Malamud* (P)
Oliver, Mary (*b.* 1935): *American Primitive* (V)
Ozick, Cynthia (*b.* 1928): *The Cannibal Galaxy* (P)
Roth, Philip: *The Anatomy Lesson* (P)
Theroux, Paul (*b.* 1941): *The Kingdom by the Sea* (P)
Warren, Robert Penn: *Chief Joseph of the Nez Perce* (V)

President Reagan proposes Strategic Defence Initiative (SDI) which becomes known as 'Star Wars'
US invades island of Grenada and overthrows leftist regime
West European countries begin deployment of US-made Pershing II and Cruise missiles; Russia protests by withdrawing from Geneva arms control talks

1984   Ammons, A. R.: *Worldly Hopes* (V)
Ashbery, John: *A Wave* (V)
Bellow, Saul: *Him With His Foot in His Mouth and Other Stories* (P)
Heller, Joseph: *God Knows* (P)
Mamet, David: *Glengarry Glen Ross* (D)
Rich, Adrienne (*b.* 1931): *The Fact of a Doorframe* (V)
Stone, Robert (*b.* 1937): *Children of Light* (P)
Updike, John: *The Witches of Eastwick* (P)
Wright, Charles: *The Other Side of the River* (V)

Geraldine Ferraro is first woman to be nominated for the vice-presidency
Jesse Jackson is first Black to mount serious bid for the presidency
Ronald Reagan is re-elected to presidency with 59% of popular vote and 49 states
US athletes excel in Los Angeles-based Olympic Games

1985   Hersey, John: *The Call* (P)
Irving, John: *The Cider House Rules* (P)
Roth, Philip: *Zuckerman Bound* (P)
Shepard, Sam: *A Lie of the Mind* (D)
Vonnegut, Kurt: *Galapagos* (P)

US hostages held in Beirut; later released
Reagan and Mikhail Gorbachev hold summit meeting in Vienna
US citizens attacked and wounded at Rome and Vienna airports
Russia returns to arms control talks despite Euromissile deployment

1986   Hemingway, Ernest: *The Garden of Eden* (posthumous P)
McMurtry, Larry (*b.* 1936): *Lonesome Dove* (P)
Miller, Sue (*b.* 1943): *The Good Mother* (P)
Minot, Susan (*b.* 1957): *Monkeys* (P)

Challenger space shuttle explodes; seven astronauts perish
US bombs Libya over terrorist links
Reagan remains popular well into second term
Robert Penn Warren designated America's first official Poet Laureate

Further reading

Titles are listed under the chapters of this book to which they most immediately refer. Many of the listed works will enlarge understanding of the literature discussed in several of the personal chapters.

1 Terms of a tradition

RUSSELL AMES, *The Story of American Folk Song* (New York: Grosset and Dunläp, 1955).

CLEANTH BROOKS, R. W. B. LEWIS and ROBERT PENN WARREN (eds), *American Literature, The Makers and the Making*, 2 vols (New York: St Martin's Press, 1973).

ALISTAIR COOKE, *Alistair Cooke's America* (London: BBC, 1973).

LESLIE A. FIEDLER, *The Return of the Vanishing American* (New York: Stein and Day, 1968).

RONALD GOTTESMAN *et al.* (eds), *The Norton Anthology of American Literature*, 2 vols (New York and London: W. W. Norton & Co., 1979).

R. W. B. LEWIS, *The American Adam: Innocence, Tragedy, and Tradition in the Nineteenth Century* (Chicago: University of Chicago Press, 1955).

LEO MARX, *The Machine in the Garden: Technology and the Pastoral Ideal in America* (New York: OUP, 1964; repr. Galaxy Books, 1967).

VERNON L. PARRINGTON, *Main Currents of American Thought: An Interpretation of American Literature from the Beginnings to 1920*, 3 vols (New York: Harcourt Brace, 1927–30).

HENRY NASH SMITH, *Virgin Land, the American West as Symbol and Myth* (Cambridge, Mass: Harvard UP, 1950; repr. Vintage Books, 1957).

ROBERT E. SPILLER, WILLARD THORP, THOMAS H. JOHNSON, HENRY SEIDEL CANBY, RICHARD M. LUDWIG (eds), *Literary History of the United States: History*, third edn revised (New York: Macmillan, 1963).

D. S. R. WELLAND (ed.), *The United States: A Companion to American Studies* (London: Methuen, 1974).

WILLIAM CARLOS WILLIAMS, *In The American Grain* (New York: A. & C. Boni, 1925).

2 The colonies

E. S. GAUSTAD, *The Great Awakening in New England* (New York: Harper, 1957).

PERRY MILLER, *The New England Mind: The Seventeenth Century* (New York:

Macmillan, 1939). *The New England Mind: From Colony to Province* (Cambridge, Mass: Harvard UP, 1953).

SAMUEL ELIOT MORISON, *The Intellectual Life of Colonial New England* (New York: New York UP, 1956).

3   The revolution

DANIEL J. BOORSTIN, *The Lost World of Thomas Jefferson* (New York: Henry Holt, 1948).

D. L. CLARK, *Charles Brockden Brown: Pioneer Voice of America* (Durham, NC: Duke UP, 1952).

BRUCE I. GRANGER, *Benjamin Franklin: An American Man of Letters* (Ithaca, NY: Cornell UP, 1964).

LEON HOWARD, *The Connecticut Wits* (Chicago: University of Chicago Press, 1943).

H. H. PECKHAM, *Gotham Yankee: A Biography of William Cullen Bryant* (New York: Vantage Press, 1950).

4   The waiting poem

MARIUS BEWLEY, *The Eccentric Design: Form in the Classic American Novel* (London: Chatto and Windus, 1959).

WILLIAM L. HEDGES, *Washington Irving: An American Study, 1802–1932* (Baltimore: Johns Hopkins Press, 1965).

D. H. LAWRENCE, *Studies in Classic American Literature* (London: Heinemann, 1924).

HARRY LEVIN, *The Power of Blackness: Hawthorne, Poe, Melville* (New York: Alfred A. Knopf, 1958; repr. Vintage Books 1960).

DAVID SINCLAIR, *Edgar Allan Poe* (London: Dent, 1977).

PHILIP YOUNG, *Three Bags Full: Essays in American Fiction* (New York: Harcourt Brace Jovanovich, 1972).

5   Renaissance

MARIUS BEWLEY, *The Complex Fate; Hawthorne, Henry James, and some other American writers* (London: Chatto and Windus, 1952).

ABRAHAM CHAPMAN, *Literature of the American Indians: Views and Interpretations* (New York: New American Library, 1975).

RICHARD CHASE, *The American Novel and its Tradition* (New York: Doubleday, 1957).

DENIS DONOGHUE, *Connoisseurs of Chaos: Ideas of Order in Modern American Poetry* (London: Faber & Faber, 1966).

CHARLES FEIDELSON, jun., *Symbolism and American Literature* (Chicago and London: University of Chicago Press, 1953).

LESLIE FIEDLER, *Love and Death in the American Novel* (New York: Criterion Books, 1960). *No! In Thunder: Essays in Myth and Literature* (Boston: Beacon Press, 1960).

MARTIN GREEN, *Re-appraisals: Some Commonsense Readings in American Literature* (New York: Norton, 1965).

DANIEL G. HOFFMAN, *Form and Fable in American Fiction* (New York: OUP, 1961).

F. O. MATTHIESSEN, *American Renaissance: Art and Expression in the Age of Emerson and Whitman* (New York: OUP, 1941).

ROY HARVEY PEARCE, *The Continuity of American Poetry* (Princeton: Princeton UP, 1961).

TONY TANNER, *The Reign of Wonder: Naivety and Reality in American Literature* (Cambridge: CUP, 1965).

EDMUND WILSON, *Patriotic Gore: Studies in the Literature of the American Civil War* (New York: OUP, 1962).

YVOR WINTERS, *In Defense of Reason*, third edn, (Denver: Alan Swallow, 1937). 'Maule's Curse' discusses Hawthorne, Cooper, Melville, Poe, Emerson, Dickinson, Henry James, etc.

6 Realisms

LIONEL TRILLING, *The Liberal Imagination: Essays on Literature and Society* (New York: Macmillan, 1948). Essays on Henry James, Mark Twain, etc.

MICHAEL MILLGATE, *American Social Fiction: James to Cozzens* (New York: Barnes and Noble, 1964).

JAMES K. FOLSOM (ed.), *The Western, A Collection of Critical Essays* (Englewood Cliffs: Prentice-Hall, 1979).

7 Modernisms

JOHN M. BRADBURY, *The Fugitives: A Critical Account* (Chapel Hill: University of North Carolina Press, 1958).

ALAN DOWNER, *Fifty Years of American Drama, 1900–1950* (Chicago: Regnery, 1951).

IRVIN EHRENPREIS (ed.), *American Poetry, Stratford-upon-Avon Studies 7* (London: Edward Arnold, 1965).

LESLIE FIEDLER, *Waiting for the End: The American Literary Scene from Hemingway to Baldwin* (New York: Stein and Day, 1964; repr. Penguin, 1967).

FREDERICK J. HOFFMAN, *The Twenties: American Writing in the Postwar Decade*, new revised edn (New York: Collier, 1962).

ALFRED KAZIN, *On Native Grounds: An Interpretation of Modern American Prose Literature* (New York: Reynal and Hitchcock, 1942).

HUGH KENNER, *The Pound Era* (Berkeley: University of California Press, 1971).

J. HILLIS MILLER, *Poets of Reality: Six Twentieth Century Writers* (Cambridge, Mass: Harvard UP, 1965). Chapters on T. S. Eliot, Wallace Stevens, William Carlos Wiliams.

LOUIS D. RUBIN, jun., and ROBERT D. JACOBS (eds), *Southern Renascence* (Baltimore: Johns Hopkins Press, 1953).

TOM SCANLAN, *Family, Drama, and American Dreams* (Westport, Conn: Greenwood Press, 1978).

ROBERT PENN WARREN, *Selected Essays* [Faulkner, Hemingway, Frost, *et al.*] (New York: Random House, 1958; repr. Vintage Books, 1966).

8   War and post-war and
9   Diversity

DONALD ALLEN and ROBERT CREELEY (eds), *The New Writing in the USA* (Harmondsworth: Penguin, 1967).

CHARLES ALTIERI, *Self and Sensibility in Contemporary American Poetry* (Cambridge and New York: Cambridge UP, 1984).

C. W. E. BIGSBY (ed.), *The Second Black Renaissance, Essays in Black Literature* (Westport and London: Greenwood Press, 1980).

ROBERT BONE, *The Negro Novel in America*, revised edn (New Haven and London: Yale UP, 1965).

ABRAHAM CHAPMAN (ed.), *Black Voices: An Anthology of Afro-American Literature* (London: New English Library, 1968).

RUBY COHN, *New American Dramatists 1960–1980* (London and Basingstoke: The Macmillan Press, 1982).

DANIEL HOFFMAN, *Harvard Guide to Contemporary American Writing* (Cambridge, Mass. and London: Harvard UP, 1979).

RANDALL JARRELL, *Poetry and the Age* (New York: Alfred A. Knopf, 1953; repr. Vintage Books, 1955).

R. W. B. LEWIS, *Trials of the Word: American Literature and the Humanistic Tradition* (New Haven and London: Yale UP, 1965; repr. Yale Paperbound, 1966).

STAN SMITH, *A Sadly Contracted Hero: The Comic Self in Post-War American Fiction* (British Association for American Studies: BAAS Pamphlets in American Studies, 5, 1981).

TONY TANNER, *City of Words: American Fiction, 1950–1970* (London: Jonathan Cape, 1971).

GEOFFREY THURLEY, *The American Moment: American Poetry in the Mid-Century* (London: Edward Arnold, 1977).

HELEN VENDLER, *Part of Nature, Part of Us: Modern American Poets* (Cambridge, Mass. and London: Harvard UP, 1980).

Index